Teaching Social Skills to Children and Youth

Related Titles of Interest

Improving Social Competence: A Resource for Elementary School Teachers
Pam Campbell and Gary N. Siperstein
ISBN: 0-205-13757-1

101 Ways to Develop Student Self-Esteem and Responsibility Volume I: The Teacher as Coach
Jack Canfield and Frank Siccone
ISBN: 0-205-13368-1 Paper   0-205-13370-3 Cloth

100 Ways to Enhance Self-Concept in the Classroom, Second Edition
Jack Canfield and Harold Clive Wells
ISBN: 0-205-15415-8 Paper   0-205-15711-4 Cloth

Successful Mainstreaming: Proven Ways to Detect and Correct Special Needs
Joyce S. Choate
ISBN: 0-205-14349-0

Self-Esteem Enhancement with Children and Adolescents
Alice W. Pope, Susan M. McHale, and W. Edward Craighead
ISBN: 0-205-14455-1 Paper   0-205-14456-X Cloth

101 Ways to Develop Student Self-Esteem and Responsibility Volume II: The Power to Succeed in School and Beyond
Frank Siccone and Jack Canfield
ISBN: 0-205-14068-8 Paper   0-205-14067-X Cloth

Behavior Management in the Schools: Principles and Procedures, Second Edition
Richard M. Wielkiewicz
ISBN: 0-205-16459-5 Paper   0-205-16458-7 Cloth

Third Edition

Teaching Social Skills to Children and Youth

Innovative Approaches

Gwendolyn Cartledge

The Ohio State University

JoAnne Fellows Milburn

Columbus, Ohio

Allyn and Bacon

Boston • London • Toronto • Sydney • Tokyo • Singapore

Copyright © 1995 by Allyn and Bacon
A Division of Simon and Schuster, Inc.
160 Gould Street
Needham Heights, Massachusetts 02194

Library of Congress Cataloging-in-Publication Data

Teaching social skills to children and youth : innovative approaches /
  Gwendolyn Cartledge, JoAnne Fellows Milburn. — 3rd ed.
      p. cm.
    Rev. ed. of: Teaching social skills to children. 2nd ed. c1986.
    Includes bibliographical references (p.   ) and index.
    ISBN 0-205-16507-9 (paper)   ISBN 0-205-16073-5 (case)
    1. Social skills in children—Study and teaching. I. Cartledge,
  Gwendolyn. II. Milburn, JoAnne Fellows.
  III. Teaching social skills to children.
HQ783.T43 1995
303.3′2′07—dc20   94-12135
                                                                    CIP

Printed in the United States of America

10 9 8 7 6 5 4 3 2 1   98 97 96 95 94

Contents

Preface

The first two editions of this book were published in 1980 and 1986. The current edition provides updated material and several new contributed chapters. As with the previous books, the intended audience is regular and special education teachers and clinicians who work with children and youth in school, residential, or community settings. It also is intended as a text to be used in preservice programs for teachers and clinicians in fields such as social work, counseling, and psychology. Parents who wish to improve their ability to teach social skills to their children also may find *Teaching Social Skills to Children and Youth* useful.

The book is concerned with social behaviors, broadly considered as skills to be taught, and emphasizes building prosocial, adaptive, new behaviors rather than eliminating problem behaviors or developing motivational systems to increase the performance of behaviors already in the child's repertoire. The social skills approach to treating children with problems is a positive one that assumes children can be taught the skills necessary to behave in different, more acceptable ways. The authors are convinced that social behaviors can and should be taught specifically as part of a school curriculum or remedial therapy program, and that the skills for such teaching should be in the repertoires of all teachers and clinicians. Although parents may less often feel the need to provide systematic teaching in the home, some knowledge of how social skills are taught, both purposefully and inadvertently, can add immeasurably to parental effectiveness. The importance of parents or caretakers in the maintenance and generalization of social skills taught to children in other settings increasingly is being recognized.

Much of the rationale for teaching social skills in the schools comes from studies of the relationship between social behaviors and school achievement (Cartledge & Milburn, 1978). It has been suggested that the teaching of social skills goes on in the classroom all the time as a "hidden curriculum," even when the teacher does not deliberately engage in social skills instruction. The instructor, like the parent, is a powerful and influential person in the child's life and, as such, serves as a model for social behaviors. He or she shapes the child's social behaviors, intentionally or not, through the process of reinforcement. Studies of teacher attitudes and behavior suggest that the student's social behaviors help determine how the teacher interacts with him or her. Students who respond in prosocial ways to the teacher (seeking out the teacher, initiating contacts about work assignments, attempting to answer questions, smiling at the teacher, and paying attention) generally receive more positive attention and have a higher rate of academic success.

Some studies indicate that the most efficient target for classroom behavior change efforts may be academic responses rather than task-related social behaviors because, for some populations, improvement in academic achievement appears to result in improved social skills as well as the reverse. A reciprocal relationship appears to exist between improved curriculum, reinforcement of academic responses, and the development of relevant social behaviors. Task-related social behaviors and academic behaviors are highly correlated: It is difficult to reinforce academic responses without simultaneously reinforcing the social behaviors that make the academic responses possible (e.g., attention to the required stimuli, complying with teacher directions, and responding under circumstances specified by the teacher).

Specifically teaching social behaviors seems particularly relevant for children with very low levels of the social behaviors essential for academic success. Social skills instruction increasingly is being included in Individual Education Plan (IEP) goals written for children in special education classes (Baumgart, Filler & Askvig, 1991), and a current definition of *learning disabilities* includes social skills deficits among the disorders that make up this condition (Gresham, 1992, McKinnie & Elliott, 1991). Gresham, Elliott, and Black (1987) stress the need for social skills instruction for successful mainstreaming of disabled children, a point even more important at a time when "inclusiveness" is becoming a salient goal in the structure of educational programs.

A case can be made for teaching interpersonal skills to children in clinical as well as school settings and for regarding instruction in social interaction skills as a tool for prevention as well as remediation of problems. In an often-quoted longitudinal study, Cowan, Pederson, Babigian, Izzo, and Trost (1973) found that children who were identified in primary grades as more vulnerable or at risk showed up in disproportionately high numbers in a community psychiatric register 11 to 13 years later. Peer ratings were the best predictor of later psychiatric difficulties. Studies of resilience in youth suggest that social skills, such as the ability to involve peers for social support, provide a protective factor against stress (Luthar, 1991; Luthar & Doernberger, 1992).

The value of social skills training in prevention of later psychological problems also is being documented in longitudinal studies. Elias, Gara, Schuyler, Branden-Muller, and Sayette (1991) found that students receiving a two-year social skills curriculum in elementary school "showed higher levels of positive prosocial behavior and lower levels of antisocial, self-destructive, and socially disordered behavior when followed up in high school four to six years later than did the control students who had not received this program" (p. 415).

Children with poor peer relationships increasingly are being targeted for social skills instruction. There are longitudinal data suggesting that early peer rejection tends to persist over time for both externalizing (aggressive) children and internalizing (isolated) children (Hymel, Rubin, Rowden, & LeMare, 1987). There also is strong evidence that children who are rejected by peers because of aggressive behavior are at risk for later difficulties—for example, dropping out of school and criminal behavior (Parker & Asher, 1987). As with social skills and academic achievement, there is a kind of reciprocal relationship between social skills and peer relationships. Children with better interpersonal skills have more opportunities to engage in the activities with peers that, in turn, enhance the learning of social behaviors.

The *prescriptive teaching, diagnostic teaching,* or *directive teaching* model (Stephens, 1977) has served as the framework for this book. The elements are:

1. Define in specific behaviorally-stated terms the behavior to be taught;
2. Assess the level of competence possessed by the learner to determine his or her initial level of performance;
3. Teach the behaviors defined through assessment as lacking in the learner's repertoire;
4. Evaluate or reassess for results of teaching; and
5. Provide opportunities for practice and generalization or transfer of behavior to new situations.

In teaching social skills, all these steps need to be present to some degree. The chapter headings in Part 1, therefore, correspond to these steps: Chapter 1 on selection of skills, Chapter 2 on assessment and evaluation, Chapter 3 on teaching procedures, and Chapter 4 on maintenance and transfer. Ideas for enhancing the effectiveness of instruction in social skills are presented in Chapter 5, as well as an example of how the instructional model might be applied to a specific social skill. It is our thesis that any practitioner who understands pedagogical principles can write his or her own social skills curriculum. Social skills can then be taught not only in a planned, systematic way but also by seizing the "teachable moment" to instruct children in social skills when events in the child's life reveal a need for such teaching.

Because material presented in this book involves the assumption that social skills contain cognitive and affective as well as overt behavioral aspects, approaches to teaching these dimensions of social skills are included. Although reviews of research evaluating the effects of cognitive-behavioral interventions indicate that these are producing equivocal outcomes (Ager & Cole, 1991; Gresham, 1985; Pellegrini & Urbain, 1985), there is at the same time a recognition that cognitive deficits and distortions contribute to a lack of social competence and are an important target for remediation. To change values and basic assumptions, particularly about the value of prosocial rather than aggressive and antisocial behaviors in problem situations, is one task of the social skills instructor, and one which cannot be done quickly and without careful programming for maintenance and generalization. Just as an academic skill, such as the learning of a foreign language, requires extensive practice over a long period of time and then opportunities for application, so the acquisition of new ways of thinking about how to relate to others requires supervised practice and long-term reinforcement.

Part 2 presents material on social skills teaching with specialized populations. A new chapter by Hughes and Cavell outlines some promising approaches to social skills programming for aggressive children. In another new chapter, Mize presents procedures for social skills training with preschool children. The updated material by Schleien, Heyne, and Dattilo shows the reader the basic level on which social skills training needs to be approached with developmentally disabled youth. And Goldstein and his colleagues expand on and update the previously published material on social skills interventions for adolescents. A chapter by Cartledge, Lee, and Feng on the implications of multicultural understanding for social skills instruction has been added to reflect the authors' concern that social behaviors must be viewed in a cultural context and taught with respect for the diversity in children's origins. Although throughout the book the authors use terms such as *appropriate, desirable, prosocial, positive,* and so forth, when speaking of a social behavior, it should be understood that the social and cultural context of the behavior must ultimately define those terms.

The material included in this third edition of *Teaching Social Skills to Children and Youth* does not constitute an exhaustive review of current literature on the social skills of children but does present approaches that have empirical foundations or have been demonstrated to be effective with children and youth in bringing about improved social functioning. In programming for children with multiple problems and skill deficits, there is an increasing recognition that social skills instruction is not a "quick fix" but should be considered one tool in an armamentarium of interventions, which might include other forms of treatment and remediation and involve greater attention to the role of the family and the community.

Acknowledgments

We would like to thank the many people who helped us with various aspects of this book. Persons deserving special recognition include graduate research assistant James Dunne and Elaine Madwar, Mary Rou Rozell, and Barbara Heinlein—the secretarial support staff in the Department of Educational Services and Research at The Ohio State University. We wish to thank Patricia Nettles of the Hillside Children's Center in Oswego, NY, Frank Gresham of the University of California–Riverside, and Frank Kohler of the Allegheny-Singer Research Institute in Pittsburgh, PA, for reviewing the manuscript.

We also would like to thank our families and friends for all the less tangible but equally appreciated kinds of help and support.

About the Contributors

Gwendolyn Cartledge (PhD, The Ohio State University) is an associate professor at The Ohio State University in the College of Education where her primary responsibility is the preparation of teachers to work with students with behavioral and emotional disorders. Professional interests center on developing academic and social skills in learners with disabilities.

JoAnne F. Milburn (MSW, UCLA; PhD, The Ohio State University) has worked with children and families in clinical and school settings, served on the faculty of the College of Social Work at The Ohio State University, and directed a multiservice children's mental health facility for a number of years. She currently works in child advocacy and child abuse prevention.

Timothy A. Cavell (PhD) is an assistant professor of psychology at Texas A&M University. He received his doctorate in 1988 from Louisiana State University (major, clinical; minor, developmental) and interned at the Morrison Center for Youth and Families in Portland, Oregon. His primary research interests include the assessment of adolescent social competence and the use of family therapy and parent training to treat childhood aggression. Professor Cavell's own approach to parent training—*Responsive Parent Training*—relies extensively on attachment theory to blend two existing models of parent training: behavior management and relationship enhancement. His research has been published in such journals as *Journal of Clinical Child Psychology, Journal of Marital and Family Therapy, Professional Psychology: Research and Practice, and Behavior Therapy.*

John Dattilo (PhD) is an associate professor in the Department of Recreation and Leisure Studies at the University of Georgia. As a C.T.R.S., he has been examining effects of interventions on leisure patterns of people with disabilities. Professor Dattilo has published extensively on the topic, including two coauthored textbooks, *Leisure Education Program Programming: A Systematic Approach* (1991) and *Be-*

havior Modification in Therapeutic Recreation (1987). He received his Ph.D. in Leisure Studies at the University of Illinois at Urbana–Champaign and has taught therapeutic recreation at the University of Nebraska and Pennsylvania State University.

Hua Feng (PhD student) is a doctorate student in special education at The Ohio State University, under the supervision of Dr. Gwendolyn Cartledge. She was a school counselor in Taiwan for three years before commencing her graduate studies in the United States. Her major research interests focus on behavior disabilities and social skills development among culturally diverse populations.

N. Jane Gershaw (PhD, Syracuse University) is Chief of the Mental Health Clinic at the Veterans Administration Medical Center in Syracuse, New York. She holds faculty appointments at Syracuse University and the State University of New York Health Sciences Center in Syracuse. She also maintains a private practice. Dr. Gershaw has had a long-term interest in therapeutic groups, having worked with this modality for over twenty years.

Arnold P. Goldstein (PhD, Pennsylvania State University) is a professor of special education at Syracuse University; Director, New York State Taskforce on Juvenile Gangs; and Member, American Psychological Association Commission on Youth Violence. His research and training interest is in teaching prosocial behavior to antisocial youth.

Linda A. Heyne (PhD) has worked extensively in the area of inclusive community recreation services for individuals with developmental disabilities. She has participated in numerous conferences, contributed to several publications, and served on national committees to promote inclusive recreation services. Dr. Heyne has coordinated the Leadership Training and Therapeutic Recreation Grant Projects at the University of Minnesota. She also has served as coordinator for a model inclusive recreation program for children and youth with disabilities at the Jewish Community Center of the Greater St. Paul area.

Jan N. Hughes (PhD) is a professor of educational psychology at Texas A&M University, where she directs the doctoral program in school psychology. She received her doctorate in school psychology from the University of Texas at Austin. Dr. Hughes has authored two books in child-clinical psychology and edited a text on cognitive behavioral psychology in educational settings. She has authored over 40 scientific papers in the areas of school psychology and child psychopathology and serves on the editorial boards of three scientific journals. She is active in national leadership in professional psychology and maintains a private practice in a pediatric clinic.

Jeanette W. Lee (PhD, The Ohio State University) is an associate professor at West Virginia State College in the Department of Education. Her primary role is instructing prospective teachers of children with exceptionalities. Professor Lee has been a classroom teacher of children with learning disabilities, behavior disorders, and mental impairments. Her major research interests include interventions for academic and affective growth and empowering parenting skills.

Jacquelyn Mize (PhD, Purdue University) is an associate professor of family and child development at Auburn University. Her research interests focus on peer relationships and social skills during the preschool years. Currently, she is engaged in research on the processes by which parents contribute to young children's social competence.

Stuart J. Schleien (PhD) is a professor of therapeutic recreation and director of graduate studies at the University of Minnesota. He holds an adjunct appointment in the Department of Educational Psychology–Special Education Programs. His research efforts involve the development of technology to integrate children and adults with developmental disabilities into community leisure environments. Dr. Schleien has written over 60 journal articles and book chapters, in addition to six books. He has presented his work at professional conferences and symposia throughout the United States, and in Canada, Israel, Australia, and Sweden. Dr. Schleien is currently the chairperson of the Leisure and Recreation Committee of the Association for Persons with Severe Handicaps (TASH) and has served on the President's Committee on Mental Retardation. He was recognized by the ARC of Minnesota as the Minnesota Educator of the Year in Mental Retardation and by the Minnesota Recreation and Park Association as the Researcher of the Year in Therapeutic Recreation and Leisure Education.

Robert P. Sprafkin (PhD, The Ohio State University) serves as chief of the Day Treatment Center at the Department of Veterans Affairs Medical Center in Syracuse, New York, and is also Director of their Psychology Training Program. He holds academic rank as an adjunct professor of psychology at Syracuse University and clinical associate professor of psychiatry at the State University of New York Health Science Center. Dr. Sprafkin maintains a private practice in Syracuse. Along with Drs. Goldstein and Gershaw, he has written extensively on social skills training with various populations.

Part 1

Steps in Teaching Social Skills

Chapter 1

Selecting Social Skills

What are social skills? A number of reviewers and researchers have offered definitions that range from the narrow and specific to the broad and general. In 1973, Libet and Lewinsohn described *social skill* as "the complex ability both to emit behaviors that are positively or negatively reinforced, and not to emit behaviors that are punished or extinguished by others" (p. 304). Another definition is that of Combs and Slaby (1977): "The ability to interact with others in a given social context in specific ways that are socially acceptable or valued and at the same time personally beneficial, mutually beneficial, or beneficial primarily to others" (p. 162).

According to the situation-specific concept of social skills presented by Hersen and Bellack (1977), the effectiveness of behavior in social interactions depends on the context and parameters of the situation. Along with behavioral skill is the individual's ability to perceive the situation and be aware when a particular set of behaviors will result in positive outcomes. Trower (1980) breaks social skills into behavioral and cognitive dimensions: skill components and skill processes. *Skill components* are single elements, such as looks or nods, or sequences of behavior, used in social interactions such as greetings or partings. *Social processes* refers to the "individual's ability to generate skilled behavior according to rules and goals and in response to social feedback" (p. 328). This distinction suggests the individual's need to monitor situations and vary behavior in response to feedback from other persons. Eisler and Frederiksen (1980) similarly describe social skills as having both observable aspects and nonobservable cognitive elements. The latter include "expectations, thoughts, and decisions about what should be said or done during the next interaction," and abilities such as "the accurate perception of the other person's wishes or intentions, or insight into which response will be the most likely to influence his or her partner's opinion" (p. 9).

Some definitions of social skills emphasize outcomes. Morgan (1980) points out that not only do social skills involve the ability to initiate and maintain positive interactions with other people, but they also include "the ability to achieve the objectives that a person has for interacting with others. . . . The more frequently, or the greater the extent to which a person achieves his objectives in interacting with others, the more skilled we would judge him to be" (p. 104). Gresham and Elliott (1984) provide a social validity definition, which refers to social skills as

> those behaviors which, within a given situation, predict important social outcomes such as (a) peer acceptance or popularity, (b) significant others' judgments of behavior, or (c) other social behaviors known to correlate consistently with peer acceptance or significant others' judgments (pp. 292–293).

The term *social competence* often is considered synonymous and is used interchangeably with social skill. Hops (1983) makes the distinction between these two concepts clear:

> Competence is a summary term which reflects social judgment about the general quality of an individual's performance in a given situation. The concept of social skills from a behavioral perspective is based on the assumption that specific identifiable skills form the basis for socially competent behavior (p. 4).

Cavell (1990) offers a model that views social competence as a "multi-level construct made up of social adjustment, social performance, and social skills." He suggests that skills and performance in and of themselves are necessary but insufficient to define social competence and must be looked at in relation to their contribution to social adjustment, that is, the achievement of important developmental goals.

Schloss, Schloss, Wood, and Kiehl (1986) point out limitations of more general definitions: social skills vary according to chronological ages and developmental levels, and some broad outcome-oriented definitions even include maladaptive or antisocial responses as well as desirable behaviors. In their view, the lack of generally accepted definitions has hindered the development of a comprehensive body of knowledge that can be translated into effective teaching procedures. To overcome some of these limitations, they suggest that social skills be defined as specific behaviors described in ways that allow reliable observation and take the subject's age and specific social context into consideration.

Discussion of social skills in this book focuses, for the most part, on social behaviors that involve interaction between the child and his or her peers or adults where the primary intent is achievement of the child's or the adult's goals through positive interchanges. As Part II shows, persons with disabilities may need to be taught some simple nonsocial behaviors as prerequisites to learning social skills.

Factors in Social Skills Selection

In determining what social skills should be taught to children, it is possible to apply both a general set of norms, defined by various experts as behaviors necessary for competence as a child in our culture, and specific criteria for the behaviors needed by an individual child to be regarded as competent. Recently, considerable attention has focused on selecting target behaviors for social skills instruction (Hughes, 1986; Kazdin, 1985; Kratochwill, 1985; Pray, Hall, & Markey, 1992; Strain, Odom, & McConnell, 1984; Weist & Ollendick, 1991; Weist, Ollendick, & Finney, 1991). All these writers emphasize the importance of careful selection of skills for successful instruction and long-term maintenance of the acquired behaviors. Among the variables involved in selecting of target behaviors are the individual characteristics of the learner, for example, skill deficits, sex, age, and developmental level; social factors such as the social and cultural milieu in which the skills are to be used; social validity—the legitimacy, in the view of the learners, their peers, and relevant adults, of the skills being taught; the purposes and desired outcomes of the instruction; and what constitutes the critical behaviors to be taught in order to achieve the desired results.

Learner Characteristics

Although a case may be made for teaching interpersonal coping skills to *all* children as a means of preventing later adjustment problems (Durlak, 1985; Elias & Branden, 1988; Elias, Gara, Schuyler, Branden-Muller, & Sayette, 1991; Kendall, Lerner, & Craighead, 1984), much social skills instruction in educational and clinical settings is initiated as a means of remediating problems in social adjustment. Regardless of whether social skills instruction is undertaken as primary prevention, for secondary prevention with high-risk youth, or to help children overcome existing problems, the first task for the practitioner is to assess the characteristics of the learners and their environment in order to tailor instruction to their needs.

Developmental Level
Developmental levels is one set of learner characteristics used in identifying social skills to be taught. It may be debated whether behavior always develops according to stages outlined by various theorists, whether some behaviors can be more easily taught and maintained at one stage than at another, and which behaviors need to be taught or simply result inevitably from maturation and accompanying experience. At the same time, stage theories do provide broad indices for social development and assist in the task of determining the sequence in which social behaviors are taught.

Two developmental theories stressing psychological factors contributing to socialization are those of Erikson (1963) and Freud (1961). These models present similar developmental systems of socialization extending from infancy through adulthood, with a set of conflicts to be mastered at each stage, primarily through the development of social behaviors resulting from interaction with significant figures in the environment. In both theories, early socialization is centered around the mother or other principal caregiver with a gradual widening of relationships to others in the home and outside. Social behaviors, such as the child's ability to take, to give, and to get others to care for his or her needs, are taught by parents and caregivers through their responses and their examples. As the child develops, social responses learned early become expressed and modified through interaction with siblings, peers, and other adults. These socializing experiences assist the child in developing a personal identity and a sense of mastery over his or her environment, with resultant feelings of self-esteem and eventual ability to become independent. An example of a developmental stage-oriented curriculum using psychodynamic concepts is that of Wood (1986).

The moral development theories of Piaget (Inhelder & Piaget, 1964) and Kohlberg (1969) are also relevant to social skills. In the sequence hypothesized for moral development as it relates to children's play behavior, Piaget specifies first a motor development stage, in which play is largely motor and individualistic, followed by an egocentric stage (approximately ages 2 to 5) where the child applies rules to daily activities based on external control of adults and older children. Then follows a stage of mutual cooperation in which the child begins to establish rules according to particular social circumstances, considering the interests of others. The final stage, at around 11 or 12 years, involves recognition of moral principles, the importance of the rights of others, and the functional importance of rules in the social order as a mechanism for protecting individual rights. Piaget considers the elements of all these stages to exist at all levels, differing only in the degree to which specific behavior patterns are found in the respective stages.

Kohlberg (1969) built on these ideas with a six-stage developmental theory suggesting that morality evolves from primarily egotistical considerations (Stages 1 and 2) to interest in maintaining order and stability (Stages 3 and 4) to the highest levels (Stages 5 and 6), where the individual adheres to inner principles, defining his or her behavior according to conscience and convictions rather than simply by laws and regulations. Within Kohlberg's model, children with delinquent behaviors are operating at the lower egotistical levels, where the emphasis is on personal gain and the avoidance of punishment. Using this framework, direct instruction, gradually moving through the developmental stages, would be recommended to improve social behaviors.

If one accepts these hierarchies related to moral development as presented by Piaget and Kohlberg, the implications for selection of social skills would be, for example, that behaviors such as sharing and cooperative play could most easily be taught after the age of two, and that acceptance of authority through following directions and understanding consequences can be taught earlier than behaviors involving independent decision making. Also implied is that social skills involving understanding another's point of view could most easily be taught at a later stage, and that principles based on one's inner beliefs are best established after the child has accepted the importance of order and regulation. The Skillstreaming program of Goldstein (Chapter 9) incorporates Kohlberg's moral development concepts.

There is an increasing trend toward viewing social skills and social competence within a developmental context. Waters and Sroufe (1983) regard social competence as a "developmental construct," pointing out that not only are specific skills situation- and age-specific, but "competence in one development period . . . should have consequences for subsequent development" (p. 80). Eisenberg and Harris (1984) suggest that among important capacities for social competence that change with age are the child's ability to take the perspective of another person, the conceptualization of friendship, problem-solving ability, and communication skills.

Developmental considerations have relevance not only for selection of social skills but also for the teaching approaches to be used. An early step in devising social skills instruction is to view the child according to developmental standards and to identify the progression needed for desired performance. To respond to social skills training, the child first may need to learn to attend to and identify relevant stimuli. Every set of social skills has prerequisites. Brooks-Gunn and Luciano (1985) point out, for example, that until the young child acquires a concept of self, reciprocal relationships are not possible, and that complex social behaviors and social emotions such as empathy require that the child has "a concept of self and is capable of taking the role of another or being influenced by someone 'Like me'." At the same time, although it is debatable at what point young children can differentiate their internal states from those of others, there is evidence that children as young as 18 months can engage in sympathetically-motivated prosocial acts (Eisenberg & Miller, 1987). Obviously, social skills requiring the use of language can more easily be taught to older children who employ verbalization in social interactions more often than do younger children (Selman, Schorin, Stone, & Phelps, 1983).

Along with developmental levels, there are age considerations. Social skills trainers need to be aware of qualitative differences in behavioral norms between children and adults. Weist and Ollendick (1991) provide an example of such differences with a detailed analysis of assertive behaviors exhibited by boys identified as interpersonally successful. They found that behaviors traditionally associated with adult assertiveness (i.e., eye contact, ability to praise, duration of speech, refusing unreasonable requests) did not significantly differentiate assertive from nonassertive youth. Smiles and lively speech were significant, along with other behaviors identified through observation: body orientation, lower number of grammatical speech errors, higher energy level, ability to state consequences, and context-appropriate behavior. The authors cite evidence from other studies (for example, Charlesworth & Hartup, 1967; Feidler & Beach, 1978; Ollendick, Hart, & Francis, 1985) to question whether assertive behaviors as defined by adult criteria are functional for children. The same questions may be asked about a variety of social behaviors.

Gender
In addition to age and developmental level differences, there are apparent sex differences in how children handle interpersonal relationships. Chung and Asher (1992) found that fourth-, fifth-, and sixth-grade boys use more hostile/coercive strategies in conflict situations, whereas girls employ more prosocial and passive strategies. Similar results were obtained by Miller, Danaher, and Forbes (1986) with five- and seven-year olds and by Fabes and Eisenberg (1992), who found that preschool boys express anger in a more direct and inflammatory way, while girls tend to use strategies that would mitigate or resolve the conflict. These findings, of course, suggest a need to instruct boys, especially, in nonviolent alternatives to conflict situations.

In discussing the implications of well-documented gender differences for social skills training, Crombie (1988) points out that girls and boys differ in the size of groups with whom they play during preschool and middle childhood; girls have a preference for smaller groups and for exclusive friendships. She suggests that group entry skills may be of greater importance for boys. Similarly, boys play more at team sports with direct competition than girls do. Specific implications are a need for "learning to deal with dominance attempts . . . to discriminate mock fighting from true aggressive behavior" and, in competitive play, "learning self-control and depersonalizing the attack" (p. 119). Whereas peer influence is more important for boys, girls are more oriented toward adults and toward the teachers in school. Crombie suggests that social skills are a "more important component of the traditional feminine gender role," especially because females tend to place greater emphasis on interpersonal relationships.

Although the gender differences described here have been identified through empirical efforts, they may not be widely accepted as valid. Gender differences are affected by factors such as cultural norms and socio-economic levels, as well as by the continually changing and evolving roles of males and females in the larger society. The practitioner needs to avoid overgeneralization in making decisions about selection of social skills based on gender considerations.

Cognitive and Behavioral Deficits

When a social skills program is undertaken because of problems in social relationships, an important aspect of target behavior selection is the identification of the specific deficits to be remediated (Maag, 1989). Weist et al. (1991) similarly argue for the identification of deficits in selecting target behaviors for treatment of the child. They suggest assessing, for example, whether deficits are in the child's cognitive skills, involve an inability to perform the desired behaviors, or result from an emotional state such as anxiety, that would interfere with performance. Considerable literature exists describing the social skills deficits of children with disabilities of various sorts (e.g., Gerber & Zinkgraf, 1982; Gresham & Elliott, 1989; Gresham, Elliott, & Black, 1987; Landau & Moore, 1991; McKinnie & Elliott, 1991; Schneider & Yoshida, 1988; Thapanadilok, 1992). Rubin and Krasnor (1986) examined the social problem-solving behaviors of children according to social status with peers, and found clear differences between socially withdrawn or isolated children and socially rejected children in their abilities to problem-solve in social situations. Socially rejected children tended toward more aggressive, impulsive, and less flexible strategies. The socially withdrawn or isolated children did not show deficits in social cognition, but rather lacked social confidence and the ability to be assertive. The authors suggest social problem training for rejected children and "confidence-boosting peer experiences" for isolated children. Akhtar and Bradley (1991) reviewed research on social information processing deficits of aggressive children with similar findings. They found that aggressive children lack a number of abilities necessary for positive social interactions. Among these deficits are the inability to encode relevant environmental cues and to generate solutions for problematic situations, along with a lack of ability to enact many social behaviors. In addition, they tend to "assign hostile intentions to social partners," and pursue inappropriate social goals. The authors conclude that treatment approaches for aggressive children need to include training in social information processing as well as possible retraining of social beliefs and goals.

Social Criteria in Skills Selection

The Cultural Context

In selecting target skills for a particular child or group of children, a number of social criteria need to be considered in addition to the factors outlined above. There is a variety of opinion in different parts of society, among groups of professionals, even within families, and certainly over time, about how children should act. For example, rather than being "seen and not heard" as in "days of yore," children are now being taught assertiveness and are expected to know how to respond in interpersonal situations with both adults and peers. The cultural context of social behaviors is an important consideration for the selection of social skills to be taught. As Argyle (1986) points out

> . . . optimum skills vary greatly with the cultural setting. Assertiveness may be successful in the United States, but it would not be so in Japan or Indonesia. Democratic-persuasive supervisory skills do not work in India or Japan. Similar differences are found between social classes, ethnic groups, and age groups inside any one culture; this is a major problem for social skills trainers (p. 680).

There are numerous other examples of cultural differences: people from different cultures stand at different distances from one another; children in some cultural groups are taught not to look directly at others; children in some families or subcultures are taught to hit back rather than engage in some alternative to aggression. Chapter 10 discusses cultural differences and the implications for social skills instruction in more detail.

Situation Specificity

Along with cultural considerations, situation-specificity is a relevant concept in identifying skills to teach. Social skills considered to be appropriate in one setting may not be so in another. Kendall et al. (1984) describe the competent child as one with behavioral flexibility, with an ability to evaluate the demands of a particular context and change behavior to fit the demands of the setting. Providing the child with an awareness that different situations require different behaviors may be a necessary prerequisite to teaching specific skills. Achenbach, McConaughy, and Howell (1987) stress the need to gather data about a child's functioning from more than one setting (both home and school, for example) to determine appropriate intervention goals. Dodge, McClaskey, and Feldman (1985) propose that "children's social behaviors are best understood as responses to specific situations or tasks" (p. 351) and suggest that assessment should identify the particular social contexts, tasks, or situations in which problem behaviors occur. For example, they found that aggressive children were particularly subject to maladaptive responses when they were being provoked by a peer (e.g., being teased, hit, or insulted) or when they needed to respond to social expectations from the teacher. As discussed in Chapter 4, situational variables also play an important role in the transfer and maintenance of skills after training.

Peer Relationships

Relationships with peers are among the most important elements in a child's life and contribute in a variety of ways to the child's social learning. Childhood peer rejection has been clearly demonstrated to be a factor in later life adjustment problems such as dropping out of school, criminality, and psychopathology (Parker & Asher, 1987). The role played by social skills in peer relationships has lately become a major focus in socialization research, and attempts are being made to determine the social skills that will encourage peer acceptance.

An early review by Hartup (1970) identifies correlates of peer acceptance. These include friendliness, sociability, and outgoingness; frequency of dispensing social reinforcers; social participation; kindness; being helpful; and being "good company" or the "life of the party." Dygdon, Conger, Conger, Wallanda, and Keane (1980) found that characteristics of "liked" children, as defined by sociometric measures, were altruism and participation in play activities, "entertainingness," vocabulary, quantity of speech, motor prowess, and academic efficiency.

Strain, et al. (1984) suggest that because of the importance of peer relationships, the selection of target behaviors for young children should involve those that will be used when relating to peers outside the instructional setting and result in positive reciprocal social interaction. Some of the behaviors they suggest are social initiations, imitation, sharing, and affectionate behavior. Kohler and Fowler (1985) point out that social behaviors, such as invitations to share, have a natural reinforcement function and may lead to a series of positive exchanges.

Play behavior emerges repeatedly as important in distinguishing competent from incompetent children, with "entry" identified as a key skill because it serves as a prerequisite for further interaction. Dodge, Schlundt, Schocken, and Delugach (1983) present a model of social competence in children's peer group entry situations involving a series of tactics to gain entry. The tactics involve various degrees of risk of being rejected. Successful tactics "avoid interrupting the group activity by calling attention to the entering child" and instead allow the activity to continue as the child becomes integrated into the group. Specific successful tactics include waiting and observing the peer group, moving progressively closer, mimicking the activity in which the peer group is engaged, followed by making a statement about the peer group. (See Putallaz and Wasserman, 1990, for a review of research on children's entry behavior.)

There are data to suggest that children regarded as socially competent have strategies for handling anger in ways that avoid aggression (Fabes & Eisenberg, 1992). Brochin and Wasik (1992) found that responses to conflict management problems significantly differentiated popular from unpopular kindergarten-level children. In their study of preschool children, the categories of anger-causing behaviors Fabes and Eisenberg describe are:

(a) physical causes—anger provoked by something done to target child's person (e.g., hitting, kicking, pushing, etc.); (b) verbal—anger provoked by something said to target child (e.g. teasing, name calling, etc.); (c) rejection—anger provoked by being ignored or not allowed to play with others; (d) material—anger provoked by someone taking or destroying the target child's property or space; (e) compliance—anger provoked by being asked or forced to do something (e.g., teacher's requests) (p. 119).

Children's responses to different sources of provocation differed, with conflict over possessions being the most common cause of anger and physical assault second. Conflict management skills, anger control, and constructive responses to provocation all appear to be important target behaviors for social skill instruction.

Although positive behaviors tend to be associated with peer acceptance and negative behaviors with rejection, this relationship is not clear. Foster, Delawyer, and Guevremont (1986), for example, find that while positive behaviors exceeded negative behaviors, grade-school children report "friends" to engage in a significant number of negative behaviors. In a study of the behavioral correlates of peer acceptance among elementary-aged non-LD children toward an LD-labeled child, Cartledge, Frew, and Zaharias (1985) found that even though the positive behaviors of being kind and saying nice things were more commonly attributed to the LD child, that child was less likely to be selected for friendship and social interaction.

Although many children with obvious behavior problems are accepted by their peers, the research literature consistently associates peer rejection with aggression and conduct disorders and peer neglect with internalizing behaviors and anxiety disorders (Asarnow, 1988; Gresham & Little, 1993; Strauss, Lahey, Frick, Frame, & Hynd, 1988). Milich and Landau (1984) suggest that aggressive children be divided into subgroups of aggressive and aggressive-withdrawn. They find some aggressive boys to be rejected, but many are viewed positively as well. On the other hand, aggressive-withdrawn boys, those with low peer interaction rates, have significantly higher rejection rates and are considered to be at greater risk for later adjustment problems. Hymel, Wagner, and Butler (1990) point out that peer relationships are influenced by such variables as social perception, reputation, and popularity.

> Behavior that is perfectly acceptable to peers when enacted by popular children is somehow less acceptable and less memorable when enacted by unpopular children. There appears to be a double standard in the peer group that ensures that popular children will continue to be viewed positively and that unpopular children will continue to be viewed negatively, regardless of actual behavior (p. 174).

Coie (1990) summarizes questions identified by Asher and Williams (1987) as key aspects of social acceptance by peers: "Is the other child fun to be with? Trustworthy? Similar to me? Does this child facilitate and not undermine my goals? Make me feel good about myself? Do we influence each other in ways I like?" (p. 374). Answers to these questions may explain why some children who have problem behaviors may still be accepted as friends and even be considered popular. This phenomenon presents a challenge for the social skills instructor in selecting peer relationship target behaviors and involves issues such as social validity, which is discussed in the next section. In addition, children with behavior problems who are popular with peers may especially need social skills training aimed at helping them use their influence with peers in constructive ways.

Two techniques for identifying peer-oriented target behaviors are the "known groups" approach in which successful children are observed to determine what they do that the target children fail to do, and "template matching" (Hoier & Cone, 1980, 1987)—an empirical approach recommended by Weist et al. (1991) for use in selecting target behaviors for children judged to be deficient in peer-related social skills. In the latter process, behaviors of successful children are examined to create a template of behavior judged to be desirable in a specific context. Descriptions of behavior can be obtained either from informants or from direct observation. A list of behaviors of the successful children is compared with those of the target child; discrepancies become the target behaviors for social skills training. This procedure has the advantage of including the situation in which the desired behaviors occur. At the same time, Rathjen (1984) points out that these approaches do not ensure that the critical behaviors that account for success have been identified. Identifying such behaviors is currently one of the most active areas in social skills and social competency research.

Social Validity

A basis for selecting social skills is implied in Wolf's (1978) discussion of social validity as a criterion for determining what are socially significant problems for behavior change efforts. Social validity, according to Wolf, can best be established by consumers or representatives of the relevant community according to such criteria as whether the behaviors have social significance in relation to goals desired by society, whether the procedures used to bring about behavioral change are acceptable, and whether the effects or results of behavior change are satisfactory to the relevant consumers. Schwartz and Baer (1991) identify consumers as (1) direct—in the case of social skills training of children, the children themselves; (2) indirect—peers, and relevant adults, who could include members of the immediate community; and (3) members of the extended community. They point out risks of undertaking behavior change programs without the agreement of the involved consumers regarding target behaviors and procedures selected. Adverse consequences could include unwillingness to participate, undermining and sabotage, and failures in long-term maintenance of skills.

For the selection of socially valid skills to teach, the views of target children themselves as direct consumers and those of the peer group as indirect consumers about desirable ways to act and respond in interpersonal situations are important considerations. Those beliefs will affect both the learner's motivation in acquiring alternate behaviors and interest in continuing to perform the behaviors once learned. In Chapter 9, Goldstein addresses this concern by having adolescents select the target skills themselves from among a group of skills. Although Schwartz and Baer (1991) assert that practitioners "are not usually and not properly in the business of shaping our consumers' values," (p. 202), both they and Hawkins (1991) discuss the importance of consumer education as an aid to acceptance of treatment goals and procedures.

Akhtar and Bradley (1991) suggest that determining children's views may also signal the need for retraining. Before teaching children alternatives to aggression, for example, the trainer will need to consider the sociocultural context and the beliefs of the children about the value of aggression and then incorporate into the training a convincing rationale for the value of learning alternatives. That rationale also may need to be provided to the adult indirect consumers—the parents, for example—if the alternatives are to be practiced in the future and in other settings.

Teachers constitute another group of indirect consumers, as well as implementers of social skills training. Much data exist related to what social behaviors teachers regard as important for children to exhibit. In contrast to the behaviors that children value mentioned earlier, teachers would emphasize social behaviors that facilitate their task of teaching academic skills. In a study by Milburn (1974), a group of teachers rated the skills concerned with order, cooperative behavior, accepting consequences, following rules and directions, avoiding conflict, and basic self-help behavior as more important. They rated as less important the skills that involved initiating contact with others, greeting and conversation, being assertive in interpersonal relationships, and performing for others. Findings such as this have been paralleled in a number of other studies (Cartledge et al., 1985; Gresham & Elliott, 1988; Meadows, Neel, Parker, & Timo, 1991; Pray et al., 1992; Williams, Walker, Holmes, Todis, & Fabré, 1989).

In one of the early social skills research efforts, a set of specific classroom "survival skills" which correlate highly with academic success for primary students is identified by Hops and Cobb (1973). These skills include attending, volunteering answers, complying with teacher requests, following teacher directions, and remaining on task. A school survival skills curriculum for secondary school students (Schaeffer, Zigmond, Kerr, & Farra, 1990; Zigmond, Kerr, Schaeffer, Brown, & Farra, 1986) emphasizes similar skills: attending class regularly; arriving on time; bringing necessary materials such as pencils, paper, and books; turning in work on time; using an assignment book; being on-task, following directions; and answering and asking questions.

The fact that youth in general may not value the same social skills as do teachers does not necessarily mean the teaching of skills considered important by adults should be abandoned. Meadows et al. (1991) suggest that "a major component in the training of social skills would have to be teaching children . . . to value interacting with adults," and that the extent to which youth and teachers agree might be considered a measure of socialization toward adult values. At the same time they suggest that because students prefer immediate social goals to those with more long-term, less direct rewards, schools need to "realign their priorities to include peer-focused social skills training" (p. 207).

Kazdin (1985) points out that a validational approach to selecting target behaviors needs to look at both long-term outcomes (predictive validity) and impact on everyday functioning (concurrent validity). In applying the concept of social validity to children's social skills, Gresham (1986) suggests that socially important outcomes of social skill training for children might include: "(a) peer acceptance or popularity, (b) significant others' judgments of social skill (e.g., parents, teachers), and/or (c) other social behaviors known to consistently correlate with peer acceptance/popularity and judgments of significant others" (p. 7). It seems apparent that in selecting target social skills, the desired outcomes will be a major factor in determining the instructional focus. The emphasis could be quite different if the goal were, for example, increased peer acceptance as opposed to classroom success or improved home relationships.

The potential social skills trainer has been presented in this section with an almost overwhelming array of variables to be considered in selecting target social skills. The age and developmental level of the child, gender, cognitive and behavioral deficits, cultural and situational context of skills to be taught, views of peers and relevant adults, goals for carrying out the instruction and social validity in terms of desired outcomes, the potential for generalization, and long-term maintenance of the skills are all important considerations. In advocating empirical methods for selecting target behaviors, Weist et al. (1991) recognize limitations having to do with time and expense and suggest that a practical approach would be to review relevant literature and make informal asssessments of successful children to identify the behaviors that are associated with success and failure in a particular setting. Similarly, Hughes (1986) recognizes the difference between research and clinical practice in selection of target skills. She suggests that the "practitioner evaluate the research evidence for the social validity of the targeted skills . . . assess whether a particular child-client is deficient in the skills . . . and attempt to determine what individual child characteristics contribute to the observed performance deficits" (p. 245).

The above suggestions are consistent with the model on which this book is based. In selecting social skills to be taught, the practitioner or researcher will be guided first by the goals underlying the instruction—whether for prevention, for remediation of deficits, or for specific research purposes. The instructor subsequently will assess the environment to determine the skills that are most salient and socially valid for success in that setting and, if relevant, will assess target children for skills lacking in their repertoires that need to be developed in order for them to succeed.

Inventories of Social Skills

A number of empirically derived constellations of social skills have been identified and developed into social skills inventories, many with associated curricula and assessment instruments. Because of the number of variables involved in determining the selection of social behaviors, it may be difficult to find a social skills inventory that meets all the needs of the individual child or specific group at any one point in time. It may be necessary to add more behaviors or delete some that are not relevant to the child or social situation. Inventories and published curricula may provide a useful place to start nevertheless.

The Social Growth Program of King and Kirschenbaum (1992) is an early intervention program aimed at young primary-grade children. The content involves: *Who am I?* (the development of self-understanding and positive self-image); *Who are we: What are social skills?* (the meaning and importance of positive social behaviors); *Active listening; Warm messages; Asking questions; Sharing feelings; Standing up for me; Self-control; Social problem solving.* Fiechtl, Innocenti, and Rule (1987) have developed a *Skills for School Success* curriculum to assist preschool children with disabilities transition to kindergarten. Activity areas are divided into component skills or tasks with performance criteria based on the speed and accuracy with which typically developing children perform the skills (Rule, Fiechtl, & Innocenti, 1990). The nine activity areas include:

1. entry routines (hanging up coat, selecting toys, and playing until the teacher signals the next activity);
2. sequence tasks (individually completing a series of tasks announced daily);
3. Pledge of Allegiance;
4. group circle activities (discussion of weather, etc.);
5. individual tasks;
6. large-group activities using commercially available curricula;
7. workbook tasks;
8. quiet time activities (child-selected, child-guided activity); and
9. transition activities (getting coat and materials to take home, lining up, and walking in line through the building) (p. 81).

The developmental teaching model for students with social, emotional, or behavioral disabilities (Wood, 1975, 1986) presents specific behavioral goals and objectives according to five stages of development, identified as preschool through age 16; the stages do not involve a rigid correspondence between age and developmental level. There are four curriculum areas for each stage: behavior, communication, socialization, and (pre) academics. Table 1-1 outlines goals for each stage.

Most published skills inventories are aimed at the school-age child. One of the earliest was Stephens' social skills inventory and curriculum (1978, 1992) on which an assessment instrument is also built (Stephens, 1992; Stephens & Arnold, 1991). The behaviors are grouped into four major categories (environmental, interpersonal, self-related, and task-related behaviors), which are further analyzed into 30 subcategories and 136 specific skills. Table 1-2 lists subcategory headings. Specific responses have been identified for each subcategory. A sample category, subcategory, and skill listing follows (1992, p. 187):

Major category: INTERPERSONAL BEHAVIORS
Subcategory: Playing Informally
Skills: To ask another student to play on the playground
                   To ask to be included in a playground activity in progress.
                   To share toys and equipment in a play situation
                   To give in to reasonable group wishes in a play situation.
                   To suggest an activity for the group on the playground.

TABLE 1-1 Goals for Curriculum Areas

Goal	Behavior	Communication	Socialization	(Pre) Academics
Responding to the environment with pleasure	Trusting body skills	Using words to gain needs	Trusting an adult sufficiently to respond	Responding to the environment with processes of classification, discrimination, basic receptive language and body coordination.
Responding to the environment with success	Successfully participating in routines	Using words to affect others in constructive ways	Participating in activities with others	Participating in classroom activities with body coordination, language, and processes of ordering, classifying, and numeration.
Learning skills for successful group participation	Applying individual skills successfully in group processes	Using words to express oneself in the group	Finding satisfaction in group activities	Participating in the group with basic expressive language concepts.
Investing in group processes	Contributing individual effort to group success	Using words to express awareness of relationship between feelings and behavior in self and others	Participating spontaneously and successfully as a group member	Successfully using signs and symbols in formalized school work and in group experiences.
Applying individual and group skills successfully in new situations	Responding to critical life experiences with adaptive, constructive behavior	Using words to establish and enrich relationships	Initiating and maintaining effective peer group relationships independently	Successfully using signs and symbols for formalized school experiences and personal enrichment.

TABLE 1-2 Behavior Categories and Subcategories

Self-related Behaviors	Environmental Behaviors
Accepting consequences	Care for the environment
Ethical behavior	Dealing with emergencies
Expressing feelings	Lunchroom behavior
Positive attitude toward self	Movement around environment

Task-related Behaviors	Interpersonal Behaviors
Asking and answering questions	Accepting authority
Attending behavior	Coping with conflict
Classroom discussion	Gaining attention
Completing tasks	Greeting others
Following directions	Helping others
Group activities	Making conversation
Independent work	Organized play
On-task behavior	Positive attitude toward others
Performing before others	Playing informally
Quality of work	Property: own and others

For a complete skill listing, the reader is referred to the Social Skills List in Appendix C.

A listing of social skills developed by Walker also forms the basis for a curriculum (Walker, McConnell, Holmes, Todis, Walker, & Golden, 1983). The target population is composed of children with mild to moderate disabilities in the elementary school grades. Their skill listings are shown in Table 1-3. Both the Stephens and the Walker et al. skills listings were developed through social validation processes in which teachers rated the importance of specified social behaviors for classroom success (Milburn, 1974; Walker et al., 1983).

Based on an analysis of correlates of peer acceptance in elementary school (Hartup, 1970), LaGreca and associates (LaGreca & Mezibov, 1979; LaGreca & Santogrossi, 1980) identify nine areas for social skill instruction that contribute to positive peer relations. They also divided these into skill components. The nine areas include:

- Smiling and laughing with peers
- Greeting others
- Joining ongoing activities
- Extending invitation
- Conversational skills
- Sharing and cooperation
- Verbal complimenting
- Play skills
- Physical appearance/grooming

TABLE 1-3 Skills of Handicapped Children

Area I: Classroom Skills

- Listening to the teacher (sit quietly and look at . . .)
- When the teacher asks you to do something (you should do it)
- Doing your best work (follow directions and write neatly)
- Following classroom rules

Area II: Basic Interaction Skills

- Eye contact
- Using the right voice
- Starting (finding someone to talk to)
- Listening (look at the person and pay attention)
- Answering (saying something after someone talks to you)
- Making sense (talking about the same things)
- Taking turns talking
- Asking questions
- Continuing to talk (keeping the talking going)

Area III: Getting Along Skills

- Using polite words (saying nice things at the right time)
- Sharing
- Following rules (everyone plays the game the same way)
- Assisting others (doing nice things for others when they need help
- Touching the right way

Area IV: Making Friends

- Good grooming (wash hands and face, brush teeth, wear clean clothes)
- Smiling
- Complimenting
- Friendship-making (starting, taking turns talking, inviting)

Area V: Coping Skills

- When someone says no (find another way to play)
- When you express anger
- When someone teases
- When someone tries to hurt you
- When someone asks you to do something you can't do
- When things don't go right

Skill components for the "Joining Sequence" include:

- Smile
- Look at the person
- Use their name
- Stand near-by
- Greet them
- Ask to join nicely (e.g., "Can I sit with you?")
- Ask a question to enter the conversation

An example of an inventory generated by Goldstein, Sprafkin, Gershaw, and Klein for use with adolescents in either a classroom or clinical setting is presented in Chapter 9. This group of skills has aggressive adolescents as a target population but is applicable to younger children as well. These skills form the basis for the *Skillstreaming* curriculum that Goldstein and his colleagues describe and that has also been adapted for use with younger children (McGinnis & Goldstein, 1984). Each skill is analyzed into a set of behavioral steps that can be translated into specific teaching objectives. The *ACCESS* curriculum of Walker, Todis, Holmes, and Horton (1983) is another program that teaches skills designed for helping adolescents with self-management and relationships with peers and adults.

There is considerable similarity between many of these inventories and curricula, even taking the differing intended populations into consideration. Most are multi-dimensional, including specific observable behaviors and cognitive and affective processes. Some additional behaviors related to cognitive or affective dimensions of social skills are described next.

Selecting Cognitive and Affective Behaviors

Affective and cognitive processes are increasingly being recognized as important determinants of social functioning and, therefore, necessary elements in the development and use of social skills. That emotions and cognitive processes are closely related is well established, although as Lewis and Michalson (1983) point out, there are several theoretical positions regarding the nature of this relationship. In some views, the expression of emotion is the consequence of cognitive processes; in others, emotional responses are seen as independent events not based on cognitive antecedents. In the view of Lewis and Michalson:

> . . . simple linear models of the relationship between cognition and emotion are inadequate. The relationships between these domains is quite complex, is continuous, and is more finely tuned than is usually depicted by traditional models. In conceptualizing the relationship between emotion and cognition, neither process should be described as causing the other. Rather, the best model is of two processes continually and progressively chasing each other, weaving their separate strands of behavior into a single composition not unlike that of a musical fugue (pp. 92–93).

In a discussion of current thinking about emotional development and regulation of emotion, Campos, Campos, and Barrett (1989) define emotions as not mere feelings, but rather "processes of establishing, maintaining, or disrupting the relations between the person and the internal or external environment, when such relations are significant to the individual" (p. 395). They agree that cognitive, motoric, and neurophysiological systems are all involved in the process of regulating emotions, and they see emotion as "a single relational process with many facets that act in concert" (p. 399). In this view of emotion, the transactions of the person with the environment take on central importance in emotional development. Factors, such as the individual's goals and strivings, emotional communications from others, and ecological concerns—exposure to various emotions in others and the emotional climate in the home, all play an important role in the generation and regulation of emotion. This view of emotional development clearly has implications for the teaching of social skills.

Training in social skills related to cognitions and affect concerns internal processes rather than observable discrete social behaviors, and most training programs dealing with these two dimensions include both cognitive and affective elements. Children most often identified as needing such training are characterized as lacking self-control, being impulsive and aggressive, possessing negative self-evaluations, and having poor peer relationships.

Social Skills Related to Affect

Although emotions or feelings are private events, difficult to measure except through their overt behavioral expressions, the emotions and their manifestations have a role in social skills training. Izard (1977) defines certain emotions (i.e., interest-excitement, joy, surprise, distress-anguish, anger-rage, disgust-revulsion, contempt-scorn, fear-terror, shame-shyness-humiliation, and guilt) as fundamental emotions, which in combination form other emotional states (anxiety, depression, love, hostility, and hate). Some of the undesirable behavioral manifestations of emotional states, for example, violent expressions of anger, indicate a need for social skills training to teach alternate behaviors. Similarly, fear, anxiety, and resulting shyness can interfere with learning and performing social behaviors.

The affective dimension of empathy has received considerable attention in recent social skills literature. *Empathy*—the ability to experience the emotions of others—is considered important if children are to master such interpersonal skills as making and maintaining friendships and resolving conflicts with others. Empathy in young children appears to have a positive relationship to prosocial behaviors such as cooperation and altruism (Eisenberg & Miller, 1987). Lewis and Michalson (1983) describe empathy as first requiring the development of a concept of self in order for children to see themselves in the place of another and thus experience the feelings of another. They also suggest that another aspect of empathy is the child's knowledge of social rules and expectations about what feelings are appropriate in specific situations. According to Harris (1989), children younger than age two or three will reach out to comfort other people, not only reacting to another person's current emotion but actively seeking to change the emotional state of another person. At the same time, how early empathic behaviors can be successfully taught to very young children is still an empirical question.

Feshbach, Feshbach, Fauvre, and Ballard-Campbell (1983, p. 3) identify the following as essential components of empathy:

1. *Recognition and discrimination of feeling*—The ability to use relevant information to label and identify emotions
2. *Perspective and role-taking*—The ability to understand that other individuals

may see and interpret situations differently; the ability to assume and experience another's viewpoint
3. *Emotional responsiveness*—The ability to experience and be aware of one's own emotions.

A fairly extensive literature of suggested teaching approaches to affective education has developed over the past several decades. One of the conceptual foundations is the taxonomy developed by Krathwohl, Bloom, and Masia (1956), which presents a hierarchy of affective-cognitive behaviors. According to their sequence, the child's affective development follows a pattern in which he or she first becomes aware of his surroundings, then learns to comply with existing rules and regulations in his or her environment, and finally moves through the process of developing a personal value system. One's behavior and value system are considered to be inseparable, in that beliefs are reflected by behavior. Therefore, the instructional goal is to help the child acquire values that foster humane, positive attitudes toward others, anticipating that the child's social behaviors will develop accordingly.

An affective education area that has not typically been emphasized in social skills research and training programs is that of values clarification. In light of current thinking, however, which points to the importance of children's values and goals in determining the strategies they use in interpersonal situations, the ways in which they process social information and potentially the motivation to improve their social behaviors, practitioners would do well to include values clarification as a prerequisite to social skills training. The goal of values clarification is to assist youth to "explore their beliefs and values and become more aware of how these beliefs and values influence their choices and behavior. . . . Values clarification is concerned more with the valuing process than with specific values" (Abrams, 1992, p. 30). Teaching materials available with values clarification activities can be found in Casteel and Stahl (1975); Curwin & Curwin (1974); Hawley and Hawley (1975); Howe and Howe (1975); Simon, Howe, and Kirschenbaum (1972); and Smith (1977).

Among programs developed for teaching specific skills related to affective behavior are the *Developing Understanding of Self and Others* (DUSO) program (Dinkmeyer, 1982), and *Toward Affective Development* (Dupont, Gardner, & Brody, 1974). These curricula, and others designed to teach children about feelings, present a number of common themes:

1. The child's sense of himself or herself, self-identity, and the development of self-esteem, which encompasses the ability to:
   - See oneself objectively, realistically.
   - Identify one's individual characteristics.
   - Identify one's positive attributes, assets, strengths.
   - Identify and accept one's negative attributes, imitations, imperfections.
   - Accept and deal constructively with negative experiences, such as failure and rejection.
   - Maintain a consistent positive self-concept in the presence of varying external feedback.

2. The child's awareness and expression of his or her own feelings, which involves the ability to:

- Recognize his or her feelings associated with different external events.
- Use words to label and describe to others both positive and negative feelings.
- Use appropriate nonverbal as well as verbal means of expressing emotions.
- Understand the function of emotional expression in his or her life, including the relationship between his or her feelings and interpersonal events.
- Change emotional expression to fit the demands of the situation.

3. The child's awareness of the feelings of others, including the ability to:

- Infer others' feelings from their verbal communication; for example, tone of voice, words, timing.
- Infer others' feelings from their nonverbal behavior; for example, facial expressions, posture, gestures.
- Infer others' feelings from knowledge of social expectations about which emotions are considered appropriate to specific situations.
- Be sensitive to the feelings of those who are different from himself or herself.

4. The child's awareness of complexities of emotional expression, for example:

- The ability to recognize when emotions in himself or herself and others are mixed
- The recognition that feelings can vary over time and among situations
- The recognition that an emotion can be changed by engaging in alternative thoughts and activities.

Harris (1989) identifies an additional dimension to the themes presented above, that of "hiding emotion." He points out that cultures teach their members to express some emotions and suppress others. He observes that normally developing children learn by age three or four to hide their true feelings to conform to expectations to be polite and well-behaved, and by age six have learned to mask their expressions of emotion to protect themselves from ridicule or anger from others. He suggests children at that point also have learned to hide their feelings to protect other people from information that would cause them to be unhappy.

Social skills training dealing with emotions can have several interrelated aspects having to do initially with assisting children to identify and label their own emotions and to recognize and label the emotions of others. The ultimate goal involves learning appropriate or acceptable ways to express a variety of feelings under varying conditions and to make constructive responses when confronted with emotional expressions of others. Helping the child find positive ways to express feelings in interpersonal situations is complex. It involves not only the child's ability to identify her or his own feelings, but the development of the ability to exercise control and selectivity over responses. This latter task involves the interaction of emotion, cognition, and motor activity.

Social Skills Related to Cognition

Dodge (1986) presents a theory for social information processing that is widely used in research on cognitive social skills. Dodge describes social information processing as a series of sequential processes in which information is encoded, represented mentally and stored, then accessed later for behavioral responses to situational stimuli. According to Dodge, the processing steps are: (1) *encoding* relevant aspects of sensory input or stimuli, which involves attending selectively to social cues and storing the cue information in short-term memory; (2) *applying* meanings that relate the stimuli to the person's emotional needs and goals through a process of mental representation; (3) *accessing* a behavioral or affective response, which is associated with the mental representation; (4) *evaluating* the response in terms of acceptability or anticipated consequences; and (5) behaviorally *enacting* the selected response.

Research applying Dodge's model to aggressive or depressed children (Akhtar & Bradley, 1991; Quiggle, Garber, Panak, & Dodge, 1992; Weiss & Dodge, 1992) has identified ways in which these children have information processing deficiencies. For example, aggressive children attend to fewer cues and are more sensitive to hostile cues; aggressive children are less able to "read" the emotions of others and are more likely to attribute hostile intent, while depressed children are more likely to engage in self-blame. The kinds of responses generated by aggressive children are qualitatively different from those of nonaggressive children, being more coercive, less effective, and more inflexible, while the responses of depressed children tend to be irrelevant and also ineffective. Aggressive children are often impulsive, failing to evaluate and consider the consequences of behavior, or anticipating positive outcomes from aggressive behavior, while depressed children in evaluating possible responses expect failure or perceive themselves to lack control over the outcomes of their behavior.

Dodge (1993) stresses the importance of goals and values in influencing how information is processed at all steps, through, for example, selective attention to cues, the kinds of responses that are accessed, and the kinds of evaluation responses that take place. Aggressive children value coercive behavior and hostile, competitive goals. Boldizar, Perry, & Perry (1989) found that aggressive children, for example, placed more value on achieving control of the victim and had little concern for negative outcomes of aggression such as suffering by the victim, the possibility of retaliation or peer rejection.

The apparent social-cognitive deficiencies of children with problems makes the need for training in cognitively oriented skills particularly salient. Hughes and Cavell present a more extensive discussion of social cognition in aggressive children and an intervention program in Chapter 6. Many of the curricula related to affective behavior mentioned above also present ways to teach cognitive skills. Some of the cognitive skills identified as important aspects of social skills training include those involved in social perception, problem solving, self-instruction, cognitive restructuring, and self-evaluation.

Social Perception

Social perception is considered to be the person's ability to perceive the parameters of a situation and vary behavior according to feedback from others. It is an important prerequisite to social skills and it involves both cognitive and affective elements. In addition to the affective skills of identifying and labeling feelings, role-taking, or *empathy*—the cognitive and affective ability to take the perspective of another person—is an important skill. Another prerequisite involves a skill mentioned earlier; that is, the ability to make inferences about others' feelings and thoughts from nonverbal cues such as tone of voice, gestures, and facial expression, as well as from verbal content. A number of studies demonstrate that children can, through systematic training, increase their understanding of others' thoughts, feelings, and perceptions.

Problem Solving

A large body of research data and a number of specific teaching programs have been developed around methods of teaching children to solve interpersonal problems. Training in problem solving differs from training in observable social skills. It presents a process for finding answers rather than a specific set of behaviors or solutions. As noted earlier, children with problems, such as depression or aggressiveness, have difficulties in generating effective alternative responses in problem-solving situations. In addition, Rubin and Krasnor (1986) found that children identified as socially rejected differ from popular and socially isolated children in their ability to think about and attempt to solve social problems.

A widely used definition of the problem-solving process developed by D'Zurilla and Goldfried (1971) includes these steps:

1. *General orientation*—the ability to recognize that a problem exists and that a solution can be found;
2. *Problem definition and formulation*—identifying the various issues involved in the situation;
3. *Generation of alternatives*—similar to "brainstorming," in which as many solutions as possible are considered;
4. *Decision-making*—in which a course of action is chosen, based on an assessment of its likelihood to resolve the identified problem; and
5. *Verification*—implementing the decision and evaluating the extent to which the problem has been resolved, possibly returning to more problem solving if the solution was not effective.

The work of Spivack, Platt, and Shure (Spivack & Shure, 1974; Spivack, Platt, & Shure, 1976; Shure & Spivack, 1978) has made a major contribution to the area of teaching problem-solving skills to children. Their *Interpersonal Cognitive Problem-Solving Program* (ICPS) was oriented first to preschool children and later expanded for use with older children. Aspects of this program are described in Chapters 2 and 3. The specific skills addressed in ICPS training, as Goldstein, Carr, Davidson, and Wehr (1981, pp. 226–228) outline, include:

1. Alternative solution thinking, ability to generate different solutions;
2. Consequential thinking, ability to predict the possible outcomes of various courses of action;
3. Causal thinking, ability to see cause and effect relationships;
4. Interpersonal sensitivity, awareness that interpersonal problems exist;
5. Means-end thinking, identification of the steps necessary to achieve a goal; and
6. Perspective taking, recognition of differences in motives and viewpoints, similar to empathy or role taking.

Variations in problem-solving training have been developed by others into programs for use with different age levels. The *Rochester Social Problem-Solving* (SPS) program (Weissberg, Gesten, Liebenstein, Doherty-Schmid, & Hutton, 1980), for example, involves teaching children to identify feelings, think of alternative solutions, and anticipate consequences of behavior.

Strategies and Goals

An area of social skills research related to social problem-solving procedures is the identification of strategies used by children and the goals they are attempting to achieve (Chung & Asher, 1992; Crick & Ladd, 1990; Neel, Jenkins, & Meadows, 1990; Renshaw & Asher, 1983). Rubin and Krasnor (1986) identify a series of social goals inferred from observations of children's play. These include: eliciting action from another, object acquisition, gaining attention or acknowledgment, information acquisition, giving and/or seeking help, soliciting permission to act, defense, avoiding anger and/or "loss of face," and initiating social play (p. 17). The categories identified to describe strategies include:

1. Prosocial—asking, politeness, waiting, sharing or taking turns, loaning;
2. Agonistic—direct imperatives, forcing, grabbing, physical attacks, property damage;
3. Authority intervention (appealing to an adult);
4. Bribing, trading, or finagling; and
5. Manipulating affect—"I'll be real happy if you give me that ball." (p. 29).

Much of the research on children's goals and strategies is carried out by asking children to consider hypothetical problem situations and then relate what they would do or say in those situations. Rubin and Krasnor emphasize the value of inferring goals from observations of naturally occurring behavior as an alternative. A study using such direct observation of preschool children's behavior (Neel et al., 1990) found that in accomplishing their goals, nonaggressive children sought alternative strategies involving verbal behavior more often than did aggressive children, with the latter moving more quickly to "intrusive" goals and strategies if their initial prosocial strategy was not successful.

Looking at a child's problem-solving strategies could be useful for the practitioner in identifying dysfunctional strategies and assisting the child in developing more appropriate ways to achieve his or her goals. Renshaw and Asher (1983) point out that the effectiveness of certain kinds of social skills training may be due not only to helping the child acquire strategies for accomplishing social goals but to the "goal construal processes," giving as an example changing the goal in a game situation to having fun rather than a goal such as winning. It appears that goals themselves and assisting the child in defining or redefining his or her goals in interpersonal situations may be an important target for social skills training.

Self-instruction

Self-instruction and related skills having to do with self-control constitute another cognitive area relevant to building social skills. Most self-instruction programs are built on an adaptation of a model developed by Vygotsky (1962) and Luria (1961). As described by Meichenbaum (1977):

> Luria proposed three stages by which the initiation and inhibition of voluntary motor behaviors come under verbal control. . . . During the first stage, the speech of others, usually adults, controls and directs a child's behavior. In the second stage the child's own overt speech becomes an effective regulator of his behavior. Finally, the child's covert, or inner speech assumes a self-governing role (pp. 18–19).

Various studies with children demonstrate that young children talk out loud to themselves when performing a task, and as children grow older, the private speech becomes internalized—"goes underground." The assumption is that much behavior is guided by internalized self-statements, and that the child's behavior can be changed by alterations in his or her self-statements.

Self-instruction with children generally involves teaching children a series of problem-solving steps similar to those outlined previously, along with self-controlling verbal statements. The *Think Aloud* program (Camp, 1977; Camp, Blom, Herbert, & van Doorninck, 1977; Camp, Zimet, van Doorninck, & Dahlem, 1977; Bash & Camp, 1980, 1986) is a curriculum that makes use of Meichenbaum's procedures. Another curriculum for teaching self-control through verbal self instruction (VSI), also built on the Meichenbaum model, was developed by Kendall (1981). Self-instruction statements include (Kendall & Braswell, 1985, p. 120):

> Problem definition: "Let's see, what am I supposed to do?"
>
> Problem approach: "I have to look at all the possibilities."
>
> Focusing of attention: "I better concentrate and focus in, and think only of what I'm doing right now."
>
> Choosing an answer: "I think it's this one. . . ."
>
> Self-reinforcement: "Hey, not bad. I really did a good job."
>
> or

Coping statement: "Oh, I made a mistake. Next time I'll try and go slower and concentrate more and maybe I'll get the right answer."

Kagan and Kogan (1970) distinguish between the differing cognitive processes of reflective and impulsive children. Both may be motivated to appear competent, with doubts about their ability. In the case of some impulsive children, anxiety about competence may result in too rapid, nonreflective responses, whereas in the case of reflective children similar anxiety may result in overly cautious responses. Cognitive self-control techniques are considered to be most appropriate for impulsive children who need to learn to "stop and think." These skills are important for aggressive children, provided anti-social goals and values are addressed. Self-control techniques may be less appropriate for anxious, inhibited, reflective, or depressed children who might profit more from cognitive restructuring approaches.

Cognitive Restructuring

A further aspect of cognitive training related to self-instruction is the alteration of dysfunctional self-statements. A major example of this approach is the *Rational Emotive Therapy* (RET) model of Albert Ellis (1962). Ellis proposes that maladaptive behavior results from irrational belief systems based on a set of imperatives about what one should or must do or must have happen. Cognition, emotion, and behavior are interrelated; irrational beliefs are responsible for disturbing emotions, which then result in dysfunctional behavior. An RET program developed for children by Knaus (1974) presents the following areas for learning: (a) helping children learn about feelings; (b) challenging irrational beliefs, helping children recognize their irrational belief systems; (c) challenging feelings of inferiority, helping children learn to evaluate themselves and others in positive terms; (d) helping children become realistic about issues related to perfectionism; and (e) teaching children to think in terms of what they would like to have happen rather than what (irrationally) "*must* and *should* happen." This program is described in more detail in Chapter 3. Roush (1984) suggests that three basic processes are involved in RET programs for youth:

> First, young people must understand the principles of rational thinking . . . be able to discriminate between rational and irrational beliefs about themselves and their environment. Second, they must have a working knowledge of core irrationalities, that is, beliefs expressing self-denigration, intolerance of frustration, or blame and condemnation of others. . . . Third, youth must develop a usable system for identifying and disputing the components of irrational thinking . . . (p. 414).

Bernard (1990) presents the primary goal of RET as that of helping the young person reduce extreme levels of negative emotions (anger, anxiety, depression), which make it difficult for him or her to overcome problems. The modification of emotional responses is accomplished by changes in the youth's irrational assumptions, inferences, evaluations, expectations, and beliefs.

A related cognitive area, which is receiving attention, is the child's attributions—an aspect of the "mental representation" step in the Dodge information-processing model described earlier. Kendall and Braswell (1985) distinguish between expectancy and attribution, the former preceding an event or situation and the latter following the event. Attribution is the attempt to explain the event or account for its cause. These authors point out the importance of attributions for generalization of improvement and also for motivation to learn self-control. Children who attrib- ute failures in interpersonal relationships to outside causes, for example, will be less motivated to engage in training to improve interactions with others. Rubin and Krasnor (1986) found that children who attributed social failure to external sources appeared less likely to attempt another solution after the initial failure, with those attributing failure to internal factors appearing to produce more adaptive strategies. Glenwick and Jason (1984) see the restructuring of attributional style as one of the desired outcomes of cognitive self-control training, suggesting that children who can learn to see themselves as causal agents can enhance their self-esteem and sense of self-efficacy (i.e., the expectation of being successful).

Other Self-control Procedures

A set of cognitive self-control procedures which have potential for changing behavior and for maintaining behavior over time is that of self-monitoring, self-evaluation, and self-reinforcement. *Self-monitoring* is the ability to observe and report one's own behavior. Studies have demonstrated that teaching children skills in self-monitoring is more effective for changing behavior if children are trained to evaluate their own performance in a way that corresponds with others' objective evaluations (Bolstad & Johnson, 1972; Santogrossi, O'Leary, Romanczyk, & Kaufman, 1973; Wood & Flynn, 1978). At the same time, another body of data exists to suggest that the act of self-recording alone, regardless of accuracy, can significantly change behavior (Nelson & Hayes, 1981). With children the difficulty of the task and the type of child involved may be factors; self-evaluation is most useful for children already motivated to improve their behavior (O'Leary & Dubey, 1979).

Self-evaluation refers to the comparison between self-observed behavior and the criteria or performance standards one has set for the behavior. Such standards can either be acquired through direct training (making the standards explicit to the child) or through modeling influences (the child observing how other people evaluate the behavior). The kinds of criteria established for evaluation clearly affect whether the criteria can realistically be met and the evaluation can be positive. Many children seldom make positive self-evaluations, possibly because they set excessively high standards for their own performance. Research on the effect of goal setting on behavior suggests that training children to set realistic performance goals might help to increase motivation and, hence, performance (Sagotsky, Patterson, & Lepper, 1978).

Self-reinforcement is the process of rewarding oneself for the performance of specific behaviors according to some criterion. An explanation for the effect of self-evaluation on behavior change is that the process of attending to one's own behavior and comparing it to a criterion triggers self-reinforcing or self-punishing thoughts, which may in turn serve to increase or decrease the behavior (Nelson & Hayes, 1981). Skill in self-reinforcement involves the child's ability to monitor his or her behavior, identify positive aspects, and deliver a reward, for example, a positive statement that could be expressed either overtly or covertly. Effective self-reinforcement, according to Jones, Nelson, and Kazdin (1977), depends on prior training with external reinforcement, which provides information regarding desirable behavior, the setting of reasonable goals, self-monitoring, and the availability of some external monitoring and external contingencies to encourage self-reinforcement. The importance of self-monitoring, self-evaluation, and self- reinforcement in maintaining social skills over time is discussed in Chapter 4.

The documented deficits and distortions in thinking processes of children with problems would suggest that interpersonal problem-solving skills, cognitive restructuring, self-instruction training, and related self-control procedures would all be important target behaviors for social skill instruction. The effectiveness of cognitively oriented social skills training in producing socially valid outcomes has been questioned, however, by some researchers. In a review article, Gresham (1985) concludes that "the effects of self-instruction and social problem solving upon the social relationships of children have not been adequately demonstrated" (p. 420). Pellegrini and Urbain (1985) also indicate that cognitive problem-solving training alone clearly has not been demonstrated to increase peer acceptance or ameliorate clinical problems. They point out the lack of valid assessment measures and the difficulty in determining the long-term effects of such training. At the same time, there are studies reporting favorable results from cognitive-behavioral interventions. Yu, Harris, Solovitz, and Franklin (1986), for example, provided social problem-solving training to children with psychiatric problems and found a decrease in behavior problems and an increase in social-cognitive skills and behavioral competencies compared to controls. They speculate that one possible reason for success was parent involvement, a variable also identified by Pellegrini and Urbain as important to consider. An issue stressed by Yu et al. is the importance of looking at cognitive and behavioral changes in a longer time frame. They suggest that behavioral changes that result from changes in social-cognitive processes cannot be evaluated adequately on a short-term basis because of the time required for such changes to "become integrated and consolidated," again suggesting the need for more follow-up studies.

Individualizing Skill Selection

In the process of selecting and developing specific social skills for instruction to meet individual needs, two sets of procedures are particularly useful: formulating behavioral objectives stated in positive terms, and analyzing broadly stated social behaviors into subcomponents, using procedures similar to those appropriate for academic behaviors. As mentioned earlier, the need for social skills training often is identified because of a problem or deficit. Social skills training involves helping children discard some behaviors and substitute more acceptable ones. Many of the problem behaviors displayed by children have opposite or incompatible desirable behaviors that could be taught or increased in frequency (see Table 1-4).

TABLE 1-4 Undesirable versus Desirable Behaviors

Problems	Social Skills
The child calls others by uncomplimentary names	The child makes positive remarks to others.
The child frequently interrupts the conversation of others	The child waits for pauses in the conversation before speaking.
The child makes negative statements about his or her ability.	The child identifies something he or she does well.
The child cheats when playing a game with peers.	The child plays games according to rules.
The child throws tantrums when teased by peers.	The child responds to teasing by ignoring or some other appropriate responses.
The child laughs at or ignores individuals in need of help.	The child assists individuals in need of help.

As previously indicated, the social goals adults have for children are generally conceptualized in global terms; for example, to "play cooperatively" or to "assume responsibility." Breaking down such goals into their subcomponents or a series of objectives assists the process of defining behavior to be taught. Although there are several models for analyzing a task, the essential steps involve (a) specifying the desired behavior, (b) identifying the subskills of the composite behavior, (c) stating the subskills in terms of observable behaviors, (d) listing the subskills according to sequence of instruction, (e) identifying and implementing appropriate instructional strategies, and (f) evaluating the results.

Howell (1985) outlines the dimensions for tasks as: content, behavior, conditions, and criteria (accuracy and/or rate proficiency). He stresses that "because social behavior is contextual and one aim of instruction is to produce changes in behavior across situations, it is important to note the conditions of task performance" (p. 26). He suggests that tasks have these components: subtasks (sometimes referred to as prerequisites) and strategies. Strategies are conceptualized as *general,* for example, "problem recognition, self-evaluation, and procedures for recognizing alternatives and resources" and *specific,* "procedures and mechanisms of problem solving which are required by a narrow content domain" (p. 28). As an example of applying this model, Table 1-5 gives Howell's analysis of the social skills task of "making friends" adapted from Walker et al. (1983, p. 29).

Performance and evaluation are facilitated by the process of specifying the exact responses desired and their prerequisites, the conditions, and the criteria for success. The task analysis process makes it possible to individualize instruction, enabling both the child and the evaluator to know what is expected and when the responses are to occur: essential aspects of social skill instruction.

TABLE 1-5 Component Definitions and Examples for the "Making Friends" Task

Component Definition	Examples
A. Subtask Knowledge Knowledge of the vocabulary, rules and facts pertaining to the content of making friends	A.1 Employs personal hygiene skils A.2 Selects appropriate clothing A.3 Recognizes potential friends A.4 Uses adequate conversational vocabulary A.5 Knows when to speak and when to listen A.6 Knows appropriate ways to ask for additional contact
B. Specific Strategy Knowledge Knowledge of a step-by-step procedure for completing the task	B.1 Seeks out appropriate others B.2 Initiates conversation B.3 Takes turns talking B.4 Asks person to spend time with him or her
C. General Strategy Knowledge Knowledge of self-regulatory and problem-solving procedures	C.1 Recognizes need C.2 Recognizes and/or generates a procedure for meeting the need C.3 Carries out the procedure C.4 Monitors activity C.5 Adjusts activity as needed

Source: From A task-analytical approach to social behavior by K. W. Howell, 1985. *Remedial and Special Education,* 6(2), 29. Copyright 1985 by PRO-ED, Inc. Reprinted by permission.

Summary

Before social skill instruction can take place, it is necessary to determine what skills are important for children to learn. Careful attention to selection of target behaviors will help facilitate the learning process as well as enhance the probability that learned skills will be retained and used. Many considerations enter into the identification of target social skills, among them the child's developmental level, which may facilitate or retard learning and retaining skills; the cultural and situational context and views of those who make up the child's environment; and the likelihood that social skills will be valued and reinforced by others once they are learned.

Selection of social skills for instruction can be based on inventories of social behavior, many of which accompany social skills curricula. Most of these combine behavioral, affective, and cognitive dimensions of skills to be taught. Although a broad spectrum of social skills can be taught for preventive purposes, most often the need for social skills training for an individual child is identified because of an excess of some behavior considered to be undesirable, and because the child does not have the related acceptable behaviors in his or her repertoire. Skill selection can be based on an assessment of individual deficits in social skills. The clinician or teacher can turn the child's problem behaviors into opportunities for social skill instruction by developing positively stated objectives and further analyzing specific components through task analysis.

Chapter *2*

Assessment and Evaluation of Social Skills

Assessment can take many forms, from fleeting observational impressions to systematic recording and the use of standardized instruments. Why should a social skills teaching program involve assessment? Social skills can certainly be taught without the sometimes difficult and time-consuming task of prior assessment to determine the extent to which a skill is in the child's repertoire.

For researchers, assessment is a necessity in order to create a basis for measuring the effects of social skills teaching on behavioral change. For teachers and clinicians, the most effective interventions also involve assessment, because they too must be concerned with the results of their efforts.

Purpose of Assessment

Assessment helps determine whether the goal for the practitioner should be teaching a new behavior or, instead, arranging the environment to encourage the performance of a behavior the child has in his or her repertoire but does not display. Mager and Pipe (1970) have a simple paradigm that is useful as a place to start in looking at assessment for social skill instruction. They suggest that problem behavior (in this case, lack of social skills in some area) may exist because the desired behavior is not known or has not been taught, because the reinforcing conditions are not sufficient to encourage the desired behavior, or because there is reinforcement for the undesirable problem behavior. A social skill may, thus, be missing because the child lacks information or ability to perform the behavior; because the environment does not provide sufficient encouragement for the child to engage in the behavior even though he or she may know how to do it; or because there is a payoff for not carrying out the desired social behavior.

Another related reason for not engaging in a desirable social skill may be the existence of unpleasant feelings, such as fear or anxiety, associated with the behavior performance that are avoided by avoiding the behavior. For example, a child may fail to be constructively assertive in a conflict with another child because (a) he or she does not know how to go about saying or doing appropriately assertive things; (b) he or she does not perceive any benefits from saying or doing something he or she knows how to do; or (c) by withdrawing in a nonassertive way, he or she is able to avoid the anxiety experienced when taking risks in conflict situations. As suggested in Chapter 1, behaviors defined as social skills usually have some goal associated with them, and a child may be faced with having to choose from among several competing goals. Through assessing which of these alternatives is operating (i.e., whether the problem is one of skill deficit or motivation), the teacher or clinician can determine the most appropriate intervention.

Problems in Assessment

Situation Specificity

In the assessment of social skills, there are many problems that interfere with obtaining valid and reliable measures. For example, many behaviors are situation- specific; a child may display a behavior in one situation but not in another. Such a discrepancy may exist because the conditions that encourage the behavior are different or are perceived by the child to be different in various situations.

In this context, the question arises of whether one is assessing the knowledge of a social skill or the ability to perform the behavior. As Bandura (1977b) points out, because people learn many behaviors by observing others, a child may have some cognitive understanding of what would be desirable social behavior, but may not be able to translate that understanding into actions. It becomes necessary, therefore, to assess both the child's knowledge of a behavior and whether she or he can perform it under appropriate circumstances. Because motivational factors in the form of reinforcing conditions in the environment also may have an effect on the child's performance of a social behavior, the most accurate assessment of performance would likely take place under highly reinforcing circumstances. Hence, the teacher or practitioner also needs to know what contingencies of reinforcement are operating in order to structure assessment situations in a highly positive way.

Respondent Reliability

A further problem in social skills assessment is that of reliability among different persons. There are many sources of data about a child's social behavior, including a variety of adults, peers, and the child himself or herself. Various studies have determined that there is often little agreement between researchers and parents, between parents and teachers, and between adults and children in their ratings of subjects on social behavior (Achenbach et al., 1987). Children's self-perceptions about their social behavior do not correlate highly with others' perceptions, but the child's view is still an important piece of assessment information, particularly in relation to motivation for change and response to social skills teaching. In addition to problems with validity and reliability related to the situational aspects of social skills performance, there are wide variations among persons and groups about what is acceptable social behavior on the part of children, as discussed in the preceding chapter. Such lack of agreement creates difficulties in establishing criteria for when a behavior should be taught or for mastery of a newly taught behavior.

Developmental Levels

Developmental levels also must be taken into consideration when establishing criteria. A high school student might be considered to have good greeting skills if he or she can establish eye contact, smile, say "hello," provide his or her name, ask for or say the other person's name, and shake hands. A preschool child might be considered to have adequate greeting skills with only the first three or four behaviors. In discussing criteria, it may be sufficient for the teacher or clinician to determine only whether the behavior occurs at all in the desired situation. If the behavior does not occur or occurs infrequently in a given situation, teaching the behavior in that context is indicated. If the behavior occurs with low frequency and with poor quality, teaching the behavior also may be indicated to increase the child's ease with the behavior. For example, a child who is only able to greet an adult with stammering and a lack of eye contact may need practice in greeting skills based on the quality of the responses even though he or she demonstrates knowledge of what to say. There may also need to be attention to motivational factors.

Forms of Assessment

Of the assessment methods that will be outlined, some involve questionnaires or rating scales of various kinds that can be completed by those knowledgeable about the child: teacher, parent, other children, or the child himself or herself. Other methods involve observing the child's actual performance of various behaviors, either in the natural environment or in a situation set up to be analogous to the natural environment. Still other procedures involve ways to test the child's knowledge of social responses, apart from whether he or she can actually perform the behaviors in social situations. Assessment procedures selected by the practitioner depend on several factors, for example: (a) the nature of the behavior being assessed; (b) whether one is assessing an individual child or a group of children; (c) what other resources, in terms of observers and equipment, are available; (d) the availability of informants knowledgeable about the child; and (e) the developmental level of the child and his or her ability to read and to provide self-reports.

Because there are problems of validity and reliability with most social skill assessment approaches, the accuracy of assessment results is enhanced by the use of multiple methods, more than one setting, and input from more than one person. As

Ollendick and Hersen (1984) point out, there also needs to be assessment of "multiple targets of change," that is, overt behaviors, affective states, and thoughts or cognitions, because all contribute to social competence and learning social skills. In the material that follows, social behavior assessment approaches to be employed by adults knowledgeable about the child (primarily teachers, clinicians, and parents) are outlined first. These are followed by peer assessment techniques, those based on self-reports, and finally approaches to be used for assessment of cognitive and affective behaviors.

Assessments by Adults

Methods most commonly used by knowledgeable adults in assessing a child's observable social behaviors include a variety of scales, inventories, and observation techniques. The observations can be made in the natural environment or in situations structured to produce the behaviors of interest. In the next section some of the most commonly used standardized instruments are described, followed by inventories associated primarily with social skills curriculum materials, and individually tailored rating scales designed for specific situations.

Behavior Checklists and Rating Scales

A first step in the formal assessment process may be the employment of rating measures or checklists, wherein individuals closely associated with the child—such as parents, teachers, or mental health workers—indicate the presence, absence, or extent of certain behaviors in the child's repertoire. In format, checklists tend to be binary (i.e., involve one of two responses indicating whether the behavior does or does not exist), whereas rating scales provide more choices along a continuum indicating the extent of the behavior. As an initial procedure, checklists or ratings are generally considered to be a method of screening for identification rather than an in-depth comprehensive assessment of social competence. Rating instruments may be classified according to either the person providing the behavior evaluation or the nature of the reporting form as well as by content and subject of the rating. Behavior checklists or rating scales can be published versions (usually backed up with data related to validity and reliability) or instruments devised by the practitioner to meet a specific need. Social skills inventories designed for teaching programs also can be used as checklists for assessment.

As adults closely associated with children, teachers are often called on for behavior ratings. Although individual variation among teachers on accuracy of ratings may occur, partly attributed to the extent of opportunities to observe the relevant behavior (Bain, Houghton, & Farris, 1991; Reardon, Hersen, Bellack, & Foley, 1979), there is evidence that teacher ratings compare favorably with other kinds of assessment of social behavior (Bolstad & Johnson, 1972; Greenwood, Walker, & Hops, 1977; Greenwood, Walker, Todd, & Hops, 1979). Some researchers argue that a strong database exists for documenting the "accuracy of teacher judgement of child behavior and performance" (Walker, Severson, Stiller, Williams,

Haring, Shinn, & Todis, 1988, p. 8). An advantage of teacher ratings, as Beck (1986) points out, is that teachers observe children in a standardized environment which enables them to make comparisons among children of the same developmental level.

Parents are the other group of adults most often called on to provide assessment data. In contrast to teachers, there are problems with reliability of parent reports; typically, they do not correlate highly with other measures. Parents may not have experience with various types of deviant behavior and may either overreact to or underreport deviant child behaviors (Beck, 1986). Humphreys and Ciminero (1979) suggest, in fact, that parent reports should be included and compared with other assessment data because parent perceptions and attitudes may be part of the problem requiring remediation.

From a somewhat different perspective, Achenbach et al. (1987) propose that the differences may be due largely to behavior specificity. That is, social behaviors vary according to the social situations, and the ratings obtained from different sources may be more a function of these varying situational demands than inaccurate or unreliable informants. In a meta-analysis of behavior assessments with varied respondents, these authors found the highest correlations (.60) between pairs that observed the child under similar conditions (e.g., pairs of parents, pairs of teachers) and the next highest correlations (.28) between adults with different roles (e.g., teacher/parent/mental health worker). The lowest correlations (.24) were found between the child's self-assessments and those of adults (e.g., parent/ teacher/mental health worker). A comparable pattern was observed by Keller (1988) in the teacher/parent/self ratings of the adaptive behaviors of seven-year-old children. In this study another variable of culture was observed, in that greater teacher-parent discrepancies resulted for minority (i.e., African-American and Hispanic-American) children than for European-American children.

Behavior checklists and rating scales have certain advantages. They are easy to administer and easy to analyze, making it possible to use copies of the same instrument to obtain responses from several different informants about the same child. For example, one child could be rated by the parents, the teacher, a school counselor, and so forth. A comparison of the multiple responses would aid in identifying behaviors to address and in gaining understanding of how the child functions in various settings.

Standardized Instruments

Behavior checklists and rating scales, both published and unpublished, exist in large numbers, and in recent years have increased both in technology and quantity (Maag, 1989). As long ago as 1977, Walls, Werner, Bacon, and Zane discovered over 200 and published a review of 166 of them. Many checklists and rating scales have been subjected to research to determine their reliability and validity. In addition to the advantages noted here, McConaughy (1993) points out that special features of standardized instruments also would include greater reliability than that of subjective measures, the ability to compare target children to their normative peers, and the ability to assess clusters of problem behaviors. Some of the instruments most often used in behavioral assessment are described here.

The *Revised Quay-Peterson Behavior Problem Checklist* (Quay & Peterson, 1987) is a rating scale for children and adolescents that originally emerged from the identification of problem behaviors among normal public school children (grades K–8) and special populations (institutionalized juvenile delinquents, children in classes for the emotionally disturbed, and children seen in child guidance clinics). The revised form has six major factors that include: conduct disorder, socialized aggression, attention problems/immaturity, anxiety-withdrawal, psychotic behavior, and motor tension-excess. Although the authors state that the items refer to easily observable behavior, the items tend to refer more to classes of behavior such as impertinence, lethargy, and irresponsibility, than to specific responses. The Quay-Peterson checklist has undergone extensive empirical validation, with reports of high internal consistency (Edelbrock, 1988) and adequate to low interrater reliability (Edelbrock, 1988; Simpson, 1991). It is used more for classifying children according to the designated categories of social/emotional disturbance than for the identification of specific behavior deficits.

Two other instruments with a similar purpose but that provide for the rating of more specific behaviors are the revised *Walker Problem Behavior Identification Checklist* (WPBIC) (Walker, 1983) and the revised *Child Behavior Checklist* (CBCL) (Achenbach, 1991). Standardized on fourth-, fifth-, and sixth-grade children, the WPBIC contains 50 items that have been factored into five scales of disturbed behavior: (a) acting-out, (b) withdrawal, (c) distractibility, (d) disturbed peer relations, and (e) immaturity. One feature of this scale is that it discriminates between boys and girls, allowing for more problem behaviors among boys because this is typical in the general population. A girl who receives a score of 12 or higher could be considered maladjusted, whereas a boy would need a score of 22 for the same classification, suggesting an interesting distinction that may change as sex roles become redefined in our culture.

The revised CBCL includes a series of instruments and procedures designed to provide a "multiaxial" evaluation of the child's behavior and emotional problems (McConaughy, 1993). Data are to be provided by parents or parent surrogates, but the accompanying *Teacher's Report Form* (TRF) and the *Youth Self-Report* (YSR) provide for assessments across settings and informants. As with the two preceding instruments, the CBCL classifies children more according to classes of behavior disorders than according to specific social skills and is considered to be particularly useful for special education placement and programming (McConaughy, 1993).

A scale developed specifically for rating social skills is the *Matson Evaluation of Social Skills for Youth* (MESSY) (Matson, Rotatori, & Helsel, 1983). It uses items fitting the definition of social skills selected from standardized instruments such as those described previously. The scale was developed through research with children ages 4 to 18. Teachers rate 64 items on a five-point scale as to how often the child demonstrates the behavior. There is also a self-report version. Sample items include:

- Becomes angry easily.
- Gripes or complains often.
- Brags about self.
- Slaps or hits when angry.
- Helps a friend who is hurt.
- Is a sore loser.
- Smiles at people he or she knows.
- Asks questions when talking with others.
- Explains things more than needs to.
- Talks a lot about problems or worries.
- Thinks that winning is everything.

The MESSY is particularly useful in the assessment of social skills because its focus is specific to social behavior (Maag, 1989), and it is comprehensive rather than emphasizing a limited domain such as assertive behavior (Spence & Liddle, 1990). With some exceptions that call for considerable inference on the part of the adult rater (e.g., "Feels angry or jealous when someone else does well. . . . Is afraid to speak to people. . . . Thinks good things are going to happen."), the items describe observable behavior.

A more recently developed assessment instrument that targets the social skills of children and adolescents is the *Social Skill Rating System* (SSRS) (Gresham & Elliott, 1990). Including teacher, parent, and self (third grade and above) assessments, the system provides assessment measures from preschool through high school. It allows for cross-informant comparisons and includes normative data according to age, gender, and disability differences. The teacher form assesses behavior in three areas: (1) social skills (e.g., "initiates conversations with peers"), (2) problem behaviors (e.g., "fights with others"), and (3) academic competence (e.g., on a scale from 1 to 5, the child's academic performance is compared to that of other children in the classroom). For social skills, teachers rate the behaviors on two scales: how often the behavior occurs, and how important that behavior is for success in the teacher's classroom. Behaviors considered to be important but occurring at low rates probably should be targeted for intervention. Parents give similar ratings for comparable behaviors with the exception of the area of academic competence. The self-reports only require the frequency ratings of social skills that reflect skills listed on the teacher and parent forms. The rating system is considered easy to use, and its built-in intervention plan enhances its utility (McLean, 1992).

Other commonly used measures for assessing overt behaviors include the *Devereux Behavior Rating Scale* (Spivack & Swift, 1967), revised by Naglieri, LeBuffe, and Pfeiffer (1992), and the *Walker-McConnell Scale of Social Competence and School Adjustment* (Walker & McConnell, 1988). Some behavior scales are designed for special populations. The *AAMD Adaptive Behavior Scale-School Edition* (Lambert, Windmiller, Cole, & Tharinger, 1974) was revised as the AAMR (Nihira, Lambert, & Leland, 1993) and is intended specifically for persons with mental retardation. The *Conners Teacher Rating Scale* (CTRS) and *Conners Parent Rating Scale* (CPRS)

(Conners, 1970, 1989) are designed to measure hyperactivity and evaluate the effects of drug therapy.

To be most useful, rating scales should have items that are clearly enough defined to have the same meaning for all raters, should be descriptive rather than inferential, should be relatively simple and quick to complete, should have established reliability and validity, and should take age and sex differences into account (Rie & Friedman, 1978), as well as cultural and disability factors. Guidelines provided by Edelbrock (1988) further specify that the selection be guided by intended purpose. A test designed for general classification of behavior disorders, for example, would be less useful for devising specific strategies for social skills intervention.

Instruction-Evaluation Inventories

A number of social skills curricula have checklists or inventories that can be useful either for pre- or postevaluation of the application of the curriculum or as independent assessment instruments. One example is the *Social Behavior Assessment* (SBA) (Stephens & Arnold, 1992), a 136-item inventory corresponding to a social skills classroom curriculum (Stephens, 1992). It is designed to be completed by an informed teacher or classroom observer. Scores denote areas in which instruction is needed. The items were developed through a social validation process (Milburn, 1974), and there is good evidence for reliability and validity (Gresham & Elliott, 1984; Stephens, 1992b). (See Appendix C, Social Skills List, for the specific skills on which the SBA is based.)

Similar instruments include the PEERS program *Social Interaction Rating Scale* (Hops, Fleischman, Guild, Paine, Street, Walker, & Greenwood, 1978), developed for withdrawn children; the RECESS program (Walker, Street, Garrett, Crossen, Hops, & Greenwood, 1978), which is a rating scale related to a curriculum for aggressive children; and the ACCEPTS *Placement Test* (Walker et al., 1983), involving 28 items corresponding to the ACCEPTS social skills curriculum. The rating received by the child on each item suggests whether the child should receive instruction in that skill. Other examples are the skill checklists developed for use with Goldstein's structured learning curriculum (McGinnis & Goldstein, 1984) and with the *Taking Part* social skills curriculum by Cartledge and Kleefeld (1991).

Informal Scales and Inventories

In assessing social skills, one is often concerned only with particular aspects of the child's interpersonal skills such as the ability to participate in a group project with a peer, engage in a conversation with an adult, demonstrate an ability to make friends, or show appropriate affect in various situations. Here, the examiner is concerned with identifying the specific responses that constitute that general behavior or attitude and with determining the presence of that response in the child's behavioral repertoire, rather than describing the child along the entire range of interpersonal social skills. For such purposes, the most practical checklists are probably those developed by the practitioner.

Mager (1972) provides a model for developing observable objectives for nonbservable goals. For example, perhaps the concern is for the child to demonstrate a more "positive attitude" toward his peers. Once the goal is stated, the next step is to determine the specific behaviors children exhibit that are indicative of positive peer attitudes. Responses may include smiling at peers, giving compliments, participating in games with peers, making positive statements about peers, and helping peers when asked. After progressing through various steps of refinement, a list of observable behaviors is produced that can be used as a checklist for the designated behavioral goals. Thus, for the goal of positive attitudes, a specific behavioral listing may include responses, such as those listed before, as well as additional ones specific to the child and setting. For example, Table 2-1 shows what an examiner constructed behavior checklist might state.

This scale shows behavior categories analyzed into more specific responses on which the child is to be rated. With informally constructed scales, the examiner would concentrate on the behaviors that are of concern for a particular child or setting. For example, assessment in a residential setting might include more interpersonal, as opposed to task-related, behaviors, while the opposite would be more appropriate at a school. Finch, Deardorff, and Montgomery (1974) suggest that individually tailored behavior rating scales, such as the one just described, may be used for assessing and recording behavior change in settings where the staff has insufficient time to obtain ongoing observational data. They propose individualized rating scales made from descriptions of the subject's behavior gathered from knowledgeable people, clinical notes, the individual's self-descriptions, and direct observation. An individualized scale is consistent with criterion-referenced procedures in that the

TABLE 2-1 Examiner-constructed Behavior Checklist

	Child demonstrates				
	No skill	Little skill	Adequate skill	Good skill	Considerable skill
Politeness					
1. Makes eye contact	1	2	3	4	5
2. Smiles	1	2	3	4	5
3. Says thank you	1	2	3	4	5
4. Says please	1	2	3	4	5
5. Offers to assist others	1	2	3	4	5
6. Makes appropriate apologies	1	2	3	4	5
7. Addresses others appropriately	1	2	3	4	5
8. Makes positive comments to others	1	2	3	4	5
Cooperation					
1. Follows group rules	1	2	3	4	5
2. Complies with reasonable requests	1	2	3	4	5
3. Takes turns	1	2	3	4	5
4. Shares appropriately	1	2	3	4	5
5. Participates in group activities	1	2	3	4	5

assessment focuses on the child's ability to perform the particular skill rather than comparing the child to his peers, as with the previously described standardized instruments.

Behavior checklists are quick, easy-to-administer screening devices for children and adults. Although they may be useful in documenting global impressions, they have limitations for social skills assessment. Checklists and rating scales are subject to bias on the part of respondents, as well as to errors related to respondents' ability to remember accurately. Checklists are useful as pre- and posttest measures if items are highly specific. Despite various shortcomings, behavior checklists can be of value as an initial procedure in assessing social skills and deficits, particularly in combination with other assessment measures.

Observation of Performance

The most obvious, but not necessarily the easiest, way to assess the performance of social behaviors is to observe the child and see what he or she does. Behavior observation, according to Wildman and Erickson (1977), is often regarded as the "ultimate validity criterion" against which other forms of assessment are measured. Because of the differences in behavior in different situations, it may be necessary to gather observational data from persons who see the child in different contexts. The following discussion includes procedures for assessing behaviors in the natural environment and in contrived situations, which include the interview and analogue measures.

Assessing in the Natural Environment

Observing the child in everyday surroundings produces a wealth of information of varying degrees of relevance. In order to capture and process all the data available through observation, a number of different methods have been devised. One approach to documentation of observation is a written description in the form of diaries or narratives, sometimes called continuous recording. Bijou, Peterson, and Ault (1968) suggest a four-column format for this kind of recording, which involves documenting the time, antecedent events, child responses, and consequent events. Recording events in a temporal sequence makes it possible not only to describe specific behaviors but also to form hypotheses about the relationships between a behavior and its antecedents and its consequences. In other words, a functional analysis is developed, similar to that described in more detail later. Such hypotheses are particularly useful in determining the conditions that facilitate the expression of desirable social behaviors.

Narrative recording is used to describe any behaviors that occur, without focusing on particular behavior. Methods for systematic recording of specific behaviors include (a) event recording by means of tally marks, wrist counters, and other counting devices; (b) duration recording; (c) time sampling techniques involving time intervals; and (d) the use of coding or rating systems related to the observed behavior.

Assessing social skills as alternatives to some identified problem behaviors usually involves dealing with nonexistent or low-frequency behaviors. Mann (1976) suggests that event recording—that is, the recording of each occurrence of each event (behavior)—is a preferred process with infrequent behaviors. It is probably the simplest method, requiring only a means of recording and a set of discrete behaviors that can be reliably identified by the observer. The kinds of social skills that might be documented using event recording could include asking or answering questions, greeting skills, raising hand in class, or saying "please" and "thank you."

Cooper, Heron, and Heward (1987) detail a set of devices and procedures for event recording that include: (a) a counter, such as a golf counter, worn on the wrist; (b) a hand-tally digital counter, such as the grocery store counter; (c) a "wrist tally board," which is a note pad worn on the wrist or clothing of the observer or the child; and (d) objects such as buttons or paper clips that can be transferred from one place to another (pockets, for example) when the event occurs; or (e) a simple clipboard, paper, and pencil. Eisler (1976) suggests that for the most reliable recording, the observer should limit the number of behaviors recorded to no more than two at a time.

Duration recording, or recording how long the behavior occurs, is more appropriate for social behaviors that occur for an extended period and have a clearly defined beginning and end. Cooper, Heron, and Heward (1987) also suggest duration recording for behaviors that occur at a high rate such as rocking, running, or tapping objects. Duration recording is useful when the teaching goal is to lengthen or shorten the period of time. For example, one might wish to lengthen the amount of time the child spends in constructive play or in conversation with peers, or shorten the amount of time the child delays before complying with an adult request. A watch or wall clock with a second hand or, ideally, a stop watch, are generally used for duration recording, along with a means of noting the numbers obtained. Cooper et al. (1987) suggest that duration recording may be used in two ways: as a simple time duration (e.g., 5 minutes); or as a percentage of some specified time period, obtained by dividing the total time into the recorded time duration.

A time sampling or interval-recording process involves recording the occurrence or nonoccurrence of a behavior during or at the end of a specified time interval. It is used when it is not practical to observe for extended periods of time, for high-rate behaviors, or for behaviors that do not have a clear-cut beginning or end. Interval recording, to be accurate, requires considerable training of observers, practice, and the observers' undivided attention. It gives an estimate of frequency or duration of behavior across time intervals.

Many methods of observational recording are complex and thus more appropriate to a research setting where more resources are available. One such method involves the application of codes or checklists for recording, which helps to enhance agreement among observers as well as to condense the vast amount of observational data in any social situation. Foster and Ritchey (1979) point out that observational code categories referring to specific behaviors help minimize the need for inference. They further note that "reliability of observational data is largely under experimenter rather than subject control and can be enhanced with code refinements and good observer training" (p. 630).

At the same time, codes tend to omit data related to situational factors (Michelson, Foster, & Ritchey, 1981). The use of codes requires clear objective definitions of behavior and observers trained to use the codes. There are few, if any, commonly used codes for recording social skills. Michelson, Sugai, Wood, and Kazdin (1983) suggest that existing observation codes vary considerably in the behaviors observed and complexity of observation systems, because of factors such as "situational specificity and the idiosyncratic characteristics of social behavior" (p. 17). These authors have developed a social skills observation checklist, and Michelson and DiLorenzo (1981) have developed a peer interaction observation code for assessing children's behavior in semistructured settings.

The use of more than one observer to establish reliability related to interobserver agreement is considered essential in gathering accurate data. Individual perceptions can be biased by expectations and prejudices, and observers can vary in their speed and efficiency in recording. Cooper et al. (1987) provide detailed guidelines on procedures for developing observational codes and establishing interobserver agreement.

Considerable concern is expressed in empirical circles about the reactive effect of observation, or the possibility that the fact of observation will serve to change the observed behavior. To lessen reactive effects, observation should be as unobtrusive as possible. Kent and Foster (1977), in reviewing studies on reactivity of observation procedures, conclude that although the presence of an observer may sometimes affect the observed behavior, such findings are not always present, and not all behaviors are affected by observers. Some data suggest that when reactivity is present, its effects usually occur at the beginning of observation but weaken over time. For social skills assessment, where the goal is to determine skills and deficits for teaching purposes, observation effects could be considered an asset if they serve to strengthen the incentives operating in the assessment situation and thus motivate the child to display his most positive behaviors.

For more detailed information regarding observation techniques, consult the following resources: Barrios (1993), Barton and Ascione (1984), Cooper et al. (1987), Gelfand and Hartmann (1984), Kent and Foster (1977), and Wildman and Erickson (1977).

Functional Assessment

Functional assessment is an observational process that focuses on examining the environmental context to determine variables controlling maladaptive behavior, effective ways to modify the environment, and the social skills that need to be taught (Durand & Carr, 1991; Foster-Johnson & Dunlap, 1993). Proponents of this approach note that behavior is related to the various events that are operating in the environment at a given time and that "challenging" behaviors often persist because they serve some desired function for the individual in the current circumstances. For example, tantruming that is consistently consequated with time-out might be one child's means for regularly escaping an undesired classroom task.

Dadson and Horner (1993) further point out that these "setting events" may be so powerful or reinforcing that ". . . typical rewards such as teacher praise, completing a task, and peer attention may become less reinforcing than usual" (p. 53). To illustrate, these authors present a case study of a student with mental disabilities who unpredictably had days of resisting instruction. Using a functional assessment, they determined that the student was inclined to cry, swear, and tantrum on days when she slept poorly the previous night or when the bus was late. This information, transmitted by her parents, enabled the classroom teacher to prepare alternative and more effective activities on these days.

In their two-step process for conducting a functional assessment, Foster-Johnson and Dunlap (1993) suggest first collecting data and then developing a hypothesis about the behavior. For the first step of data collection, the authors identify several substeps needed to formulate possible rationales for the observed behavior. As with all behavioral assessments, it is first necessary to specify the behavior so that it is clearly defined and easily targeted and measured by others.

The second substep requires that the target behavior be put into context. That is, a description is needed of the conditions (e.g., physiological, classroom environment, instructional demands) under which the behavior does and does not occur. Through direct observations over an extended period of time and interviews of others in the child's environment, it may be determined that the target behavior occurs at specific times (e.g., immediately before math class) or under certain conditions (e.g., when asked to perform a new or unfamiliar task). Videotaping the child's classroom behavior may be an effective means for observing and analyzing the child's behavior (Cooper, Peck, Wacker, & Millard, 1993).

This information then leads to the third and final substep of collecting information—determining the function of the behavior. Foster-Johnson and Dunlap (1993) contend that behavior occurs either to get something or to escape something, and at this point one must determine what is being achieved and what is maintaining this undesired behavior. Is the child being disruptive or uncooperative, for example, to escape some unpleasant assignment or to gain peer attention?

Once the major step of information gathering has been accomplished, the teacher then moves to developing and testing out a reasonable hypothesis. Through the systematic manipulation of variables and consequences, the teacher can assess the accuracy of this hypothesis and devise plans for developing more adaptive behaviors. Foster-Johnson and Dunlap (1993) give an example of hypothesis testing and possible interventions (see Table 2-2).

Evolving from the Bijou et al. (1968) continuous recording procedure described earlier, functional assessments also emphasize observing the individual throughout the day and obtaining information from informants in other settings. Case studies using functional assessment to analyze and modify behaviors include independent performance on math assignments (Cooper et al., 1993) and clothes shredding behavior (Redmond, Bennett, Wiggert, & McLean, 1993). Durand and Carr provide several reports of functional analysis as a means for targeting functional communication skills (Carr & Durand, 1985; Durand, 1990; Durand & Carr, 1991).

TABLE 2-2 Hypothesis Testing and Possible Interventions

Hypothesis Statements	Modify Antecedents	Teach Alternative Behavior
Jack gets into arguments with the teacher every day during reading class when she asks him to correct his mistakes on the daily reading worksheet	Get Jack to correct his own paper. Give Jack an easier assignment.	Teach Jack strategies to manage his frustration in a more appropriate manner. Teach Jack to ask for teacher assistance with the incorrect problems.

Source: From Foster-Johnson and Dunlop (1993, p. 49).

Permanent Products

Cooper (1974) defines permanent products as tangible evidence of behavior that can be measured after the behavior occurs. Although permanent products may have more applicability in academic assessment, there are approaches to social skill assessment through observation that involve a product. Because behavior goes by quickly and accurate observations are difficult, an increasingly practical means of assessing behaviors in the natural environment involves the use of video- and audiotapes to capture the behavior and make it accessible for later evaluation. Such devices are particularly useful for the researcher concerned with reliability of assessment. In a social skills program to increase appropriate dinnertime conversation, for example, tape recordings were made at home during the dinner hour and analyzed according to conversational categories, making both assessment and ongoing evaluation possible (Jewett & Clark, 1976). Audio- and videotapes also are valuable where the behaviors of more than one child are being assessed at the same time. For the teacher and therapist, recordings can be a useful tool to assess the child's social skill deficits, enable the child to assess his or her own skill deficits, and demonstrate improvements by comparing tapes before and after training.

Permanent products play a role where behaviors cannot be directly observed in the natural environment but must be inferred from observable results (e.g., assessing the degree of a child's compliance with a request to clean his or her room). Other social skills may involve the production of a product: for example, the ability to write a thank-you note or take a phone message, or the tangible results of a group project designed to assess ability to work cooperatively in a group and share materials.

Setting Up "Contrived" Situations

Because sometimes it is inefficient to wait for a behavior to occur to collect observational data, Stephens (1992b) suggests arranging the natural environment to require or facilitate the behavior, then watching for its occurrence. An example of such a contrived assessment situation would be the following, for the skill, "To share toys and equipment in a play situation":

> During a free-play or recess period, have the target student play with some available toys or equipment alone for a short time. Then send another student over to play with the same toys or equipment. Observe whether the first (target) student willingly allows the second to play with the toys, and if he plays together with the second student. Or, establish a small group activity, such as drawing pictures with one set of magic markers or pens given to target student for all to share. Observe the target student for sharing behavior (p. 293).

Observe how a child handles winning or losing by setting up a competitive game. Or establish a task-oriented group to assess, for example, the child's ability to: follow rules related to the task, ask permission to use another's property, stay on-task, share materials, work cooperatively, ask for and give help, or use "please" and "thank you."

Wood, Michelson, and Flynn (1978) use a systematic and structured approach to the contrived naturalistic scene in which trained confederates participate (described in Michelson et al., 1983, and Beck, Forehand, Neeper, & Baskin, 1982). Michelson et al. (1983) call this strategy a "candid camera" method. Beck et al. (1982) assess skill at entering a group by directing a child to join two peers who are playing a game. The peers have been instructed in responses that vary, depending on the approach behaviors exhibited by the subject. The Wood et al. measure, the *Children's Behavioral Scenario* (CBS), is a contrived interview conducted by an adult. It involves both questions to elicit assertive or nonassertive responses and arrangement of the physical environment in ways that invite assertive or nonassertive behaviors. The contrived aspects of the environment include inviting the child to sit down in the only available chair, which is covered by an attaché case, or asking the child to write something, offering him or her a pencil with a broken point. Another instrument described by Shapiro and Kratochwill (1988), the *Contrived Test of Social Skills* (CTSS) (Shapiro, Stover, & Ifkovits, 1983; Shapiro, Gilbert, Friedman, & Steiner, 1985), employs similar procedures to assess classroom social skills.

This assessment approach is easy and efficient, its main disadvantage is an ethical one. Michelson et al. (1983) suggest that because this kind of assessment involves deception, it is important that children be debriefed afterward, that parental approval be obtained, and that there are no harmful aspects to the experience.

The Interview as an Assessment Situation

The clinical interview is a common form of assessment that can yield useful initial information about a child's social skills. The interview as a method for assessing social skills has not received a great deal of empirical attention, but as Gresham and Elliott (1984) point out, children are often referred for social skills instruction after data have been gathered through interviews with parents or teachers. Interviews with adult sources can provide important information about the child's social skill deficits and the conditions under which various social behaviors are exhibited or are lacking. Similarly, interviews with parents and teachers can add to the social validity of assessment data by revealing what social behaviors they are likely to approve of and reinforce. Such interviews can be most productive and the data gathered most accurate if questions are standardized and gather specific information.

Gresham and Davis (1988) give a three-phase behavioral model as an example for conducting interviews with parents and teachers. The first phase, the problem identification interview (PII), focuses on objectively defining the behavior, its related environmental conditions, and the means for data collection. The problem analysis interview (PAI), the second phase, categorizes the behavior according to data collected and devises an intervention plan. The problem evaluation interview (PEI) evaluates the effects of the intervention on the problem behavior and determines subsequent actions. The authors give specific steps for carrying out each component of this interview process.

An interview with a child is one kind of contrived situation that can provide observational data on a variety of social behaviors, as well as self-report information. Interviews with children old enough to be verbal provide data on how the child regards his or her own social behavior and perceives his or her own strengths and deficits in dealing with others. Perhaps as important, it can serve as an opportunity to observe the social skills manifested in the interview situation. For example, these can include:

- The child's ability to sit quietly, pay attention to the adult, maintain eye contact, and listen.
- The child's ability to communicate about behaviors and feelings, ability to describe situations and her or his role in them, and ability to put thoughts into words; the child's vocabulary, voice quality and articulation, length of answers, relevance of replies, and ability to initiate as well as respond.
- The nature of affect displayed by the child, whether she or he is comfortable in a one-to-one situation with an adult, and her or his greeting skills.

A small group interview reveals a different set of behaviors for observation, especially those related to peer interactions:

- The nature of the child's interaction with peers, whether she initiates or follows, whether she is easily influenced into group misbehavior, and how she participates in a group task.
- The nature of the child's verbal behavior with peers, whether he initiates and carries on conversations, makes relevant comments, listens to others, and is positive with peers.

The child's knowledge of appropriate social behaviors also can be assessed in the interview. Eisler (1976) provides a list of interpersonal behavior situations that might be explored in interviews with adult clients about their history of interpersonal response patterns. Adapted to children, the list could include the ability to:

1. Express opinions contrary to those of peers, parents, teachers.
2. Ask favors of someone.
3. Initiate conversations with peers and adults.
4. Refuse unreasonable requests from friends and strangers.
5. Invite a peer to play.
6. Compliment someone.
7. Receive compliments.
8. Ask for help in solving problems.
9. Resist pressure from peers to behave in an unacceptable way.

In the treatment of an adult, the interview is probably the primary source of information about the client. When dealing with children, the interview may present special problems. Responding to another person in a one-to-one interview situation involves a complex set of communication skills that the child may not yet possess. Children are much less likely than adults to be able to self-monitor feelings and responses and report about them to someone else. In addition, children seldom present themselves to a teacher or therapist expressing concern about their own problems or behavior deficits. A discussion about identifying their difficulties can engender resistance and avoidance. To counter such responses, Goldman, L'Engle Stein, and Guerry (1983) stress the need for the interviewer to keep the child comfortable through an attitude of acceptance and to use techniques to relax the atmosphere such as lessening demands, allowing the child to move around, or taking a break for snacks. It is often useful to have food and play materials, such as clay and crayons, available to help make the interview situation less formal.

Because of the child's limited behavioral repertoire, the skill of the interviewer in communicating with children is particularly important (Evans & Nelson, 1977; Witt, Cavell, Heffer, Carey, & Martens, 1988). In interviewing children, for example, the typical approach of asking questions may not be productive. Witt et al. suggest that, for younger children, open-ended questions may be inhibiting and limit the amount of useful information obtained. They also advise reducing the complexity of questions asked and the complexity of responses to be made by children. Permitting young children to point to pictured faces depicting emotions is one example they give to reduce response complexity.

Recently, the low reliability of the unstructured interview as a source of social behavior data has led to a trend toward the structured interview. Witt et al. (1988) cite research (e.g., Bierman, 1983; Paget, 1984) recommending structured interview instruments to obtain objective, comprehensive assessments that allow for comparisons across informants and time. The authors list several such instruments and report that some of them, such as the *Diagnostic Interview Schedule for Children* (DISC) (Costello, Edelbrock, & Costello, 1985), can be administered by lay persons with minimal training within 50 to 60 minutes.

The interview is one of the most easily available and convenient methods to start gathering assessment information. To the extent that the child can recognize and talk about his or her interpersonal problems and conflicts, the interview can help provide a rationale for social skills instruction and thus enhance the child's motivation. Combined with other assessment procedures, information obtained from skilled interviews can be useful in devising plans for social skill interventions.

Analogue Measures

Because many social behaviors are difficult to structure and observe in a natural situation, the analogue is an approach that has been used for many years to provide access to more complex or infrequent social behavior, particularly a simulation or role-play representing an interpersonal encounter. Role-playing has the advantage of permitting the practitioner to study the environmental conditions under which the response occurs as well as the response itself (Goldfried & D'Zurilla, 1969). The interviewer also can arrange a variety of conditions so that many responses can be studied. In addition, according to McFall (1977), analogue measures, such as role-playing, enable the researcher to control extraneous variables, avoid the possibility of the harmful consequences that could occur in similar real-life situations, and offer the practical advantages of efficiency and economy.

Goldfried and D'Zurilla (1969) define standards used in the development of role-play assessment instruments. These are:

1. Situational analysis—an environmental survey to identify the most meaningful, problematic situations an individual typically encounters.
2. Response enumeration—possible alternative responses to various problem situations.
3. Response evaluation—which responses are most likely to receive favorable reactions in the natural environment.
4. Development of measurement format—the mode of responses to be used by the child to assess competence in various social situations (e.g., role playing, written responses, naturalistic observations).
5. Evaluation of the measure—whether the assessment procedures adhere to recognized psychometric principles (i.e., are valid, reliable, computed according to sound scoring procedures, and standardized so that they provide for performance comparisons across populations).

Situation analysis and response enumeration are particularly important in role-play assessment, because assessment research demonstrates that the quality of role-playing increases when the person being assessed can relate to or identify with the assessment situation.

An example of role-play tests using the Goldfried and D'Zurilla model is that of Edleson and associates (Edleson & Cole-Kelly, 1978; Edleson & Rose, 1978). The authors identify problem conditions common to children and incorporate them into role-play assessment scenes covering interpersonal skill in various situations. The *Problem Inventory for Adolescent Girls* (PIAG), in which extensive interviews are held with adults and adolescents to identify problem situations and responses (Gaffney & McFall, 1981), follows the same model.

Role-Play Assessment Instruments

Common aspects of role-play instruments for children include

- Practice situation. Prior to the actual testing situation, scenes are used to determine if the child understands what is expected. They can also be used as a mechanism for warming up to the role-playing situation.
- Standard script. To ensure uniformity of testing conditions, scripts are developed and delivered by a narrator.
- Prompts. Following each scene, the child is expected to respond to a prompt. For example, a scene is described by the narrator in which the child is being teased, and the prompter actually delivers the taunting statement to which the child is to respond. Prompters who are within the child's peer group can provide an additional element of realism to the situation.
- Videotaping and rating. Videotaping the role-played scene makes it possible to review and evaluate.

This sequence is consistent with the format Merluzzi and Biever (1987) refer to as a "structured role play"— it is conducted according to a script and the confederate does not respond to the target child's response. In contrast, according to these authors, unstructured role-plays permit the target child and confederate to interact for an extended period (approximately five minutes) and children are instructed to act "naturally," pretending they are actually in the described setting. Under these conditions, target children are given ample opportunity to talk, perhaps providing a more realistic assessment of the specified behavior.

One of the most extensively researched role-play instruments for children is the *Behavioral Assertiveness Test for Children* (BAT-C), which was developed by Bornstein, Bellack, and Hersen (1977) and has since been refined and modified, for example, in the *Behavioral Assertiveness Test for Boys* (BAT-B) (Reardon et al., 1979) and the *Children's Interpersonal Behavior Test* (CIBT) (Van Hasselt, Hersen, & Bellack, 1981). Focusing on assertive behaviors in school, examples from the original nine-scene instrument include (Bornstein et al., 1977, p. 186):

Female Model

NARRATOR: "You're part of a small group in a science class. Your group is trying to come up with an idea for a project to present to the class. You start to give your idea when Amy begins to tell hers also."

PROMPT: "Hey, listen to my idea."

NARRATOR: "Imagine you need to use a pair of scissors for a science project. Betty is using them, but promises to let you have them next. But when Betty is done she gives them to Ellen."

PROMPT: "Here's the scissors, Ellen."

NARRATOR: "Pretend you loaned your pencil to Joannie. She comes over to give it back to you and says that she broke the point."

PROMPT: "I broke the point."

Michelson et al. (1983) also developed the *Social Skills Role Play Test* for children, which corresponds to their *Social Skills Observation Checklist* and assesses several social skills areas.

To increase the similarity to the natural environment, role-playing assessments may be provided through audio- or videotapes. Under these conditions, the individual must respond to various situations presented on the tapes. Every effort is made to make the scenes realistic, employing theatrics such as background sound effects, actors, and confederates who are as similar as possible to the type of person being described in the scene. For example, if the assessment situation consists of one child responding to another on the playground, appropriate noises would be included in the background and a child (confederate) would be used to record the comments to which the child being assessed would respond. Responses made by the child being assessed may be either oral or physical; it is assumed that the closer the approximations are to reality, the more natural the child's responses will be.

A third alternative is paper-and-pencil responses—multiple-choice questionnaires, where the child must indicate which of the listed behaviors he or she would perform under the conditions presented. Although somewhat more difficult for children, another type of paper-and-pencil response has an open-ended format, requiring the child to generate his or her own natural reaction to the taped situation.

Audio- and videotape assessment conditions are similar to those in role-playing; that is, the child is instructed how to respond, a narrative describing the situation is provided, a confederate actor makes a comment to which the individual being assessed must respond, and the response is made according to some predetermined mode. These measures have special advantages: (1) they more closely approximate real-life conditions, (2) it is possible to structure audiotapes to assess characteristics specific to a particular child, (3) they may be administered without an examiner present, (4) one may employ nonverbal as well as verbal communications with videotapes (Nay, 1977), and (5) they make it possible to present identical stimuli to more than one child. Hughes and Hall (1985) and Hughes, Boodoo, Alcala, Maggio, Moore, and Villapando (1989) present some successful examples of videotaped role-plays with children. These authors argue that the videotape format facilitates assessment by permitting the teacher to focus only on the child's response rather than on setting the scene, providing for uniform assessments and a novel effect that motivates children to respond.

One of the previously noted disadvantages of using videotapes as an assessment tool, that is, equipment costs, has been addressed somewhat by the increased use and availability of this equipment in most schools. Nevertheless, limitations for videotaped assessments include the time involved in staging scenes and the fact that responding to the taped situations requires only single responses and does not allow for ongoing interaction. In live role-playing, the interaction may be continued beyond the initial response, resulting in a more thorough and possibly more accurate assessment of how the child would respond under such conditions.

Several researchers (Bellack, Hersen, & Lamparski, 1979; Bellack, Hersen, & Turner, 1978, 1979; Matson, Esveldt-Dawson, & Kazdin, 1983; Van Hasselt et al., 1981) question the validity of role-play tests in predicting actual social behavior in real-life situations. Lack of role-taking ability, anxiety associated with role-playing, and the relative brevity of required responses are factors identified by Bellack et al. (1979) that may limit the external validity of role-play tests for children. McFall (1977) states:

> Analogue methods . . . invariably require certain compromises with reality. While they may help generate interpretable solutions to simplified experimental problems, their solutions may or may not have relevance for the "real life" problems that initially prompted the research. Reasoning by analogy necessarily involves making abstractions about certain ways in which two things seem to be similar, while ignoring all of the other ways in which they may be different. It is assumed that the abstracted similarities somehow capture the essence of the phenomenon being studied, and that little of essence is left among the overlooked differences. Whether the solutions generated by analogue methods actually have relevance, or external validity, is a function of the particular analogies chosen . . . (p. 153).

More recent studies, however, with college students (Conger, Moisan-Thomas, & Conger, 1989; Merluzzi & Biever, 1987) and adult patients (Bellack, Morrison, Mueser, Wade, & Sayers, 1990), as well as with school-age children (Hughes et al., 1989), lend support to the value of role-play assessments. Closely tailoring measures to behaviors and populations being assessed appears to be one factor critical to the success of these measures. For example, Hughes et al. (1989) contend that in the past role-play assessments with children were inadequate partly because adults were used to deliver prompts, and the assessment measures were based on research conducted with adults.

To counter these perceived defects in their study with elementary-aged children, the researchers used children rather than adults to deliver prompts for role-plays and used ratings from socially competent children as criterion measures for the children's role-plays. They also rated the children's performance according to the content of their response rather than by discrete skill components. For example, a child's score was based on whether an appropriately assertive response was made, instead of on eye contact or the number of words uttered. Significant correlations were found between children's role-play performances and teachers' ratings of social competence and peer ratings. Popularity and intelligence emerged as significant variables, with children who received higher peer ratings and better scores on measures of cognitive ability performing better in the role-plays.

Despite some empirical evidence of its legitimate use with children (Hughes et al., 1989) and obvious advantages, such as flexibility of assessment and ease of administration (Bellack et al., 1990; Shapiro & Kratochwill, 1988) like all other social skills assessment approaches, role-play tests are best when used with other measures.

Assessment by Peers

Sociometric Procedures

In addition to parents and teachers, peers provide another important source of data about social behavior. Evaluations by peers typically are obtained through one of two means: peer assessments or sociometric techniques. Although these two measures are commonly confused, McConnell and Odom (1986) point out the need to distinguish the two evaluations, because they tap different concepts. Peer assessments are designed for children to rate their peers according to some behavior or trait, but sociometrics assess how a child *feels* about a peer. In responding to the former the child might be asked to identify the best student or worker in the class, but with a sociometric assessment the child would be asked, "Who do you *want* to work with?" The latter is more affective and indicates personal preference.

Sociometrics may be used to supplement other social skill assessment techniques to identify children with social skills deficits. Because researchers have established a relationship between childhood peer rejection and later-life social maladjustment, such as juvenile delinquency or emotional disturbance (Parker & Asher, 1987; Roff, Sells, & Golden, 1972), sociometric assessment may have a potential for prediction. The predictive validity of sociometrics is not yet clearly established (Foster, Bell-Dolan, & Berler, 1986; Gresham & Stuart, 1992). Yet McConnell and Odom (1986), in their extensive review of these studies, conclude that "sociometric assessment, as a measure of children's social relationships with peers, may help identify children who could be at risk for adjustment problems as adults" (p. 227). Sociometric methods differ in format and are classified according to the way they are implemented—that is, nominations, paired comparisons, and roster-ratings (Hops & Lewin, 1984; Hymel, 1983).

Nominations

Nominations are the most commonly used and simplest form of sociometric assessment. Individual children are required to nominate their peers according to degree of acceptance or nonacceptance. Positive measures and responses (e.g., "Who do you like the most?") are generally preferred, but it has been determined that negative responses (e.g., "Who do you like the least?") are also necessary to distinguish between those who are disliked and those who are simply ignored. Children who are not identified when using positive measures may not necessarily be rejected but rather are overlooked during the selection process. Negative nominations often are viewed dimly by adults who assume such assessments may harm children and their peer relationships. Using the sociometric procedure, Hayvren and Hymel (1984) found that children engaged in relatively brief conversations about the assessments, concentrating on positive nominations and making no reference to disliked peers. To date no additional studies of this nature have been conducted, but as Gresham and Little (1993) note, there is no documented evidence of negative nominations having a deleterious effect on children, and the failure to include them substantially compromises the reliability of sociometric nominations.

In using peer nominations, the child typically is directed to identify three children he or she likes the most and then three children he or she does not like or likes least. This number may vary, however, so that the child may make an unlimited number of nominations for any one question, or make as few choices as desired. The latter option might be advised in the case of negative nominations to avoid forcing the child to make a false negative choice. If using either of the two previous options, the researcher is required to employ a weighted scale for data analysis.

Obtaining valid peer nominations is a major consideration with sociometric assessments, especially with young children. Moore and Updegraff (1964) developed a sociometric procedure for use with nursery school children, ranging in age from 3 to 5 years. Individual interviews were conducted, wherein the responding child was presented with a board containing individual pictures of each child in the group. The examiner assisted the child in identifying each picture, then the child was asked to find someone he or she especially liked. After four choices were made, the child was directed to identify someone he or she did not like very much for four more choices. Following this step, the examiner pointed to the pictures of children not selected and asked the responding child if he or she liked or disliked that child. Responses were scored according to positives, negatives, and order of choice, with weights being assigned to the respective choices. For example, a child selected first as being liked received +8 points, while the first disliked child selected received –8. Similarly, the second liked child received +6 and second disliked child –6, with the remaining two choices scored 4 and 3. Positives and negatives selected because the examiner pointed to them received +1 and –1 point. Computation of the points yielded composite sociometric scores for each child, with well-liked children receiving the highest scores.

In addition to votes based on affect, peer choices can be made within the context of specific activities such as play and academic tasks. For example, children taking Miller's (1977) *Sociometric Preference Test* might be given a list of classmates and directed, "Choose five persons you would most like to work with" (p. 20). The five choices are designated by ordinal numbers as illustrated.

Mark A.	3rd
Peter B.	1st
John B.	4th
Mary C.	2nd

As social competence data obtained from peers have gained in popularity, there has been a corresponding increase in the sophistication of assessment procedures and peer status categories. Initially, researchers focused on targeting the socially isolated child, later differentiating within this group, the rejected and neglected child (Gottman, 1977). In 1982, Coie, Dodge, and Coppotelli conceptualized a five-category peer status paradigm consisting of popular, rejected, neglected, controversial, and average children. Popular children receive many most-liked votes and few least-liked; rejected children receive many least-liked and few most-liked votes. Neglected children receive a few of both most-liked and least-liked votes; controversial children receive many of both most-liked and least-liked votes. Average children are a referent group that falls midway between the other four extremes.

Within this model, Coie et al. (1982) present the polar opposites of popular-rejected children and neglected-controversial children. Whereas neglected children receive few acceptance or rejection nominations, controversial children receive many of both. Although the category is a point of contention (Newcomb & Bukowski, 1983), Coie (Coie & Dodge, 1983; Coie et al., 1982) asserts that controversial children are a distinct, high-risk group that should be considered in sociometric assessments. Controversial children are described as having leadership characteristics but also as being disruptive, a profile consistent with juvenile delinquents. In a one-year follow-up study Coie and Dodge (1983) found the ratings of rejected children to be most stable and those of controversial children to be least stable. These findings were confirmed by Gresham and Stuart (1992), who also observed that when shifts did occur they were more likely to be from negative status categories (i.e., rejected, neglected, and controversial) to positive status categories (i.e., average or popular).

Paired Comparisons

One concern with sociometric assessments through nominations is that children, particularly young children, will name peers impulsively or fail to nominate a peer, not remembering that child's name. Paired-comparison sociometric assessment is designed to circumvent these limitations. With this procedure, the names or pictures of only two peers are presented at a time, and the responding child is directed to indicate either a positive or negative nomination for one of the pair. Each child in the group is paired with every other child in the group, thus avoiding the possibility that a classmate might be overlooked and ensuring the stability of any particular nomination. Sociometric scores are derived according to the number of positive or negative choices each child receives from her or his peers. This procedure yields a large number of data points that contribute to the greater reliability of the paired-comparison measure (Hops & Lewin, 1984; Hymel, 1983).

An obvious disadvantage of paired-comparison assessments is the time needed for administration. Vaughn and Langlois (1983) employed a complete paired-comparisons procedure with 40 preschool children. The individually administered assessments necessitated two to three 15-minute sessions. Total time estimates for this group assessment ranged from 20 to 30 hours. Compare this to the one five-minute individual session required for an assessment using nominations (Hymel, 1983), which would have a total time estimate of $3\frac{1}{4}$ hours for the same population. A reliable and less time-consuming subsample approach developed by

Cohen and Van Tassel (1978) still involves more time than nominations (Hymel, 1983).

Roster and Rating

A method used more with school-aged children is the roster and rating sociometric questionnaire. The roster is an alternative to the more common fill-in instrument, where the child is expected to write in names of peers. The roster-rating instrument provides children with a listing of classmates and a rating scale for indicating peer attitudes. The *Spontaneous Choice Test* (Miller, 1977) specifies ratings according to a three-point scale labeled "like," "dislike," and "indifferent." The child places a check opposite each name, based on which term most accurately conveys his or her feelings toward the child being rated. When encountering Mary J.'s name, for example, her best friend probably would check the column under *like* as shown below (adapted from Miller, 1977, p. 20):

	Like	Dislike	Indifferent
Mary J.	X		
Others			

The more popular format is the alphabetized roster with a five- or seven-point scale following the name of each child in the group. The respondent rates each member listed on the scale according to how much he or she likes or dislikes the named child. Each child's score is the average of all of his or her ratings. This method has certain advantages: It allows for ratings by all group members and, by providing ratings on a continuum, it avoids some of the unpleasant ethical aspects of negative ratings (Hymel & Asher, 1977). An example of a five-point rating scale is shown in Table 2-3.

Ratings tend to indicate general likeability of a peer, not whether that peer is chosen for friendship (Connolly, 1983; Schofield & Whitley, 1983). For example, in studying the effects of race on peer preferences in a desegregated setting, Schofield

TABLE 2-3 Example of a Five-point Rating Scale

	I like this person a lot	I like this person	Don't know very well	Don't care for this person	Don't like this person at all
Directions: How do you feel about your classmates? Circle the number that best tells how you feel about each classmate.				
John E.	5	4	3	2	1
Roy P.	5	4	3	2	1
Linda W.	5	4	3	2	1
Others	5	4	3	2	1

and Whitley found stronger racial preferences with peer nominations than with roster-rating measures. Schofield and Whitley's (1983) meta-analysis of previous research in this area corroborated their findings, supporting their contention that "peer nominations reveal friendships, whereas the roster-and-rating technique assesses interpersonal acceptance, a much less intimate form of relationship" (p. 243). Hymel (1983) points out that, although rating scale scores are more related to social competence, they are less useful in identifying rejected children and determining social impact.

Peer Assessments

A major limitation of sociometric procedures is that knowing a child's level of acceptance or rejection does not specify the personal attributes or shortcomings that contribute to that social status (Connolly, 1983; Foster & Ritchey, 1979; Hymel, 1983). Therefore, more structured peer assessments such as *Who Are They?* (Bowman, DeHaan, Kough, & Liddle, 1956) and *Class Play* (Bower, 1960) are recommended. The *Who Are They?* test requires each child to identify a classmate who she or he feels is best described by various statements, designed to measure leadership, aggression, withdrawn behavior, and friendship. Sample items include: "Who are the good leaders?" and "Who are the boys and girls who make good plans?" Coie et al. (1982) adapt the *Bower Class Play Test* into 24 behavioral questions such as, "This person starts fights. He or she says mean things to other kids and pushes them and hits them" (p. 559). The children in this study nominated three children they felt characteristically exhibited each type of behavior. These data yield behavior correlates of cooperativeness, support, and physical attractiveness for accepted children, while correlates for the rejected group were disruptiveness and aggression.

The *Adjustment Scales for Sociometric Evaluation of Secondary School Students* (ASSESS) (Prinz, Swan, Liebert, Weintraub, & Neale, 1978) is an instrument designed for the peer evaluation of secondary students. ASSESS consists of five scales, each divided into several observable behaviors indicative of the category. The scales and representative behaviors are (p. 497):

1. Aggression-Disruptiveness; e.g., "Are rude to teachers."
2. Withdrawal; e.g., "Are sort of ignored."
3. Anxiety; e.g., "Are nervous when called upon to answer in class."
4. Social Competence; e.g., "Can work well in a group."
5. Academic Difficulty; e.g., "Do poorly in school."

Students put an X beneath the names of peers they feel are characterized by these various descriptions. The authors report the instrument to be a reliable and valid peer assessment for adolescents.

Sociometric and peer assessments can be administered in various ways and are useful in providing valuable information about children's social development. There are, however, several considerations or cautions to note. For very young children, sociometric evaluations should be obtained through individual interviews, making certain the child understands the directions and responds properly. Similar procedures may be necessary for somewhat older children with special needs. By third grade, the child is probably able to make sociometric ratings through paper-and-pencil tasks. Another consideration important for school-aged children is preference for same-sex and same-race peers. For that reason, choices may be based largely on these variables rather than on social interaction factors, and this needs to be taken into account when analyzing the results. Foster et al. (1986) suggest that group designations may change depending on whether ratings are conducted according to the same sex or include both sexes. They speculate that by changing the gender of the raters, a rejected group in one study could become a neglected group in another study. Similarly, physical appearance plays a role in peer assessments, particularly for girls, and thus may unfairly distort the social competence evaluations of individual subjects. Vaughn and Langlois (1983) also found physical attractiveness to correlate with social status with preschool children, particularly girls. Using pictures as part of an assessment may result in peer judgments of social competence being biased by physical appearance. McConnell and Odom (1986) also specify the likeability of one's name, the presence of a disability, and ecological factors as correlates to peer ratings. Relative to class environment, they found fewer social isolates in open versus traditional, large versus small, and secondary versus elementary classes.

To correct for the tendency of children to base ratings of a peer on a recent negative experience, it is recommended that the sociometric procedure be administered two or more times over a period of weeks to obtain accurate results. Rating scales appear to be better indices of tolerance or likeability and, thus, may be a more appropriate peer measure of social skill but not of social impact. Ratings also seem to have greater reliability than instruments that require children to write in or nominate names of peers.

A final issue to consider is the biasing effect of parental consent. Foster et al. (1986) point out that consent is more likely to be obtained from parents with professional/managerial occupations, whose children tend to fall within the average or above intelligence range. This phenomenon limits the opportunity for adequate study of the full range of peer interactions and may exclude children evidencing significant social skill deficits.

Self-assessment

Another approach to social skills assessment is to involve children in assessing their social competence through the use of various scales, checklists, and self-monitoring techniques. Although one may question children's ability to perceive their social behavior accurately or their effect on others, these reports may provide valuable assessment data. The responses may be used to compare discrepancies between self-perceptions and assessments by others, to identify critical areas for instruction based on misperceptions of behavior, and to determine changes in self-assessment pre- and posttreatment. Self-reports are observable behaviors in themselves.

There are numerous problems with self-reports. Gresham and Elliott (1984) stress that "children's self-report measures have not been found useful in predicting peer acceptance, peer popularity, teacher ratings of social skills, role-play performance, or social behavior in naturalistic settings" (p. 297). Michelson et al. (1981) point out further difficulties in reading and comprehension and developmental factors, along with "misreading, misinterpretation, cheating, indifference, and external environmental factors." On the other hand, several researchers argue for the inclusion of self-reports in comprehensive assessments, noting an improvement in methods and instruments over recent years that has resulted in more valid, reliable self-assessments (e.g., Witt et al., 1988; Spence & Liddle, 1990). It is important to note that the child's self-perception is an influential factor related to motivation for learning social behaviors and the lasting effects of social skills training. The next section presents several means of obtaining self-report data related to social behavior, measures of self-esteem and perceived social competence, and procedures for self-monitoring social behavior.

Self-assessment of Social Behaviors

The assertiveness scale is a self-report measure designed to assess overt social behaviors. The *Children's Assertive Behavior Scale* (CABS) (Michelson et al., 1983) is a 27-item pencil-and-paper, multiple-choice instrument designed for elementary school–age children. It measures specific responses to brief situations, reflecting behavior categories such as empathy, conversation making, requests, and compliments. The authors report extensive data for this instrument, indicating positive reliability and validity (Michelson & Wood, 1982). For each item, the child chooses one of five possible options, indicating how he or she would respond in that situation if the "someone" in the situation was (a) another youth, or (b) an adult. The range of choices include very passive, passive, assertive, aggressive, and very aggressive responses. The authors also have developed a second instrument with the same items to be rated by the teacher. A sample item of the instrument, with the responses labeled on an aggressive/passive continuum, might read (Michelson et al., 1983, p. 222):

   1. Someone says to you, "I think you are a very nice person." You would usually:
      a. Say "No, I'm not that nice." (very passive)
      b. Say, "Yes, I think I am the best!" (very aggressive)
      c. Say, "Thank you." (assertive)
      d. Say nothing and blush. (passive)
      e. Say, "Thanks, I am really great." (aggressive)

The *Matson Evaluation of Social Skills for Youth* (MESSY) (Matson et al., 1983), referred to earlier, is a self-report instrument broader in scope than the previous measure, focusing on a range of social behaviors, feelings, and cognitions. The MESSY has been found to have good psychometric properties (Spence & Liddle, 1990). It requires children to rate themselves on a five-point scale. The items are similar to those on the teacher scale it accompanies but is translated into the first person: "I become angry easily.". . . "I gripe or complain often."

Another self-report instrument, designed to assess a wide range of social behaviors and provide for multiple respondents (teachers and parents), is the *Social Skill Rating System—Self* (SSRS-S) (Gresham & Elliott, 1990). There are two levels, one with 34 items for elementary-aged children—starting at the third grade, and a second with 39 items for secondary students—beginning at grade seven. Students rate themselves on a three-point scale (0 = never, 1 = sometimes, and 2 = very often) according to the degree to which they feel they perform the designated behavior, for example, "I ask before using other people's things." The specific items reflect four classes of behavior—cooperation, assertion, empathy, and self-control—so the student receives scores according to these subcategories, as well as a total social skills score. Standard scores and percentile levels also are provided.

Self-esteem Measures

Self-report scales dealing with self-concept or self-esteem attempt to measure the child's sense of self-worth, acceptance, success, and competence in various areas. Such measures may be useful to assess the effects of social skills training on children's self-perceptions.

Several such instruments exist (see Witt et al., 1988), but two of the most widely used are the *Self-Esteem Inventory* (Coopersmith, 1967) and the *Piers-Harris Self Concept Scale (The Way I Feel About Myself)* (Piers, 1984). Both are unidimensional measures of children's self-concept and require children to indicate whether a particular statement describes them, for example, "I'm pretty sure of myself" (Coopersmith, 1967).

A more recently developed instrument, *The Perceived Competence Scale for Children* (Harter, 1982), makes an attempt to measure the child's sense of personal competence across several domains rather than as a unitary concept. There are subscales for cognitive, social, and physical competence, and an independent subscale for general self-worth. The 28-item scale can be used for elementary and junior high students. The question format is different from other self-worth measures in that it makes possible a broader range of responses and, thus, according to the author, reduces the tendency to give socially desirable responses. This example is from the general self-worth category (Harter, 1978, p. 2):

Some kids feel good about the way they act.	*but*	Other kids wish they acted differently.
Really true for me		Sort of true for me
Sort of true for me		Really true for me

Since one subscale specifically measures the child's perceptions of his or her social competence with peers, this instrument has particular relevance for social skills assessment. Harter reports a fairly high correlation between sociometric ratings and social subscale scores. The structure and usefulness of this instrument is documented in the empirical literature (Marsh & Gouvernet, 1989; Witt et al., 1988).

The validity of self-report measures of competence is open to question. Harter (1982) suggests, however, that low correlations between the child's perceived competence and indices of competence, such as teacher ratings and achievement tests, do not necessarily indicate poor validity for the competence measure. She suggests that such findings "have implications for program-evaluation efforts, suggesting that a goal should be to foster a realistic sense of competence rather than enhancement per se. That is, reduction in the magnitude of discrepancy scores may be as critical as outcome variables as a mean increase in the competence score" (p. 96).

Self-monitoring

Self-monitoring, or having the child observe and record his or her own social behavior, is used as an assessment technique even though it has a number of limitations. Self-recording has been identified as reactive, since the child knows the target behavior and the purpose of the recording, and the self-recording can thus result in behavior change. Shapiro (1984) points out that it is difficult to differentiate between the use of self-monitoring as an assessment strategy and self-monitoring as intervention. In a number of studies, self-recording alone has been successfully employed as an intervention to bring about positive behavior. Reliability is another major problem with self-monitoring. Shapiro and Cole (1993) suggest that the accuracy of reports can be influenced by the use of rewarding contingencies, focus on behaviors that are pleasant rather than aversive to the child, and the use of subtle, efficient recording devices. Self-recording can be monitored by others if the behavior is observable, and this improves its accuracy. If the child is recording private events, such as thoughts and feelings, however, reliability becomes more problematic.

Self-reporting is a skill that needs to be taught before it becomes a useful means of assessment. It is necessary to make sure first that the child can identify the presence of the target behavior when emitted, then provide the child with a means of recording the behavior. Any of the observation techniques discussed earlier could be used by the child with some instruction—for example, using a counter, a tally sheet, or a timepiece—to record frequency or duration of a specific behavior. A child trying to develop the skill of ignoring another child who teases him or her could record each attempt at ignoring on a wrist counter.

For children, it is particularly important for the behavior to be simple and easily defined and for only one behavior to be selected at a time. It may be easier, for example, for children to monitor behavior that is nonverbal (e.g., in-seat or task-completion) rather than verbal (e.g., talk-outs or contributing to discussion) (Gardner & Cole, 1988). As discussed earlier, self-reports have questionable reliability as assessment tools and are most useful when combined with data from other sources. The skill of self-monitoring, however, may be useful in enhancing social functioning as well as in assisting in generalization of social skills over time. Self-monitoring is discussed further in Chapters 3 and 4.

Assessment of Affective and Cognitive Behaviors

The point was made earlier that thoughts and feelings are relevant to social skills instruction because how children feel and think in social situations affects their social behavior, and because socialization involves learning culturally defined, acceptable public ways to express these inner events. Because cognitions and affect are difficult to measure directly, assessment usually begins with verbal self-reports even though these are difficult to validate independently.

Self-reporting of inner events is a complex set of behaviors involving the ability to recognize and label one's own thoughts and feelings and report them verbally to someone else. Programs to teach such behavior should be part of a social skills training program and may have to be carried out before self-reporting can be useful as an assessment technique. Roberts and Nelson (1984) point out the need to assess inner events in the context of developmental levels since children improve on self-reporting skills as they grow older.

Assessing Affect

Assessing affect has an advantage over assessing cognitions per se—there are physiological manifestations of feelings that can be measured more directly. Physiological arousal accompanies negative emotions such as fear, anxiety, apprehension, and anger; these bodily changes can often be observed. Technological means, such as measures of skin response and cardiac activity, have been used in research studies with adults to measure physiological aspects of fear and anxiety. Practical considerations, however, make it unlikely that these will become popular assessment procedures with children in schools or clinical settings.

Self-reports of Affective Behavior

A number of scales and checklists have been developed for self-reporting affective states such as fear, anxiety, and depression. In recent years, interest in these assessments has increased, partly due to the relationship between certain emotional states, such as depression, thoughts of suicide, academic performance, and later mental health problems (Witt et al., 1988).

The *Revised Children's Manifest Anxiety Scale* (R-CMAS) (Reynolds & Richmond, 1985), is a scale developed for the self-reporting of anxiety by children. It is based on two formerly revised instruments: the *Children's Manifest Anxiety Scale* (Casteneda, McCandless, & Palermo, 1956) and the *What I Think and Feel* (Reynolds & Richmond, 1978). Children 6 to 19 years of age respond by circling yes or no to 37 statements designed to measure their anxiety. The revised form was altered to increase its readability for a wider audience and is considered to be a reliable and valid measure of anxiety (Witt et al., 1988). The *General Anxiety Scale for Children* and the related *Test Anxiety Scale for Children,* both by Sarason, Davidson, Lighthall, Waite, and Ruebush (1960), are similar in format. Another approach to anxiety assessment is the *State-Trait Anxiety Inventory for Children* (STAIC) and *State-Trait*

Anxiety Inventory (STAI) for adolescents and adults (Spielberger, 1973). These scales involve two separate parts, one to measure "state" anxiety—feelings at a particular moment in time—and the other to measure "trait" anxiety—the frequency of anxious behaviors.

One common approach to assess anxiety and fear in adults is the *Fear Survey Schedule,* in which the individual indicates on a scale the degree of his or her fear of listed objects or events. Variations of the fear survey technique have been developed for use with different groups (Hersen, 1973). These scales have differing degrees of reliability and ability to predict adult behavior in potentially fear-inducing situations. A *Fear Survey Schedule for Children* (FSS-FC), developed by Scherer and Nakamura (1968) and later revised by Ollendick (1983), calls for children to rate their degree of fear related to such items as "Being in a crowd . . . The sight of blood . . . Strange-looking people."

The revised instrument, the *Fear Survey Schedule for Children—Revised* (FSSC-R), kept the original items but modified the response format so that children now report their degree of fear on a three-point scale (none, some, a lot). The previous five-point scale was thought to be confusing to young children and those with disabilities. The psychometric properties also were addressed in the revised form to produce reliability, validity, and norming data. These changes are considered improvements over the original form; however, the rather small sample used makes the norms for the FSSC-R questionable (Witt et al., 1988).

To assess depression in children ages 7 to 17, the *Children's Depression Inventory* (CDI) (Kovacs, 1992) has been developed as a modification of the *Beck Depression Inventory.* The CDI is an extensively researched instrument (Reynolds, 1993; Witt et al., 1988). The child rates 27 statements reflecting depressive symptoms on a three-point scale as to degree of applicability. The items are intended to reflect the child's feelings during the past week, related to symptoms of depression, such as insomnia, withdrawal, sadness, shame, and pessimism: "I have trouble sleeping every night. . . . Things bother me all the time. . . . I feel like crying every day." Witt et al. (1988) suggest the CDI may be the best measure to assess depression in children.

Another self-report instrument is the *Children's Depression Scale* (Lang & Tisher, 1978; Tisher & Lang, 1983), which contains similar depressive statements and includes positive statements as well. It yields both a depressive score and a positive score, along with scores on a range of subscales representing different areas of depression. Reynolds (1993) presents two other measures to assess depression—for children, the *Reynolds Child Depression Scale* (RCDS) (Reynolds, 1989) and, for adolescents, the *Reynolds Adolescent Depression Scale* (RADS) (1986). Both employ a four-point Likert-type format for self-reporting depressive symptomatology.

Affective Assessment by Adults and Peers

Although most measures of affect are self-reports, the behavioral manifestations of feelings lend themselves to other types of assessment as well. For example, a measure of anxiety, the *Test Anxiety Scale for Children* (Sarason et al., 1960), has a teacher rating scale as well as the self-report scale. The *Louisville Fear Survey for Children* (Miller, Barrett, Hampe, & Noble, 1974) was developed to be used by either a parent, another adult, or the child to rate the intensity of fear generated by various stimuli. The *Children's Depression Scale* has an accompanying adult form intended for use by parents or teachers, which makes it possible to compare the child's and adults' responses.

An additional approach to depression assessment is the *Peer Nomination Inventory for Depression* (Lefkowitz & Tesiny, 1980). According to its authors, this sociometric measure correlates well with teacher- and self-ratings. It is read aloud to a group of children, who are given a class roster and instructed to draw a line through names of classmates who can be described by questions such as, "Who often plays alone? . . . Who thinks they are bad? . . . Who doesn't try again when they lose?" Thirteen of the items describe depression; six of the items describe happiness and popularity.

Observation of facial expression and various "body language" manifestations of inner states is a frequent means of gathering data on affect in children. Many behaviors are interpreted to be outward signs of inner reactions. Some of these include:

- The condition of body stiffness or relaxation
- Tensing of neck and shoulder muscles
- Flushing
- Trembling hands or hand wringing
- Chewing fingers
- Nail biting
- Thumb sucking
- Stroking, twisting, or pulling out hair
- Biting or licking lips
- Frequent throat clearing
- Frequent trips to the bathroom or many drinks of water
- Heavy breathing
- Signs of anguish such as tears, wailing, moaning, or sobbing
- Signs of happiness such as smiling and laughing
- Speech indicators such as stammering, inability to speak out loud, hesitation in speech, voice tremors, or talking to oneself
- Reports of physical symptoms such as headaches, stomachaches, or vomiting

A very stressed child may regress and wet or soil his or her pants. The hyperactive child may attempt to reduce feelings of anxiety through continual verbal and bodily activity. Conversely, a child in a state of panic can be immobilized and mute. And, of course, the child's face can present a variety of clues from which inferences about thoughts and feelings can be made.

In reviewing studies predicting altruism and empathy from facial expressions and gestures, Goldstein and Michaels (1985) conclude that use of facial expressions is a promising approach: "Trained raters can make reliable discriminations of emotions from children's . . . facial behavior." Glennon and Weisz (1978) devised a 30-item scale, the *Preschool Observation Scale of Anxiety* (POSA), using observable behavioral indicators such as those just outlined to assess anxiety in preschool children. In a study in which children were observed in a testing situation, Glennon and Weisz report high correlation of POSA scores with three independent measures of anxiety completed by parents and teachers. They also report sensitivity to situational variation in stressors—anxiety scores were significantly lower in a second session designed to be less anxiety-producing. Making use of overt manifestations such as those described above to assess inner events can serve as a basis for hy- potheses to be tested in other ways.

Assessing Cognitive Behaviors

In the process of assessing cognitive factors relating to social skills, the goals are to determine (1) whether the child has cognitive understanding of the behaviors being taught, (2) whether he or she is engaging in faulty cognitions that interfere with desirable social behavior, or (3) whether he or she is lacking in problem-solving strategies that would facilitate desired social interactions and overall competence. Although a child may show behaviors under assessment conditions that she or he may not translate into behavior in the natural environment, this information in itself is valuable. As indicated previously, teaching approaches should differ considerably for the child who knows what a desirable social response would be but for various reasons fails to perform, as opposed to the child who behaves inappropriatly because he or she doesn't know what to do.

Generally, measures to assess the child's knowledge of desirable social re- sponses use the analogue format described earlier. The further the assessment conditions are removed from real-life events, the more likely one is assessing cognitions rather than actual responses the child would make within the described situation.

Paper-and-pencil analogues (more than other analogue categories) may be important primarily for gathering information about how much the child is able to specify rather than whether he or she performs the correct social response (Nay, 1977). This assessment approach presents a social situation, typically in writing, to which the child must give the appropriate social response in open-ended or multiple-choice form. Wood and Michelson's *Children's Assertive Behavior Scale* (1978) (presented earlier under self-report scales) is one example of the multiple-choice format. In the *Purdue Elementary Problem-Solving Inventory* (PEPSI) (Feldhusen, Houtz, & Ringenbach, 1972), children select among alternative solutions to problem situations presented in cartoon slides. Open-ended instruments require the child to tell what should be done or how he or she would act under the conditions presented. Examples of this open-ended method include the Spivack and Shure (1974) measures described later in this section. Social knowledge measures, which ask students what they would do in hypothetical social situations presented in pictures or videotapes (LaGreca & San- togrossi, 1980), are related to analogue approaches.

Another aspect of cognitive process assessment is that of determining faulty cognitions such as maladaptive self-statements, assumptions, and beliefs; perfectionistic thinking; and inaccurate attributions, where the child fails to accept responsibility for her or his behavior and attributes her or his actions to external factors (Meichenbaum, 1977). Based on his information-processing model, Dodge (1993) proposes that socially unskilled children often interpret social situations from a biased, dysfunctional perspective. Aggressive children, for example, are likely to draw on previous negative experiences and attribute hostile intentions to the behaviors of others. That is, an aggressive child excluded from a peer social group will, more often than an average child, label the exclusion as deliberate rather than simply an oversight.

Meichenbaum (1976) identifies several techniques to assess a child's cognitions. One of these involves videotaping the child during assessment on some behavioral measure such as role-play test. The tape is replayed, and the child is asked to share the thoughts he or she experienced during the enactment. The interviewer probes cognitions, particularly in scenes where social skill deficits are observed. Attention is then given to other similar situations to determine to what extent this particular pattern indicates the child's general thought processes.

In a 1993 assessment of deviant information processing, Dodge describes a procedure where children are shown videotapes of social situations involving other people and are asked to provide a running commentary of the action. Dodge reports preliminary studies showing that children who tend to describe the behaviors of others from an aggressive schema also have high rates of aggressive acts.

There are few well-developed and tested means for assessing children's attributions and self-efficacy thinking styles. Bugental, Whalen, and Henker (1977) looked at attributions related to internal/external locus of control by means of structured interviews in which children were asked to explain their school success and failure. Kendall and Braswell (1985) suggest that self-efficacy could be assessed by asking children, prior to a testing session on a problem-solving task, how confident they are that they will complete the task, then comparing the responses to actual task performance.

A third aspect of cognitive assessment is to determine the child's ability to engage in constructive problem solving. Spivack and Shure (1974) developed several instruments for measuring the cognitive problem-solving skills of young children. The *Preschool Interpersonal Problem Solving Test* (PIPS) assesses the child's ability to think of alternative solutions, the *What Happens Next Game* (WHNG) measures consequential thinking, and the *Means-Ends Problem Solving Test* (MEPS) investigates the child's ability to conceptualize means toward a goal.

The PIPS test has two parts, one presenting conflict situations with a peer, the second with the child's mother. In the first part, the child is given seven basic stories involving one child playing with a toy a second child wants. The child being assessed tells what the child in the story who wants the toy might do to resolve the situation (Spivack & Shure, 1974):

Here's (child A) and here's (child B). A is playing with this truck and he has been playing with it for a long time. Now B wants a chance to play with the truck but A keeps on playing with it. Who's been playing with the truck for a long time? You can point. That's right, A. (Point to A.) Who wants to play with it? That's right, B. What can B do so he can have a chance to play with the truck?" (If there is no new relevant response: "What can B say . . . ?) (p. 194).

Next, the child is given five stories where the child in the story does something to anger his mother—for example, "A broke his mother's favorite flowerpot and he is afraid his mother will be mad at him. What can A do or say so his mother will not be mad?" (p. 195). Again, the child gives solutions to these problems. The interviewer encourages the child to give as many different solutions as possible. Each alternative is counted as one point, yielding a total PIPS score for both parts of the test.

A modification of the Spivack and Shure PIPS, the *Social Problem Solving Test* (Rubin, Daniels-Beirness, & Bream, 1984; Rubin & Krasnor, 1986), provides for both qualitative and quantitative assessment of problem-solving skills. It asks children to describe what story characters would do to resolve problem situations. The experimenter tallies the number of relevant alternatives presented and probes for further responses. Answers are also coded according to type of problem-solving strategy presented—"prosocial, agonistic, authority-intervention, bribe, trade or finagle, or manipulative affect."

The second test, the *What Happens Next Game,* is designed to determine whether the child is able to anticipate consequences to certain behaviors. It is described as a game because the examiner begins telling a story, and the child completes it. The child is given five stories of peer conflicts with toys and five stories involving the child doing something without adult permission. Examples of both types include (Spivack & Shure, 1974):

1. "A had a truck and he was playing with it. B wanted to play with that truck. So B grabbed—you know, snatched—that truck. Tell me what happens next . . ."
2. "Here's A and this is Mrs. Smith. A saw Mrs. Smith's little poodle dog on her porch and took it for a walk. But A did not ask Mrs. Smith if he could take it. What happened next in the story?" (p. 198).

The focus is on whether the child is actually able to specify realistic consequences to various events and, if so, the number of different consequences identified.

The *Means-Ends Problem Solving Test* involves the child in attempting to fill in the middle part of a problem situation for which the beginning and ending are presented. For example (Spivack et al., 1976):

Al (Joyce) has moved into the neighborhood. He (she) didn't know anyone and felt very lonely.

The story ends with Al (Joyce) having many good friends and feeling at home in the neighborhood. What happens in between Al's (Joyce's) moving in and feeling lonely, and when he (she) ends up with many good friends? (p. 65).

The child's response is scored in terms of "means" (inputs that lead to problem solution), "obstacles" (additional problems the child adds to the script that interfere with a solution), and "time" (using time as a means to solve the problem). The children's MEPS is designed for elementary school children and is given orally to maintain attention and minimize problems caused by the inability to read.

Pellegrini (1985) provides support for the relationship between social problem solving and social skill. The study obtained positive correlations between performance on the MEPS and social competence measures of peer and teacher assessments for children in grades 4 through 7. Meisel (1989), however, fails to attain similar results with primary grade children using an alternative problem-solving test—*The Open Middle Interview* (Polifka, Weissberg, Gesten, Flores De Apodaca, & Piccoli, 1981). Meisel speculates that the open-ended and more detailed responses elicited by the MEPS tap ". . . more of the cognitive processes that mediate social responding . . ." (p. 44).

Roberts and Nelson (1984) suggest the need to teach and reinforce correspondence between verbal reports of inner events and observable motor behavior. If assessment is to be used to evaluate the effects of treatment on the cognitive domain, they stress the need for behavioral measures such as observation along with rating scales and checklists. Other researchers point to limitations of currently available cognitive assessment measures (Krasnor & Rubin, 1981; Meisels, 1989; Rubin & Krasnor, 1986)—for example, the possible lack of personal relevance for the child; the higher-level thought processes possibly occurring during assessment, compared to "knee-jerk" reactions under real-life conditions; the relatively narrow content areas; the predominately verbal nature of the responses; weak psychometric strength; and a lack of direct relationship to actual strategies children use. Krasnor and Rubin (1981) recommend that episodes of problem-solving behavior in real or simulated situations be content-analyzed along several dimensions to determine the child's actual effectiveness in problem solving and draw inferences about cognitive processes.

A more recent development that somewhat addresses these concerns is presented by Irvin, Walker, Noell, Singer, Irvine, Marquez, and Britz (1992) in their use of interactive videodisc assessments. Pointing out the need to capture as much reality in social assessments as possible, the authors assert that this technology permits the assessor to adequately convey the details of real-life conditions such as critical nonverbal/paralanguage cues (i.e., voice tone, warmth, and humor), while simultaneously providing consistency and necessary control of stimulus conditions. Additional features include: (1) response ease—young children or children with disabilities are able to point to the stimulus item on the screen and not be penalized in the assessment process for language deficits, and (2) a branching format—the examiner may make hypotheses about the child's social cognitions and solicit responses to test the hypotheses.

The basic assessment format consists of a video presentation of some social situation with a voice-over narration. The child is directed by the narrator to respond by touching the screen. The authors describe the application of this format in "peer group entry" assessment. Situations of children's group play are depicted, and the child being assessed is directed to touch the screen when the "best times to join in" occur. Appropriate times would be during natural breaks in the game; an inappropriate time would be during an argument over rules.

This step is followed by an assessment of possible game entry strategies. The child is given five options, only one of which is considered socially skilled (i.e., asking to join at the first natural break). The inappropriate responses are externalizing and internalizing behaviors such as aggressing/bragging or hovering/waiting too late to join. The response options are presented in a standard format, and children may respond more than once. Afterward, to assess understanding of the consequences of these various responses, the child is asked if the children would let him or her join in if he or she performed the various behaviors. The child is also questioned about the type of emotional reactions the strategies might cause in the other children.

The authors used research literature and children's focus groups as content and criterion measures to develop interactive videodisc assessments for the skill areas of compliance, joining ongoing group activities, and responding to peer provocation. Empirical validation of the psychometric properties of this assessment method, particularly as it predicts social competence in children, is not yet available.

Assessing Social Perception

Social perception is a complex process involving cognitive and affective subskills such as the ability to identify and label the feelings of others, role-taking (the ability to take the cognitive or affective perspective of another), and social inference (the ability to draw causal inferences from social situations). Well-established means to assess different aspects of social perception are not abundant. Those that exist relate primarily to cognitive and affective *role-taking ability*—the ability to think about what another is thinking and infer how another is feeling, along with *empathy*—the ability to share the feelings of others.

The ability to take the role of another is frequently assessed through the presentation of scenarios, such as those originally developed by Flavell, Botkin, Fry, Wright, and Jarvis (1968) and modified by Chandler (1973), in which the child knows more about a story than someone else and is asked to tell the story from the point of view of the less-informed person. In Chandler's process to assess affective and cognitive role-taking, a story is portrayed in a cartoon sequence with a new character introduced midway in the sequence—a "bystander" who is unaware of preceding events. The child is asked to explain events from the perspective of the new unenlightened character, leaving out the facts that he or she knows.

For example, a series entitled "Fear" shows a boy breaking a window and running home, the neighbor with the broken window knocking on the boy's door, and the father observing the boy crouching in fear as he hears the knock on the door. The unenlightened character in this sequence is the father. The student is asked to describe what the father is thinking as he observes his son's response to the knock on the door. The respondent is able to take the role of this character accurately if he or she ascribes to the father a recognition of the emotional reaction in his son but does not attribute it to the antecedent events described in the pictures. If the respondent gave a response such as, "The father probably thinks he broke a window," she or he would be reacting according to her or his own perspective rather than that of the uninformed character. Comparable role-taking assessments have been developed by Feffer and Gourevitch (1960), using background scenes and cut-out figures from the MAPS test (Shneidman, 1952), and by Selman and Byrne (1974) with filmstrips.

Empathy and affective role-taking are often confused. In reviewing definitions of empathy, Goldstein and Michaels (1985) conclude that empathy combines several meanings:

1. Taking the role of another, seeing the world as the other sees it, and experiencing the feelings of the other;
2. Being able to read nonverbal communication and interpret the feelings expressed; and
3. Conveying a feeling of caring or sincere effort to understand and help.

Feshbach (1982) describes a similar three-component model of empathy.

A study by Feshbach and Roe (1968) forms the basis for much of the research on empathy assessment. The assessment technique, the *Feshback & Roe Affective Situation Test for Empathy* (FASTE), involves a series of slides showing real children in one of four affective situations: happiness, sadness, fear, and anger. Themes used for each of the four affects were:

1. *Happiness*—birthday party, winning a television contest;
2. *Sadness*—a lost dog;
3. *Fear*—child lost, frightening dog; and
4. *Anger*—the toy snatcher, false accusation.

A narrative accompanied each. There were identical sequences with both male and female figures. After viewing a slide sequence, children were asked to state how they felt, with the answers used as an index of empathy. *Empathic responsiveness* was defined as the degree to which the child's reported emotional state matched that of the story character. By asking "How does the child on the screen feel?" the FASTE was also used in this study as a measure of social comprehension. Feshbach and Roe found that degree of empathy could not be accounted for solely by degree of comprehension of others' feelings.

Eisenberg-Berg and Lennon (1980) point out some disadvantages of this approach: The stories might be too brief to evoke vicarious emotional responses; emotions like fear and anger may be too complex for very young children to understand; asking for verbal responses might be inappropriate for very young children; and having unfamiliar persons as experimenters might create anxiety in subjects. Their variation used four longer stories, accompanied by three illustrations each, which assessed only sadness and happiness. Empathy was assessed both verbally and nonverbally: after children were asked to describe how they felt, they were asked to point to pictures with children's facial expressions registering happiness, sadness, anger, and no emotion, and instructed to "Point to the picture that tells me how this story made you feel."

Feshbach's (1982) measures attempt to assess different dimensions of empathy. These include the *Affective Matching Measure,* the *Emotional Responsiveness Measure,* and the *Feshback and Powell Audiovisual Test for Empathy.* In the *Affective Matching Measure,* children are presented with black-and-white drawings of children in situations that evoke different emotions. Affective facial cues of the main character have been deleted. Subjects are asked to choose from a sheet displaying five faces (with expressions of happiness, pride, anger, sadness, and fear) the one that matches how the character in the picture feels. In the *Emotional Responsiveness Measure,* children are presented with five $1\frac{1}{2}$-minute taped vignettes, designed to evoke pride, happiness, anger, fear, or sadness. After each tape, the child is asked to rate the degree to which he or she feels the indicated emotion on a nine-point scale.

The *Audiovisual Test for Empathy* involves a series of two-minute videotapes of stories with children experiencing the same five emotions. A child can be tested individually, shown the videotapes, and asked how much he or she feels the emotions—a little, some, or very much. In groups, children are given response sheets listing eight emotions and are asked to circle the emotion that describes that feeling and then indicate on a ten-point scale how much they feel the emotion. An empathy score is based on the degree to which emotional responses correspond to the affect conveyed by the child in the videotape. All the above measures were developed with third- and fourth-grade children and based on self-reports of situations in their lives that evoked various emotions. All the measures had versions for both boys and girls and attempted to control for both sex and racial bias.

Another approach to assessment of empathy is the *Index of Empathy for Children and Adolescents* (Bryant, 1982), a paper-and-pencil adaptation of an adult emotional empathy measure (Mehrabian & Epstein, 1972). Children are asked to respond yes or no to 22 statements such as, "It makes me sad to see a girl who can't find anyone to play with . . . I get upset when I see a girl being hurt . . . Even when I don't know why someone is laughing, I laugh too." Bryant demonstrates satisfactory reliability and preliminary construct validity and suggests that this is a convenient and practical measure for studying the expression of empathy in children. She cautions, however, that this is not a direct measure of empathy, but rather requires the child to think about and report on his or her own empathic responses.

A measurement developed by Barrett and Yarrow (1977) assesses another aspect of social perception, *social inference.* The child is shown five videotapes of social interaction that involve a child or young adult. In each sequence, an affective experience is followed by an abrupt change in behavior. For example, one sequence shows a child working successfully on a manual task. His parents are heard arguing angrily, and the child is then shown having difficulty with the task. Subjects are tested for retention of events, asked to explain why the character behaved as he did, and scored on the basis of their ability to explain the final events by using information from the earlier events. Another similar instrument, the *Test of Social*

Inference (Edmonson, DeJung, Leland, & Leach, 1974), developed primarily for an adult population with disabilities, also can be used with nondisabled children ages 7 to 13.

Few of the instruments designed to measure aspects of social perception have been subjected to extensive validity and reliability studies. Enright and Lapsley (1980), in a review of role-taking instruments, conclude that only the cognitive role-taking measures of Chandler and Selman possess sufficient validity to be used in educational programs, and no affective role-taking measures to date meet that criterion. Morrison and Bellack (1981) stress the need for more instruments to assess social perception skills, in particular ones that account for the variability of social perception across situations and that assess some of the several possible reasons for social perception deficits (e.g., failure to listen or attention to irrelevant cues, failure to look, failure to integrate what is seen and heard, and lack of understanding of what is seen and heard). The videodisc assessments by Irvin et al. (1992) might be useful in the assessment of social perception as well. In that assessment process, children are required to interpret social situations, make inferences about behavior, and read affect—for example, "Touch the picture when someone gets angry."

Summary

Assessment prior to teaching social skills helps determine which social behaviors are missing from the child's repertoire and need to be taught, and which behaviors need only to be increased through altering motivational conditions. Assessment also assists in determining the effectiveness of teaching and clinical interventions.

Adults, such as parents and teachers, are the major sources of information about children's social behavior. Rating scales and inventories are frequently used to gather data for screening purposes from adults, because such measures are easy to administer and lend themselves to comparisons among raters. Such instruments include standardized behavior checklists and rating scales, inventories associated with social skills curricula, and informal scales and inventories designed for specific settings or situations.

Observation and recording of the child's performance of social skills in the natural environment provide the most specific and relevant information. Observational data can be gathered in a variety of spontaneous situations, or events can be structured to elicit the behavior being assessed. An interview can serve as one such contrived situation, lending itself to the observation of several interpersonal behaviors as well as yielding information about the child's perceptions of his or her situation. Other data can be gathered in the natural environment through permanent products, especially by using video- and audiotapes.

Simulations of events in the environment through role-playing provide another source of observational data, particularly for behaviors that would be difficult to observe in the child's everyday situations. Assessment through role-playing can be carried out using spontaneous enactments of problem situations or through more standardized means, using prepared scripts that prompt responses. Simulations can be delivered by live players or through audiotaped, videotaped, or interactive videotaped presentations. Simulated approaches to social skills evaluation, however, have limited validity in predicting social behavior in actual situations.

A number of sociometric procedures have been devised to gather data from peers about children's degree of acceptance and social behavior deficits as seen by peers. The most commonly used procedures are nominations, in which children nominate peers according to degree of acceptance or nonacceptance; paired comparisons, in which children make choices between pairs of peers; and roster-ratings, in which children are presented with rosters of the entire group to rate. Like other social skills assessment procedures, sociometric techniques cannot be relied on as a sole measure of social behavior.

Another source of information about social behavior is the child himself or herself. Approaches include self-report measures, in the form of paper-and-pencil checklists or rating scales assessing social behavior; and self-esteem and self-monitoring procedures, in which the child observes and records her or his own social behavior. Self-monitoring is limited as an assessment technique by reactive effects and by the amount of skill needed to observe, measure, and report on one's behavior. These approaches are most useful when combined with data from other sources.

Along with behaviors the child emits in various social situations, it is also important to identify emotions and cognitions that may interfere with or facilitate social competence. The child's ability to perceive and interpret various aspects of social situations is another significant aspect of social skill. Because of outward manifestations of emotion, affective responses can be observed and thus measured more easily than cognitions or social perception. There are a number of scales and checklists for both assessment by others and self-reporting of emotional states such as fear, anxiety, and depression. Cognition-related assessment includes paper-and-pencil and open-ended measures of social skills knowledge and problem-solving techniques. Aspects of social perception, such as role-taking ability, empathy, and social inference, are assessed primarily through the presentation of scenarios, followed by questions to determine the extent of the child's understanding or involvement.

Although there is an increasing number of approaches to the assessment of social skills, each one has limitations. When doing assessments, it is important not to rely on a single method but rather make use of multiple methods and more than one informant in more than one setting if possible, and to measure not only observable social skills but cognitive and affective dimensions as well.

Chapter 3

The Teaching Process

Learning social skills takes place primarily through observation, imitation, and feedback from the environment; children learn social skills in much the same way they learn academic concepts. The steps in instruction can be seen as first, presenting a stimulus; second, eliciting a response to the stimulus; and third, providing feedback about the correctness of the response, followed by further refinement of responses and practice in correct responses.

In social skills instruction, the first step can be a demonstration, a verbal description, a picture or diagram, or other stimuli describing the behavior. The desired response from the learner is an attempt to reproduce the stimuli through imitation. The feedback provided for the response can take a variety of forms, but essentially needs to convey information about whether and how the response should be repeated or changed. The learner then needs opportunities for further imitation, feedback, and practice.

This chapter deals with the instructional process and outlines the salient features of social skills teaching, many of which have been described in research literature with empirically demonstrated positive results. Procedures for teaching observable social behaviors almost always involve some aspect of social modeling or learning by imitation. Social modeling also is important for teaching adaptive ways of thinking and feeling in social situations, particularly where the internal events can be reflected in some overt behavior. Chapter 5 discusses other elements necessary for effective social skills instruction.

Social Learning Modeling and Role-Playing

Social learning theory provides the framework for the procedures most commonly employed in social skills training. The first of these, *social modeling*, is the process of producing a model of social behavior that enables another to learn by observation and imitation. An individual observes another person's behavior and then imitates that behavior, behaving similarly under similar circumstances. Social modeling is the method whereby most social behaviors are learned, especially during the developing years when children learn to imitate the behaviors of significant others in their lives such as parents, teachers, and peers. For example, young children playing with dolls are observed to care for and speak to their dolls in a manner similar to the way their parents treat them or a sibling. In later years, these same children may note aspects of their parenting behavior that reflect those of their parents, even though in many cases there is a conscious desire not to emulate their parents' child-rearing practices.

On a broader scale, the presentation of models through the mass media (e.g., television and films) has so extensively affected our lifestyles that it influences the products we consume and the entertainment we pursue. Whether through the mass media or direct observation, there is evidence that social models also influence the degree to which we engage in aggressive, passive, or assertive behaviors (Bandura, 1973).

The power of social modeling in modifying behaviors and in developing new ones has been thoroughly documented under laboratory conditions. Investigators in pioneering studies have used these procedures to help children acquire such behaviors as increased social interaction for isolated children (O'Connor, 1973), an increased tendency to give to charity and to help others (Rosenhan & White, 1967), and improved conversation skills involving asking for and giving information (Zimmerman & Pike, 1972). Social modeling also has been used extensively to develop assertive behaviors (McFall & Lillesand, 1971) and has shown to be effective in eliminating or reducing such maladaptive behaviors, such as aggression in children (Chittenden, 1942). In addition to facilitating the development of novel responses, it is likely that new behaviors acquired through modeling will be maintained following treatment, compared to those developed through operant techniques only (Combs & Slaby, 1977).

Over the past two decades a specific paradigm has emerged, commonly referred to as *social skills training* (SST), consisting of social modeling, behavior rehearsal, and (usually) reinforcement conditions. The research literature provides numerous examples of this model's positive effects on the development of social behaviors, including play behaviors, greetings, compliant behaviors, self-control, social interactions, and alternatives to aggression (Knapczyk, 1988; Zaragoza, Vaughn, & McIntosh, 1991). According to Bandura (1977b), observational learning depends on the learner's ability to attend to and understand the models' presentations, the learner's ability to code and retain these responses for future use, and the presence of incentive conditions that motivate the learner to perform the observed behavior. Therefore, skill training using this model typically consists of

1. *Instructions*—the identification of specific skill components, including a social skill rationale, and information on skill performance encompassing both verbal directions and social modeling;
2. *Skill performance*—learner reproductions of the target skill, trainer feedback, and trainer reinforcement; and

3. *Practice*—production of the behavior at future times and under a variety of conditions.

Giving Instructions

Providing a Rationale

At the initial stage of instruction, the learner needs to be given a purpose or rationale for the skill, particularly if the target behavior is not one typically valued by the learner or the significant others in his or her environment. One goal in establishing the social skill purpose is to provide the learner with information about the usefulness and inherent advantages of the social skill, rather than simply presenting it as something one is expected to do. Skill-deficient children often persist in their maladaptive responses because they fail to connect their behavior with aversive consequences or are unable to identify and perform alternative behaviors that would produce more desired results. The emotional rush and sense of satisfaction one typically experiences immediately following some act of aggression, for example, may be rewarding and serve to reinforce such aggressive behaviors in the future. This is particularly true if children fail to associate long-term destructive outcomes with their aggressive actions. Therefore, at this point, instruction needs to be geared toward helping the learner recognize the value of behavior based on potential consequences and benefits. Stories, scenarios, and films might be useful for this purpose.

To illustrate, in their curriculum for primary-aged children, Cartledge and Kleefeld (1991) used simple stories to set the stage for a series of social skill lessons. One story, "The Apple Pie Plan" (p. 143), told of Ross Raccoon who consistently responded with physical aggression when he was teased by Felicia Fox. Ross's fighting did not stop the teasing; as a matter of fact, it was shown that his continued fighting reinforced the teasing. Ross was helped by his classmate, Will Rabbit, to realize that one solution to this dilemma was to try to ignore his tormentor. This was accomplished through a combination of self-statements and an image of a piece of apple pie, reminding him of the dessert he would obtain for refraining from fighting. After a few days, the newly learned ignoring behavior was effective in eliminating Felicia Fox's teasing.

Following the story, discussion questions are used to help the children understand the specific productive and nonproductive actions of the principal character, as well as the affective and cognitive dimensions of social problem solving. That is, although Ross disliked the teasing and taunting, he found the consequences to his counter-aggression to be even more distressing. It was not fighting but ignoring, through the use of constructive self-statements, that helped to produce the desired effects.

For older, intermediate-aged students, Cartledge and Kleefeld (in press) employed folktales to provide a rationale for the skill. Folk tales have a special appeal for social skill instruction since they were created largely to pass along social and behavioral mores. For the skill of negotiating conflict, a Russian folk tale personifying two major rivers shows how gentle persuasion rather than brute force or aggression can resolve conflict to the benefit of both parties.

A final example is provided for adolescents. At this level real-life situations or stories are most useful. Michelson et al. (1983) present adolescent scenarios for resolving conflict. The same scene is presented twice (e.g., a classmate is unjustly angry at you), one with successful and one with unsuccessful conflict resolution. After discussing both scenes, students can be helped to analyze them to determine the most desirable outcome and the specific behaviors producing those results. In the preceding example, students would be shown that one is more likely to resolve conflict when he or she displays respect for the other person, makes a sincere attempt to discuss the problem, and avoids making the other person more angry by getting angry himself or herself. Another alternative for adolescents is biographical excerpts showing how recognized heroes use various social skills to address and overcome problem events in their lives. For example, learning to ignore the taunts he received at the beginning of his career not only helped Jackie Robinson experience great success in his personal career but also had a positive impact on the entire field of baseball.

Regardless of the form for the initial motivating activity, it will be most meaningful to students if they are assisted in relating the problem situations to their own lives. Follow-up discussions should be structured so that students reflect on comparable personal experiences where this skill would be useful. At the appropriate point during social skills instruction (e.g., during role-play exercises), students can be directed to act out the target skill as a possible resolution to their own problem situation.

Identifying Skill Components

Rather than simple responses, individual social skills are actually complex processes, frequently consisting of a chain of behaviors. The child needs to be able to identify the specific subskills that make up the comprehensive social skill. For example, what responses are required in greeting someone, in making a friend, or in being assertive? In the first case, the child would be expected at least to make eye contact, say "hello," give her or his name, and perhaps smile. Skills such as making friends and good sportsmanship are even more complex, but still lend themselves to analysis. The components of approach behavior for the purpose of friendship-making have been identified as greeting, asking the other child for some information (such as "Where are you from?"), inviting the other child to do something with him or her, and telling the child something like, "I like to play ball" (Gottman, Gonso, & Rasmussen, 1975).

One method for helping children determine skill components is to involve them in the process of behavior analysis. For example, for the skill of making friends, a story or role-play could be presented that depicts children successfully making friends, followed by a discussion to identify the specific responses that helped the fictional characters make friends. As the behaviors are generated, they are listed in order of occurrence—for example:

1. Say, "Hi, how are you? My name is _____. What's yours?"
2. Ask something like, "Where are you from?" or "What are you doing?"
3. Invite him or her to do something, "I want to play checkers. Would you like to play with me?"

In this approach the trainer uses the children's own words as much as possible and takes the children's developmental levels and cultural differences into consideration. For example, older youths (particularly boys) might include a handshake in this sequence, the configuration of which might differ from one cultural group to another. It might also be necessary to establish whether each child understands the nature of each behavior listed and can reproduce it in a natural rather than mechanical fashion. One approach is to ask children to demonstrate their suggested responses; for example, "George, what else might you ask a new child? Would you show us how you would ask that?"

Cartledge and Kleefeld (1991, in press) treat these skill components as *steps* that evolve directly from the motivational vignettes or stories described in the preceding section. The steps for ignoring verbal aggression include:

> When someone bothers you, try to ignore.
> 1. Don't look at the person.
> 2. Don't talk to the person.
> 3. Think about other things (p. 144).

For negotiating conflict through gentle persuasion, children are encouraged to perform the following:

> When you are in an argument, try to use gentle persuasion by:
> 1. Listening to the other person's side of the argument
> 2. Then tell your side of the argument
> 3. Try to find a solution where you both agree
> 4. Be fair and friendly
> 5. If you can't agree, don't continue to argue
> 6. If necessary, find someone else to help you.

Engage students in discussions to generate valid responses according to specific social situations they encounter.

Instructions also need to be tailored to the child's intellectual, chronological, and social skills development level. Very young or low-functioning children, for example, may have difficulty identifying, analyzing, or providing a rationale for the desired social skill. Similarly, young children may need assistance in determining what the specific responses are and how they should be made. Certain overt actions, such as sharing and joining a group, may have to be prompted physically as well. Children with limited attention spans and behavioral controls probably would benefit most from brief, direct introductions.

Presenting a Model

At this stage of the instructional process, present the learner with examples through modeling of how the composite behavior is performed. Goldstein, Sprafkin, and Gershaw (1976) provide guidelines for "modeling display," suggesting that the behaviors be presented:

   a. In a clear and detailed manner,
   b. In the order from least to most difficult behaviors,
   c. With enough repetition to make overlearning likely,
   d. With as little irrelevant (not to be learned) detail as possible, and
   e. With several different models, rather than a single model (p. 6).

The most common and perhaps easiest presentation is through live models. Because the characteristics of the model can either facilitate or inhibit the tendency of the observer to copy the modeled behavior, the model needs to be perceived by the learner as someone who is important, successful, and someone with whom he or she can identify. The competence of the model is extremely important, especially during the initial display. Therefore, the instructor and an assistant or highly competent students would be elected to conduct the first enactment.

Ideally, the social skill to be learned and its skill components would be listed on the chalkboard or in some other visual means so they can be viewed by all of the students and role-playing participants. The trainer sets the scene for the social modeling, describing the problem behavior, the conditions under which it occurs, and the roles of the respective participants. For example, in a social skills situation involving responses to verbal aggression, there are several viable options available to the child. These include engaging in certain cognitions to maintain self-control, leaving the scene, reporting the situation to an adult authority figure, and so forth. The group is asked to choose one of these responses to learn first—for example, responding to verbal aggression through ignoring—and to identify the skill components. As previously noted, these might include looking away from the aggressor, refraining from speaking to the aggressor, and saying things to oneself to keep calm. The social situation for the modeling display might be described as follows:

> You are a new student at school. Your parents bought you some new clothes and shoes for your first day at your new school. Your shoes do not look like the shoes most of the other children are wearing. On the playground one of the students, Ron, begins teasing you about your "funny-looking" shoes.

The trainer takes the role of the new student and assigns the role of Ron to an adult assistant. Student observers are directed to assess whether or not the trainer performs the skill according to the listed skill components. To increase attention, the instructor may assign individual students to evaluate specific subskills or behaviors. The teacher and the assistant then enact the modeling display, with the teacher slightly exaggerating the first two components and verbalizing out loud to demonstrate the third step. Possible verbalizations include, "I know he is just trying to make me feel bad," "If I say something back to him, he'll just keep teasing me," or "I'll pretend I don't care what he says, and maybe he will quit." After two or three taunts, Ron quits teasing and goes off elsewhere to play. The teacher then verbalizes out loud some statement of self-satisfaction, such as, "I knew he would stop if I didn't say anything to him." or "I'm glad I didn't say anything to him." Based on studies showing the greater likelihood of models being imitated if the behavior is rewarded, it is recommended that the modeling display be structured so the targeted behaviors produce the desired effect (e.g., ignoring stops the teasing) (Goldstein, 1988).

Following each enactment, a discussion would ensue to determine factors such as what skill and related responses occurred (e.g., ignoring: looking away, refraining from responding, using self-statements), whether it was effective (e.g., did it stop the taunting?), how the actor(s) felt, and what other responses one might use in this situation. Discussions of this nature are critical because individuals with social learning problems are prone to overlook the most salient features of the model's behavior. Modeling participants should receive the first opportunity to evaluate their performance, followed by observers, and then the social skills trainer. The previously specified skill components could be used as the point to initiate students' evaluation of the degree and quality of performance.

Live modeling provides the opportunity to observe and perform alternative skills, especially considering the possibility that under real-life conditions a particular social behavior may prove ineffective in achieving the desired reaction. For example, depending on the social situation, reporting to an adult may result in more taunting, which would suggest that other responses should be considered. The learning experience may be enhanced by permitting children to reverse roles—for example, being the taunter and the one taunted. The obvious disadvantage of using live models is that the trainer cannot be certain the behavior will be displayed accurately, and it is more difficult to reproduce the scene for later viewing (Eisler & Frederickson, 1980).

Another variable to be considered in presenting models is the importance of negative examples. Ladd and Mize (1983) point out that negative models may be instructional in making the parameters of the desired behavior more explicit, thus limiting the possibility of overgeneralization. To illustrate, they give the following example:

> After witnessing a variety of approach behaviors, children may have inferred a strategy such as "to play, I have to go up to other children" but overgeneralized it to include aggressive as well as prosocial initiations (p. 141).

As a rule, negative models should be used only after the learners demonstrate an understanding of the specific responses that make up the appropriate behavior. Negative examples are useful in helping the learner make finer discriminations and differentiate clearly between desired and undesired responses. In teaching children to ignore, for instance, the model might refrain from looking at or saying anything to the verbal aggressor but verbalize self-statements such as, "I don't like her," "She is so bad," "I will get back at her later," "These are terrible things she is saying to me." Although the teasing is annoying, self-statements such as these could potentially arouse additional negative feelings that may eventually interfere with one's efforts to ignore. Children should be helped to differentiate between counterproductive and more constructive self-statements such as: "She's just trying to get me in trouble, so I'm not going to react to this," "I'll really get back at her by not saying anything," "I won't let her know she has hurt my feelings," and "I'll feel better about myself if I manage to stay out of trouble."

Live models have unique advantages. The social skills trainer may find it helpful, however, to use multiple models from various sources. Several additional ways of presenting models in social skills instruction are outlined, including the use of puppets, taped models, models through books, and peer models.

Puppets as Models

Although generally considered most appropriate for the younger child, puppets can serve as effective models for the older child or adolescent as well. The determining factor with puppets, as with other forms of models, is relevance, or the extent to which the learner can identify with the characters depicted. For example, one effective social skills instruction program with junior high school youngsters used puppets in the role of the school cheerleaders, athletes, and other individuals commonly found in a junior high school. In addition to being attractive and possibly increasing attention to the learning situation, puppets can be used to depict social situations of immediate concern in a way that is less threatening and, in some cases, less embarrassing than if live models were used. Puppets provide an element of objectivity so that the learner who is unwilling to deal directly with her or his own actions may be willing to view, discuss, and eventually role-play the same behaviors with puppets.

Puppets also may take the form of fictional characters such as Winnie-the-Pooh or television favorites such as Sesame Street characters. In addition to commercially available puppets, children may be assisted in making their own puppets. Personally made puppets can contribute to model identification and attractiveness. Handmade puppets may range from rather elaborate productions made of fabric, papier-maché, or clay, to very simple models made of socks, paper bags, boxes, tin cans, construction paper with drawn features, or figures cut out and pasted on tongue depressors.

Extensive use of puppetry can be seen in commercial programs such as *Developing Understanding of Self and Others Program* (DUSO) (Dinkmeyer, 1982) and *Taking Part: Introducing Social Skills to Children* (Cartledge & Kleefeld, 1991) published by American Guidance Service. In both programs puppets are used to present the problem, to model desired behaviors, and to role-play possible alternative responses. For example, in one lesson dealing with verbal aggression (Dinkmeyer, 1982), the initial activities with the two main puppet characters help children understand the importance of avoiding making unpleasant comments to others, while the role-playing with a puppet focuses on helping children identify appropriate ways of expressing positive and negative feelings.

As the child develops more skill and becomes more comfortable in dramatic activities, it is hoped that he or she will learn to engage in live role playing, discarding symbols and props such as puppets. Responses practiced under live role-playing conditions should be easier to transfer to everyday situations.

Taped Models

Models may also be presented through media such as films, television, radio, audio- and videotapes, magazines, and newspapers. Although references can be made to positive role models found in the mass media, these sources lend themselves less easily to formal social learning instructions because of the difficulty in controlling content and ensuring that the most desirable material will be viewed or read. Greater control can be exercised with specific video- and audiotapes designed for social skills instruction. The efficacy of film-mediated models in producing new social responses has been thoroughly documented (Bandura, 1969). The typical method of presentation is to show a model demonstrating a skill—for example, encountering and effectively resolving a conflict situation.

Goodwin and Mahoney (1975) describe one such modeling videotape that involves controlling aggression while being provoked. The tape shows the model coping with verbal aggression from peers by engaging in various self-statements such as, "I will not get angry" and "I will not fight." The self-statements were dubbed onto the tape to illustrate the model's thought processes. While viewing the tapes, the coping mechanisms used by the models (i.e., cognitive self-statements) were highlighted so that the observers were aware of the exact behaviors (in this case cognitions) that helped the model cope successfully with the situation.

Knapczyk (1988) successfully used videotaped models to reduce the aggressive behaviors of adolescent males with behavior disabilities. In this study, videotapes were made with competent students depicting the maladaptive behaviors typically displayed by the target students, along with alternative adaptive behaviors that might be used in place of the aggressive responses. The students were taught individually. The students viewed examples of their characteristic behaviors and the more desired alternatives, as enacted by their peer models. During instruction the teacher pointed out the possible consequences of both sets of behavior. The students rehearsed adaptive responses to daily encounters and received feedback on how closely responses matched expected standards.

Although audiotapes have not been used as extensively for social modeling, they are particularly useful for modeling skills in verbal communication and demonstrating affect. For example, audiotapes may be used to model the delivery of assertive statements with appropriate tonal quality and emotion. Taped modeling instructions allow for additional presentations so that, where necessary, the behavior may be reviewed repeatedly until learned.

Models Through Books

Along with tapes and films, books may serve as a source of symbolic modeling for children and adolescents. Stories, realistically written with believable and significant characters, can be used to teach a child how to respond to various social situations.

For example, Swimmy, in the book *Swimmy* by Leo Lionni (1963), may serve as a model for how to overcome loneliness by using creative problem solving to initiate a play activity with others. In discussion after reading the story, the teacher would help students use Swimmy as a model by pointing out the most critical actions—(1) thinking of various things the fish might do, (2) deciding on something in which everyone could participate, (3) making sure everyone knew what he or she was to do, and then (4) doing it. Stories and books may be particularly powerful social learning tools, for they present models with an additional dimension and in greater depth. As Eisley and Merrill (1984) point out:

> Stories have a somewhat unique advantage over even actual observation of individuals behaving virtuously or unvirtuously. Stories are able to report the inner thoughts, beliefs, desires, and motivations of the actors. Stories have another advantage for educators. Although many contexts naturally occur in which human virtues are manifest, pedagogically and ethically they are not as susceptible to classroom demonstration and manipulation as are concrete and defined concepts. Therefore, the most practical tools left to an instructor for teaching human virtue concepts are stories and certain kinds of dramatization (p. 4).

In one study (Cartledge, 1984), brief stories were used to introduce the social skill strategies taught to elementary school children. When reviewing appropriate responses for previously taught skills, the children were observed to make frequent references to story characters and situations. This indicated that the stories not only provided social skills rationales and models, but facilitated the subsequent recall and execution of the desired behaviors as well. A resource for identifying stories dealing with children's problems is the *Book Finder*, published by American Guidance Service. The reader is also referred to the materials list in the Appendix of this book.

Peers as Models

Peer models may be highly effective in social skills instruction and can assist in individualizing social skills lessons. Research shows that peer imitation can begin in infancy, that reinforcement contingencies may facilitate peer modeling, and that peers have been used successfully in social skills development among both very young and older children (Rubin, 1982). The facilitating effects of peers in social skills training can be seen in a study conducted by Bierman and Furman (1984), where children were taught conversational social skills. Children instructed under conditions with competent peers were found to experience greater peer acceptance and enhanced self-perceptions compared with subjects receiving individual instruction without peer involvement.

Children functioning on low levels, who fail to benefit from traditional social modeling or role-playing techniques, may profit from individual instruction where they are assisted by peers in copying and reproducing the desired social responses. Ascher and Phillips (1975) describe such a procedure, labeled *guided behavior rehearsal,* in which socially-competent peer guides used modeling and behavior rehearsal to help adult clients gain greater social competence. The guide accompanied the client to various social situations in order to model appropriate behaviors, conduct training sessions where specific responses were rehearsed, and provide feedback and reinforcement for approximations to desired responses. In one case, these procedures were successful in teaching a young man, who was neurologically impaired, exactly how to initiate and engage in conversation, with the result that his social skills improved and he was able to sustain relationships.

This second method of peer intervention has been labeled *prompt and reinforce* (McEvoy & Odom, 1987). Successful use of these procedures with children is described by Csapo (1972). A socially skilled child is assigned to a peer with social deficits to assist in areas such as playing with peers, resisting aggression, and engaging in conversations. The peer model is trained in modeling techniques for the target behaviors to be developed and in techniques for prompting and reinforcing the incompetent child.

A third, more common form of peer involvement is through *peer-initiation* strategies (McEvoy & Odom, 1987). Socially competent peers are taught to initiate social interactions with children with behavior problems. Several studies reviewed by McEvoy and Odom (1987) show that trained "interveners" can be effective in increasing the social behaviors of their less competent peers.

Although promising, researchers caution that peer-mediated interventions may produce more vertical than horizontal relationships (Gaylord-Ross & Haring, 1987). Under these conditions, it is more difficult to sustain peer initiations without teacher prompting and to effect natural contingencies of reinforcement. Another caution relates to the possible stigmatizing effect and peer abuse that might occur when certain students are singled out for peer-mediated strategies. Teachers might avoid such pitfalls through strategies such as establishing reciprocal conditions, where skilled and skill-deficient children are paired or grouped to prompt and reinforce each other. In this situation, problem children are not identified, but the pair or group is to work together toward some predetermined goal—for example, 15 minutes of conflict-free cooperative play during recess. Other possible precautions include establishing the target child as the behavior change agent and using interdependent group contingencies. These are described further in Chapter 4 in the discussion of peers as trainers. To the extent possible, children selected to serve as models should be respected by the target student, should be skilled in the social behaviors to be developed, and should be similar in background—age, gender, and socioeconomic status.

A major consideration in presenting the model is ensuring that the observer attends to and understands the most important aspects of the modeling situation. Such understanding may be encouraged by discussing the modeling display afterward, helping the learner identify what happened and the events that should be given the most attention. In videotaped presentations, trainers frequently use narration, in which the narrator points out the most salient features as the scene develops. Furman (1980) points out the importance of this procedure in facilitating recall and understanding and in minimizing the learner's tendency to overlook what appears irrelevant but is actually germane.

Skill Performance

Guided Rehearsal

Observed behavior will not necessarily be learned unless some mechanism is put into operation whereby the behavior display is remembered and subsequently reproduced. Trying out the modeled behaviors under supervised conditions will help the child produce them successfully in real-life situations. Behavior rehearsal (Rose, 1972) represents a form of structured role-playing that enables the child to act out and practice the new behaviors. Bandura (1977b) suggests that practice be conducted through covert responding, verbal responding, and motoric reproduction.

Covert Responding. Essentially, covert responding refers to cognitive images about a particular event. Imagery can be used effectively to develop both academic and social behavior. Behaviors coded through imagery can be retrieved later for appropriate responding. When engaged in social skills instruction, the use of imagery or covert responses can be prompted by helping the learner imagine or reproduce in his or her mind the behavior that previously was modeled. For example, the child has just been exposed to a modeling session designed to teach appropriate responses to verbal aggression. The child may then be directed to imagine the scene and possible responses—for example: "You are walking home from school and two pupils from your class are following you. They begin to tease you because you struck out during the baseball game, and your team lost. Imagine what you will do next."

Imagined resolutions to this scene may include:

1. An assertive statement such as "I know I struck out but everyone does sometimes," and "I won't feel bad because I did this time."
2. An empathic statement such as "I know you are upset because we lost the game and I am too, but I tried my best."
3. Physical avoidance, for instance, leaving the scene by taking another route home or going into a public building such as a store or library.

Obviously, the responses employed would depend partly on the circumstances and the particular students. For example, in one situation, verbally assertive statements may serve to extinguish undesirable behavior while in another situation they may provoke more aggression. Children may generate undesirable responses from a verbally aggressive statement like, "Maybe I'm not such a good baseball player, but neither are you." Through imagining consequences, children may be helped to recognize that although the immediate results may be rewarding, the long-term effects of counter-aggression may be aversive. Rather than identifying one solution for each conflict situation, the aim is to help children recognize that a variety of alternatives exist, and that the ones used should be those most likely to resolve rather than worsen the situation. The imagery procedure may include:

1. Child closes eyes while scene is depicted by practitioner.
2. Child is directed to imagine performing the designated response.
3. Child is directed to imagine reactions to her or his response.
4. Practitioner directs child through some scene with alternative responses.
5. Child and practitioner identify the most natural and appropriate responses the child would employ under similar circumstances in the future.

Covert responses could be used as a desensitizing device for the shy or inhibited child. After a period of imagining various personal enactments, the youngster may become more relaxed and willing to participate in overt rehearsals. Another advantage, identified by Eisler and Frederickson (1980), is that covert rehearsal can be employed more easily under a variety of circumstances. The youngster could be directed to imagine appropriate responses immediately before some anxiety-producing event. As the child approaches a verbally-aggressive peer, for example, he or she may covertly practice assertive, empathic, or avoidance behaviors as possible solutions to this problem situation. An obvious shortcoming of covert responding, particularly for young children, is that it cannot be observed and, thus, there are limited possibilities for corrective feedback and performance evaluation. For this reason, covert rehearsal probably should be employed in addition to, not instead of, overt behavior rehearsal.

Verbal Responding. An extension of the steps used for covert responding or imagery is verbal responding. Retention and appropriate performance can be enhanced by having the child talk through the desired responses, elaborating on the previous imagery sequence. At each step, the child describes the scene again in her or his own words, restating the alternatives and verbalizing possible consequences to proposed resolutions.

Motor Responding. Although the two previous response types may be used independently, they are viewed best as preparation for making motor responses. Here the child is required to act out (typically in a role-playing format) the responses that he or she has observed, visualized through imagery, and verbalized. Role-play essentially consists of four basic parts:

1. *Setting the stage*—practitioner describes the scene, selects participants, and assigns and describes participant roles.
2. *Enactment*—participants interact with each other, dramatizing respective roles.
3. *Discussion/evaluation*—performances are evaluated by participants and observers, and alternative responses identified.
4. *Reenactment*—scene is played again, incorporating suggestions from step 3; different participants may be identified.

As previously discussed, the practitioner may choose live enactments or symbolic representations such as puppets.

In addition to providing practice of desired behaviors, responding through role-playing has other advantages. It allows for switching roles so that participants can view both sides of the situation. This is especially important for the child who tends to exhibit behaviors that are annoying to others. For example, the child who frequently engages in teasing may be the object of the taunting in the role-play. Another advantage is the opportunity to observe consequences of specific responses. The child who chooses to counter aggression with more aggression or with extreme passivity may realize that she or he has simply negatively escalated rather than resolved the situation. By observing the consequences, children begin to recognize the importance of alternative behaviors. A third advantage of enactment through role-playing is that it facilitates memory. New behaviors are more effectively learned and maintained if the memory of practice incorporates a motor component such as overt role-playing (Star, 1986).

Feedback

As with all learning, feedback is critical to social skills development, because by receiving information about his or her performance, the child is able to make the necessary corrections to improve the skills. Feedback may take a variety of forms—for example: (1) verbal feedback, where the child receives corrective instructions or praise; (2) reinforcement systems, where correct responses earn tangible reinforcers; and (3) self-evaluation, where a system is devised to enable the child to evaluate himself or herself. As indicated above, the typical role-play situation incorporates a discussion/evaluation phase for the purposes of either indicating better ways to perform the behavior or suggesting other ways to respond such as "Smile and look pleasant when you congratulate the winner, George," or "Another way to make friends with Marie is to ask her to play a game with you."

For behaviors performed correctly, the trainer should compliment the child, being careful to praise specific responses—"You really did a good job of following the rules when you played checkers, George." Van Houten (1980) points out the facilitating effects of feedback when given immediately, frequently, and publicly to the group as well as individually. The last condition refers to the importance of informing the group of how well they are doing to promote and foster a group spirit that contributes to social skills development.

Video- and audiotapes are valuable self-evaluation tools and may be especially effective for the adolescent who has difficulty accepting feedback from other sources. The simulated social interactions are taped and afterward the participants evaluate their performance according to specified criteria. The effects may be somewhat dramatic in cases where the youngster is completely unaware of how he presents himself or the effect she has on others. The child who tends to scowl or yell, for example, may recognize how negative these behaviors are by observing them on tape. Teaching children how to monitor and evaluate their own behavior involves assisting them in understanding the goals of various social interactions and how to determine whether a particular encounter was successful. Self-evaluation is another aspect of the role-play discussion/evaluation phase. This may be provided by guiding the child through a sequence of questions. For example, using the previous scene of verbal aggression.

1. What happened after you responded to teasing?
2. What did you want to happen?
3. Did they stop teasing you?
4. What else did you do?
5. How do you feel about what happened?
6. What do you think you will do the next time this happens?

Ladd (1981) helped third-grade students evaluate themselves by conducting self-evaluation sessions. Following the behavior rehearsal of the target skill with a peer, the researcher met with the individual child and "reviewed observed skill performance, elicited children's perceptions of peers' responses, discussed reasons for undesirable outcomes, and encouraged children to adjust their performance accordingly" (p. 174). Kendall (1981) suggests training the child to use a self-evaluation chart with adult monitoring over a period of time to assess how closely the child's evaluations match those of the trainer.

Reinforcement Systems

Feedback may also be provided through reinforcement systems. Contingencies frequently are attached to social behaviors so that correct performance results in desired reinforcers. If the social skills instructor determines feedback through verbal reinforcement is insufficient to motivate the child or children to increase desirable social responses, tangible or token reinforcement systems may be established. It may be necessary to differentiate between reinforcers given for participation regardless of the quality of the responses and those that provide positive feedback for the desired responses. As a suggested set of procedures:

1. Clearly *define what behaviors* will be rewarded. For example, in role playing to teach assertive behavior, reinforcers can be given for such target behaviors as looking at the person you are speaking to, speaking in an appropriate tone of voice, smiling at the person you are relating to, making verbal responses without hesitating, and making positive or relevant verbal statements.

2. *Provide reinforcers* in a form appropriate to the child, for example: (a) edibles, such as cereal or candy, for a very young or low-functioning child; (b) poker chips or other tangible token; or (c) points on a chart or on the chalkboard.

3. *Deliver reinforcers* either (a) during the activity immediately following the target behavior, along with verbal feedback (e.g., "Good eye contact, John," or "That was a good reply"), provided it is not disruptive of the activity; or (b) in an individual or group evaluation session after the activity (i.e., "In that last role-play, how many points should we give John for eye contact?").

In the last situation, the discussion around awarding points can serve as corrective verbal feedback. For this purpose, the most ideal arrangement would be the availability of videotapes to review, discuss, and use as the basis for awarding points. The trainer should determine whether tokens or points need to be exchanged for backup reinforcers in the form of privileges, activities, or tangible items, based on an assessment of existing motivation levels. It is important to remember to reinforce liberally for steps in the right direction, because initial attempts at learning social skills are likely to be awkward and far from perfect.

There is some evidence that social skills training will be most effective if consequences are applied to competing negative behaviors as well as to the positive responses being developed. Several studies demonstrate the value of applying the behavioral principles of prohibitions and response cost as well as contingent reinforcement in developing social skills (Zaragoza et al., 1991). Bierman, Miller, and Stabb (1987) used skill training procedures to develop positive peer behaviors in primary-aged aggressive boys. Treatment consisted of (1) instructions on prosocial behaviors, (2) instructions on prosocial behaviors plus prohibitions for negative behaviors, (3) prohibitions only, and (4) no treatment. During training for conditions 1 and 2, students received praise and tokens for performing specific social skills. Prohibitions involved clearly establishing rules for undesired behaviors (e.g., "no hitting"), and briefly removing the opportunity to earn rewards when an infraction occurred. The authors report prohibitions to be effective in causing immediate reductions in the negative behaviors, but more sustained positive effects were found with the combination of instruction and prohibitions.

Bierman et al. (1987) argue that reductions in negative behaviors alone will not directly lead to increases in social skill/status and vice versa. Schirtzinger (1990), for example, used social skills instruction and tokens to increase "friendship-making" behaviors in middle-school students with learning disabilities, but corresponding decreases in negative peer comments were not observed.

Practice

Practice for Maintenance

Behaviors are more likely to become an established part of the learner's repertoire and to persist over time if the learner is regularly prompted or cued about the desired actions, if extensive practice and overlearning are provided, and if reinforcing contingencies are appropriately arranged. Bulletin boards, games, role-plays, written assignments, and other such activities provide a forum wherein students can continually practice and be reminded of the behaviors to emit.

The practice format and the responses required from the learner may vary. As discussed in the previous section, the child is first expected to practice the behavior through some overt and/or cognitive enactment directed by the social skills trainer. These enactments, accompanied by prompting and feedback, are continued until some acceptable level of proficiency is attained. Once this performance standard is reached, practice under less structured and closely-supervised conditions can be programmed. Children might be organized into small groups to engage in social skills games or informal role-plays.

To dramatize the actions primary-age children should take when ignoring verbal aggression, role-plays could be devised where friendly and unfriendly statements are presented. Direct the children to look at and walk toward the friendly face, accompanied by statements such as "I like you" and "You have a nice smile." When the unfriendly face is shown along with unkind statements, such as "That's an ugly picture you drew" or "I don't like you," the children are to look and move away. This activity may be repeated numerous times, using statements typically expressed and gradually eliminating the use of faces so students are reacting solely to the statements.

For older students, independent practice in the form of a worksheet may be useful in situations where group size and structure are not conducive to extensive overt enactments under the trainer's supervision. The format for these worksheets varies widely so for any particular skill, the child may be asked to:

1. Write a brief essay indicating appropriate behaviors to be performed under specified conditions.
2. Complete a cartoon sequence depicting appropriate responses for a problem situation.
3. Complete a crossword puzzle, where the target words refer to appropriate social behavior.
4. Draw a picture depicting appropriate social action.

An example of a worksheet is presented in Chapter 5 (Figure 5-1) in the sample teaching strategy section. If worksheets are used, take care to vary them, make them enjoyable, and not use them as busy work; otherwise, the activities might become aversive and counter the effectiveness of the social skills instruction. It should be emphasized, however, that worksheets are not replacements for behavioral rehearsal but simply provide a means for more frequent practice opportunities along with occasional behavioral enactments.

Practice for Generalization

Finally, provide opportunities to practice the behavior in other conditions and with other people. After the child has consistently made appropriate responses to verbally aggressive statements, direct the student to practice these behaviors when teased on the playground or at home with her or his siblings. Also, direct the student to report back the results of these practice sessions, to the trainer, at which point he or she should be praised for his successes and receive additional instructions, if necessary.

To increase the incentive to perform these behaviors in other settings where reinforcers are not present, the teacher might provide activities and reward opportunities such as the "ignoring chain" (Cartledge & Kleefeld, 1991). Children receive the explanation that ignoring provocation is a sign of strength, and if they practice ignoring, they will be as strong as the chain. One paper or plastic loop is displayed in the classroom. An additional loop with the child's name will be added for each observed or reported occasion of ignored provocation.

Morales (1992) describes the "I" card technique that is used with secondary students with behavior disorders. For the practice component of their social skills lessons on ignoring disruptive peer behaviors, students were instructed that each time they ignored such a behavior (or on returning to the classroom if it occurred outside the class), they could raise their hand and simply say, "I." The teacher immediately gave the student a small colored sheet of paper that began with the statement "I ignored . . . ." The student completed the statement with a description of the event. When verified, the ignoring reported could earn the student a specified number of bonus points. Activities of this nature can be used to accentuate what ignoring is for the student, how it can be employed, and the beneficial effects of ignoring. Within an appropriate period of time, such activities would be faded and students would rely on social and internal cues for using this skill.

In practicing behaviors in other settings, it is important to determine if the child is able to assess social situations and make the most appropriate responses. For example, making an assertive remark and leaving the scene may be an appropriate way to respond to verbal aggression from a peer or sibling but not necessarily from a parent or teacher. Techniques and procedures for behavior maintenance and generalization are discussed in greater detail in the next chapter.

Coaching

Closely related to social modeling is a procedure termed *coaching,* which also provides for instructions, behavioral rehearsal, and feedback as a means to develop social skills. The most obvious differences between these two methods are that coaching frequently is taught one-on-one and verbal instructions are stressed, while modeling activities, such as those presented in this chapter, are minimized. Oden (1986) describes coaching as follows:

> The child is first instructed in social concepts (e.g., cooperation) by an adult, who encourages the child to suggest specific behavioral examples and adds examples when a child does not provide any. Throughout, the coach repeats and reviews the concepts and gives feedback on how well the child understands their applicability. More general social reality concepts may be included, such as taking into consideration the perspectives or viewpoints of others and considering the consequences of various behaviors for all persons involved (p. 260).

Mize further discusses and illustrates coaching in Chapter 7 of this book.

Cognitive and Affective Methods

Another dimension of social skills instruction relates to internal thinking and emotional states. The mediational processes (thinking) that occur between the presentation of environmental events (stimuli) and the individual's reactions to these events (responses) direct behavior and thus are highly relevant to teaching social skills. Thoughts about a social encounter are greatly determined by how the social situation is perceived. Therefore, interventions geared toward improving social perceptions need to be considered. Emotions that can be triggered either by internal or external events also influence social responses. Feelings and thoughts interact and cannot be separated easily.

In social skills training, the intent is to help the child become aware of her or his feelings and thoughts and to develop styles of behavior that facilitate positive social interaction. Instructional approaches are presented in the following section. These are designed to help children become aware of the impact thoughts and feelings have on social behavior and, accordingly, develop ways to produce more adaptive behaviors. To accomplish the latter, children need to be able to be able to interpret social situations, to understand their feelings and those of others, and to employ various cognitive strategies as needed.

Social Perception

Social perception refers to one's ability to interpret a social situation accurately. Every human interaction presents a myriad of interpersonal events—facial expressions, physical gestures, verbal statements, and tones of voice—all of which are to be taken in, synthesized, and interpreted. There is a direct relationship between the ability to read social situations and overall social skill (Chandler, 1973; Morrison & Bellack, 1981; Rothenberg, 1970). Social perception has been variously defined and, as Morrison and Bellack (1981) point out, it is a complex process involving many factors. For example, if an individual misreads a social situation, is it due to misunderstanding what is seen or heard, attending to irrelevant stimuli, or failing to attend at all?

McFall (1982) discusses social performance in terms of decoding, decision-making, and encoding systems. He proposes that within any social situation the individual must decode or read environmental cues, use a set of decision-making skills, and then act on the environment with motoric responses. *Decoding skills,* which can be equated with social perception, are described as "the processes by which the incoming sensory information is received, perceived, and interpreted" (p. 24). McFall stresses the importance of social perception, in that deficient decoding will likely result in inadequate social performance.

Yeats and Selman (1989) present a developmental model of social perception designed to analyze how children resolve conflicting goals within dyadic situations. This model, called interpersonal negotiation strategies (INS), is an attempt to integrate problem-solving procedures (e.g., Spivack & Shure, 1974; Shure, 1992) and developmental models of social cognition (e.g., Kohlberg, 1969; Piaget, 1965). Interpersonal negotiation strategies are specified according to four levels: impulsive, unilateral, reciprocal, and collaborative. Each level requires children to employ a set of problem-solving skills that reflect their level of development and sophistication. At the lowest level, for example, children's perspectives will be limited to their own personal interests, and decision making will likely resort to physical means to get what they want. At the highest (collaborative) level children are more objective in their perspective; problem solving focuses on actions that have mutual positive social effects and future benefits.

In a series of studies, Yeats, Schultz, and Selman (1991) assess elementary and junior high students on the use of these strategies with stories like the following:

> Randy (Mary) and Tom (Sue) are friends. They have been assigned to work together on a science project in school and only have two days to finish the project. They meet after school and Randy (Mary) says he (she) wants to start working on the project right away, but Tom (Sue) wants to play softball first (p. 404).

Students' responses were found to correlate with social adjustment and social status as determined by teacher ratings and peer sociometric assessments. These findings underscore the importance of role-taking, as well as moral understandings and problem-solving skills, to social perception.

For instructional purposes, social perception is viewed largely as either (1) a communication process where nonverbal and verbal communication are stressed, (2) a psychological process where the role of emotions predominate, or (3) a decentering process where one learns to develop understanding of others and to take the role of the other. A few distinct methods for teaching social perception that reflect these theoretical positions have been identified.

Communication

Improved communicative competence is one approach to heightening the learner's social understanding. Within this orientation, social perception deficits are considered to indicate an inability to interpret and relate the various signals and symbols in the environment accurately. The child who fails to recognize that a certain situation demands reverence or that a particular voice inflection signifies anger or sarcasm will probably respond inappropriately, possibly resulting in negative consequences. Programs attempting to develop social perception through instruction in nonverbal communication tend to emphasize the understanding of what is being communicated through facial expressions, through physical gestures and body movement, through voice cues, and through other physical/environmental cues such as physical proximity and physical appearance (Minskoff, 1980a, 1980b; Wiig & Semel, 1976).

Minskoff (1980a, 1980b) outlines a remedial social perception program focused on nonverbal communication. The curriculum provides for learning in four major skill areas to help the child:

1. Comprehend body language such as facial expressions, gestures, and posture;
2. Understand the significance of spatial elements in social situations—for example, the distance people maintain between them, which may provide valuable information about their personal relationship;
3. Interpret vocal cues—loudness, and paralanguage—yawns;
4. Become aware of artifactual cues, such as cosmetics and clothing, e.g., to note the significance of an individual wearing a policeman's uniform and its related authority.

For each of these areas Minskoff recommends that children be directed to discriminate, use, and apply cues in staged social situations. Although suggestions for instruction are given, a packaged curriculum program is not provided. According to Minskoff, such programs would have limited value because "the teaching materials must be tailored to the specific social problems of the students and therefore have to be created by the teachers" (1980a, p. 121).

In addition to nonverbal communication, social perception training attempts to help the learner develop increased understanding and skill in positive verbal communication. Such skills are useful for evoking positive responses in others, as well as for enabling one to communicate needs and feelings more clearly. Teaching positive communication skills can begin with having children identify the statements of other people that make them feel happy and warm toward that person, then using those behaviors as the basis for role-playing. Such a list might include greeting someone in a positive way, giving another person a compliment, saying something nice about someone to a third person, or expressing appreciation. Fagen, Long, and Stevens (1975, p. 166) present a series of questions that have the goal of teaching positive communication with others in situations that could otherwise result in negative interactions:

1. If someone did not agree with you, how would you want him to tell you? How could you tell someone that you don't agree with him, in a way that is not mean?
2. If someone did not like what you did, how would you want him to tell you? How could you tell someone that you don't like what he did, in a way that is not mean or hurtful?
3. If someone did not like what you said, how would you want him to tell you? How could you tell someone that you don't like what he said to you, in a way that is not mean?
4. If you were not sharing, how would you want someone to tell you? How could you tell someone that he is not sharing?
5. If you lost a game, what could someone say to make you feel better? What could you say to someone who has lost a game?
6. If you make a mistake, what could someone say to make you feel better? What could you say to someone who has made a mistake?
7. If you got into trouble, what could someone say to make you feel better? What could you say to someone who has gotten into trouble?
8. If someone were angry with you, how would you want him to tell you? What could you say to someone who has made you angry?

9. If you were afraid, what could someone say to make you feel better? What could you say to someone who is afraid?
10. If you were crying, what could someone say to make you feel better? What could you say to someone who is crying?[1]

Wiig (1982) provides a comparable, more structured program, termed prosocial communication skills designed to develop positive communication skills among incompetent children and youth. The prosocial communication skills are divided into four categories: ritualizing, informing, controlling, and feeling. *Ritualizing* refers to communication rituals commonly found in everyday speech such as greetings, introductions, and responses. *Informing* involves the way one goes about giving, obtaining, and responding to information such as asking questions ("What is that?") and reacting appropriately to information received ("It is a robot"). *Controlling* pertains to speech acts used to control another's behavior and ways they may be used most effectively—for example, "No, I won't" versus "I would rather not do that." The last category, *feeling,* addresses expressing feelings ("I feel great today") and comprehending attitudes and feelings ("You are worried"). The skills within each of these categories are taught according to a structured learning approach, which includes directions, modeling, and practice, similar to what was outlined earlier in this chapter.

Role-Taking

Egocentric thought, one's inability to take on the perspective of another, interferes with social perception and thus contributes to maladaptive behaviors. As the child develops and experiences a steady improvement in the ability to identify and understand emotions in others, there is a corresponding decline in egocentrism. Training in role-taking involves teaching participants to assume various roles in interpersonal situations. An informal version of role-taking is frequently employed in conflict resolution strategies where participants in the conflict are required to reenact the event but to take the role of the other person. Role-playing and social modeling, predominant methods for teaching social skills, have considerable value in teaching social perception through role reversal techniques.

Chandler (1973) describes an intervention procedure used with delinquent youth designed to help them see themselves and to improve role-taking abilities. Under the supervision of trainers, the youths designed dramatic skits that they enacted, videotaped, and reviewed. Although developed and produced by the youth, guidelines for these dramas were that:

1. The skits developed by the participants be about persons their own age and depict real-life situations (i.e., not episodes involving TV or movie characters),
2. There be a part for every participant,
3. Each skit be rerun until each participant had occupied every role in the plot,
4. That the video recordings be reviewed at the end of each set or tape in an effort to determine ways of improving them (p. 328).

---

[1]Fagen, Long, and Stevens extracts in this chapter are from *Teaching Children Self-Control.* Copyright © 1975 by Merrill Publishing. Reprinted by permission.

The investigation showed that the youths receiving this training made significant improvements over their control group peers, both on the role-taking posttest and in an 18-month follow-up of reported delinquent behaviors.

Empathy

Another component of social perception pertains to the way in which emotional responsiveness and the understanding of feelings influence human behavior. Empathy may be viewed as an extension of role-taking, labeled by Greenspan (1981) as *affective role-taking*. The emphasis here is on affective behavior—that is, the degree to which the observer is able to identify and understand the other's feelings, to take the perspective of the other, and to become emotionally aroused over the circumstances of the other. Empathy is considered to be the foundation of prosocial behaviors such as altruism, sharing, and cooperation. Accordingly, a logical assumption is that individuals with higher levels of empathy also will display more prosocial behaviors. Although some studies have failed to support this position (Cartledge, Stupay, & Kaczala, 1986; Hansen, 1983; Maheady, Maitland, & Sainato, 1982), Schonert-Reichl (1993) reports a review of more recent investigations showing increasing evidence of positive correlations between measures of empathy and social interaction skills, particularly friendship. In her study of adolescent males with and without behavior disorders, Schonert-Reichl found males with behavior disorders had lower indexes of empathy and poorer interpersonal relationships compared to their nondisabled counterparts.

Empathy generally is defined in terms of one individual's response to the emotions of another. The child who observes a friend suffer some misfortune, for example, and experiences sad feelings, is demonstrating empathy. The response may be based on the extent to which one either recognizes the feelings of the other or experiences the same feelings as the other (Strayer, 1980).

Bengtsson and Johnson (1992) suggest extending the dimensions of empathy to encompass the importance of focusing on inner thoughts or experiences as well as obvious feelings, and on one's ability to take the perspective of both the victim and the victimizer. In a study conducted with 60 ten- to eleven-year-old children, the tendency to "focus on inner experiences" was assessed through the presentation of affective scenarios such as a boy having to sell his dog after learning he is allergic to it. Responses such as "I guess he thinks it is awful to have to sell the dog" and "If I had to sell my dog I would feel miserable" (p. 14) were examples of spontaneous reflections on the inner states of the distressed individual. This ability to adopt the inner perspective of the other was found to relate to enhanced empathic arousal.

The second construct, ability to take more than one perspective, was studied by presenting children's conflict situations where there is a victim and victimizer; for instance, one child accidentally ruins another child's highly valued drawing. *Extended empathic reasoning* was the term used to describe responding that not only considered the thoughts and feelings of the protagonist but also expressed concern for the victimizer—for example, "I don't think he intended to spoil the drawing, but he should have stopped playing with the balloon when the other boy asked him to do it" (p. 16). Prosocial behaviors were strongly related to children's abilities to view conflict situations from the perspective of both parties.

Although all the processes described above relate to emotions, some may be more cognitive than affective. The respective roles of affect and thought processes are not easily delineated. If a situation is defined narrowly or limited to one perspective, emotional arousal and social behaviors are likely to be limited or aligned accordingly. Therefore, skill in displaying emotional responsiveness is based on one's ability to judge social events accurately and comprehensively, to recognize and label emotions or feelings in oneself and others, and to find constructive means for expressing feelings in interpersonal situations. The next section describes approaches to teaching about emotions.

Affective Behavior

Most affective education programs begin with teaching the child to identify and label the emotions of others from various observable indicators, that is, facial expression, body language, voice tone, and verbal content. Teaching the child to *read* emotions from facial expressions is probably the most important place to start. Developmental psychologists point out the significance of facial expressions in early communication between mothers and infants. They consider the human face an important factor in social development: The face provides the most immediate and specific information about a person's emotional state. Another part of this task is teaching the child to connect emotions with preceding events in the environment so she or he understands that emotions do not occur randomly but have antecedents. A further task is acquainting the child with the range of possible human emotions and enabling him or her to make discriminations about them.

Some initial approaches to teaching children how to identify feelings involve presenting various emotions in a variety of ways, asking the child to label and enact them. Sample activities include:

1.   Present pictures of faces from books or magazines to help the child learn to identify and label emotions. Have the child make up stories about why the people in the pictures are happy, sad, or otherwise.

2.   Have the child draw faces reflecting emotions and tell stories explaining the emotions. Provide a scene for the child to relate to; for example, "Draw a face of someone who:

- Just had his money stolen.
- Just won a prize, or
- Is being chased by a bully."

3.   Have an adult model facial and bodily gestures and have children identify what emotions are involved.

4.   Have children pick cards with names of emotions written on them and role play emotions for others to identify in a guessing game. A variation could ask for the child to role play the emotion with facial expressions, body language, voice tone, or words.

5. Have the children develop a vocabulary of feelings, a "feelings dictionary," making lists of synonyms for words describing feelings, using them to label pictures, for spelling words, or as the basis for games. Pictures of faces might be displayed on a bulletin board labeled with a list of descriptive words.

In order to teach children to be aware of and label their feelings, an adult initially may need to make inferences about the feelings and provide information to call attention to the cues each child is giving out: "You are smiling, Mary. Are you feeling happy?" "You have a frown on your face, John. Can you tell me what you are feeling? What happened to make you feel that way?" The adult also can provide a model by identifying and labeling his or her own feelings, and provide information to explain the feelings. Along with learning to identify their own feelings, children can learn that others may have different feelings in the same situations. Some activities for teaching children to label their emotions include:

1. Have each child draw his or her own face or role-play how he or she would feel in different situations; for example, "Draw the face that shows how you would feel if:

- You fell in the mud with your new clothes on,
- Your pet had not come home all day, or
- You were opening presents on your birthday."

2. Provide an exercise using sentence completion—for example, "For me, happiness is . . ." accompanied by drawings. Have children compare notes on their answers in a discussion.

Formal lessons on emotions can be found in existing curricula. Labeling the four basic emotions (happy, sad, anger, fear) is one lesson provided by Cartledge and Kleefeld (1991) in a social skills curriculum for primary-aged children. Through the use of animal puppets, the instruction begins with a story where the main characters learn to recognize and name feelings. Questions are interspersed throughout the lesson, aimed at helping students identify the emotions correctly and associate them with the precipitating events. In the discussion that takes place after the story, the children are encouraged to relate the feelings presented in the story with their own personal experiences.

To increase awareness of these feelings in themselves and others, children are directed to role-play the events of the story. For example (Cartledge & Kleefeld, 1991):

> Give the puppets to four children. Ask Felicia Fox and Benny Frog to pantomime the events of the story: Felicia happily chews bubble gum; Benny enters, discovers the missing gum, and shows anger; Benny directs his anger toward Felicia, who responds with fear. As each emotion is portrayed, Will Rabbit and Sally Deer describe what's happening and name each feeling. Coach the children as necessary.

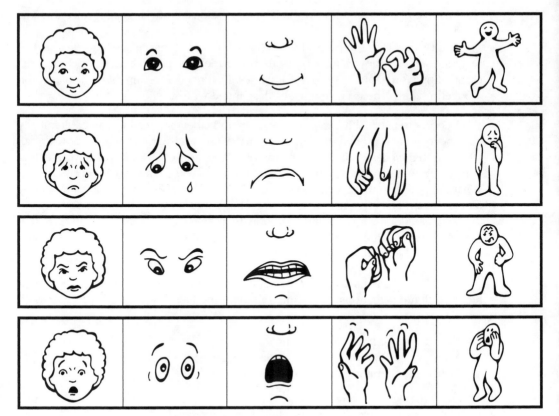

Blackline Master 7

Taking Part: Introducing Social Skills to Children
©1991 AGS® American Guidance Service, Inc., Circle Pines, Minnesota 55014-1796
Permission to the purchaser to reproduce this worksheet for instructional use is hereby granted by the publisher.

FIGURE 3-1 Blackline Master

After the role play, discuss how the characters portrayed and named each feeling. Then have the children exchange roles and role play again. As time permits, allow each child to take a turn with a puppet. When all have participated, have various children role play the four feelings again, this time without using puppets. They can use either the story events or another story that you or they devise. Encourage the group to offer the players feedback on the way they portrayed and named their feelings (p. 37).

Social perception and increased abilities to label emotions are emphasized through additional practice activities. In the subsequent pantomime activity, individual children act out feelings to be named by the other students. This activity is followed by a worksheet focusing attention on specific body movements/gestures as well as total affect. (See Figure 3-1.) Children use this worksheet to make associations with various situations such as the following (Cartledge & Kleefeld, 1991):

1. You are eating an ice cream cone.
2. You are being chased by a barking dog.
3. You tear your new shirt.
4. You are having a birthday party.
5. You are startled by someone wearing a mask.
6. You hear someone call you a bad name.
7. You find out that your pet has run away (p. 38).

Act out or draw.

voice

Further practice is given by helping the children attach verbally presented scenes with each of the four emotions. For sadness, the teacher reads the following with verbal and physical expression:

> My dog Feiffer is dead. He was playing in the yard, and then he ran out into the street. A car was coming and couldn't stop in time. I played with Feiffer every day. Now I won't ever see him again. I feel . . . (p. 39).

Children are helped to verify the emotion assigned to that scene by responding to questions such as these (Cartledge & Kleefeld, 1991, pp. 38–39):

1. What did you hear in the story that told you I felt (sad)?
2. What words made you think of (sadness)?
3. What changes did you see in my face?
4. How did my mouth look?
5. How did my mouth change?
6. How did my eyes look?
7. How did my eyes change?
8. How did my eyebrows look?
9. How did my eyebrows change?

As part of maintenance, teachers are encouraged to observe students daily for opportunities to compliment those who correctly name feelings. Rewards, such as the Will Rabbit stickers included in the curriculum, might be used for this purpose, particularly for those students who are either reluctant or less able to perform this skill. The curriculum also recommends reading children's books—such as the Susan Riley (1978) series of *Afraid, Angry,* and *I'm Sorry*—and creating a Feelings bulletin board where children routinely display pictures of designated emotions. Some guidelines suggested by Fagen et al. (1975) are relevant to the task of teaching children to recognize and label their feelings. For group discussions related to emotions they suggest the following:

> No individual should be pressured to respond or to divulge his feelings: Teacher or peers might question one another out of interest, but an explicit norm should be established for the "right to privacy" or the "right to pass."
> It should be recognized that participation by pupils may be verbal, nonverbal, or vicarious: Students can be learning without saying or doing anything. The right to be silent, to listen, and to observe should be respected at all times. The watchful member is often learning more about emotions and acceptance of them (including his own) than is the rapid talker (pp. 66–67).

Practice with more impersonal and less anxiety-laden issues should be provided before taking up any directly personal or high-anxiety issues. For example, feelings about television, the weather, sports, and so on can be introduced before beginning to talk about feelings toward parents, teachers, or other students. In this way, students can learn first that differences are acceptable, that retaliation or hurt is not a consequence of honest expression, and that feelings are not right or wrong. The teacher should continually reiterate that feelings can be pleasant or unpleasant and enjoyable or painful, but he or she should emphasize that they are never bad or wrong. A clear distinction should be made between a person's right to own any and all feelings and her or his responsibility to place limits on acting out feelings. It is most useful to introduce feelings by focusing on some present event, experience, or issue. Questions introduced by "How do you feel when . . .?" or "What thoughts or feelings do you have . . .?" or "When do you feel that way?" are preferable to questions in the past tense.

Beyond labeling, instruction in this area also needs to focus on the role of emotions and appropriate ways to respond to them. *Emotional responsiveness*—the ability to identify and share the emotional experiences of others—is based on the individual's understanding of his or her own emotions. In addition to teachings geared to the child's feelings such as the ones just given, the child should have the opportunity to learn to respond to the feelings of others. An example of teaching for emotional responsiveness is given by Feshbach et al. (1983) in their curriculum designed to teach the spectrum of empathic behaviors to elementary school-aged children. The children are given an excerpt from the book *A Tree Grows in Brooklyn*, informed that it is about children of their ages, and then, following the story, are engaged in a discussion about how they feel and the causes of these feelings. A variety of activities is included in this curriculum: problem solving, role-playing, and simulations. Feshbach et al. (1983) field tested this curriculum empirically and reported encouraging findings of improved prosocial behaviors among empathy-trained children.

Caring, empathic behaviors may be promoted through daily learning in the classroom. The following are some actions teachers can take for this purpose:

1. Establish ongoing procedures such as silent cheers (thumbs up signs) or applause where each child's success (which may be as small as recognizing a sight word) is recognized by the class.
2. Make certain each child has frequent opportunities to give and receive group affirmation.
3. Make certain children know you are aware of and value the caring kind acts they express toward others.
4. Encourage students to call or send notes to a fellow student who experiences some misfortune such as death of a relative, an accident, or illness.
5. Provide opportunities for students to tutor a peer in the classroom or in another classroom.
6. Structure community projects that promote caring behaviors such as contrib-

uting toys to orphaned or impoverished children or visiting older people in nursing homes.

7. Emphasize the feelings associated with conflict situations; help children understand how their actions may have hurt others.

8. From films shown in class, discuss acts of caring or how the characters might have been more empathic.

9. Discuss disasters in the news such as hurricanes, earthquakes, famines, and wars. Note how the victims of these events might be feeling and what you might do to assist them.

10. Encourage students to keep logs of caring acts they performed for the last week. Arrange for each child's actions to be recognized by the entire class and display the logs on the "caring" bulletin board.

The ultimate goal in learning about one's own and others' feelings is to help the child find constructive ways to express feelings in interpersonal situations. This is complex because it involves not only the child's ability to discriminate and respond internally but the development of the ability to exercise control and selectivity over overt responses as well. This latter task involves a three-way interaction between emotion, cognition, and motor activity. Social skills training aimed at teaching behavioral control of emotion is most effective if it develops awareness in the child of his or her feelings in a situation, awareness of the cognitive evaluations he or she is making about the situation and his or her own feeling state, and a mastery of the range of behaviors related to the situation in which to engage. In helping children make a distinction between their thoughts and feelings and their behavior, Fagen et al. (1975, p. 178) suggest using the following points as the basis for discussion:

1. All thoughts and feelings are OK and normal to have.
2. Thoughts and feelings can be private property; complete freedom is possible for thoughts and feelings.
3. All actions or behaviors are not OK; some are illegal, harmful to self or others, or against the rules.
4. Behaviors or actions cannot be private property; complete freedom is not possible for behavior.
5. Thoughts and feelings are different from behavior; you can think and feel things without needing to do them or without blaming yourself for having mean or "bad" ideas.

Several of the cognitive approaches discussed later in this chapter also are geared toward helping the child make the connection between thoughts, feelings, and behavior.

Training in communicative processes, empathy, and role-taking may be effective in enabling the individual to become more socially perceptive. Because this is a relatively new area, literature on training procedures is limited. Even more sparse is research demonstrating the effectiveness of the instructional techniques currently identified. There is a need not only for efficacy studies but also for an investigation of specific emotions and perceptions as they relate to the developmental process.

For example, Moyer (1974), in a study with kindergarten and third-grade children, found that expressions of happiness were the easiest to identify and communicate, with anger second. Fear and sadness were next, being of equal difficulty. Surprise was the most difficult, especially for the kindergarten subjects. Most programs present these emotions in a parallel fashion without allowing for differences in difficulty or the additional time it would take to develop understanding of a particular emotion. The exact nature of social perception problems is not entirely clear. Some children, for example, may misperceive because they focus on only one part of the social situation; that is, they will look only at the face and not the body movements, or they may attend to the apparent smiling face and miss the angry words.

Although there is a tendency for social perception and social skills to be equated in the literature, Morrison and Bellack (1981) view social perception as a precursor of social skills. They differentiate between having a "repertoire of response skills" and social perception, which is knowing when and how to make the particular response. When teaching social perception, be aware that improvement in reading the social environment does not automatically lead to improved performance without direct social skill instruction. The reverse also appears to be true (Morrison & Bellack, 1981). Therefore, the social skills trainer should incorporate environmental cue comprehension into instruction on specific social skills.

Cognitive Approaches

Cognitive approaches to social skills instruction focus on helping the child acquire thought patterns necessary for social competence. Although various models exist, they may be grouped according to two primary intentions: to alter the statements the child makes to herself or himself, or to develop cognitive problem-solving skills. The common element present in all models is the theoretical position that cognitions play a major role in directing behavior and, thus, the child's maladaptive behavior may be indicative of inadequate thinking styles.

Altering Belief Systems

One theoretical framework for altering belief systems stems from the *Rational Emotive Therapy* (RET) model developed by Albert Ellis (1962). The basic premise is that maladaptive behaviors largely result from irrational belief systems that influence what we say to ourselves and thereby control our behavior. Ellis (1977) takes the position that inappropriate behavior is less a function of a particular event than of what one says to oneself about the event. The student who receives a failing mark, for example, may react inappropriately if she tells herself that she is worthless and dumb or that it is terrible and catastrophic to fail. The objective of rational models is to help the individual identify the events leading to specific behaviors, to analyze irrational belief systems considered to be controlling these reactions, and to replace these systems with rational ones that are more likely to lead to adaptive behavior. In examining irrational belief systems, Ellis (1977) suggests looking for the things a person tells himself he should or must do or must have happen. Examples of these beliefs that Gambrill lists (1977) include:

1. The idea that it is a dire necessity for an adult human being to be loved or approved by virtually every significant other person in his community;
2. The idea that one should be thoroughly competent, adequate, and achieving in all possible respects, if one is to consider oneself worthwhile;
3. The idea that certain people are bad, wicked, or villainous and that they should be severely blamed and punished for their villainy;
4. The idea that it is awful and catastrophic when things are not the way one would very much like them to be;
5. The idea that human unhappiness is externally caused and that people have little or no ability to control their sorrows and disturbances;
6. The idea that if something is or may be dangerous or fearsome, one should be terribly concerned about it and should keep dwelling on the possibility of it occurring;
7. The idea that it is easier to avoid than to face certain life difficulties and self-responsibilities;
8. The idea that one should be dependent on others and needs someone stronger than oneself on whom to rely;
9. The idea that one's past history is an all-important determinant of one's present behavior, and that because something once strongly affected one's life, it should indefinitely have a similar effect;
10. The idea that one should become quite upset over other people's problems and disturbances; and
11. The idea that there is invariably a right, precise, and perfect solution to human problems, and that it is catastrophic if this correct solution is not found (pp. 498, 499).[2]

The principles of RET have been adapted into a therapeutic program for children (Bernard & Joyce, 1984), which focuses on understanding the variety and range of emotions, and how our thoughts, rather than people and events, produce specific feelings. Various techniques are used to help the child employ more rational beliefs: (1) challenging and restating irrational thoughts and (2) performing new adaptive behaviors that force the children to discard previously held self-defeating thoughts. One classroom application is an activity by Knaus (1974), in his *Rational Emotive Educational* program, to help children understand that the feelings come from thoughts. In the Happening-Thought-Feeling-Reaction diagram, an event is presented on the chalk board in diagram form. Using name calling as the problem event, the diagram would be:

[2]From Gambrill, E. D., *Behavior Modification,* 1977. Copyright © Jossey-Bass. Reprinted by permission.

Happening	+	*Thought*	=	*Feeling*	*Reaction*
Arthur calls James' mother a name		It's terrible to have my mother called a name . . . I can't stand it . . . I have to get him for that . . .		Strong anger (out of control)	James hits Arthur; fight results

To demonstrate how different thoughts could lead to different feelings and actions, the same diagram can be developed with alternative thoughts, feelings, and reactions generated by the children,

Happening	+	*Thought*	=	*Feeling*	*Reaction*
Arthur calls James' mother a name		He doesn't even know my mother . . . He wants me to get angry . . . I don't have to do what he wants . . .		Mild anger or annoyance	James ignores Arthur, and walks away.

According to the author, the program is geared to children from fourth to eighth grades but can be adapted for younger or older youngsters. It is intended to be presented several times weekly for approximately a 9-month period.

Altering Self-statements

Although RET utilizes self-statements, its primary aim is to change one's philosophy or basic belief system, whereas other cognitive approaches employ self-speech as a means to alter some problem behavior. Two examples are stress-inoculation training and self-instructional training (Meichenbaum, 1977). *Stress-inoculation training* is designed to develop thinking skills or verbal mediators that enable the individual to cope successfully with stressful situations. Presented as a three-step process, the individual is helped to understand what the problem situation is, how to develop cognitive coping skills, and how to apply the skills under stressful conditions. In the first step, the child is aided in understanding the antecedent events and the cognitive and physiological aspects of the problem (what events provoked the emotional event), the physical responses that accompanied the emotions (increased heartbeat, sweating), and the self-statements that directed the emotional overt behaviors such as flight in fear or fighting in anger. To illustrate, a student may be helped to understand that (1) the problem occurs whenever he makes an incorrect response to his academic work; (2) he is reacting physically also, feeling hot and starting to breathe hard; (3) he is telling himself he is a dummy and no good when he gets something wrong; and (4) he subsequently starts to cry, to yell, to destroy his papers, and to throw things.

After understanding the events that precipitate his behavior, the student is then trained to practice certain coping self-statements. Meichenbaum (1977, p. 155)

presents a four-phase model with sample self-statements to be employed for re-hearsing coping cognitions:

1. Preparing for a stressor—recognizing the nature of the situation ("What is it you have to do?" or "You can develop a plan to deal with it");
2. Confronting and handling a stressor—using statements to increase courage and self-confidence ("Just 'psych' yourself up—you can meet this challenge" or "One step at a time; you can handle the situation");
3. Coping with feeling overwhelmed—recognizing that reactions to the situation will occur and trying to keep these feelings under control ("You should expect your fear to rise" or "Don't try to eliminate fear totally; just keep it manage-able"); and
4. Reinforcing self-statements ("It worked; you did it" or "You can be pleased with the progress you're making").

A similar sequence for anger based on this model was devised by Novaco (1975). Adapting these categories for children, self-statements for the example given above (the child overreacting to corrective feedback) might include:

- Preparing for provocation
  - If the teacher marks something wrong, I can handle it.
  - I know what to do if I get upset.
  - Making a mistake is not so bad; I can correct it.
- Impact on confrontation
  - Keep calm.
  - Think about the ones you got correct.
  - It's silly to get angry about one problem.
  - The teacher is really right to show me what I did wrong.
  - Being corrected helps me learn.
- Coping with arousal
  - I'm beginning to breathe hard; I should relax.
  - Stop and think about all the good work I did today.
  - Try to keep cool.
- Reflection on provocation when conflict is unresolved
  - It partly worked.
  - I can do better next time.
  - This is hard to do but I'll keep trying.
- Reflection on provocation when conflict is resolved or coping is successful
  - I did a good job that time. I even smiled at the teacher.
  - I can be a good student. The teacher likes me to keep calm when I make a mistake.
  - I feel better about myself when I keep calm.

In teaching a child to apply coping skills under different stressful conditions, the teacher might stage various scenarios reflective of real-life events to be enacted by the child. Using the example presented previously of a child who overreacts to making mistakes on schoolwork:

> Pretend that you are in class and you just finished taking a spelling test. What can you say to yourself that will help you prepare for the teacher correcting your paper?
>
> The teacher has returned the paper, and you have two wrong and eight correct. What can you say to yourself to keep from being upset?
>
> You told yourself to keep cool, but you still felt hot and shaky inside and you started to cry. The teacher tells you that you did better on this test. What can you say to yourself?
>
> You were successful in keeping from being upset about your spelling test. Now what should you do?

Role-playing such scenes will provide a more explicit demonstration of behaviors and thus greater opportunity for feedback and self-evaluation.

Self-instructional training (SIT) focuses on controlling impulsive or aggressive behaviors. Instructional techniques include cueing the child that a problem situation exists and that he or she must stop and think out how to proceed. Labeled *thought stopping* and initially used with adults, this procedure was devised to help the individual discontinue nonproductive or self-defeating thought processes. For example, the individual who tends to engage in excessive self-denigrating thoughts might say "stop" out loud or to himself or herself to terminate the thoughts, and then direct his or her thinking along a more productive path. In adapting thought stopping for children, environmental or physiological stimuli are identified and used as signals for the child to stop and employ prescribed thinking skills. Palkes, Steward, and Kahana (1968), in a program to train hyperactive boys to perform paper-and-pencil tasks, used large cue cards that included statements such as "Before I start any of the tasks I am going to do, I am going to say 'STOP!'"

Thought-stopping procedures have been incorporated into several social skills instruction programs (Camp & Bash, 1981; Harris, 1984; Lochman, Nelson, & Sims, 1981), where some cue is provided to help the learner stop and think before acting impulsively and inappropriately. Harris (1984), in his *Making Better Choices Program,* presents a red traffic STOP sign on a poster board as the first step in the social skills cognitive sequence. The learner is directed to relax and be calm before devising a plan and taking action. Etscheidt (1991), in an adaptation of the Lochman et al. (1981) model, employed verbal and motor cues to get aggressive children to stop and think before acting. To inhibit verbal aggression, students were directed to engage in self-instruction with the statement "Don't say it!" and then place a fist over the mouth. For physical aggression, the self-statement was "Don't do it!" and the motor response was to tuck their hands under arms.

After the interruption, the child is expected to use internal mediators or talk in order to guide himself or herself through the problem situation. Training for such thought structuring is exemplified by a sequence developed by Meichenbaum and

Goodman (1971) to show a child how to think through a difficult task (Meichenbaum, 1977, p. 32):

1. An adult model performed a task while talking to himself out loud (cognitive modeling);
2. The child performed the same task under the direction of the model's instructions (overt, external guidance);
3. The child performed the task while instructing himself aloud (overt self-guidance);
4. The child whispered the instructions to himself as he went through the task (faded, overt self-guidance); and finally
5. The child performed the task while guiding his performance via private speech (covert self-instruction).

An example of the modeling situation might be (Meichenbaum & Goodman, 1971, p. 117):

> Okay, what is it I have to do? You want me to copy the picture with the different lines. I have to go slow and be careful. Okay, draw the line down, down good; then to the right, that's it; now down some more and to the left. Good, I'm doing fine so far. Remember go slow. Now back up again. No, I was supposed to go down. That's okay. Just erase the line carefully. . . . Good. Even if I make an error I can go on slowly and carefully, Okay, I have to go down now. Finished. I did it.

In this example, impulsive second-grade children were trained to use self-talk to monitor their behavior and respond more accurately. The problem situation was performance on various paper-and-pencil cognitive tasks such as the Porteus Maze tests. As noted from the model, training is designed to move the child gradually from copying the verbalization of the model, to independently making these statements out loud, to finally internalizing them in the form of thoughts. The ultimate goal is, through repeated presentations, that the child will be taught to use this thought pattern automatically when confronted with problem situations.

Problem Solving

In addition to stress-innoculation and self-instructional training, many cognitive-based social skills curricula include problem-solving sequences designed to help children and adolescents successfully resolve problem situations. Research findings indicate that good problem solvers tend to evidence better social adjustment than those with limited skills in this area (Richard & Dodge, 1982; Spivack & Shure, 1974), and the effects of training in social problem solving appear to be promising for students with adjustment problems (Ager & Cole, 1991; Yu et al., 1986). The instructional steps for social problem solving typically include determining the problem, alternative responses, the appropriate solution, and the possible effects.

Problem Definition and Formulation. Before an individual can pursue the solution to a problem, she or he must be able to recognize that a problem exists

(Meichenbaum, 1975). The task of helping a child recognize a problem may be approached, for example, by identifying and compiling problem situations encountered by a particular child or by children of a younger age group, or by having older students list their own problematic situations. The situations are discussed with the learner to help her or him understand the nature of the problem and the related environmental and emotional factors. It is important that the learner define the problem in terms of an event or situation over which she or he has some control rather than focus solely on the maladaptive behaviors of others or on her or his emotional state. The following vignette is given to illustrate.

> It is time for recess and the teacher announces that the students in row one may get in line. Larry and Ron both try to be first in line. Larry tells Ron that he got there first and moves in front of Ron. Ron tells Larry that he got there first and tries to get in front of Larry. A scuffle breaks out and the teacher makes both Larry and Ron return to their seats. As punishment, they are made to remain in the classroom during recess and work on academic assignments. Both boys are very upset about missing recess and blame each other. Later, in discussing the problem with the teacher, [each boy insists] that the problem centered on the other boy's not recognizing his first position in line.

In the above scenario, both boys present themselves as victims, powerless to exercise positive control over the events that occurred. The problem needs to be defined more objectively before the students can respond constructively. A series of questions might be used to help achieve that goal; (1) identify what the learner wanted to have happen, (2) identify what did happen, (3) identify how this made the learner feel, and (4) state why the learner is feeling this way. Using the previous scene, the teacher might question as follows:

TEACHER: Ron, what is it you wanted to happen?

RON: I wanted to be first in line for recess.

TEACHER: What happened so that you weren't first in line?

RON: Larry said he was first. He pushed me out of the way.

TEACHER: How did this make you feel?

RON: Angry. Mad. (Teacher prompts student to identify disappointment as an important emotion here.)

TEACHER: Why did you feel this way?

RON: Because he pushed me. Because I wanted to be first in line.

TEACHER: So the problem is that you and Larry both wanted to be first in line.

This sequence of questions would be repeated with Larry so that both boys are focused on the fact that the problem is that each wanted to be first in line and the scuffle was a maladaptive attempt for them to solve the problem, not the cause of the problem. The goal of this first step of problem identification is to help the learner develop a thinking style to use to define problems independently. Once the child clearly understands what the problem is, she or he can begin to consider solutions.

Determining Alternatives. In this step, the learner is assisted in generating various alternative responses and the possible consequences to these solutions. For data collection, the learner would list as many alternatives as possible, including those that might be undesirable. Alternatives for the example just presented might include:

- Pushing the other person out of the line
- Complaining to the teacher
- Negotiating with the other person the position of being first in line in exchange for some other privilege such as first at bat during recess
- Letting the other person be first, and saying nothing
- Telling the other person she can be first if she lets you be first the next time she is first in line
- Asking the other person to let you be first, and the next time you will let him be first
- Letting the other person be first, and later discussing with the teacher ways you could get to be first in line

In a formal teaching situation, the list of alternatives and their corresponding consequences might be presented visually to aid memory and understanding. For young children the responses may be depicted through simple stick pictures and displayed on a bulletin board (Spivack & Shure, 1974). Older, more competent students may simply write the behaviors and possible outcomes on the chalkboard. Data analysis occurs when youngsters are required to review their suggested responses in terms of possible consequences; for example, "If you let the other person be first and later discuss with the teacher ways you could be first in line, what do you think would happen?" Consequences for each of the alternatives would be listed and discussed in terms of possible outcomes.

Some empirically based findings on these procedures are worth noting. First of all, teachers need to attend to the type of alternatives generated. Although the procedure is designed to identify both prosocial and antisocial alternatives with the notion that the latter would be eliminated through thoughtful analysis, there is evidence that this policy might be counterproductive. In some studies higher levels of aggressive behaviors were found to erupt following social problem-solving training where many antisocial alternatives were generated (Olexa & Forman, 1984; Weissberg et al., 1981). This suggests that it would be better to emphasize positive over negative alternatives. The exception might be when an undesired behavior has already occurred with negative consequences such as in the above scene, and the listing provides the opportunity to analyze the action and determine its future desirability.

A second concern pertains to the number of alternatives generated. The assumption that good problem solvers are those who are able to identify many alternatives for any one problem situation needs further examination (Amish, Gesten, Smith, Clark, & Stark, 1988; Neel et al., 1990). Amish et al., for example, taught 25 children with behavior disorders to produce significantly more alternatives to problem situations but found no adjustment differences during posttesting.

Finally, it is important to note the kind of strategies employed by socially appropriate children. Neel et al. (1990) observed that when initial efforts were unsuccessful, nonaggressive children tended to redirect themselves or seek clarification on what was expected. In contrast, aggressive children tended to use intrusive strategies to achieve goals and relied less on verbal information gained from questioning or the use of descriptive comments. Therefore, in helping learners specify alternatives that will result in the greatest adjustment return, teachers should minimize the focus on the number of alternatives, stressing instead the most prosocial and realistic options. Strategies that help children mediate problem situations verbally also should be targeted.

Determining Solutions. This decision-making step involves matching the alternatives and consequences that have been generated. Following the Spivack and Shure suggestions mentioned previously, the pictured or listed behaviors could be coordinated so the child sees that response *X* could possibly lead to consequence *Y*. For older learners, words may be substituted for pictures. Also, at this point, behaviors may be ordered so that children list the alternatives from most preferred to least preferred. Another consideration is the need to identify the exact way to carry out the most desirable alternative (Goldfried & Goldfried, 1975). Once the most desirable solution is determined, the learner should be assisted in trying it out. The behaviors first may be practiced through role-playing. Behavior rehearsal is especially important if the actual problem situation is anxiety provoking and if the desired response consists of complex behaviors unfamiliar to the child. Depending on the nature of the problem and suggested solutions, the application sequence may entail

- *Modeling of the suggested response*—the trainer demonstrates how the responses should be made.
- *Behavior rehearsal*—the child acts out the desired behavior in a manner similar to that demonstrated by the trainer. Under role-play conditions, a variety of responses may be considered and tried out to assess the relative effects.
- *Application in real-life conditions*—the child tries the solution in a actual situation. The trainer aids the child in assessing the results and in determining alternatives, if necessary. The child is encouraged to use problem-solving strategies in his or her daily living.

Evaluation. The evaluation is conducted with the child to determine the effectiveness of the applied strategy. As with problem identification, the learner may need guidance in deciding whether he accomplished what she wanted. If desired goals have not been met, the child is then helped to find other or additional ways to approach the situation.

The effective use of problem-solving strategies is partially based on the child's abilities to understand the nature of the problem, identify alternative responses, to think through various responses and their consequences, and to evaluate the alternatives in terms of desired ends. However, before embarking on problem-solving instruction incorporating the above steps, note that this model demands certain prerequisite abilities that the learner, especially a young child or a child with special needs, may not have. Problem solving requires that the learner possess basic language skills, reasoning skills (ability to understand relationships, to identify realistic alternatives, and to anticipate consequences), ability to engage in sustained attention, and sufficient memory skills to retain learning.

Spivack and Shure (1974) address this issue in their problem-solving training program for preschool inner-city children through the use of instructional activities for systematic teaching of preproblem-solving skills, consisting of the following abilities and concepts:

1. *Language*—basic language skills assumed to be prerequisite to the child's ability to go through a problem-solving process. For example, knowing words for expressing alternatives (or, not, and), words for describing emotions (happy, sad, mad), words for alternative solutions (maybe, might, if-then), and words for consequential thinking (why, because).
2. *Emotions*—labeling emotions, identifying emotions in others, and learning to cope with various feelings.
3. *Situation analysis*—recognizing that any situation consists of several factors that must be considered before acting.
4. *Preferences*—understanding that people have preferences and that these differ among individuals.
5. *Causal relationships*—understanding the relationship among events and the effect one may have on another's behavior.
6. *Fairness*—considering the rights of others.

Using a game format, the authors provide for extensive instruction in the preliminary skills before directly engaging the child in problem-solving strategies. The remainder of the script focuses on skills directly related to problem solving—that is, identifying alternative solutions, anticipating consequences of specific acts, and matching the consequences to their respective solutions. During training, the teacher conducts several sessions designed to help the child identify as many alternatives as possible to a problem situation. For example, "Robert is riding on the bicycle but George wants to ride also. What can George do?" The teacher assists the children in listing solutions, such as these:

- Ask Robert to let him ride.
- Asking the teacher for help.

- Grab the bicycle from Robert.
- Give Robert something to let him ride the bicycle.

The next set of sessions deals with identifying consequences for certain events. An act is presented, such as George pushing Robert off the bike, and the children are guided in thinking out what might happen next. A list of consequences might include:

- Robert may cry.
- Robert may hit George.
- Robert may tell the teacher.
- Robert may get hurt.

The two previous skills are combined in the final series of lessons: A problem is presented, the child is prompted to think of a solution for the problem and to identify immediately the possible consequence to these actions. Values are not attached to the solutions suggested by the child, but it is hoped that the child will think through the various alternatives and choose the best course on her or his own. The authors stress that the program is not designed to teach children *what* to think but *how* to think in problem situations.

Perhaps the best means for promoting and reinforcing this ability is to use problem-solving "dialoguing" with children on an ongoing basis whenever conflict situations arise in the natural environment (Amish et al., 1988). Before exercising authority to arbitrate the situation, the teacher can briefly prompt children to pinpoint the problem and to "think about what you might do to solve it." Praise and even tangible reinforcers for successful resolutions might encourage regular use of this strategy. A published curriculum of this model exists for children from preschool through the elementary grades (Shure, 1992).

Weissberg et al. (1980) present a similar problem-solving curriculum for second- to fourth-grade children. An important feature of the instruction is to encourage children to persist and to think of other solutions when the previously chosen alternative is unsuccessful. During the role-play enactments, the teacher often takes the role of the spoiler, ensuring that the suggested behavior will fail. The teacher then prompts pupils to generate and to try another solution. An example from one of the strategies follows (Weissberg et al., 1980, pp. 100–101):

GEORGE: We're upset because Pete took our ball and there's nothing else to play with.

KAREN: Our goal is to get the ball back.

GEORGE: (to Karen) What do you think we should do?

KAREN: We could . . . (propose a solution and its consequence).

GEORGE: We could . . . (propose another solution and its consequence).

KAREN: Let's try . . . (the best solution from the previous activity).

When George and Karen try their solution to get the ball back, Peter (played by the teacher) SHOULD REFUSE TO GIVE IT. Then the role-play is interrupted and what took place is reviewed:

Class, George and Karen stated their problem and goal. They even thought of some solutions and their consequences. (Solution X) seemed like a good solution but it didn't work. They didn't reach their goal of getting the ball back.

How did George and Karen feel when their solution didn't work? Disappointed, discouraged, sad, tired, mad, let down. Have a brief discussion of the fact that this is natural and that the person may be tempted to give up.)

Class, what do you think George and Karen should do next? (The answer you want here is: "Try again!").

That's right. It's important for good problem solvers to try again!

Problem-solving procedures have been used extensively to train and assess groups of children and youth. The research literature, although generally showing improved performance in problem-solving cognitive skills resulting from training, reports equivocal effects of problem-solving training on social behavior and adjustment. Weissberg et al. (1981) found that problem-solving training positively affected social adjustment of suburban but not urban third grade students.

Although there are reports of positive effects of problem-solving training on social behavior (Elardo & Caldwell, 1979; Spivack & Shure, 1974), other investigations have failed to obtain similar relationships (Amish et al., 1988; Kendall & Fischler, 1984; Olexa & Forman, 1984; Schneider & Yoshida, 1988). These mixed findings call into question some basic assumptions about problem solving: (1) the degree to which problem-solving abilities will be used to mediate social behaviors, (2) the accuracy of existing assessment procedures, and (3) the appropriateness of this training for differing groups.

The observation that socially maladjusted subjects performed worse on measures of problem-solving cognitive skills logically led to the assumption that problem-solving training would contribute to more adaptive behaviors. The consistent failure to find a problem-solving/behavioral link has caused researchers to search for other influences. Some initial evidence indicates that cognitive skill (Kendall & Fischler, 1984) and maturity (Durlak, Fuhrman, & Lampman, 1991) may be factors in the problem-solving, behavioral-adjustment equation. In their literature review, Durlak et al. found that more advanced children benefitted more than less advanced children from treatment.

A final and critical consideration is the appropriateness of this training for special populations such as urban learners and students with learning disabilities or behavior disorders. Although Spivack and Shure (1974) report favorable results with urban preschool children, they identify language difficulties as a potential interference. For successful implementation, Spivack and Shure found it necessary to develop vocabulary, word meaning, and language concepts such as the understanding of conditional If . . . , then . . . statements.

Beyond language, however, some researchers (Olexa & Forman, 1984; Weissberg et al., 1981) point out difficulties with urban populations due to the tendency for these children to generate more aggressive behavior alternatives as part of training procedures geared toward identifying a variety of alternative solutions. Under these conditions, problem solving was considered to be counterproductive: aggressive, maladaptive pupil behaviors seemed to increase in proportion to training. This phenomenon provides support for emphasizing quality of alternatives over quantity (Amish et al., 1988; Hopper & Kirshchenbaum, 1979; Neel et al., 1990). It may be necessary, under such conditions, for trainers to exercise more control so that aggressive, antisocial alternatives are minimized and prosocial solutions are maximized. If, indeed, aggressive alternatives are causing negative behaviors to escalate, then the reverse also should be true.

In addition, as suggested in Chapter 1, children's beliefs about the relative value of aggressive as opposed to more prosocial alternatives may need to be explored and challenged. Coie and Koeppl (1990) suggest the technique of "reframing" to encourage aggressive children to consider nonaggressive alternatives—for example, interpreting provocation as an attempt to get them to lose their temper and do something to get them into trouble. In this case the child is challenged to resist letting others control him or her.

Hazel, Schumaker, Sherman, and Sheldon-Wildgen (1982) assessed the relative effects of social skills and problem-solving training on adolescents with learning disabilities (LD), adolescents without learning disabilities (non-LD) and adolescents who had been court-adjudicated. They found that although the LD group acquired the social skills to a level comparable with the other two groups, they failed to demonstrate progress in problem solving commensurate with the non-LD and court-adjudicated peers. Amish et al. (1990) found increases in problem-solving abilities did not mediate the social behaviors of students with behavior disorders, causing the authors to speculate that the lack of impulse control interfered with the students' ability to apply their newfound knowledge in conflict situations.

Students' self-management problems have led curriculum developers increasingly to incorporate anger-control and coping strategies into their social skills programs. Lochman, for example, found the combination of stress inoculation, self-instruction, and problem-solving procedures to be effective in improving the adaptive behaviors of aggressive, school-age males (Lochman et al., 1981; Lochman, Burch, Curry, & Lampron, 1984; Lochman & Curry, 1986). Chapter 6 of this book discusses this model with aggressive learners in greater detail. These findings indicate the need for differential application of social problem-solving training with special populations to address the specific needs and differences of the respective groups. These concerns notwithstanding, social problem solving continues to be a promising strategy for increasing social competence. There is an obvious need for a refinement of procedures to assess the effects of interpersonal problem-solving training adequately and to implement the training procedures more discriminantly.

In employing cognitive and affective methods for social skills training, certain considerations and cautions are warranted:

1. Training should be presented in a relaxed rather than rigid manner, establishing rapport and individualizing the curriculum according to the child's developmental and skill levels. For very young children, play may be used as the point of initiating self-instruction training. For example, the trainer might talk his or her way through a skill game and assist the child to perform in a similar manner. In another case, for older children who may be less inclined to reveal their self-statements or to verbalize outwardly, the trainer may use tapes or scenarios of others in problem situations and have the child suggest what the fictional character might be thinking. For the child who has difficulty talking out loud during training, the trainer may monitor self-statements by periodically interrupting the child and ask "What are you saying to yourself?"

2. Due to heavy reliance on language and cognitive abilities, the child with language, cognitive, and attentional deficits may require extensive, systematic instructions before cognitive mediation procedures can be taught. As identified in the discussion on problem-solving strategies, attention must be given to prerequisite skills. After acquiring the basic skills, the child can be involved as a "collaborator" in determining the training procedures to be used. Through questioning, the trainer may get the child to identify an effective self-training strategy rather than imposing one on him or her. The child's own language should be used whenever possible. There is good evidence that this instruction needs to be tailored to meet the unique needs and idiosyncracies of specific populations.

3. One major pitfall encountered in training children in self-talk is that the statements may become mechanical, in which case they are not controlling the maladaptive behavior. To counter this, the trainer should impress on children that they are only to say what they mean. A serious learning climate should be established, possibly placing reinforcing contingencies on behaviors that are commensurate with self-statements.

4. Training can be enhanced by including modeling, behavioral rehearsal, and relaxation techniques. The opportunity to practice modeled cognitions is a critical factor that may determine the effectiveness of the training. Kendall and Morison (1984) stress the importance of integrating cognitive and behavioral methods: "The judicious utilization of cognitive and behavioral methods will maximize treatment efficacy" (pp. 279–280).

5. A final consideration is the quantity of instruction. The various procedures outlined here are designed to be presented over an extended period of time, ideally on a daily basis. Using cognitive approaches, the trainer should be committed to regular instruction. During training, monitoring is important to make certain the child's self-talk and overt actions are congruent and that the child continues to use internal mediators to direct appropriate responses.

Summary

Teaching social skills involves many of the same procedures as teaching academic concepts—that is, exposing the child to a model for imitation, eliciting an imitative response, providing feedback about the correctness of the response, and structuring opportunities for practice. One method for teaching complex social behaviors is through the imitation of a model or social modeling. The social modeling process requires that the learner recognize the value of the behavior to be learned and identify the specific responses that make up that behavior, that the behavior be modeled in a way that is attractive and understandable to the learner, that the learner be provided with opportunities to practice the behavior using various response modes, and that the learner receive feedback on his or her performance from others as well as through self-evaluative procedures. A behavior may be demonstrated, but if the child is unable to conceptualize the responses involved or does not recognize the importance of the behavior, social modeling is unlikely to occur. The trainer should also expect that initial efforts to produce novel behaviors may be awkward and unnatural, with a need for continued practice and feedback.

Thoughts and feelings also are relevant to social skills training. Various approaches have been developed for teaching social perception skills, along with affective and cognitive behavior. The focus of social perception training can involve both verbal and nonverbal communication; it can include training in cognitive role-taking; and it can emphasize training in empathy, often viewed as an extension of role-taking.

Approaches to teaching social skills related to emotions involve the child in recognizing and labeling her or his own feelings and those of others, along with learning socially desirable ways to express emotions. Activities for teaching about feelings also involve helping the child recognize the differences in her or his emotional responses and those of others in similar situations and develop some understanding about the role of thinking processes in generating feeling states. In teaching the child to express emotions in constructive ways, a problem-solving approach can be applied in which the child identifies and role-plays problem situations, alternative responses, and outcomes, along with examining alternative thoughts and feelings that could be associated with the problem.

The use of cognitions in teaching social skills focuses on efforts to structure thinking styles that are functional for directing social behaviors. One area of emphasis is the elimination of irrational, self-defeating, or faulty thought patterns, replacing them with more rational or productive ones. A second focus is the development of structured thought patterns to be used under certain conditions or for specific behaviors—that is, Meichenbaum's stress-inoculation training and self-instructional training. Problem-solving procedures geared toward modifying the child's cognitions help the child analyze social situations accurately and make decisions based on possible alternatives and consequences. Although cognitive models vary, they share a common reliance on language, some prerequisite skills on the part of the learner, and intensive instruction over an extended period of time.

The models this chapter describes are not mutually exclusive. As a matter of fact, most efforts toward social skills instruction employ elements of each of these approaches, and there is good evidence that the most efficacious approaches incorporate all the methods—behavioral, cognitive, and affective.

Chapter *4*

Generalization and Maintenance of Social Skills

Once social skills have been selected, assessed, and successfully taught, the remaining task is to make sure the child can exhibit the skills when and where it is desirable to use them. Social behaviors need to be generalized from the instructional setting to other settings where they would be appropriate, and from interactions with one set of people to others. They also need to be maintained over time. Research reviews related to behavior generalization (Kirby & Bickel, 1988; Landrum & Lloyd, 1992; Stokes & Baer, 1977; Stokes & Osnes, 1986, 1988; 1989) point out that generalization does not automatically occur but needs to be planned and programmed as part of the training process. Some techniques that will be described as effective for generalization include: (1) varying the aspects of training, (2) training mediators, and (3) changing the contingencies of reinforcement.

Aspects of Training

The ways in which social behaviors are taught appear to influence whether the new behaviors will occur in settings beyond the training site and whether they will occur with persons other than the trainer. Two specific strategies for the training process are varying settings for training and varying trainers.

Training in Different Settings

A frequent occurrence in behavior change programs is that newly acquired behaviors are established only in the setting where the child is instructed and do not naturally transfer to other settings. Researchers have found that newly taught behaviors do not automatically generalize from one location to another, such as from home to school (Wahler, 1969), or even within the same environment such as from clinical settings to mainstreamed classrooms (Berler, Gross, & Drabman, 1982). Although exceptions may occur, for the most part social skills learned under one condition will not be expressed elsewhere unless specific steps are taken to program such a transfer. Smith, Young, West, Morgan, and Rhode (1988) used a self-monitoring system to reduce the disruptive and off-task behaviors of three male adolescents with behavior disorders and one female adolescent with learning disabilities. The desired behaviors were produced in the special classroom but did not expand to the regular classroom. Sasso, Melloy, and Kavale (1990) report similar findings— prosocial gains obtained in the special/treatment classroom failed to be reproduced in the mainstreamed classes where no special procedures were put in place by student or teacher.

Stokes and Osnes (1986, 1988) suggest the need to provide "sufficient stimulus exemplars," or to employ multiple training settings and conditions to simulate the diversity that typically occurs in the natural environment. Social skills instructors should first analyze the settings in which the skill is to be emitted and then devise a training plan that will reflect these varied conditions. An example of teaching a skill in multiple settings is provided by Murdock, Garcia, and Hardman (1977) in a study where students with developmental disabilities were taught to articulate words. Each child was taught by one trainer in a small room, by a second trainer in the corner of a regular classroom, and by a third trainer in a learning center for individualized activities. Not only did the children learn to say the words consistently in these settings, but they also generalized the words to other settings where training had not been conducted. A significant aspect of this study was that the behaviors did not begin to generalize to other environments until they were taught in at least two settings.

Analogue Conditions

It is not always possible to provide instruction under natural conditions. The trainer must aim to approximate realistic conditions, including physical surroundings, participants, problems, and encounters closely representative of the ones the learner is most likely to experience in real life (Eisler & Frederiksen, 1980; Favell & Reid, 1988). Walker and Buckley (1974) used a procedure of "equating stimulus conditions": The special class where the behaviors were developed was altered so that it more closely resembled the regular class where students were expected to manifest these behaviors. Changes included increasing the workload and using social rather than tangible reinforcers.

In a study to reduce aggressive behaviors in two adolescent males, Knapczyk (1988) illustrates another means for instructing for multiple settings. Prior to the study, the generalization settings were identified (i.e., special class, shop class, and gym class) and the respective environments were analyzed to determine behavioral standards set by nonaggressive peers and the requisite social skills needed by target students for successful adjustment in each situation. Training involved the use of three 10-minute videotapes depicting each of the settings. Model students were used as actors to demonstrate both the undesired behavior typical of the target student in the respective settings and the socially appropriate alternative response. Three days of videotaped instruction were followed by five days of teacher monitoring, reinforcement, and corrective feedback in the generalization settings. The videotapes eliminated the need to provide instruction in each setting, and aggressive behaviors were reduced for both students in all three class situations.

While learning to generalize, the child must learn to discriminate according to environmental stimulus conditions, and these skills need to be explicit in the instructional program. To illustrate, one uses different greetings to authority figures, such as teachers, peers, and family members, and different communication styles in the academic classroom than in the gym. A particular advantage of the Knapczyk procedure just described is that it allowed the trainer to note and visually depict the salient features of each setting so students could learn to alter their behavior according to the unique social demands found in each situation.

When teaching for transfer, the social skills trainer should structure the procedures to ensure the child's behavior is controlled by explicit aspects of the training, not incidental factors. In a study with children with autism, Rincover and Koegel (1975) found that behaviors learned in instructional settings failed to transfer to a second setting because the children were responding to incidental stimuli, such as the trainer's hand movements instead of his verbal commands. When these unintentional behaviors were introduced into the second setting, the children responded as they had under treatment conditions. An important consideration with this study is that, although the desired responses were produced, they were not under the control of the intended stimulus.

These findings emphasize the importance of analyzing the social skills instructional situation to ensure that the child's behavior is being triggered by the appropriate social stimuli. A child, for example, may learn to make assertive responses only in the presence of a supportive peer group, or a child may depend on certain nonverbal behaviors, such as eye contact from the teacher, to signal actions such as making appropriate greetings. When these cues are lacking, the child may be less inclined to make assertive responses or appropriate greetings even though the behaviors are dictated by the situation.

Stokes and Osnes (1986) specify the need to program common physical stimuli that will cue the desired responses into the training and generalization settings. To be most effective, they suggest that these stimuli be associated with some reinforcer and be able to be easily transported across environments. In an example provided by Cartledge and Kleefeld (1991), a teacher who is trying to show her students constructive reactions to peer teasing might incorporate a chain link made with plastic paper clips into her instruction. Students are instructed that ignoring and other constructive behaviors are signs of strength, not weakness, and just as the chain gets stronger with each link, they get better each time they respond appropriately to unkind peer actions (Cartledge & Kleefeld, 1991). During instruction, each correct enactment is rewarded by praise and a plastic link/clip, to be exchanged for points or backup reinforcers following the instructional session. After terminating instruction, a visual reminder—a bulletin board with a picture of a chain link/clip and sign—of possible reactions like the following might be displayed:

When someone says something that is unkind, show how strong you are by

- Ignoring and walking away, *or*
- Telling them why you didn't like what they said, *or,* if necessary,
- Getting help from the teacher.

Smaller versions of this sign might be posted in generalization settings, including hallways, lunchrooms, and gyms, where the staff are trained and authorized to dispense points (which are later converted to real or pictured links/clips) to students who respond appropriately. Over time the use of clips and tangible rewards gradually would be faded, but the visual cues and praise would be retained.

To introduce a broader range of stimuli similar to real-life conditions, the instructional setting should vary according to group constellation and size, allowing for different responses and environmental conditions. The most effective training conditions (i.e., individual or group) are determined primarily by the behaviors to be learned, the child's skill level, and the natural conditions under which the child will have to perform the behavior (Phillips, 1978). For example, the child learning to talk in class should receive instruction in large groups; however, it may be necessary to conduct training sessions that gradually move the child from individual to large group settings. On the other hand, small-group instruction may be necessary for the child being taught to engage in conversation with a peer.

Training with Different People

To avoid the possibility that new behaviors will remain under the control of one trainer and will fail to generalize, as in the Rincover and Koegel (1975) study described earlier, use more than one trainer. Two trainers can alternate in sessions, keeping conditions similar but requiring the child to respond to the social situation rather than the trainer. A study by Stokes, Baer, and Jackson (1974) illustrates this point: More than one trainer was used to teach institutionalized, mentally retarded children to greet others by waving. The first trainer, using prompting and shaping procedures, taught the child to make the greeting response. A second trainer was used when probes revealed no generalization or only transitory generalization to other staff members. The researchers found that the greeting response expanded to encompass staff that were not involved in the training most effectively when the child was taught by more than one trainer. This study and others in the research literature point to the need for multiple trainers or models to effect generalization (Gunter, Fox, Brady, Shores, & Cavanaugh, 1988; Stokes & Osnes, 1986). Other members of the child's natural environment, such as teachers, parents, and peers, can be trained to instruct, prompt, and reinforce the desired social behaviors as well.

Teachers

In the Smith et al. (1988) study on self-monitoring mentioned earlier, the authors attributed the failure of the behaviors to generalize to the mainstreamed classroom partially to the fact that the teachers in these classrooms did not consistently match the students' self-ratings. Although the time and skill the teachers needed to complete these ratings were minimal, researchers may have underestimated the investment required to engage teachers successfully in collaborative efforts to develop social skills.

Walker and Buckley (1974) found instructions to mainstreamed teachers in behavior modification procedures to be less effective than precise descriptions, discussion of the procedures, and periodic classroom visits to provide direct assistance. For example, in a maintenance strategy, the teacher was given detailed information on the child's academic materials, reinforcement system, and exactly how the reinforcement program for academic and social behaviors should be implemented.

Parents

The first and perhaps most important teacher for each child is the parent. Increasingly, researchers recognize the importance of the parents' role, and in recent years more attention has been given to parent involvement to facilitate behavior generalization. Parents often are unaware of the specific social skills needed by their children to be successful in other environments, the specific skill deficits of their children, or the most effective ways to develop the desired behaviors. Furthermore, parent actions inadvertently may be at cross purposes with the development of certain social skills. Schreibman (1988), for example, describes a study where parents of children with autism were helped to increase the verbal behavior of their children. During baseline it was observed that the parents requested that their children respond more nonverbally than verbally. The treatment, involving increases in parent verbalizations to their children and requests for verbal responses from their children, resulted in greater verbal imitations, verbal responses, and spontaneous speech by all the children.

Often extensive parent instruction is not possible; however, at the very least, parents should be informed of the skills being taught, the importance of these skills to their child's overall development, and actions they may take to assist in the development of these behaviors. This information may be transmitted through brief meetings and daily/weekly communication forms. Wiig and Bray (1983) coordinated teacher and parent instruction of prosocial communication skills in young children by providing a "home activity sheet" that corresponded with each social communication skill taught in the classroom. The sheet included instructions to parents and a series of home-based activities designed to reinforce the target social communication skill.

Peers

Along with significant adults in the child's life, the peer group can be used to provide social skills training and maintenance. Peers offer special advantages because they generally are found in both training and generalization settings (Stokes & Baer, 1977; Stokes & Osnes, 1986; 1988). Children exercise considerable control over each other, and in many cases it is critical to enlist their involvement in social skills instruction. Consider, for example, the child whose peers reward verbal and physical aggression—behaviors that may be incompatible with the social skills being taught. In their review of the empirical literature, Mathur and Rutherford (1991) conclude that peer-mediated interventions could effect positive behavior change and produce lasting results, given systematic programming for generalization.

One form of peer-mediated intervention involves using multiple competent peers as models or participants during social skills instruction. Gunter et al. (1988) used eight typically developing, intermediate-aged students as participants in developing peer interaction skills in two same-aged students with autism. During social skills instruction, the teacher verbally and physically prompted each autistic student to initiate an interaction with one of four nondisabled peers. The competent peer responded to this initiation and continued to interact as long as the target student persisted. As a result of these procedures, one target student began to initiate spontaneously with peers without disabilities who had not served as trainers and in nontraining settings.

Fowler (1988) presents three models of peer-mediated interventions that emphasize supervision or monitoring by peers. In the first form, *subject as client,* peers are trained to monitor and consequate the behavior of a target student with significant skill deficits. In one study described by Fowler, a student with negative peer interaction rates was alternately monitored by six socially skilled classmates. Training for the target student and the monitors consisted of role-playing positive and negative interactions, as well as disbursing points and fines to the target student for positive and negative behaviors. Following training, the monitors assumed responsibility on a rotating basis for supervising the client's behavior during recess. Generalization occurred across conditions, that is, A.M. recess, P.M. recess, and noon, as treatment conditions were introduced. The effects were maintained three months after treatment conditions were removed, and negative reactions from peers decreased substantially.

In the second model presented by Fowler, the student serves both as *subject and therapist.* In this format, students with behavior problems alternate between being monitored by peers and serving as the peer monitor for other students. In the reported study, these procedures were effective in reducing the disruptive behaviors of six students with learning and behavior disorders.

The third model, *subject as therapist,* uses students with significant skill deficits to monitor the behaviors of other, more skilled students. According to Fowler, this intervention was effective in reducing the negative peer interactions for three first-grade males. For two of the three students, however, baseline interactions returned once treatment conditions were removed. Based on her review of these and other studies, Fowler concludes that peer-mediated interventions are likely to produce more durable treatment effects and generalize across subjects, but less often across settings.

Group contingencies are another means for encouraging peer support and getting desired behaviors to generalize. Walker and Buckley (1974) employed *peer programming procedures,* where the target child, on making the desired responses, was able to earn a specified number of points to be exchanged for a reward for the entire class. The objective was to make it profitable for the peer group or other members of the child's environment to support and reward appropriate rather than inappropriate behaviors. This was a group-oriented contingency, the type described by Greenwood and Hops (1981) as a *dependent* system. In their research review, Greenwood and Hops determined the most effective group-oriented systems to be *interdependent* systems, in which contingencies are based on the ability of the group as an aggregate to meet some preestablished criterion or goal.

Lew and Mesch (1984) used an interdependent group-oriented contingency to help students improve their academic and social behavior. Less academically and socially competent subjects were assigned to small groups with more competent peers. The combination of performance standards and contingent reinforcement was found to improve social interaction and academic achievement. The effects were maintained for most subjects, even after contingencies were removed.

Salend, Whittaker, and Reeder (1992) described another type of interdependent, peer-mediated group system. Pairing self-management and group contingency procedures, the researchers trained middle-school students with learning and behavior disorders to use self-evaluations to manage their talk-out behavior. The students were divided into teams of four. They were taught to evaluate the presence and absence of the target behavior and rate their team's talk-out behavior on a six-point scale (0 to 5), representing a range from excellent to unacceptable. At specified intervals the teams collaborated and submitted a group rating. Students were rewarded according to the frequency of talk-out behavior during that interval and how closely the team's rating matched that of the teacher. Student talk-outs were reduced substantially during treatment periods.

In employing group-oriented contingency systems, the social skills trainer should attend to the following factors:

- Make sure that reasonably attainable goals are established. Goals that are set too high initially may be frustrating, giving little incentive to try. As progress is made, goals may be raised gradually.
- Make sure that target children (in dependent systems) do not become victims, receiving punishment for inadequate responses instead of praise and encouragement for approximations.
- Make sure that the peer group understands what the target behaviors are and exactly how to provide support and encouragement. Peer understanding may be developed through instruction sessions that include role-playing the target behaviors and appropriate peer responses.
- Make sure that rewards to be earned are highly desired by the group. Program

rewards should be faded gradually once the behaviors appear to have stabilized and become maintained and supported largely by social and other natural reinforcers.

Although peers have been shown to be effective behavior-change agents, a review of the research regarding peer effects on withdrawn children's maintenance and generalization of social interaction behaviors reveals that peers still interact minimally with these children (Strain, Kerr, & Ragland, 1981). Studies show that when trained children are returned to natural environments, competent children do not automatically interact with and reinforce their less competent peers. These findings led Strain et al. to advocate more extensive intervention strategies, such as structuring peer social systems, similar to those described earlier, to create peer environments more supportive of trained subjects. Another recommendation (Strain et al., 1981) was to train skill-deficient children in social skills more consistent with those of their more competent peers.

Bierman and Furman (1984) provide supportive evidence for this position. In their study, preadolescent children either (1) were coached individually on conversation skills, (2) were engaged in a group experience, (3) received coaching and the group experience, or (4) received no treatment. Coaching was found to increase and maintain conversation skills. Peer acceptance, however, was found to persist only among subjects trained in the groups with competent peers. According to the authors, another contributing factor was the use of a "superordinate goal" as part of the group experience. The children were informed that they were to work together on a group project, that is, "make friendly interaction films for the university" (p. 155). Collaborating on this larger goal appeared to promote positive peer attitudes, which were enhanced by the improved conversation skills of the skill-deficient subjects. Thus, peers may be instrumental in behavior maintenance and generalization, if the social skills taught parallel those of the more competent peers, if competent children are included in training sessions, and if conditions enhancing group cooperation are established.

Several investigators emphasize the importance of instructing surrogate trainers, such as peers (Fowler, 1988; Salend et al., 1992) and parents (Schreibman, 1988), to help bring about generalized behaviors. More than one researcher (e.g., Gunter et al., 1988; Smith et al., 1988) attributed generalization failure, at least partially to lack of skill or will on the part of these auxillary trainers. Therefore, the training of other social skills trainers should not be underestimated. The following guidelines for instruction are adapted from Gelfand and Hartmann (1975):

1. Generally outline the instructional program.
2. Provide trainees with a written description of the instructional session, and invite them to observe your training.
3. Following observation, discuss procedures in detail.
4. If necessary, provide additional observations.
5. Rehearse training sessions through role-play where the trainee provides instruction.

6. Observe trainee's social skills instruction of child.

7. Provide corrective feedback either during or following session.

8. Provide tape recordings of training sessions for the trainee to listen to and practice.

Gelfand and Hartmann (1984) also note the importance of varying training examples. Real-life events rarely occur exactly as presented under treatment conditions. Therefore, children need the opportunity to respond to a variety of examples to avoid rigid, situation-specific behavior. In teaching parents to increase the speech of their children with autism, Laski, Charlop, and Schreibman (1988) found a task-variation procedure, such as using the same word with different referents (e.g., "open" the door and "open" the box), contributed to generalization. Similarly, in teaching a set of social interaction behaviors, such as dealing with conflict, the child needs to be presented with a variety of possible problem situations and learn an array of adaptive responses for any one event.

Training Mediators

A promising approach to programming for generalization is developing cognitive mediators to assist the child in maintaining appropriate behaviors in settings, times, and conditions beyond those explicitly involved in training. According to Bandura (1977b), response patterns are represented in memory and retained in symbolic form primarily through imagery and verbalization. Behavior learned through observation is acquired and retained more effectively with mental and verbal rehearsal in addition to behavioral rehearsal. A number of questions have been raised (Franks & Wilson, 1978) about the utility of cognitive strategies for generalization. Yet others (e.g., Meichenbaum, 1977; Stokes & Baer, 1977; Stokes & Osnes, 1986) see the development of cognitive mediators as having considerable potential, particularly when they are deliberately programmed as strategies for generalization.

Language as a Mediator

Because most cognitive processes are verbal rather than visual, language is the mediator most often involved in training for generalization. Stokes and Baer (1977) point out that language serves as a common stimulus "to be carried from any training setting to any generalization setting that the child may ever enter" (p. 361). A simple method for using language as a mediator is having the child state what she or he did or might do while engaging in a social behavior. For example, the child learning to exhibit appropriate behavior after winning a game might verbally list these responses:

1. After my partner congratulates me, I will say, "Thank you" and smile.

2. I will compliment him for playing a good game.

3. Then, I will ask him if he wants to play another game.

4. If he says "yes," I will let him go first.

Statements of this kind will be effective, however, only if they represent real actions on the part of the child. Stokes and Osnes (1986) emphasize the importance of bringing the child's behavior under the control of the child's language, through procedures such as *correspondence training*—the child is rewarded for truthful reports of social behavior. Clark, Caldwell, and Christian (1979) provide an example of this procedure in a study using self-reports to generalize conversation skills to other settings. Children who had been taught conversation skills in the classroom were directed to practice these skills during lunch period. Following lunch, the students indicated on a questionnaire whether they had made certain responses; for example, "Did I ask a classmate about his or her mom, dad, brother, or sister?" The accuracy of these reports was ascertained through a video monitoring system that taped the children during lunch. Rewards were given for making the desired statements at lunchtime and truthfully reporting them. According to the authors, the combination of accurate self-reports and delayed reinforcement were effective in maintaining conversational skills. In another study, Barton and Ascione (1979) found that sharing behavior among young children persisted and generalized only when children were taught to use language to accompany their sharing.

Self-instruction and problem-solving cognitive approaches also show promise for behavior generalization. Because these procedures employ language to develop problem-solving strategies, it is reasoned that the skills developed will be more lasting and more easily transferred to a variety of situations and behaviors. In a review of self-instruction research with children, Kendall (1978) concludes treatment that stresses "metacognitive development" (i.e., awareness of one's thinking processes) is most likely to lead to generalization. Meichenbaum (1977) presents evidence that self-instruction for behavior generalization and durability was more effective when the training required overt, rather than covert, self-instructions and the training was conducted over extensive periods of time. A variation of self- instruction is the stress-inoculation model (see Chapter 3), which Meichenbaum presents as a proce-dure explicitly developed for generalization training.

Support for problem solving's effects in facilitating behavior generalization can be seen in a study by Park and Gaylord-Ross (1989), where three students with mental retardation were taught job-related social communication skills. The training consisted of role-playing and problem solving, but the latter proved much more effective in causing behaviors to endure and generalize to the work setting. The basis for this success may have been the reliance on the decision making and extensive verbali-zations inherent in problem-solving procedures. It should be noted, however, that in this study students were required to act out desired behaviors as part of the problem-solving process, and it may be that cognitive approaches were enhanced by behavioral rehearsal.

Therefore, multimethod strategies are probably most effective for this purpose. Other researchers have used combinations of these cognitive interventions to produce generalized behaviors from clinical settings to the classroom (Kendall & Braswell, 1985), from school to home (Lochman et al., 1984), and from residential settings to the classroom (Maag, Parks, & Rutherford, 1988).

A somewhat different perspective on language is provided in a series of studies on functional communication for individuals with severe disabilities by Durand and Carr (Carr & Durand, 1985; Durand & Carr, 1987; Durand & Carr, 1991). The intervention involved teaching students specific speech acts as alternatives for previously held nonproductive, "challenging" behaviors. If a student previously used inappropriate behavior to escape difficult tasks, for example, the student was taught to ask for assistance. In one study, Durand and Carr (1991) used teacher modeling and prompting to replace challenging behaviors with requests for teacher assistance such as "Help me" or "I don't understand." The newly taught behaviors spontaneously generalized to other settings and were maintained for periods of up to two years. The researchers attribute this finding to the fact that they ". . . were successful in choosing behaviors [the communicative responses] that elicited maintaining contingencies" (p. 262).

Similar effects of instruction in social communication skills are reported in a study where three students with moderate disabilities were taught to initiate and expand on conversations with nondisabled peers (Haring, Roger, Lee, Breen, & Gaylord-Ross, 1986). Prior to intervention, the researchers assessed the mainstreamed student population for typical initiation and expansion statements. This information was used as the basis for training the target students and, according to the researchers, partially accounted for the durability of these behaviors and their transfer to natural settings.

These and other studies suggest that the generalization properties of language may be programmed not only to mediate behavior across conditions but to effect natural contingencies of reinforcement as well. That is, appropriate social communication is likely to be reciprocated by others, and thereby serve as a reinforcer, helping to maintain new behaviors.

Expectations as Mediators

A further cognitive mediational variable related to generalization is expectations. Bandura (1977a) speaks of *efficacy expectations* as "the conviction that one can successfully execute the behavior required to produce the outcomes" (p. 103). The greater the self-belief, the more likely one will set high standards and be motivated to achieve them (Bandura & Jourden, 1991). Bandura (1977a) suggests that efficacy expectations are generated through (1) *performance accomplishments*—awareness of one's actual successful performance; (2) *vicarious experience*—awareness of other's successful performance; (3) *verbal persuasion*—*suggestions and exhortations from others or from oneself;* and (4) *reducing emotional arousal*—the ability to apply various means of controlling emotions in stressful situations.

Applying these dimensions to the generalization of social skills, the teacher or clinician can enhance the child's expectations of future success by

- Training in actual skills,
- Providing examples of successful models,
- Suggesting through discussion and other verbal means how the learning of social behaviors will be helpful in the future,

- Engaging the child in various kinds of learning to develop feelings of competence in stressful interpersonal situations.

Through role-play and discussion, expectations can be established about the kinds of situations in which the social skills will be appropriate in the future.

An example of verbal persuasion can be seen in a study conducted by Katz and Vinceguerra (1980). While attempting to change reinforcement schedules, the researchers found that task-related behaviors were best maintained when the student received statements stressing his or her ability and personal competence. The learner was more likely to stay on-task when told "You're doing such a good job, I don't think you need as many tokens today," as opposed to "I can't give you as many tokens today because I ran out," or when not given any reason for the absence of tokens.

Bandura and Jourdan's (1991) study with college students in a business administration class shows the effects of social comparison on self-efficacy and performance. The students were assigned a set of problems related to managerial decision-making. Following each trial, students were given a score on the efficiency of their own strategy and that of a comparative group. The latter score may not have been truthful, depending on the student's experimental group. The students also were required to indicate periodically how confident they felt in their performance and their commitment to the task. Students given feedback indicating progressive mastery displayed the highest levels of self-confidence, greatest increases in task performance, and the highest level of self-satisfaction. In contrast, students consistently receiving comparative feedback higher than their own performance showed a steady decline in their self-efficacy and evidenced lowered analytic strategies and self-satisfaction.

In developing social skills, the teacher can emphasize the child's successeš and increasing mastery rather than concentrating on failures or noting the superior performance of peers. Teachers also should try to program success experiences for newly-taught skills. The child learning to initiate activities with peers, for example, could be assigned to make such requests first of fellow students who are skilled and prepared to reciprocate appropriately.

Related to self-efficacy is the concept of attributions, which refers to the reasons an individual gives for various personal experiences. Failing a major exam, for example, may be attributed to external events such as bad luck or teacher dislike or to internal events like lack of competence. Children who internalize, attributing behavior change to personal efforts, are more amenable to social skills intervention and behavior generalization than those who externalize (Glenwick & Jason, 1984; Kendall & Braswell, 1985). Glenwick and Jason (1984) point out that a greater sense of self-control can be developed in children through strategies that create a gradual movement from external contingencies toward self-management.

Contingencies of Reinforcement

The maintenance of social behaviors, once they have been taught, also is referred to as *resistance to extinction, durability,* or *generalization over time.* The principal factors supporting maintenance of social skills over time are the contingencies of reinforcement operating in the settings where the social skills would be expressed. The learning of social skills is facilitated by reinforcement and feedback. From their analysis of generalization and maintenance in studies with preschool children, Chandler, Lubeck, and Fowler (1992) observe behavior change strategies incorporating reinforcement—that is, prompting plus reinforcement and reinforcement plus feedback—to be most effective in promoting behavior generalization. According to these authors, "combinations of antecedent and consequence strategies may be more likely to produce generalization because they address both ends of the three-term contingency (antecedents, behaviors, and consequences)" (p. 421).

For generalization to occur, the nature of reinforcement needs to be changed, and there are a number of ways this can happen. The sources of reinforcement can be changed, particularly from external to intrinsic sources of reward; the ways in which reinforcement is given can be changed; and the kinds of rewards provided can be changed.

Changing the Timing of Reinforcement

In the process of teaching new social behaviors, reinforcement needs to be provided immediately on a continuous basis for correct responses. Once behaviors are learned, behavior will occur most readily over time if the timing or schedule for reinforcement is "thinned" to occasional reinforcement provided on an intermittent and unpredictable basis. Stokes and Baer (1977) suggest introducing noncontingent reinforcement, even "random or haphazard" delivery of reinforcement to assist in generalization, with the goal of establishing conditions in which the subject "cannot discriminate in which settings a response will be reinforced or not reinforced" (p. 358).

Fowler and Baer (1981) report on a study conducted with preschool children to assess the effects of delayed reinforcement on behavior generalization. The subjects in this study were instructed to perform various social behaviors such as making statements of praise or sharing with peers. Although rewards were provided only for responses made during one (contingent) period of the schoolday, the investigators found that these behaviors were more likely to generalize to other (noncontingent) times if rewards and feedback were delayed until the end of the schoolday, approximately one-half to two-and-one-half hours later. The authors attributed the generalization effect primarily to the fact that the children were unable to discriminate between the contingent and noncontingent conditions. That is, the subjects felt they had to make the targeted responses all day to receive the desired reward. Thus, the use of delayed reinforcement in addition to assisting in the generalization of sources of reinforcement from one set of persons to others, also assists in thinning reinforcement schedules.

Rhode, Morgan, and Young (1983) provide another example in which reinforcement thinning and self-evaluation procedures were used to program behavior from a special education resource room to a regular classroom. In the resource room, students were taught to evaluate themselves and self-administer points, initially every

15 minutes. This schedule was gradually thinned to self-evaluation every 30 minutes. At this point, the procedures were transferred to the regular classroom, where self-evaluation proceeded systematically so that students provided themselves with points only every two days, then no points, then only verbal self-evaluation, and ultimately no overt, but possibly private self-evaluations.

A study conducted by Sullivan and O'Leary (1990) points out the need to attend to the reinforcement system that will produce the greatest returns when attempting to fade reinforcers and maintain treatment effects. The authors suggest that fading response cost procedures, rather than reward programs, might produce more durable behavioral change. In their study with 10 elementary-aged children, they employed a reward system where the children could earn up to four tokens during a twenty-minute academic period, depending on task-appropriate behavior. At different times with the same children they also used response cost, wherein students were given four tokens each day that they could lose, if warranted, at the point of teacher evaluation. The researchers found response-cost and reward systems equally effective in increasing on-task behaviors; however, maintenance of gains was greater for the response-cost procedures.

These findings were attributed to the more discernable differences when fading the reward program. For example, the average daily rates of contingent token delivery per child during the first treatment and fading conditions were .6 and .2 for the response-cost program but 3.2 and 1.2 for the reward program. During the fading process, Sullivan and O'Leary argue that the more obvious reductions in rewards and feedback might have been more disruptive to the children, particularly those with hyperactive/aggressive disorders, whose abnormal demands for rewards caused their behaviors to be more vulnerable to extinction. Whether using positive or negative systems, the fading of reinforcement conditions needs to be programmed so gradually that the process is nearly imperceptible to the learner, especially those with special needs.

Use of contingency contracts (Dardig & Heward, 1980; DeRisi & Butz, 1975; Guevremont, Osnes, & Stokes, 1988; Homme, Csanyi, Gonzales, & Rechs, 1969; Kanfer, 1975) can be an aid to generalization and maintenance of social skills, because contracts provide a means by which rewards can be delayed and the source of reinforcement changed from one person to another. Further, the existence of a contract can serve as a reminder for children to engage in the target behaviors beyond the training setting. The contract can be made between the child and the trainer, with rewards provided in the training setting for target behaviors to be carried out in another setting. It also could be established between the parent and child, with the trainer serving as negotiator for the target behaviors to be performed in the home. The contract can be verbal or written, formal or informal, but a written contract, signed and witnessed, may be taken more seriously by all participants. A further advantage of the contingency contract is the potential for the child to set her or his own rewards and criteria for reinforcement, thus moving the social behaviors closer to maintenance by self-reinforcement.

A social skills-related contingency contract should have the following compo-nents: (1) a clearly defined social behavior, so all concerned can agree whether it has occurred; (2) performance criteria for the behavior—that is, how much of the behavior has to occur to earn the payoff and under what circumstances it should occur; (3) the reward to be provided when criteria are met and who provides the reward; and (4) a means of determining whether the reward has been earned. Homme et al. (1969) provide some criteria for a successful contingency contract:

- The contract reward should be immediate at first;
- Initial contracts should reward small steps;
- The contract should be fair;
- The terms of the contract should be clear;
- The contract should be honest (i.e., carried out immediately according to the specified terms);
- The contract should be positive.

Changing the Nature of Reinforcement

Types of external reinforcement vary from social reinforcement (i.e., praise, smiles, positive attention, positive physical contact), to various forms of tangible reinforcers (i.e., food or toys), to generalized conditioned reinforcers (i.e., tokens or points that can stand for a variety of reinforcing events).

The work of Premack (1959) establishes that almost any high-rate, presumably more preferred, activity can serve as a reinforcer for a low-rate, presumably less preferred, activity. Because reinforcement is defined by its positive effect on behavior, effective reinforcers cannot always be predicted in advance. Determine what kinds of rewards will encourage the child to engage in social skills training or perform the social behavior he or she has learned. The child who can progress from a need for immediate edible rewards, to a token exchange system, to behavior maintained by social rewards, is considered to have become more highly socialized. If social skills instruction begins initially with tangible reinforcers, maintenance over time will be enhanced if the trainer moves toward the use of social reinforcement because praise, smiles, and attention are potentially available in almost all settings. If social rewards do not serve as reinforcers initially, they can take on reinforcing value if they are paired with whatever is actually reinforcing to the child.

Gelfand and Hartmann (1975, 1984) suggest exaggerating the praise and smiles at first so the child will attend to them, then gradually eliminate the artificial reinforcement, maintaining the behaviors with occasional praise or some other natural contingency. Social and backup reinforcers are also recommended to sustain interest and motivation and to simulate real-life situations.

Changing the Source of Reinforcement

Rewards for social behaviors come primarily from persons in the external world or from intrinsic sources: The satisfaction inherent in behaving in approved ways. The *Relevance of Behavior Rule* of Allyon and Azrin (1968) states, "Teach only those behaviors that will continue to be reinforced after training." If social skills are taught with attention to some of the criteria outlined in Chapter 1, especially the need for social validity in selection of skills, persons in the natural environment will respond in ways that keep the behaviors going. Social skills are, by most definitions, behaviors that will be reinforced by others. Skills, such as positive approaches to others, conversation skills, problem-solving skills, and ability to express emotion constructively, are all behaviors to which others will generally respond positively. As Phillips (1978) points out: "Social skills . . . imply reciprocity, interaction, and mutual reinforcement" (p. 8). Several authors (Kohler & Greenwood, 1986; McConnell, 1987; Stokes & Baer, 1977; Stokes & Osnes, 1988) speak of *behavioral traps* or entrapment—teaching entry responses that expose the child to a community of natural reinforcers. For example, providing an isolated child with the skills to make friends may open up new opportunities for positive experiences.

Although many social skills may, by their nature, evoke maintaining responses from the external environment, some planning and programming for generalization and maintenance through altered reinforcement may be necessary. It may be necessary at first, for example, to program a change in reinforcement source, from the teacher or therapist to persons in the child's larger environment. Enlisting the support of parents, peers, and other relevant people in the child's life is necessary to transfer social behaviors taught in the school or clinic to the wider environment. As Baer (1981) points out, the success of such programs is seriously jeopardized if the significant others in the child's life are not in agreement with the child's changed behavior.

With a focus on peers, McConnell (1987) argues that skill-deficit children are most likely to be caught in a community of naturally occurring reinforcers if the target skills lend themselves to peer reinforcement and if the behaviors are taught in a context of peer-mediated systems such as those described earlier in this chapter. Kohler and Greenwood (1986) provide an in-depth discussion of peer-based behavioral traps, pointing out that trainers should not automatically assume that these natural contingencies are in place. McConnell, Sisson, Cort, and Strain (1991) increased the response rates of both target children and their peers, but peer interactions failed to occur and result in behavioral trapping.

Through an analysis of the environment, as suggested by Kohler and Greenwood, one can determine if behavioral reciprocity is occurring and a functional relationship can be ascertained by controlling peer responses and assessing their effect on the target behavior. If the relationship is found to exist, the same peer contingencies can be applied to other behaviors. For example, as noted in one peer tutoring study (Kohler, Greenwood, & Baer, 1985), peer assistance, praise, and prompts by a few student tutors favorably influence tutee responding and achievement. The subsequent classwide application of these procedures produced similar results, verifying the presence and efficacy of peer contingencies.

In transferring reinforcement to the home or another setting, the social skills trainer needs to assess the parents' or others' ability to provide positive feedback. Inform the parents or others that, for example, "Our social skill of the week is paying compliments. Please respond positively when John says something nice to you, even if he is not very smooth about it," or "John will bring home a feedback slip. Please mark a point on it whenever he makes a positive comment to someone." A program to transfer the source of reinforcement can start with reinforcement provided in the training setting, based on behavior emitted there. Reinforcement can continue in the training setting, given on a delayed basis from data provided by the home. Then reinforcement can transfer to the home, based on behaviors expressed in the home.

A program using such a transfer of reinforcement was carried out by Jewett and Clark (1976): Conversational skills were taught in preschool then practiced at home during the evening meal. Audiotapes were made of the mealtime conversation and scored the next day, with a snack provided at school as a reinforcer for children who had used the trained comments at home during the previous evening meal. Ultimately, the entire program was transferred to the home.

Many parents may be able to provide praise and other reinforcers easily, possibly initiating contingency contracts to maintain social behaviors. For parents without the skills to provide contingent reinforcement, it may be necessary to build parent training into the social skills training program. Chapter 6 of this book discusses parent training.

Another way to transfer the source of reinforcement from the therapist or teacher to others in the natural environment is to provide the child with skills to elicit reinforcement as a means of learning to recruit a natural community of reinforcers to maintain or generalize behaviors (Stokes & Baer, 1977; Stokes & Osnes, 1988). To be able to self-reinforce (discussed below) and to use verbal mediators, the child needs to be able to recognize when she or he has done something praiseworthy and learn how to call others' attention to it in a way that encourages positive responses.

Seymour and Stokes (1976) report a study in which adolescent girls in an institutional setting were trained, through discussion and role-playing, how to cue staff to provide praise for their work improvement. When using this approach, try to develop cohorts in the environment who are willing to reward the child's positive remarks about herself or himself, because this behavior has some risks of being misused or misunderstood by others.

A procedure that combines several elements (i.e., practice in other settings, teaching the child to elicit reinforcement, and transferring reinforcement to others) involves giving the child a card or feedback slip to carry after he or she has learned a skill. As the child moves through the school or other environments, he or she is instructed to watch for opportunities to practice the target skill, then present the card to an available adult to mark confirmation that the behavior was performed satisfactorily.

This technique is useful in a setting where the relevant adults can be informed in advance that the children in Miss Jones's class are practicing giving compliments and will be carrying feedback slips, and that it would be helpful for the adults to mark the card and provide social reinforcement for a good attempt at a compliment. Later, the teacher or therapist can ask the child to describe verbally each of the compliments paid, and he or she can be reinforced again for the report.

Developing Self-management Skills

Perhaps the most effective source for reinforcement is the child. Self-management appears to be one of the more promising means by which behaviors can be maintained over time. Bandura (1977b) regards the ability to regulate one's behavior by self-produced consequences as the highest level of performance in the developmental hierarchy of incentives, and refers to self-reward as a "generalizable skill in self-regulation that can be used continually" (p. 144). The ability to self-regulate can be regarded as a social skill that has the following component parts: (1) adopting standards by which performance is to be evaluated, (2) monitoring one's behavior, (3) evaluating one's performance according to the standards set, and (4) providing self-reinforcement based on the degree to which the behavior meets performance standards.

Adopting Standards

Establishing standards or goal setting can be an extremely powerful tool: It may contribute to motivation and help the learner concentrate on what is to be accomplished and the corresponding strategy to be used to achieve the goal (Graham, Harris, & Reid, 1992). From the related literature, Graham et al. (1992) identify several components needed for effective goal setting. First, goals should be *specific* rather than general or vague. "Initiating at least one play activity with peers at recess," for example, provides greater useful specificity than simply "increasing social interactions with peers."

A second consideration pertains to goal *difficulty.* The goal should be sufficiently difficult to make it challenging and create the incentive to want to achieve, but, on the other hand, it should be reasonably attainable so the learner does not give up before trying. An extremely withdrawn child who has not yet mastered responding to the approach behavior of peers, for example, may find a goal of initiating peer activities too advanced for his or her current social development level. Perhaps a more realistic goal for this child would be to make at least one appropriate response to a peer initiation daily.

Proximity of goals is a third factor Graham et al. identify. Proximal goals, which are to be achieved soon (compared to distal goals to be accomplished in the future), are likely to result in greater productivity. For example, the learner is more likely to master "making a daily peer contact" than "making a good friend by the end of the academic year."

Goal setting is aided by *feedback,* which may encourage the learner to continue making progress and to increase efforts if necessary. To be most effective, the learner needs to be advised of her or his performance on a regular basis. This helps the learner remain focused on the target behaviors and improve self-evaluation abilities.

Should performance standards be determined by the children or imposed externally? Graham et al. (1992) recommend *participative goal setting,* where the teacher and student jointly engage in goal setting. On the other hand, Felixbrod and O'Leary (1973) found self-determined and externally imposed standards to be equally effective, while Dickerson and Creedon (1981) found that children who establish their own performance standards showed significantly greater academic improvement than others whose standards were set by the teacher.

Dickerson and Creedon also observed that the children in the self-selection group tended to set relatively stringent standards, which the authors speculate contributed to their superior performance. Related studies also found self-determined, more stringent conditions enhanced students' productivity and on-task behaviors (Guevremont et al., 1988; Jones & Evans, 1980).

The durability of treatment gains is a final issue relative to effective goal-setting to enhance self-management skills. Consistent with other such studies, Guevremont et al. (1988) observed a reduction in performance gains once baseline conditions were reinstated. To counter this repeated erosion, the researchers established a contracting procedure where students were prompted to set consistently higher goals and rewarded for meeting these criteria. As a result, following contracting, the children continued to respond at treatment levels and were reported to set more stringent goals.

The research literature indicates that self-determined, exacting standards are important to successful self-management among children, but children need to be prompted and reinforced for setting high and realistic standards that can be operative for superior achievements. Until the child is able to assume this responsibility independently, however, the teacher needs to perform this function cooperatively with the learner, supporting and helping the child become motivated by his or her success. It appears that standard-setting or goal-setting alone can bring about a change in behavior, but for these gains to be maintained beyond treatment conditions the use of reinforcing contingencies may be needed. As noted earlier in this chapter and in the study by Guevremont et al. (1988), contingency contracts can be particularly useful for this purpose.

Self-monitoring

Self-monitoring involves observing and recording one's behavior according to some established standard. It may be used for assessment (see Chapter 2) and/or behavior change. To be effective with children, the procedures need to be kept simple and the directions made clear. Workman (1982, pp. 46–47) gives the following guidelines for employing self-monitoring procedures in the classroom:

1. Determine exactly what student behavior (target behavior) you want to improve.
2. Design and copy the recording sheet you want to use.
3. Make the recording sheets available to your students.
4. Explain to your students exactly what behavior you want them to record, and tell them how you want them to improve.
5. Have the students begin recording and charting their own behavior.

Individual recording forms, such as the one in Figure 4-1, are prepared with the child's name and date and taped to the child's desk to be marked according to specified directions and the criteria established for the target behavior. In making the

Put an X in each square
each time you talk
out without permission.

MONDAY									
TUESDAY									
WEDNESDAY									
THURSDAY									
FRIDAY									

FIGURE 4.1. Sample Self-monitoring Card

Source: Adapted from Workman, 1982, p. 48.

standards explicit and clear, Workman advises that the behavior be defined and posted. For example:

Talking-out means

1. You said something to another student or to the whole class, but
2. You did not raise your hand, and
3. The teacher did not give you permission to speak.

Researchers report self-monitoring procedures to be effective in changing and maintaining desired behaviors (Christie, Hiss, & Lozanoff, 1984; Hughes, Ruhl, & Misra, 1989; Nelson & Hayes, 1981; Nelson, Smith, Young, & Dodd, 1991; Platt, 1991; Sagotsky et al., 1978). McLaughlin, Krappman, and Welsh (1985) required four elementary-aged students to record whether they were doing their work. These self-recordings resulted in increased on-task behaviors that persisted at follow-up checks four months after initiating treatment. Similarly, Lloyd, Bateman, Landrum, and Hallahan (1989) documented maintenance over a five-week period after using self-recording to increase the task-related behavior of five elementary students with mild disabilities. A noteworthy feature of this study, however, was the use of fading procedures to gradually eliminate treatment conditions. Fading involved first discontinuing signals while students continued to record and then, three days later, no longer requiring students to record their behavior.

Self-monitoring and fading were used also by Stahmer and Schreibman (1992) to improve the social skills and play behaviors of three students with autism. In this study, target children were required to record their behaviors at the end of predetermined intervals. By systematically lengthening the recording intervals and fading adult supervision, the children were helped to develop and maintain desired behaviors for at least twenty-minute segments. Bolstad and Johnson (1972) take the position that self-monitoring procedures are practical and inexpensive for the classroom teacher because once the learner has learned to monitor his or her own behavior, the self-evaluation process can be maintained with only occasional checks by the teacher.

Getting self-monitoring behaviors to transfer from treatment to nontreatment settings is somewhat problematic (Hughes, et al., 1989). Sasso et al. (1990) used self-recordings to maintain behaviors following social skills instruction. Three students with behavior disorders were trained to record target prosocial behaviors on a weekly basis. Following weekly recordings, students received encouragement from the teacher and booster instructional sessions on the target social skills. These procedures were effective in causing skills to persist in the special classroom, but they did not spontaneously generalize to the mainstreamed classroom where no treatment conditions existed.

Misra (1992) managed to get newly acquired social communication skills to generalize to real-life situations by teaching three adults with mild mental retardation to use a golf counter to monitor these behaviors during daily encounters. Unfortunately, as with Sasso et al. (1990), an erosion of treatment effects occurred once self-recording was discontinued. As noted by Hughes et al. (1989), the environmental events should be examined closely to determine what is truly maintaining the behavior. Another concern is that treatment conditions are of too short a duration for the behavior to become firmly established in one's repertoire and be useful in mediating behaviors in other settings. More extensive training and fading procedures might be warranted.

Although there is research evidence that self-monitoring procedures alone can be effective (Sagotsky et al., 1978), it appears the effects can increase substantially through the application of externally administered contingency systems (Baer, Fowler, & Carden-Smith; 1984; Kiburz, Miller, & Morrow, 1984). Although not addressed in the reseach literature, it is advisable for trainers to encourage students to continue monitoring their behavior indefinitely at least at the covert level. This recommendation is consistent with real-life conditions, because to live orderly, disciplined, and productive lives, it is necessary for individuals to monitor their behaviors on a consistent basis, albeit informally, according to some external or internal standard. This capacity to self-monitor, which appears to be commonplace to most individuals, may need to be kept in place overtly for extended periods and carried on covertly on an ongoing basis for individuals lacking in self-control.

Many of the studies using self-monitoring have employed correspondence training wherein the child is taught to report his or her own behavior accurately. Robertson, Simon, Pachman, and Drabman (1979), for example, implemented correspondence training by first having teachers rate the children's behavior and give the children this feedback. The children were then directed to rate their own behavior. Their ratings were matched with those of the teacher, with rewards for matching the teacher's ratings, thus increasing the probability that in the future they would make accurate assessments. After children demonstrated skill in rating their own behavior, teacher matchings were no longer required. Rewards were administered based on the children's reports. The importance of accurate recording to self-monitoring success is a debated issue: Some researchers argue that accuracy is mandatory (Bolstad & Johnson, 1972; Fixen, Phillips, & Wolf, 1972), while others point to desired behavior changes despite the learners' inaccuracies (Harris, 1986; Misra, 1992).

Self-evaluation

Self-evaluation is part of the correspondence training process—the child has to apply some evaluative criteria before rating her or his behavior. Wood and Flynn (1978) developed a self-evaluation token system with delinquent youth in which external reinforcement for room cleanliness was transferred to self-reinforcement. Accuracy of self-evaluation was developed by giving two sets of points, one for room cleanliness and the other for the extent to which self-evaluations agreed with those of an independent adult observer. After an 80 percent level of agreement was reached, the independent observation was discontinued, and accurate self-evaluation was maintained by random spot checks. More recent studies also show self-evaluations to be effective in altering and maintaining social behaviors in treatment settings while treatment conditions are in place (e.g., Salend et al., 1992; Smith et al., 1988), or by incorporating treatment conditions into the generalization setting (Clark & McKenzie, 1989).

Sainato, Strain, Lefebvre, and Rapp (1990) present a rather elaborate self-evaluation system that is effective in maintaining the class-appropriate behaviors of preschool children with disabilities even after treatment conditions are removed. In the study, children rated themselves on each of nine work-related behaviors. The teacher matched the pupil ratings and provided reinforcement accordingly. The procedures were simplified so the children only had to make a "yes" or "no" response, and pictures of the children responding appropriately were attached to their response forms. Although the relative effects were not determined, the gradual fading of treatment conditions and the photographs of the children acting appropriately may have contributed to the success of this study.

Fading has been found to be a key factor in promoting generalization in other studies as well (Odom, Chandler, Ostrosky, McConnell, & Reaney, 1992; Stahmer & Schreibman, 1992). Odom et al. taught preschool children to initiate play behavior with their peers and then gradually faded visual and verbal prompts, causing peer initiations to increase and be maintained over a specified period.

Providing visual self-evaluative feedback in the form of photographs (Sainato et al., 1990) or videotapes (Osborne, Kiburz, & Miller, 1986) appears to facilitate the development of desired behaviors as well as to contribute to their durability and transfer. Osborne et al. found videotaping aided in the use of a self-evaluation procedure to reduce the self-injurious behavior of an adolescent. Kern-Dunlap, Dunlap, Clarke, Childs, White, and Stewart (1992) used videotaped feedback, self-evaluations, and reinforcement to improve peer interactions among five preadolescent males with severe emotional disturbance. These studies show the mediating effects that visual self-evaluative feedback can have on one's behavior.

Self-reinforcement

Self-reinforcement can be viewed as a natural outgrowth of self-evaluation where positive or negative verbalizations result, depending on the degree to which one's self -evaluations meet expected criteria (Nelson & Hayes, 1981). Like reinforcement delivered by external sources, self-reinforcement can take a variety of forms. Self-reward can range from self-administered tokens or points, to self-contracting for tangible items, to internalized rewards by means of positive self-statements. The last item could be considered the ideal and an ultimate goal of social skills training. Self-reinforcement implies that the learner assumes full responsibility for the assessment, determination, and administration of the rewards, a measure of control not typically present in most classrooms.

Most studies, such as those reviewed in this chapter, tend to use student–teacher ratings, augmented by bonus points for accurate matchings. The ability of students to become more self-reliant in administering reinforcement has not been extensively researched.

In one study conducted by Ninness, Fuerst, Rutherford, and Glenn (1991), reinforcement procedures were altered systematically and transferred in part to student control. Social skills instruction and a self-management package were employed to improve the social behaviors of three junior high students with behavior disorders. As part of self-management, students moved through four levels of reinforcement, where progression to a higher level was contingent on four weeks of attainment at an established criterion. For example, at the lowest level, students were assessed every 20 minutes and could earn a possible 100 points. After earning 90 percent of these points for four weeks, the students would move to the next level, where they was assessed every 30 minutes, could earn 70 points, and could move to the next level after attaining 95 percent of these points for four weeks. At each level, there was a reduction of the number of assessments per hour and the number of points to be earned. There was a corresponding (slight) increase in the percentage of points to be earned. The study also included 20-minute periods where students were required to self-assess and determine ratings when the teacher was not in the classroom. On her return, the teacher administered noncontingent bonus points.

Although not totally student self-reliant, these procedures do represent a form of reinforcement thinning and greater student responsibility for self-reinforcement. The authors credited these techniques, at least partly, for the transfer of the desired behaviors to nonteacher-supervised settings.

Systematic instruction to help learners become skilled and effective in self-reinforcement is essential. As part of the learning process, Graham et al. (1992) suggest a gradual transition from collaborative evaluation and reinforcement to self-evaluation and reinforcement. As mentioned earlier, contingency contracts can be useful vehicles for developing self-reinforcement, since it is possible to increase the child's participation in the contracting procedure by gradual steps. Homme et al. (1969) provide the following stages for that process:

Level 1: Manager-controlled system in which the manager determines the reinforcer and the task and delivers the reward.

Level 2: Transitional step with partial control by student, where student assumes joint control with the manager either over the amount of reinforcement or the amount of task.

Level 3: Second transitional step in which manager and student share equally in determining both the reinforcer and the task.

Level 4: Third transitional step in which the student assumes full control of either the task or reinforcer and shares joint responsibility with the manager for the other.

Level 5: Student controlled contracting, in which the student has assumed full control of determining both the amount of reinforcement and amount of task.

Another aspect of self-reinforcement is the child's ability to "pat himself or herself on the back," either overtly or covertly. Children may need to be taught through specific procedures how to make positive self-statements. Chapter 3 outlines procedures for altering negative self-statements. Stephens (1992, pp. 235–236) provides a teaching strategy for social modeling of the self-positive statement:

Teaching strategy

SKILL: The student makes positive statements when asked about himself or herself

Social modeling
1. Identify a need for the behavior through a classroom discussion. Use stories, film strips or other aids where available. Bring up such points as the fact that everyone has good qualities and does some things well, even though no one is perfect. Have the class identify reasons why it's good to know about your own good qualities and recognize the things you do well. Have the class try to distinguish between behavior which could be considered "bragging" or inappropriately building oneself up at the expense of another, and behavior which involves appropriately saying positive things about oneself and what one has done. Generate with the class some positive sentences one might use to describe one's accomplishments. For example, "I like my picture." "That was a good hit I made." "I'm happy that I got 100 in spelling."
2. Identify specific behavior to be modeled. When someone asks you to tell about yourself or about something good you've done, try to think of something positive to say. (Stress that one need not be perfect or do everything perfectly in order to find good things to say about oneself.)
3. Model the behavior to the class. Describe to the class some realistic positive traits you possess and skills you have. For contrast you might insert some negative comments and have students distinguish between the two.
4. Give each student an opportunity to practice. Make up a list of positive statements as prompts. Give each student a copy of the list. Go around the class and have each student find a statement which he could apply to himself and read it in response to a prompting question from the teacher. Go around the class again and

have each student think of another statement which is not on the list. Provide prompts wherever necessary. Reward students who make appropriate responses.
5. Maintain through reinforcement the behavior of making positive statements about oneself or one's accomplishments.

The progression of the child from self-administered tangible rewards to internalized rewards—in the form of positive statements and thoughts—can be programmed through shaping and fading procedures. Based on some of the limited research in this area, the following steps are suggested for moving the child from self-provided, extrinsic rewards to self-administered, intrinsic rewards for appropriate social behaviors, with the understanding that movement from one part of the process to the next needs to be paced according to the success experienced at any one point.

1. Establish with the child the specific behavior to be rewarded and the criteria for reinforcement. Establish with the child the reward she or he will provide for herself or himself, beginning with tangible rewards, if necessary, at whatever level is appropriate.
2. Initiate correspondence training, providing practice in self-monitoring with rewards for accuracy.
3. Initiate self-reinforcement, providing verbal reinforcement from the trainer for both the social behaviors and the appropriate delivery of self-reinforcement.
4. Have the child accompany self-reinforcement with a verbal description of what was done to gain the reward. For example, have the child place a star on a chart at the end of a play period for target behaviors, such as sharing or taking turns, then describe what was done to earn the star and give an additional star for an accurate description.
5. Ask the child to think silently about what he or she did to earn the reward before making the statement.
6. Move to less frequent self-administered, tangible rewards and verbal descriptions, requiring the child to remember for a longer time what was done to earn the reward.
7. Discontinue the use of self-administered, tangible rewards but require verbal reports, reinforced by external praise.
8. Discontinue regular verbal reports but periodically use probes and reminders: "I saw you help Mary when she fell down. Did you congratulate yourself for doing something nice for someone else?"

The self-control procedures outlined here require children to "self-administer a program therapists or teachers would apply if they assumed the role of primary treatment mediators" (Gross & Wojnilower, 1984, p. 511). Gross and Wojnilower question whether behavior under these conditions is indeed "self-directed." They argue that teachers generally monitor the application of self-control procedures and, therefore, the contingencies for maintaining a particular behavior are not always clear. That is, children may continue to engage in desired actions because they are still under the control of the standards and contingencies established initially by the teachers, not because these responsibilities have been transferred to the child. With a few exceptions (e.g., Ninness et al., 1991), researchers rarely attempt to study the total transfer of self-management conditions, including reinforcement contingencies, to the child.

Another related caution is the importance of children administering self-reinforcement accurately, because inappropriate self-rewards could result in the reinforcement of maladaptive behaviors. Student training is an important contributing factor to accurate self-reinforcement (Salend et al., 1992). Workman (1982) suggests using modeling and behavior rehearsal to ensure that the child understands exactly how the target behavior is to be performed, as well as how to employ the self-management techniques.

Stevenson and Fantuzzo (1984) report using modeling, behavior rehearsal, and correspondence matching for two two-hour sessions to train one subject in a self-control sequence. In addition to self-recording, self-evaluation, and self-reward, the researchers consider other facilitating variables to include the student's booster sessions, the student's voluntary participation, and the student's opportunity to determine goals and reinforcers.

Although, theoretically, social skills may be trained and generalized across settings and persons and maintained over time through altered contingencies and self-reinforcement, realistically, it may be necessary to provide more training occasionally. Periodic booster sessions are one way to maintain behavior change (Hersen, 1979; Stevenson & Fantuzzo, 1984), although Franks and Wilson (1978) caution that booster sessions are most effective if they are timed to occur before a behavior has been allowed to deteriorate. Similarly, an instructor may need to present occasional abbreviated review lessons for previously learned social skills. Baer (1978) suggests that the concept of "savings" is relevant to the issue of generalization. Even though a behavior may be taught once and then require occasional reteaching for new settings or maintenance over time, the initial instruction will serve to decrease the time and effort required to provide additional teaching.

Summary

Specific programming needs to be built into social skills instruction to assist in the generalization of the social behaviors to different settings and people and the maintenance of the behaviors over time. Generalization-promotion strategies vary, and some may produce greater returns than others (Chandler et al., 1992). For newly learned skills to transfer from one setting to another, the training setting should be structured to resemble the real-life environment as closely as possible. It is also helpful to use more than one setting during the training and more than one trainer. Involving people from the natural environment (e.g., parents and peers) in the training is particularly helpful to facilitate generalization.

The use of mediators (in the form of language, self-instruction, problem-solving skills and expectations) can be a way to extend training into new environments, because these can be carried into any setting through the child's cognitive activities. Techniques for maintaining behaviors generally involve changes in the contingencies of reinforcement surrounding the social behaviors. Changes can be made in the sources of reinforcement from the trainer to someone in the natural environment, and in the timing of reinforcement from frequent predictable reinforcement to infrequent intermittent rewards.

Contingency contracts are a useful way to change both the source and timing of reinforcement. The kinds of external reinforcement provided also can be changed from tangible rewards to more natural social reinforcement, and efforts made to develop the child's ability to monitor, evaluate, and provide his or her own internalized rewards for desirable social behavior. Even though behaviors can be programmed to generalize over time, persons, and settings, it still may be necessary to provide occasional reteaching to make sure that the child will continue to reap the positive benefits gained from learning social skills.

Chapter *5*

Integrating the Steps:
Issues in Application

Along with the procedures outlined in the first four chapters of this book, some additional factors for effective social skills instruction need to be considered. As with all teaching, the learner's attending behaviors and willingness to engage in the learning task are basic and critical ingredients. Therefore, this chapter focuses on the conditions that motivate and reinforce learning as determined by skill relevance, performance contingencies, activity enjoyment, and external resources. Much of the social skills training reported in the literature has taken place in schools; and most of the social skills curriculum programs have been designed for classroom application for both remedial and preventive purposes. For that reason, this chapter addresses issues associated with social skills instruction in the schools; and finally, offers a sample social skills strategy that incorporates the social skills teaching steps detailed in the first four chapters.

Facilitating Instruction

Increasing Relevance

There is a direct relationship between the value the child attaches to the behavior to be taught and that child's willingness to participate in the learning and eventual performance of the behavior. Therefore, an important first step is to help the child associate a meaningful and positive value to the social skill to be learned. The trainer can initiate a discussion about the skill in question, establishing its relevance for the child: Why it is important? What benefits come from learning this skill? What disadvantages result from not knowing this behavior? Such a discussion could relate to specific problem situations children are experiencing, possibly disguised or put in a fantasy context.

Another means of increasing relevance is to use techniques appropriate to the young person's age level, making sure the behaviors selected for development are meaningful to the learner. For example, the interest elementary-age children show in forming clubs might lend itself to a "social skills club" that meets under established conditions at a desirable place and time. For adolescents, the use of media, such as videotape feedback with opportunities to operate the equipment themselves, could enhance interest, as could providing opportunities for self-direction in skill selection, developing scenarios for role-playing, and evaluating progress.

Increasing Motivation

The teacher or therapist's ability to present himself or herself as a positive stimulus is basic to motivation. In other words, the nature of the relationship that exists with the student will affect the student's involvement. There are many ways to set the stage or provide the stimulus that will encourage the learner to participate, including the adult's ability to provide support and encouragement. Depending on the type of skills to be taught, the conditions of the setting, and the ages of the learners involved, a number of procedures could be used in combination to create motivating conditions.

One procedure could be using materials, such as stories, filmstrips, films, and other audio-visual media, to set the stage. (Appendix A identifies a variety of such materials for all age groups.) Another method is to tie social skills teaching into regular curricular activities or special classroom projects with visual presentations such as pictures, photographs, cartoons, or student-produced artwork to illustrate the skill. A bulletin board emphasizing sportsmanship, for example, could present a picture captioned, "Michael Jordon/Crissy Evert says, 'Be a good sport,'" with specific sportsmanship behaviors shown below it. Cartoons, such as *Peanuts* are a fertile source for social skills ideas. The following social skills lessons, provided by a classroom teacher for a student with peer-related problems, demonstrate motivational procedures.

Yvonne was an eight-year-old second grader, who her teacher described as having a lovely smile that was infrequently displayed. Yvonne lived with her mother and four-year-old sister in a neighborhood where safety was a major issue. She reported regularly hearing gunfire, she was afraid to sleep in certain areas of her home, and she was often not permitted to go outside. These conditions may have adversely affected Yvonne's social development, perhaps causing her to be insecure and reluctant to trust others.

In terms of peer relations, Yvonne was observed to make uncomplimentary remarks constantly to the other students. According to her teacher, she would make rude noises to the other children if they bumped her or even got too close to her. She would laugh at the clothing of her peers and make abusive statements such as "you smell," "that's ugly," "don't touch my things, you're dirty." The problem behavior was making unkind statements to peers, and the social skill instruction focused on helping Yvonne learn to compliment the other students.

Social skill instruction was presented through a guided writing activity, which was an established part of the language arts curriculum consisting of a short 10- to 15-minute period of one-on-one instruction. The teacher introduced the topic of "playing with others" as a means of assessing Yvonne's understanding of her poor peer relationships and her related feelings. The following is an excerpt from Yvonne's writing, indicating that she had some awareness of this problem.

> When she comes over to me we play for a little while, then she gets mad. She says she is going to play with someone else. I tell her to go on, I don't care. It makes me mad when she says that, then I don't have no one to play with. Then I feel bad.

During direct instruction with Yvonne it was determined that a compliment should include: a) think about what you want to say, b) look at the person, c) smile, d) give the compliment, and e) be sincere. After modeling and practicing these steps, it was suggested that this instruction should be presented to the entire class through a photograph instruction book featuring Yvonne. Yvonne was delighted.

The teacher and Yvonne planned the format of the mini book and the pictures that would be needed. They reviewed the steps of the skill and practiced them with another child who would be posing for the photos with Yvonne. Each instruction and review provided Yvonne with additional practice. Presenting this to the other student gave Yvonne the opportunity to model the behavior herself. Yvonne presented the book to the entire class.

Recordkeeping by the classroom teacher showed that Yvonne's complimentary statements steadily increased from a level of .2 per day prior to instruction to 2.4 per day during and following social skill intervention. In like manner, within this period uncomplimentary statements consistently declined from a mean of 5 to 2.2 per day. Additional evidence of Yvonne's growth could be seen in a post instruction essay where she described a problem with peer relations and a plan to solve the problem by complimenting the person she previously offended.

In order to keep and build upon these gains the teacher established conditions for behavior maintenance and generalization. Environmental props were set up in order to cue the behavior to occur on a regular basis. For example, the teacher served as a model by frequently delivering compliments, Yvonne's book was displayed on the classroom library shelf, a mirror was placed in the classroom, and a photograph of each child with a caption of a student generated compliment was posted on the bulletin board.

In addition to environmental reminders, the teacher developed three other plans for generalization. First, Yvonne was required to record the number of compliments she made and the ones she heard the teacher make each day. This recording could later be extended to other settings. Secondly, using language as a mediator, Yvonne was directed to plan for specific opportunities during which she would use her new skill. An example of one of her plans was . . . "When I go home, I will tell my Mom dinner smells good. Then I will say you are a good cook. She will probably say thank you. Then we'll eat." Finally, Yvonne was fortunate to have the same teacher when she returned to school the following year for third grade. The teacher provided booster sessions early in the year and used Yvonne as a role model and peer tutor for the first and second graders in the class. At Yvonne's request, the teacher and Yvonne plan to develop another similar book to present to the class. (Fishback, 1992).

This creative and sensitive teacher not only demonstrated critical social skills teaching components outlined in this book, but employed a few additional techniques effective in engaging and committing the learner to this instruction. Understanding that Yvonne valued peer relationships and felt bad when they turned sour, the intervention was designed so that Yvonne would receive positive peer attention and respect, rather than be treated as a "patient" needing teacher and peer assistance to become more acceptable. This approach undoubtedly made the social skills instruction much more attractive to Yvonne and the other students. The project was further enhanced by using activities already in place (guided writing), adding novel features (photography), and building on skills currently in the student's repertoire (reading and writing skills).

It is important to note that the most important features for Yvonne seemed to be peer recognition and academic performance. For other students, points of greatest salience may include interests such as sports, dating, art, or music. The astute instructor will explore ways to capitalize on the relevant themes in a student's life to make social skills learning more attractive and meaningful.

Another possibility for increasing motivation is establishing expectations that positive benefits will result from engaging in the task at hand. Such benefits could include both future payoffs from knowing the behaviors and immediate benefits such as having refreshments or reduced homework assignments. It is important to schedule social skills training at a time when it will not compete with high-interest activities.

As noted in Chapter 3, the instructor needs to make sure social skills instruction does not imply that participants are deficient in some way, creating a stigma effect. When instruction is presented with humor, play, and in ways to ensure the child's success, extrinsic reinforcement may not be necessary. However, children who are less easily motivated may need a contingency contract, where activities, privileges, or tangible reinforcers are offered in exchange for engaging in social skills training. Badges, ribbons, or certificates can serve as incentives and symbols of achievement.

A contingency management system may help encourage participation or manage behavior in the group during instruction. It is important that rewards for participating not be confused with feedback for performance, because the criteria for each should be quite different. Teacher praise for participating and making good attempts at learning the social behavior is an essential aspect of encouraging motivation. For example, to reward the performance of children who are learning to make positive statements, give each child a card to carry and give points for every positive comment they are observed to make. They can exchange the points at the end of the day or the end of the week for something they value. For every ten points their name could go on cards to be placed in a fish bowl for a drawing.

Using Social Skills Games

Games are another means for enhancing social skills activities. Presenting social skills instruction in the form of games can assist the instructor in many ways. For one thing, playing a structured game requires the exercise of various social skills. The game can become a vehicle for teaching skills like taking turns, sharing materials, being a good winner or loser, teamwork, cooperation, attention to details, following rules, self-control, and various problem-solving skills. Games also can motivate children to participate, because games imply fun and an element of play rather than work. Using games is particularly useful where social skills content can evoke anxieties and resistance.

As Gordon (1972) points out, games simulate real-life situations and provide a way to test out real-world events. At the same time, games create distance from real life and involve a suspension of the usual forms of evaluation. Games provide an opportunity for the child to learn the consequences of his or her actions without actually having to suffer them. In a game, mistakes and exposure of ignorance are more tolerated. Games usually encourage laughing and joking, which can relieve anxiety and facilitate involvement.

Games can be classified as paper-and-pencil, board, role-play, or hybrid—some combination of the others (Heitzmann, 1974). Common elements for presenting social skills instruction in game format include:

- An aspect of chance such as drawing a card or spinning a wheel;
- Unknown aspects to be discovered by guessing;
- Dramatic features, elements of surprise, or novelty;
- Material presented in ways conveying humor or fun;
- Opportunities for active participation and several kinds of activities or modes of response;
- Well-defined limits and rules;
- Clearly understood goals or objectives to be reached, involving the learning of specific concepts or skills; and
- Immediate feedback about the results of one's actions.

Almost any social skills content can be put into game format through very simple means. For example, have each child pick a skill out of a hat to role-play. Or have teams take turns playing a form of charades in which a specific emotion or coping strategy is pantomimed to be guessed by the other group. Several manufacturers market do-it-yourself game kits with blank boards, dice, spinners, markers, and other game equipment (see resource materials list in Appendix A).

Board games are more complex and limit the number of players but, at the same time, provide opportunities for considerable variety. There is a defined series of activities, involving the order of player turns and the sequence of decisions or steps each player must make (Glazier, 1970). In a social skills board game, for example, players can move along the board according to a chance spin or roll of the dice, draw cards requiring the verbal or performance demonstration of a social behavior, and may land in a penalty box with some action required in order to escape.

> One teacher, for example, used a series of games for a four-year-old to practice the social skill of appropriately borrowing and returning someone else's property. The child's mother saw the absence of this skill to be a persistent and significant problem for the child and other family members. The steps for instruction and practice were: (1) identify the owner, (2) make a request, "May I use your _____?", (3) look at owner and listen for answer, (4) say "Thank you," (5) state where the item was located when borrowed, and (6) return item to same place within specified time period.

To practice steps 1, 2, 3, and 4, the children played a modified version of the game *Candyland*. Before the children could move their game marker on the game board, they had to pick a card containing a pictured object and a color matching a color assigned to another player. The child had to identify the owner by color, ask the owner, "May I use your *(name of object)*?", look at the owner and wait for an answer; and then say "Thank you." After correctly completing this sequence, the child could choose a regular *Candyland* color card and move the game marker to the designated space.

All six steps of the social skill were practiced in a game called "Climbing the Social Skills Ladder." Again using situation cards, children were permitted to move up a space on the ladder if all six steps were enacted correctly. Each game was played at a different session and some games were repeated for several sessions. The teacher reported these procedures to be effective in helping the target child specify and perform the six steps in the appropriate use of others' property. (Spitzer, 1991)

The empirical literature also documents the effectiveness of games in teaching social skills (Foxx, McMorrow, & Mennemeier, 1984; Foxx, McMorrow, & Schloss, 1983). Foxx and his colleagues adapted the Parker Brothers game *Sorry* so that the game cards indicating the number of spaces to be moved on the board also included statements to elicit responses from the participants about various social situations. For example, one of the social vocational card statements was, "You are working on an assembly task and your supervisor says, 'You're not doing that right.' What should you do?" The resulting game, *Stacking the Deck, a Social Skills Game for Retarded Adults*, is available commercially and research reports indicate significant increases in correct responding under simulated conditions (Foxx et al., 1984). (See Appendix A for more commercial social skills games.)

Some cautions about the use of games need to be presented. Games of this sort provide an excellent format for practicing desired behaviors; however, skill trainers also need to program for prompts and rewards in the natural environment for behavior transfer to occur. Social skills can be introduced or practiced in game format, but the connection between what is done for fun and its application to the real world needs to be made at some point. This could be accomplished by a discussion after the game in which practical applications are identified, or by references back to the game when a relevant problem arises. If the intent of the game is to provide practice in a specific skill, structure the game so each player has an opportunity to make the required response and cannot become a "winner" solely by chance: He or she should only win by performing the target behavior. The criteria for winning should relate to the concept or skills to be learned.

Another caution: Minimize win/lose situations in social skills games unless the target social skills are those encountered in competitive games (i.e., being able to win or lose with good sportsmanship and being able to cope with failure). If rewards are given during the game, ideally they should be given for participation rather than for winning or losing. Further, to ensure ongoing participation, the game should be constructed so players are not "out" and then eliminated from the game without an opportunity to be rotated back in quickly. Because much of the learning that takes place in games results from imitation of others' successful behavior, the group or the team needs to be structured so weak members are paired with stronger members. The following section gives examples and uses of cooperative games.

Cooperative Learning

Cooperative learning is defined as students working together for mutual benefit where they are able to encourage and support each other, assume responsibility for their own and each other's learning, employ group-related social skills such as decision making and trust building, and evaluate the groups' academic and social progress (Johnson & Johnson, 1989). In an analysis of cooperative and competitive learning situations, Johnson and Johnson (1987) contend that competition is not a great motivator, but within cooperative activities each participant has an equal chance for forward movement. They note that shared responsibility and work, as observed in many occupational settings, is often the basis of successful interpersonal relationships.

Observing that cooperative behaviors instruction can range from a single activity to restructuring an entire curriculum, Sapon-Shevin (1986) presents three models commonly used for cooperative learning in an academic context: (1) interdependent groups (The Jigsaw Method), (2) competitive cooperative groups, and (3) small group learning.

The Jigsaw Method (Aronson, 1978) is designed so each student is responsible for learning specific content of the lesson, becoming the "expert" required to teach that information to other students in the group. Interdependence is established by testing each group member on all the material studied in the group. A teacher of upper-elementary students, for example, may divide a topic, such as "Building and Maintaining a Classroom Terrarium," into five sections: (1) animals to put in a terrarium, (2) purchasing animals for a terrarium, (3) plants and rocks for a terrarium, (4) care of plants and animals, and (5) cleaning a terrarium. Students are divided into groups of five and one member of each group is assigned to research one of the topics. Members from different teams studying the same topic meet as "expert" groups to discuss their material and then return to their respective groups to teach the information to their teammates.

Competitive cooperative groups are distinguished from the other models mainly by the inclusion of team competition. In *Student Teams—Achievement Divisions* (STAD) (Slavin, 1978), students are organized into heterogeneous groups (according to gender, ability, and race) to tutor group members on instructional content. Students help each other learn, motivated partially by the knowledge that individual quiz scores will be computed into team scores. Each individual contribution, however, is based on the improvement each member made over a previous score.

A similar format is employed in *Teams Games Tournaments* (TGT) (DeVries & Slavin, 1978), except that students are organized into teams that compete to display knowledge of the subject matter. To equalize competition, group membership is routinely changed, and individual contributions to team scores are based on improvement over previous scores. *Team Assisted Individualization* (TAI) (Slavin, Leavey, & Madden, 1982) differs from the previous two formats: The emphasis is on individualization and students work in pairs of their choice to practice the material. This method was devised for classes where the skill levels are too diverse for the children to be taught as a group.

Small-group learning, described in *Learning Together* (Johnson & Johnson, 1987), engages heterogeneous groups of four or five students in a single learning activity. One group assignment is submitted and students are evaluated according to the average group achievement. Group members may be assigned roles to help the group run more smoothly and to help members observe firsthand how each person can affect the group's outcome. Roles may involve monitoring social interactions, demonstrating academic tasks, recording behaviors, and reinforcing desired behaviors.

Cooperative Games

Competitive games often include undesirable behaviors such as taunting/teasing (e.g., Lame Wolf), grabbing or snatching in scarcity situations (e.g., Musical Chairs), monopolizing or excluding other children (e.g., Keep Away), or physical force (e.g., Tag Ball). As an alternative, Sapon-Shevin (1986) suggests that cooperative games can be useful to promote positive social interaction. Desired game features involve:

1. Including children who have been left out; opening one's games or activities to others; finding a part for another child to play.
2. Sharing and taking turns.

3. Touching other children gently; helping other children who have fallen down or who are experiencing difficulty.
4. Talking nicely to classmates; calling classmates only by names they like; noticing and commenting on classmates' strengths rather than weaknesses (pp. 281–282).

Sapon-Shevin gives the following examples of fun, cooperative games and a discussion of their uses in social skills instruction:

Musical Laps (Harrison, 1976)—This is a cooperative version of *Musical Chairs*. The whole group forms a circle all facing in one direction, close together, each with hands on the waist of the person ahead. When the music starts, everyone begins to walk forward. When the music stops, everyone sits down in the lap of the child to the rear. If the whole group succeeds in sitting in laps without falling to the floor, the *Group* wins. If children fall down, gravity wins. It works best with more than 10 children about the same size.

Nonelimination Musical Chairs (Orlick, 1982)—The object is to keep everyone in the game even though chairs are systematically removed. As in the competitive verion, music is played, and more and more chairs are removed each time the music stops. In this game, though, more children have to sit together to keep everyone in the game.

Social Behaviors: Gentle physical contact; sharing, inclusion; group problem solving. Notes/Suggestions: These two games are unique in that they represent crucially different alternatives to traditional musical chairs, in which pushing, shoving, and grabbing lead to success. In Musical Laps, the obstacle is gravity; this game is ideal because it rarely works the first time, as children tend to stand too far apart. When everyone falls down, the group must then engage in problem solving; that is, "What can we try to make it work?" Even young children playing this game have been observed to engage in elaborate planning and hypothesis testing. When the group finally succeeds, there is general rejoicing. An additional positive feature of this game is the fact that when the group collapses, it cannot be identified as "Billy's fault" but, because many children fall, it usually is seen as a failure of the group.

In Nonelimination Musical Chairs, rather than the pushing and exclusionary tactics of traditional Musical Chairs, children must find ways to make room for more and more children. The verbal behavior heard during this game is generally of the form "Come sit on/with me" or "Make room for Johnny."

This game represents an ideal starting point for exploring issues of "limited resources" with children; rather than confirming the "each child must have his own material" notion. Teachers can explore ways in which children can find creative alternatives to exclusion. For example, on the playground, if more than two children want to use the seesaw, how could that be done? (For example, two children on each end; two children count, while two see-saw, then switch places, etc.) (pp. 283–284).[1]

Additional cooperative games can be found in resources such as *The Second Cooperative Sports and Games Book* (Orlick, 1982) and *Everybody Wins* (Sobel, 1983).

Studies on cooperative learning provide evidence that cooperative activities can

[1]Excerpts from Orlick, T., *The Second Cooperative Sports and Games Book,* 1982. Copyright © Pantheon Books. Reprinted by permission.

promote friendships (Berndt, Perry, & Miller, 1988), positive peer relationships, acceptance of mainstreamed students, self-esteem, academic achievement (Slavin, 1990), and acceptance of different racial/ethnic groups (Goldstein, 1988a). Based on his literature review, Goldstein (1988a) notes that the beneficial effects of cooperative learning appear to be greater for minority (African Americans and Mexican American) than majority (European American) students.

Authorities repeatedly caution that cooperative learning involves more than telling students to work together. The skills needed to participate in cooperative groups varies according to the method used, but at a minimum students need competence in initiating the learning task promptly, tutoring peers rather than simply giving answers, and encouraging and reinforcing appropriate peer behaviors. Direct, systematic instruction of cooperative learning behaviors should be undertaken, using the skills training model outlined in Chapter 3.

Implementing Social Skills Teaching in Schools

Although schools are a major socializing institution, social skills typically do not appear as part of the formal instructional curriculum, nor does the professional staff naturally or readily assume this responsibility. Thus, initiation and maintenance of social skills programs in schools are accompanied by some unique and significant considerations. These concerns are addressed in the following section.

Administrative Considerations

Social skills programs, particularly in schools, require administrative support in various forms. First, whether social skills are to be taught is usually an administrative decision. Ideally the instruction should be school- or systemwide to increase the likelihood that the behaviors taught will be valued and reinforced in the larger environment. Administrators also need to provide curriculum materials and allow for flexibility in scheduling so that social skills can be taught effectively and regularly.

Second, administrators need to be knowledgeable in ways to conduct social skills instruction so they can serve as curriculum leaders. This will enable them, when interacting with students, to employ techniques and reinforcers that are consistent with classroom instruction. Administrators also need to serve as models, making a concentrated effort to exhibit the social and problem-solving behaviors desired in the learners.

Finally, social skills instruction and development should be rewarded. Teachers need to be encouraged and reinforced for providing training, and children need to be recognized for appropriate behavior. Administrators are uniquely positioned for this purpose because, in addition to privately administered praise, they can provide schoolwide recognition through bulletins, posters, campaigns, and assemblies.

An example of a systemwide program is provided by Prothrow-Stith (1991), who describes a violence prevention program in the Little Rock, Arkansas, school system. As part of the administrative commitment, every school—elementary through high—was encouraged to teach the violence-prevention curriculum. At the junior high level, the same teachers were assigned to teach the curriculum all day for a ten-week period. This procedure was reported to be quite effective due to the teachers' resulting skill and favorable orientation toward the curriculum. The administration also sponsored poster contests and rewarded students for desired behaviors.

Trainer Considerations

A critical but rarely articulated issue is teachers' receptivity to providing formal, direct social skills instruction. Teachers readily acknowledge the importance of social competence to the child's school and eventual adult success; however, they are sometimes reluctant to assume nonacademic teaching duties, insisting instead that social skills instruction should be relegated largely to other social institutions, such as the family and church, or implemented by other school personnel. Although this position is understandable, teachers need to be reminded of the school's socializing importance. For some children the school is the primary resource for developing socially appropriate behaviors. Teachers also need to become aware of the relationship between social skills and academic achievement (Cartledge & Milburn, 1978), and of the ever-present "hidden" curriculum, which may inadvertently result in the learning of undesired social behaviors. An explicit social skills program is one remedy for this.

Although the legitimacy of formal social skills training in the school is frequently questioned, teacher resistance may emanate more realistically from issues such as time involvement, the nature of the intervention, and teacher skill. Witt, Martens, and Elliott (1984) found the amount of time needed to plan and implement behavior management procedures to be the determining factor in teacher acceptance of these strategies. The teachers were least receptive to the interventions that consumed the most time. In an earlier study with preservice teachers, Witt and Martens (1983) also found a preference for positive (i.e., praise, rewards) over reductive (i.e., time-out, response cost) strategies. Teachers frequently do find themselves unduly burdened with extraneous, nontraditional teaching and managerial duties. Yet attention to the social development of their students needs to be recognized as an explicit aspect of teachers' professional responsibility.

Issues of teacher skill and training are also related to teacher receptivity. Social skills trainers need to understand the skill-training process thoroughly, independent of commercially prepared materials, before they can be effective in their instruction. Although there are various approaches, the direct instruction model is reflected in most social skills teaching. Chapters 1 through 4 discuss the basic elements of this model, which outline methods for targeting, assessing, developing, and maintaining social behaviors. Although many social skills programs provide training scripts, a thorough understanding of the skills training model enables the trainer to innovate where necessary and provide instruction for the unique needs of the learner.

Operant technology is another knowledge base needed by the skill trainer. For some learners, particularly those with disabilities (Walker et al., 1983), social skills acquisition, maintenance, and application are contingent on the trainer's ability to manipulate environmental events so the learner is motivated to learn and experiences consequences likely to promote continued skill performance. Operant procedures can facilitate these outcomes. Shores (1987) stresses the importance of direct instruction for social skills development, but notes that ". . . programs for training teachers to implement the procedures remain problematic" (p. 239). Peterson and McConnell (1993) consider implementation integrity, or the "degree to which an intervention is delivered as planned" (p. 43), to be a key factor in effective social skills teaching. At the very least, well-developed inservice programs are warranted.

Skilled instruction also is a function of practice. Weissberg and Gesten (1982) found improved instruction with experienced teachers—that is, the quality of social skills instruction systematically improved as teachers had the opportunity to practice and refine their skills over a period of two or three years. Social skills training in the schools also demands sufficient competent trainers to consult regularly with teachers who require assistance with teaching procedures. The problems noted here are common to behavioral intervention programs, and it is obvious that measures need to be taken to ensure that teachers are effective in their instruction. As with the development of any skill, extensive practice with adequate feedback is critical.

Other school professionals, such as school psychologists and guidance counselors, are excellent resources for social skills training in schools. These professionals have some distinct advantages: They are not constrained by the limitations of classroom conditions, they can more easily restrict the size of their student groups, and their professional orientation tends to be closely aligned with the theoretical underpinnings of social skills training. The roles of these professionals, particularly the school psychologist, have been broadened (Cartledge & Milburn, 1983), establishing their potential for providing preventive social skills training, for intervening with problematic or disabled students, and for consulting with classroom teachers.

Keep in mind the previously noted pitfalls relative to behavior generalization and maintenance: It is not recommended that social skills training in the schools become the singular responsibility of ancillary professionals such as school psychologists and counselors. At the very least, a collaborative effort is in order. Separate social skills training with special personnel will be maximized if the target subjects' peer group is taught similar skills in the classroom, and if teachers and peers can be enlisted to reinforce newly acquired behaviors so that they are rewarded under natural conditions.

Instructional Considerations

To be most effective, formal social skills instruction should be institutionalized in the schools, presented on a regular basis during assigned periods for all grade levels and populations. Much has been said about the inadequacy of brief social skills programs

(Edleson & Rose, 1981; Shores, 1987; Weissberg & Gesten, 1982): As with academic skills, the merits of prolonged instruction are obvious.

Cartledge (1984) and Michelson et al. (1983) recommend at least two sessions a week, with the amount of time for each session dictated by the developmental level of the learners. For example, primary-aged children will need relatively short periods—that is, 15 to 25 minutes—whereas 45- to 60-minute sessions would be appropriate for middle-grade students and adolescents. Social skills instruction should be viewed as preventive and developmental so that it becomes a part of the formal curriculum and is taught on an ongoing basis. As students progress, the instruction moves to other skills, and the curriculum spirals, with more complex and sophisticated skills taught at higher grade levels. As with the academic curriculum, there should be periodic review or booster sessions for previously taught skills.

To maximize learning opportunities, social skills instruction can be infused into the regular academic curriculum such as in the example presented earlier on teaching peer-related social skills to Yvonne. Cartledge and Kleefeld (in press) provide another example, in which folk tales from around the world were used as motivational activities for social skills instruction with intermediate-aged students. Programs of this sort allow reinforcement of academic content (e.g., reading, language arts, and social studies), permit a natural integration of social skills instruction throughout the daily curriculum, and tend to be more attractive to classroom teachers without compromising critical social skills learning.

A formal social skills training program is advocated; however, social skills instruction can be a part of every instructional activity in the learner's schoolday. Teachers need to be flexible to take advantage of events for spontaneous incidental teaching. They can capitalize on a "teachable moment" to provide impromptu social skills instruction at the time the skill deficiency is manifested.

For example, the children are engaged in a basketball game. One child misses a thrown ball and is taunted by another child who calls him "butter-fingers," with other children joining in the name-calling. Social skills instruction can be initiated at this point by

- Stopping the game,
- Discussing with the children the preceding events,
- Enacting a role-play of what happened,
- Reversing the roles by using some of the taunting pupils as objects of name-calling, then
- Role-playing more positive things to say to someone who is experiencing difficulty.

During the discussion, the teacher attempts to elicit from the students an understanding and identification of the negative, painful effects of name-calling, of alternative positive statements such as, "Good try," or "Don't feel bad—we all miss sometimes," and of the facilitative potential of encouraging words. The game could then resume with the teacher watching for and reinforcing students who provide positive encouragement for each other.

Academic pairings or groups provide another vehicle for informal social skills instruction. In these situations children can be prompted and reinforced for various peer-related social behaviors.

The ways in which children are grouped is another variable to be considered in social skills instruction. Children may be taught social skills in varying group sizes. Small groups of 10 or fewer generally are preferred (McGinnis & Goldstein, 1984). As the group size increases, the instructor needs to be aware of potential interferences such as limited opportunities to respond, pupil inattention, limited opportunities for feedback, and so forth. There is some evidence that the most critical aspect of the training is the behavior practice (Weissberg & Gesten, 1982). For larger groups, adult co-trainers (McGinnis & Goldstein, 1984; Michelson et al., 1983) or peers trained as small group leaders (McGinnis & Goldstein, 1984) are recommended. A procedure Cartledge (1984) employed for large groups was to extend the number of sessions allotted to each skill, allowing for guided practice for each student but varying the activities to ensure pupil attention.

The grouping of children can enhance peer support and reinforcement and provide children with peer models. It is often harder to engage a single child in social skills training than (at least) a duo, where the two children can provide motivation for each other. Social skills instruction will be facilitated if groups contain both competent children and those who are skill-deficient (Bierman & Furman, 1984; McEvoy & Odom, 1987; McGinnis & Goldstein, 1984; Shores, 1987). LaGreca (1992) suggests pairing low- and high-status children and mixing children with differing degrees of social status within groups to increase peer acceptance. Elementary-age children may prefer same-sex groups. In some settings, it may be necessary to avoid stigma by using the whole class as a group, or developing groups based on criteria other than the need for social skills training.

Some problems may result from group instruction as well. It may be more difficult to bring about behavior change in group situations where peers provide reinforcement for the incompatible, maladaptive responses. According to Reppucci and Saunders (1974):

> Behavior patterns maintained by informal peer contacts in most natural settings are seldom accessible to more than partial modification by the usually less powerful contingencies available to the behavior modifier or staff mediators (p. 655).

Social skills trainers must have realistic expectations about the possible outcomes of such training. First, trainers need to be perceptive about the child's potential capacity and rate of growth. As with cognitive skills, children vary in ability and speed of learning. Therefore, instructional standards need to be established individually. Focus on helping each learner reach his or her fullest potential rather than holding to an idealized, inappropriate goal. Second, according to Michelson et al. (1983), other extraneous factors, such as home, medical, or emotional problems, may limit the effects of training—but, if nothing else, this instruction may impress on the child the need to make changes at a later time. Michelson et al. (1983) also point out that social skills training is not a panacea for all childhood disorders. It may be necessary to use the training in conjunction with more intensive professional intervention.

Parental Considerations

As noted previously, factors related to the home and parents can either facilitate or interfere with social skills instruction. To the extent possible, parents need to become an integral part of the social skills instruction program. In their discussion of children's aggressive behaviors in Chapter 6 of this book, Hughes and Cavell suggest that the greatest effects are produced if parents are integrated into a comprehensive child-centered social skills training package. As part of their involvement, parents need to be informed of:

1. The relevance of social skills development to their child's immediate and future success;
2. How current parenting practices may impede or undermine the development of critical behaviors;
3. Specific skills needed by their children; and
4. Actions they may take to promote and maintain desired skills.

Viewing parents as partners rather than "patients," social skills trainers should give them the opportunity to collaborate, jointly determining/negotiating the skills to be taught, the responses to be made, and the most effective means of instruction. Parents can be effective teachers. While taking a course in teaching social skills, one mother presented the following case study of her efforts to reduce her son's verbal aggression.

Phillip was a 9-year-old fourth-grade student who was born with a con-genital amputation of his right arm. His right arm extended halfway between his shoulder and what would have been his elbow. A single digit grew at the end of his aborted arm. He refused to wear his prosthesis or long shirts because he felt that they got in the way of many activities such as climbing trees and biking.

Phillip's exposed arm provoked much curiosity in new acquaintances, and some of them, especially younger children, often asked him what happened to his arm. Over the years Phillip's reactions to this inquiry evolved from quietly looking away or hiding behind his parents when younger to being untruthful ("A shark bit it off") or aggressive ("What happened to your head?") at his present age. His mother wisely realized that Phillip always would be con-fronted with public reactions to his arm and needed to learn constructive ways to respond to this situation. Specifically, the mother wished to help her son react to questions about his physical disability by giving a truthful, positive, and assertive response.

Before instruction, the mother engaged her son in a brief discussion to determine if he reacted this way because he felt other people were asking him about his arm to be cruel or if he just found the questions to be intrusive. If the former, the social skill instruction also should address Phillip's social perceptions. Based on their conversation, the mother concluded that Phillip felt these questions resulted from curiosity, not meanness. Although Phillip defended his responses as simply "joking," he did agree to cooperate with his mother to explore more appropriate ways to respond.

Instruction consisted of first identifying the components of an appropriate response. Phillip and his mother decided that when he was approached about his arm he would: (a) smile, (b) look at the person asking the question, (c) answer the question truthfully, and (d) use a normal tone of voice. For example, "I was born that way. It may look different, but it doesn't cause any problems at all." Phillip and his mother role played these behaviors according to various possible situations. Other family members were instructed to reinforce appropriate responses from Phillip.

Because the opportunity to respond under real-life conditions seldom occurred, Phillip's mother constructed an analogue assessment which presented various scenarios. For example, "When you are on vacation, a little girl who is 8 years old comes up and asks, 'How'd you break your hand?' Here's what you say: _____"

During the posttest, Phillip responded appropriately on 4 out of 5 (80%) compared to the pretest where he made 1 out of 7 (14%) desired responses. For the one item "missed" on the posttest Phillip refrained from making a positive statement telling what he "could" do, e.g., "I can do anything any other person can do." When questioned about this, Phillip stated that he didn't feel he had to prove anything to strangers. Phillip had a good point; it was in his best interest to be assertive rather than passive or aggressive, but he was not obliged to ingratiate himself to others.

Perhaps the best evidence of Phillip's learning came with a humorous incident following the social skill instruction. Phillip and his mother were shopping at the grocery store when a woman and a young child came down the aisle. Suddenly the child started speaking very excitedly in Japanese. As she spoke she pointed to Phillip. Phillip turned to his mother and said, "I know what I'm supposed to say, but I don't know how to say it in Japanese!" And then Phillip broke out in laughter (Altomare, 1989).

The importance of the parental role in social skills instruction can be seen in several curriculum programs that provide parent or home notes to correspond with specific skills being taught in school (e.g., Cartledge & Kleefeld, 1991; Jackson, Jackson, & Monroe, 1983; Wiig & Bray, 1983). Typically, these materials describe the social skill being taught and the related behavioral components. Parents are expected to evaluate their child on the same behaviors at home and return the sheet to the trainers. Exercises of this nature may recruit the participation and cooperation of initially reluctant or resistant parents. For children with more severe behavior disorders or deficits, it may be necessary to employ the services of professionals who can provide more intensive social skills intervention with the children and their families.

Community Considerations

Social skills trainers need to be able to communicate their social development program to the significant others in the child's environment, to teach behaviors that are likely to be reinforced by these individuals, and to enlist their support and involvement. There are occasions, however, when behaviors crucial to the child's social development are not valued by others in the natural environment. Many adults, parents, and peers view counteraggression as a requisite survival skill and will encourage children to respond to provocation almost exclusively with physical force and verbal aggression. Although the immediate results of such actions may be rewarding, the long-term effects are counterproductive, causing aggression to escalate and producing a continual conflict cycle with the child's peers and others.

Beyond its immediate emotional returns, counteraggression may be advocated largely because knowledge and understanding about more viable and constructive alternatives are lacking. Thus, significant members of the child's community must be helped to recognize the value of nonaggressive options and reinforce the child for employing these more productive behaviors. Prothrow-Stith (1991) reports that, in one community-based project, her violence prevention curriculum impacted attitudes held by direct care workers who previously subscribed to violence as an appropriate means to resolve conflict.

The media, particularly television, is an important force in the socialization of today's children and youth. Ninety-eight percent of all U.S. households possess at least one television set (U.S. Bureau of the Census, 1986), so it is safe to conclude that nearly all our children have regular access to television. Estimates of average television viewing range from 26 hours per week for school-age children in the general population (Stephens, 1986) to more than 40 hours per week for low socioeconomic and minority students (Stroman, 1991).

These data pertain to the prosocial and antisocial messages transmitted through television. Stroman (1991) reports, in her review of studies, that television can have both positive and negative effects, but that convincing data show children and youth are negatively impacted by television violence. Boys and young children, especially those from low socioeconomic groups, are most vulnerable. Stroman contends that the negative impact of television can be diminished and provides several recommendations:

1. Parents are advised to minimize television watching, to watch programs *with* their children and point out items of interest or concern, and to pressure institutions such as the Federal Trade Commission or Federal Communications Commission for more appropriate children's television.
2. Teachers are encouraged to enlighten parents about the influence of television,

to teach children to view television programs critically, and to advocate more appropriate television programs.

3. Most important, parents, teachers, and other members of the community need to provide children and youth with values and standards by which to assess the images conveyed through the media. Many of these values can be communicated through social skills instruction.

Another community resource to enhance social skills instruction is *mentoring* programs. Mentoring can be performed by a variety of individuals and can take many forms. Big Brother and Big Sister programs are perhaps the most common and enduring. Young people enrolled in these programs typically either have a missing parent or have begun to exhibit high-risk behaviors predictive of poor social adjustment. Social skills instruction under these conditions is informal at best, but young people often bring problems in personal relationships with either friends or authority figures to these mentors. For example, one young mentor was at a loss as to how to help her mentee deal with problems of peer aggression. After discussing the matter with Professor Cartledge and consulting a social skills curriculum for adolescents, the mentor identified several new approaches she could present to this youth.

Educators in an elementary self-contained inner-city school for students with behavior disorders describe a somewhat novel and attractive mentoring program (Petri, Mungin, & Emerson, 1992). The goal was to provide African-American male role models for a student body that was 88 percent male, that came from families with 89 percent single mothers, and whose professional school staff was 86 percent female. For the first year, the mentors included an architect, two policemen, two social workers, and two professionals from the private sector. The mentors spent four hours per month working with the students in their classes, performing various tutoring and monitoring duties.

A similar program for inner-city delinquents used retired persons as tutors and mentors. The close mentor–mentee relationships that emerged in these projects could be the basis for providing and reinforcing valuable social skills lessons. A special advantage of school-based mentoring programs is that regular contact is likely to occur because school attendance is required for the mentee, and the mentor can make this project part of his or her working day rather than infringing on valuable (and possibly limited) personal time. Same-race male mentors are particularly important for the social development of minority males.

There are many community organizations, agencies, and institutions that can be tapped for social skills instruction/reinforcement. These include social service agencies, mental health centers, boys' and girls' clubs, scouting organizations, recreation centers, sports teams, employers, job coaches, juvenile courts, and churches. Obviously, the community contacts to be made depend on the students' level of involvement and the organization's relevance to skills being taught. For example, one teacher sees a critical need to teach appropriate sportsmanship skills to her students. Two of her students with significant deficits in this area play on community baseball teams and participate regularly in activities at the community recreation center.

Informing the team coach and center counselor of her instructional project and ways they might reinforce these skills could be extremely fruitful.

Evaluation Considerations

Evaluation of social skills can be a major problem in natural settings, particularly as it pertains to efficiency, validity, and available resources. The most easily administered pupil assessments are paper-and-pencil measures such as self-report instruments— e.g., *Social Skill Rating System—Self,* (SSRS-S), Gresham and Elliott (1990)—or sociometric ratings. But scoring can be time consuming and, most important, the results are not necessarily congruent with pupil behavior under real-life conditions. Sociometric ratings may more accurately reflect social status than self-report measures, but the analysis can be highly complicated and the results provide little, if any, information on the nature of individual behavior change.

Behavior checklists or adult ratings can be used, but when completed by informed observers, rater bias becomes a factor. This eliminates using teachers who have provided the social skills training. Yet limited resources or available school staff mitigate against employing uninformed observers for an extended period of time. Other means of evaluation, such as recording the number of infractions for target pupils before and after training, are desirable but probably not a realistic expectation, even for a committed school staff.

Social validation is salient for this issue: Perhaps the most valuable information can be obtained through less formal means than the objective measures. First, how does the learner compare to his or her peers in social adjustment? More important than the instances of verbal aggression, in the example cited earlier, is whether Yvonne still stands out in her class as being the most negative and rejected student. Is she sought out by her fellow students for social activities? Does she enjoy the same level of peer interaction as the other students?

A second consideration is others' satisfaction with the behavior change. The social skills instruction will be viewed favorably if others find the changes to be positive and desirable. For example, do the other children find Yvonne more pleasant to be with? Did the mother note a reduction in sibling and family conflict as a result of her four-year-old learning to appropriately borrow and return other's property?

Finally, consider "consumer satisfaction," or the learner's reaction to the instruction and the behaviors learned. Does Phillip, for example, find it more comfortable, pleasant, and beneficial to respond to inquiries about his arm in the more positive, assertive manner? And does Yvonne find a greater payoff in making compliments than in being rude to her fellow students? Cartledge (1984) found that elementary-age students not only reacted favorably to the social skills instruction, indicating role-playing to be their favorite activity, but also felt that social skills teaching should continue and be a regular part of the curriculum. One student stated that she felt everyone should receive social skills instruction, *including teachers.* Another child reported that as a result of social skills instruction she had stopped fighting.

The problems with teacher motivation and skills, discussed earlier, are magnified when considering their impact on program evaluation. If effects are minimal, are these due to invalid procedures or to the limits of teachers' willingness or ability to teach? Weissberg and Gesten (1982) found that pupil improvement corresponded with refinement of teacher skill. Cartledge (1984) also observed higher ratings among pupils assigned to the teachers showing the most skill and evidence of teaching ability. To evaluate social skills instruction in the schools effectively, one must use valid procedures, such as direct objective measures, as well as address issues relative to social validity.

Applying a Social Skills Model

The instructional methods for social skills development presented in the first four chapters of this book are consistent with the *prescriptive* or *directive* teaching model (Stephens, 1978; 1992b). Essentially, the elements are:

1. Define in specific, behavioral terms the skill to be taught;
2. Assess the learner's competence to determine his or her initial level of performance;
3. Teach behaviors the assessment shows are lacking in the learner's repertoire;
4. Evaluate or reassess for results of teaching; and
5. Provide opportunities and activities to maintain the behaviors and generalize them to new situations.

These steps and procedures can be adapted to almost any social behavior that can be defined in terms of observable actions, enabling practitioners to develop their own social skills curriculum (Milburn & Cartledge, 1979). The example that follows translates a problem situation into a social skills teaching strategy.

Application of the Model

Problem

Many undesirable behaviors in children continue to occur and even increase because other children pay attention to them. Such behaviors could be decreased and sometimes extinguished by teaching children to ignore these behaviors in their peers.

Step 1 Define the Behavior to Be Taught. Teaching objective: When the child encounters teasing or annoying behavior from another child, she or he will ignore it.

Step 2 Assess the Behavior. Identify the children who are most easily distracted or who react most to annoying behavior from others. Observe what happens as a consequence of their reactions and determine:

- Do these children know what "ignoring" means and how to do it?
- Are there incentives to ignore the other child or are they, perhaps, receiving some satisfaction themselves from the results of their reactions?
- Are there cognitive and affective aspects of the problem situation that might need to be changed? For instance, is the teasing or annoying behavior interpreted by the child as a reason for anger and aggressive retaliation?

Step 3　Plan and Implement Teaching Activities. These include:

1. Motivate pupil interest by providing a rationale for the desired social behavior through an age-appropriate discussion, film, story, and the like. Students might relate personal problematic experiences they had with teasing. Or a contrived situation could be presented such as the following story for elementary-age students. In constructing his or her own story or scenario, the teacher should draw on problems observed among his or her own students, but structure the events so target students are not humiliated or ridiculed.

> Buffy came into school crying again. Buffy often came into school crying, but this morning was worse. Her face was dirty, her clothes were torn, and her books and papers were all disheveled. Patricia, one of the nicest and cleverest students in the school, came to Buffy, put her arms around her, and asked her what was the matter.
> "They are always bothering me," wailed Buffy. "They're always picking on me!"
> "Who?" asked Patricia. "Come with me, Buffy, and tell me what happened."
> Buffy went with Patricia and told her the whole story. She told Patricia that every morning on the bus some of the other boys and girls would call her names. When they did that, Buffy would cry and yell at them and call them names back. Then the other boys and girls would laugh at Buffy and call her more names. This morning Buffy became so angry she started to hit some of the boys and girls. They fought her back and that's how she got her clothes and papers torn and dirtied.
> "Well, Buffy," said Patricia, "I'm sorry these terrible things happened to you, but I think you need to learn how to handle these boys and girls."
> "I can't fight all of them," cried Buffy. "I tried today, and you see what happened."
> "I'm not talking about fighting," replied Patricia. "I'm talking about my secret weapon: ignoring. After school today, I will teach you how."
> Every day after school, Patricia helped Buffy practice ignoring. Before long Buffy was coming to school happy like the other students because the boys and girls on the school bus had stopped teasing her.

2. Engage students in a group discussion. Talk about what ignoring means, how to do it, and when to do it. Have the students give examples of behaviors that would be good to ignore, as well as times when a behavior should not be ignored. Discuss other alternative reactions, the advantages and disadvantages of each, and possible outcomes of different ways of behaving. Have students relate the discussion to actual incidents in the classroom or on the playground. The discussion can be done at a structured social skills lesson time or can take place in an impromptu fashion after a problem has occurred. The problem situation can become the scenario for role-playing.

3. Draw out of the discussion an operational definition in terms that children can understand. For example, ignoring means "Walk away," "Turn your head away," or "Don't answer." Write these behaviors on the chalkboard.

4. Identify cognitive behaviors. The Happening-Thought-Feeling-Reaction Diagram (Knaus, 1974), discussed in Chapter 3, would be useful to facilitate children's understanding of how different thoughts can help them ignore by controlling their feelings. Assist students in identifying constructive self-statements that could be used under such conditions: "I am not going to get in trouble," or "He's just trying to make me cry; I won't let him." List self-statements on the chalkboard as specific behaviors to use when ignoring. Help students practice them.

5. Set up a role-playing situation, in which the teacher and a student or two students demonstrate ignoring, using actual or hypothetical situations. For a more dramatic impact, demonstrate both appropriate and inappropriate responses. Give students an opportunity to tell you whether ignoring has occurred. Divide the students into pairs and give them problem situations to role-play ignoring: "Ignore someone who is poking you." "Ignore someone who is making faces at you." "Ignore someone who is calling you a name." Have the students reverse roles and take turns being ignorer and ignoree. Bring the group together to demonstrate and evaluate each other's ability to ignore.

6. Praise students who give good demonstrations and provide corrective feedback for those who have difficulty. It may be necessary to repeat the discussion and role-play practice on more than one occasion.

7. Provide a model by showing that many inappropriate student behaviors can be eliminated by ignoring.

8. Additional pupil practice can be provided through worksheets such as Figure 5-1. For each of the situations depicted, students should identify constructive self-statements and behavioral responses.

Step 4   Evaluate. Observe the children's behavior in problem situations to determine whether their reactions to teasing are decreasing, whether they appear to be turning away and ignoring teasing remarks and annoying behavior. Because ignoring is sometimes difficult to observe or interpret and teasing may be subtle and hard to detect, systematic evaluation would probably involve counting specific problem behaviors that could decrease as a result of ignoring—talk-outs, fights, and on- or off-task behavior. If the problem behavior is decreasing, provide adequate reinforcers to maintain positive responses. If the behavior is not changing, more assessment of the antecedents and results of the problem behavior may be necessary, along with more training sessions.

Step 5   Program for Maintenance and Transfer

1. Provide rewards to keep positive behaviors going. Praise the children when they appear to ignore teasing. To avoid calling attention to the child being ignored,

FIGURE 5-1 Integrating the Steps Worksheet

you may need to deliver the praise subtly or at a later time, with a comment such as, "Marvin, I'm proud of how well you are trying to ignore George when he kicks the back of your chair" or "Louise, I like the way you kept on working and ignored Larry's singing behind you."

Public postings might be used to remind and reward students for this behavior. One example is the use of "teasing tags," which are happy faces cut out of construction paper with room for a child's name. Children observed, by either the teacher or another child, handling teasing constructively have their names written on a teasing tag. The tag is hung on the bulletin board with a praise statement such as "Social Skills Superstars."

2.   Set up a contingency contract. A contract could be individual to the child: "If you ignore John's humming and tapping during reading period, you may help me bring in the film projector." A contract also can be a group contract: "If the class can ignore anyone who is talking out and acting silly from now until recess, we will have five minutes longer for recess."

3.   Teach children to monitor their own behavior. A child trying to develop the social skill of ignoring could, for example, record attempts at ignoring on a tally sheet or a wrist counter. Although self-monitoring may be questionable as a source of reliable data, it can have a motivational effect to keep a new social skill going.

4.   Set up role-plays and discussions to show the children how they can benefit from using ignoring in problem situations with their classmates or siblings at home and in the neighborhood. Make sure the children understand the circumstances when ignoring is appropriate. For the most successful transfer, let the parents know what you are doing and encourage them to reinforce the child's efforts to ignore in problem situations.

5.   Make homework assignments, such as the one in Figure 5-2, where students record conflict situations and the behaviors they employed to resolve the problem. These assignments can serve as reminders to practice these behaviors at other times and under various conditions. They need to be adapted, however, to the students' skill and developmental levels. Therefore, in some cases, only simple oral reporting of recent actions may be required, while for highly capable students, essay assignments of considerable detail may be appropriate.

Now that you have learned how to ignore teasing, you are ready to practice these behaviors at home as well as at school. Think about this for the next three days. Then, in the space below, tell about one time when you did a good job of ignoring teasing.

1. What was the problem behavior that you wanted to ignore?

2. How did you ignore it?

3. What did you say to yourself to help you ignore the behavior?

4. What did the other person do?

5. Did this solve the problem?

6. How did you feel afterward?

FIGURE 5-2 Homework for Ignoring Teasing/Negative Behavior

Summary

Successful social skills instruction depends on several factors including the needs and interests of the learner, the attitudes and skills of the trainer, and the teaching conditions. Learner interest and participation can be stimulated by making social skills instruction meaningful, reinforcing, or fun. Developmentally appropriate activities that help the youngster understand why it is important to learn a particular social behavior contribute to skill relevance and pupil motivation.

Techniques that either increase the reinforcing properties of the instructional activities or reward attending behavior provide additional means to promote pupil interest and involvement. Learning can be facilitated by the attractive, creative presentation of social skills lessons. When necessary, more powerful incentives in the form of rewards can be employed to sustain attention and enhance performance.

Games are particularly useful for providing motivation and introducing social skills teaching in a nonthreatening context. Social skills games can involve the use of a game board as well as simple procedures devised by the teacher or therapist. Other games use role-playing or simulation of realistic situations. Social skills games should deemphasize competition and provide sufficient opportunities to participate and practice the skills to be learned. Cooperative groups can enhance positive peer interactions for both academics and fun.

Although social skills instruction can be conducted successfully in the schools, some potentially mitigating factors pertain to teacher training and skill, administrative support, evaluation, parental participation, and community resources. Schools are uniquely structured to create an environment where social skills can be taught and systematically reinforced by immediate members (peers, teachers, administrators, ancillary staff), thereby contributing to the durability of learned behaviors. Recognizing their powerful role, the aid and participation of parents, as well as other significant persons in the child's environment, need to be solicited to further solidify the child's newly acquired skills.

Schools can be instrumental in preventing as well as providing remedies for mild to moderate social skills problems. Teacher training and support are critical ingredients for effective social skills instruction. Another important factor is the ease with which the strategies can be administered. Avoid procedures that overly tax teachers either in time or skill. The effectiveness of social skills instruction needs to be determined by adequate evaluation. School settings, however, present special evaluation problems and therefore require that additional measures are taken to ensure efficient and valid procedures.

A social skills curriculum can be developed to fit the behavioral needs of children by using some of the same processes by which children naturally learn social behaviors. With procedures such as social modeling, role-playing, and verbal mediation, accompanied by reinforcement techniques, social skills trainers can build new behaviors and increase the frequency of desirable social behaviors in children.

References

Abrams, B. J. (1992). Values clarification for students with emotional disabilities. *Teaching Exceptional Children, 24,* 28–33.

Achenbach, T. M. (1991). *Integrative guide to the 1991 CBCL, YSR, and TRF profiles.* Burlington: University of Vermont, Department of Psychiatry.

Achenbach, T. M., McConaughy, S. H., & Howell, C. T. (1987). Child/adolescent behavioral and emotional problems: Implications of cross-informant correlations for situational specificity. *Psychological Bulletin, 101,* 213–232.

Ager, C., & Cole, C. (1991). A review of cognitive-behavioral interventions for children and adolescents with behavioral disorders. *Behavioral Disorders, 16,* 276–287.

Akhtar, N., & Bradley, E. J. (1991). Social information processing deficits of aggressive children: Present findings and implications for social skills training. *Clinical Psychology Review, 11,* 621–644.

Allyon, T., & Azrin, N. (1968). *The token economy.* New York: Appleton-Century-Crofts.

Altomare, K. (1989). *A social skills project.* Unpublished manuscript.

Amish, P. L., Gesten, E. L., Smith, J. K., Clark, H. B., & Stark, C. (1988). Social problem-solving training for severely emotionally and behaviorally disturbed children. *Behavioral Disorders, 13,* 175–186.

Argyle, M. (1986). The great popularity of social skills training. *Contemporary Psychology, 31,* 678–680.

Aronson, E. (1978). *The jigsaw classroom.* Beverly Hills, CA: Sage.

Asarnow, J. R. (1988). Peer status and social competence in child psychiatric inpatients: A comparison of children with depressive, externalizing and concurrent depressive and externalizing disorders. *Journal of Abnormal Child Psychology, 16,* 151–162.

Ascher, L. M., & Phillips, D. (1975). Guided behavior rehearsal. *Journal of Behavior Therapy and Experimental Psychiatry, 6,* 215–218.

Asher, S. R., & Williams, G. A. (1987). Helping children without friends in home and school. In *Children's social development: Information for teachers and parents* (pp. 1–26). Urbana, IL: ERIC, Clearing House on Elementary and Early Childhood Education.

Baer, D. (1981). *How to plan for generalization.* Lawrence, KS: H & H Enterprises.

Baer, D. M. (1978, September). Remarks as discussant, Symposium on Research and Technological Consideration of Generalization and Maintenance Variables. Paper presented at the Convention of the American Psychological Association, Montreal.

Baer, M., Fowler, S. A., & Carden-Smith, L. (1984). Using reinforcement and independent grading to promote and maintain task accuracy in a mainstreamed classroom. *Analysis and Intervention in Developmental Disabilities, 4,* 157–169.

Bain, S., Houghton, S., & Farris, H. (1991). Teacher ratings of social skill by direct observation and through interactive video. *British Journal of Educational Technology, 22,* 196–202.

Bandura, A. (1969). *Principles of behavior modification.* New York: Holt, Rinehart & Winston.

———. (1973). *Aggression: A social learning analysis.* Englewood Cliffs, NJ: Prentice-Hall.

———. (1977a). Self-efficacy: Toward a unifying theory of behavioral change. *Psychological Review, 84,* 191–215.

———. (1977b). *Social learning theory.* Englewood Cliffs, NJ: Prentice-Hall.

Bandura, A., & Jourden, F. J. (1991). Self-regulatory mechanisms governing the impact of social comparison on complex decision making. *Journal of Personality and Social Psychology, 60,* 941–951.

Barrett, D. E., & Yarrow, M. R. (1977). Prosocial behavior, social inferential ability, and assertiveness in children. *Child Development, 48,* 475–481.

Barrios, B. A. (1993). Direct observation. In T. H. Ollendick & M. Hersen (Eds.), *Handbook of child and adolescent assessment* (pp. 140–164). Boston: Allyn and Bacon.

Barton, E. J., & Ascione, F. R. (1979). Sharing in preschool children: Facilitation, stimulus generalization, and maintenance. *Journal of Applied Behavior Analysis, 12,* 417–430.

———. (1984). Direct observation. In T. H. Ollendick & M. Hersen (Eds.), *Child behavior assessment.* Elmsford, NY: Pergamon Press.

Bash, M. A., & Camp, B. (1980). Teacher training in the think aloud classroom program. In G. Cartledge & J. F. Milburn (Eds.), *Teaching social skills to children: Innovative approaches* (pp 143–178). Elmsford, NY: Pergamon Press.

———. (1986). Teacher training in the think aloud classroom program. In G. Cartledge & J. F. Milburn (Eds.), *Teaching social skills to children: Innovative approaches* (pp 187–218). Elmsford, NY: Pergamon Press.

Baumgart, D., Filler, J., & Askvig, B. A. (1991). Perceived importance of social skills: A survey of teachers, parents, and other professionals. *The Journal of Special Education, 25,* 236-251.

Beck, S. (1986). Methods of assessment II: Questionnaires and checklists. In C. L. Frame & J. L. Matson (Eds.), *Handbook of assessment in childhood pathology: Applied issues in differential diagnosis and treatment evaluation.* New York: Plenum Press.

Beck, S., Forehand, R., Neeper, R., & Baskin, C. H. (1982). A comparison of two analogue strategies for assessing children's social skills, *Journal of Consulting and Clinical Psychology, 50,* 596–597.

Bellack, A., Hersen, M., & Lamparski, D. (1979). Role-play tests for assessing social skills. Are they valid? Are they useful? *Journal of Consulting and Clinical Psychology, 47,* 335–342.

Bellack, A., Hersen, M., & Turner, S. (1978). Role-play tests for assessing social skills: Are they valid? *Behavior Therapy, 9,* 448–461.

———. (1979). Relationship of roleplaying and knowledge of appropriate behavior to assertion in the natural environment. *Journal of Consulting and Clinical Psychology, 47,* 670–678.

Bellack, A. S., Morrison, R. L., Mueser, K. T., Wade, J. H., & Sayers, S. L. (1990). Role play for assessing the social competence of psychiatric patients. *Psychiatric Assessment: A Journal of Consulting and Clinical Psychology, 2,* 248–255.

Bengtsson, H., & Johnson, L. (1992). Perspective taking, empathy, and prosocial behavior in late childhood. *Child Study Journal, 22,* 11–22.

Berler, E. S., Gross, A. M., & Drabman, R. S. (1982). Social skills training with children: Proceed with caution. *Journal of Applied Behavior Analysis, 15,* 41–53.

Bernard, M. E. (1990). Rational Emotive Therapy with children and adolescents: Treatment strategies. *School Psychology Review, 19,* 294–303.

Bernard, M. E., & Joyce, M. R. (1984). *Rational-emotive therapy with children and adolescents.* New York: John Wiley and Sons.

Berndt, T. J., Perry, T. B., & Miller, K. E. (1988). Friends' and classmates' interactions on academic tasks. *Journal of Educational Psychology, 80,* 506–513.

Bierman, K. L. (1983). Cognitive development and clinical interviews with children. In B. Lahey & A. E. Kazdin (Eds.), *Advances in clinical child psychology,* Vol. 6 (pp. 217–250). New York: Plenum Press.

Bierman, K. L., & Furman, W. (1984). The effects of social skills and peer involvement on the social adjustment of preadolescents. *Child Development, 55,* 151–163.

Bierman, K., Miller, C., & Stabb, S. (1987). Improving the social behavior and peer acceptance of rejected boys: Effects of social skill training with instructions and prohibitions. *Journal of Consulting and Clinical Psychology, 55,* 194–200.

Bijou, S. W., Peterson, R. F., & Ault, M. H. (1968). A method to integrate descriptive and experimental field studies at the level of data and empirical concepts. *Journal of Applied Behavior Analysis, 1,* 175–191.

Boldizar, J. P., Perry, D. G., & Perry, L. E. (1989). Outcome values and aggression. *Child Development, 60,* 571–579.

Bolstad, O. D., & Johnson, S. M. (1972). Self-regulation in the modification of disruptive classroom behavior. *Journal of Applied Behavior Analysis, 5,* 443–454.

Borke, H. (1971). Interpersonal perception of young children: Egocentrism or empathy? *Developmental Psychology, 5,* 263–269.

Bornstein, M. R., Bellack, A. S., & Hersen, M. (1977). Social-skills training for unassertive children: A multiple-baseline analysis. *Journal of Applied Behavior Analysis, 10,* 183–195.

Bower, E. M. (1960). *Early identification of emotionally handicapped children in school.* Springfield, IL: Charles C. Thomas.

Bowman, P. H., DeHaan, R. F., Kough, J. K., & Liddle, G. P. (1956). *Mobilizing community resources for youth.* Chicago: University of Chicago Press.

Brochin, H. A., & Wasik, B. H. (1992). Social problem solving among popular and unpopular children. *Journal of Abnormal Child Psychology, 20,* 377–391.

Brooks-Gunn, J., & Luciano, L. (1985). Social competence in young handicapped children: A developmental perspective. In M. Sigman (Ed.), *Children with emotional disorders and developmental disabilities: Assessment and treatment.* Orlando, FL: Grune & Stratton.

Bryant, B. K. (1982). An index of empathy for children and adolescents. *Child Development, 53,* 413–425.

Bugental, D. B., Whalen, C. K., & Henker, B. (1977). Causal attributions of hyperactive children and motivational assumptions of two behavioral-change approaches: Evidence for an interactionist position. *Child Development, 48,* 874–884.

Camp, B. (1977). Verbal mediation in young aggressive boys. *Journal of Abnormal Psychology, 86,* 145–153.

Camp, B. W., & Bash, M. A. S. (1981). *Think aloud: Increasing social and cognitive skills—A problem-solving program for children (primary level).* Champaign, IL: Research Press.

Camp, B. W., Blom, G. E., Herbert, F., & van Doorninck, W. J. (1977). "Think aloud": A program for developing self-control in young aggressive boys. *Journal of Abnormal Child Psychology, 5,* 157–169.

Camp, B. W., Zimet, S. G., van Doorninck, W. J., & Dahlem, N. W. (1977). Verbal abilities in young aggressive boys. *Journal of Educational Psychology, 69,* 129–135.

Campos, J. J., Campos, R. G., & Barrett, K. C. (1989). Emergent themes in the study of emoional development and emotion regulation. *Developmental Psychology, 25,* 394-402.

Carr, E. G., & Durand, V. M. (1985). Reducing behavior problems through functional communication training. *Journal of Applied Behavior Analysis, 18,* 111–126.

Cartledge, G. (1984). *Formal social skills instruction in the schools: Report.* Unpublished manuscript.

Cartledge, G., Frew, T. W., & Zaharias, J. (1985). Social skill needs of mainstreamed students: Peer and teacher perceptions. *Learning Disability Quarterly, 8,* 132–140.

Cartledge, G., & Kleefeld, J. (1991). *Taking part: Introducing social skills to children.* Circle Pines, MN: American Guidance Service.

————. (in press). *Working together: Building children's social skills through folk literature.* Circle Pines, MN: American Guidance Service.

Cartledge, G., & Milburn, J. F. (1978). The case for teaching social skills in the classroom: A review. *Review of Educational Research, 1,* 133–156.

————. (1983). The how-to of effective social skills training. *Directive Teacher, 3,* 12.

Cartledge, G., Stupay, D., & Kaczala, C. (1986). Relationship between social skills and social perception in L.D. and nonhandicapped elementary-aged children. *Learning Disability Quarterly, 9,* 226–234.

Castaneda, A., McCandless, B. R., & Palermo, D. F. (1956). The children's form of the Manifest Anxiety Scale. *Child Development, 27,* 317–326.

Casteel, J. D., & Stahl, R. J. (1975). *Values clarification in the classroom: A primer.* Pacific Palisades, CA: Goodyear.

Cavell, T. A. (1990). Social adjustment, social performance, and social skills: A tri-component model of social competence. *Journal of Clinical Child Psychology, 19,* 111–122.

Chandler, L. K., Lubeck, R. C., & Fowler, S. A. (1992). Generalization and maintenance of preschool children's social skills: A critical review and analysis. *Journal of Applied Behavior Analysis, 25,* 415–428.

Chandler, M. (1973). Egocentrism and antisocial behavior: The assessment and training of social perspective-taking skills. *Developmental Psychology, 9,* 326–332.

Charlesworth, R., & Hartup, W. W. (1967). Positive social reinforcement in the nursery school peer group. *Child Development, 38,* 993–1002.

Chittenden, G. E. (1942). An experimental study in measuring and modifying assertive behavior in young children. *Monographs of the Society for Research in Child Development, 7*(1, Serial No. 31).

Christie, D. J., Hiss, M., & Lozanoff, B. (1984). Modification of inattentive classroom behavior. *Behavior Modification, 8,* 391–406.

Chung, T. Y., & Asher, S. R. (1992, August). *Children's strategies and goals in resolving conflicts with peers.* Paper presented at the Convention of the American Psychological Association, Washington, DC.

Clark, H. B., Caldwell, C. P., & Christian, W. P. (1979). Classroom training of conversational skills and remote programming for the practice of these skills in another setting. *Child Behavior Therapy, 1,* 139–160.

Clark, L. A., & McKenzie, H. S. (1989). Effects of self-evaluation training of seriously emotionally disturbed children on the generalization of their classroom rule following and work behaviors across settings and teachers. *Behavioral Disorders, 14,* 89–99.

Cohen, A. S., & Van Tassel, E. (1978). A comparison of partial and complete paired comparisons in sociometric measurement of preschool groups. *Applied Psychological Measurement, 2,* 31–40.

Coie, J. D. (1990). Toward a theory of peer rejection. In S. R. Asher & J. D. Coie (Eds.), *Peer rejection in childhood* (pp. 365–399). New York: Cambridge University Press.

Coie, J. D., & Dodge, K. A. (1983). Continuities and change in children's social status: A five-year longitudinal study. *Merrill-Palmer Quarterly, 29,* 261–282.

Coie, J. D., Dodge, K. A., & Coppotelli, H. (1982). Dimensions and types of social status: A cross-age perspective. *Developmental Psychology, 18,* 557–570.

Coie, J. D., & Koeppl, G. K. (1990). Adapting intervention to the problems of aggressive and disruptive rejected children. In S. R. Asher & J. D. Coie (Eds.), *Peer rejection in childhood* (pp. 309–337). New York: Cambridge University Press.

Combs, M. L., & Slaby, D. A. (1977). Social skills training with children. In B. B. Lahey & A. E. Kazdin (Eds.), *Advances in clinical child psychology,* Vol. I. New York: Plenum Press.

Conger, J. C., Moisan-Thomas, P. C., & Conger, J. J. (1989). Cross-situational generalizability of social competence: A multilevel analysis. *Behavioral Assessment, 2,* 411–431.

Conners, C. K. (1970). Symptom patterns in hyperkinetic, neurotic, and normal children. *Child Development, 41,* 667–682.

————. (1989). *Conners' rating scales.* Austin, TX: PRO-ED.

Connolly, J. A. (1983). A review of sociometric procedures in the assessment of social competencies in children. *Applied Research in Mental Retardation, 4,* 315–327.

Cooper, J. O. (1974). *Measurement and analysis of behavioral techniques.* Columbus, OH: Merrill.

Cooper, J. O., Heron, T. E., & Heward, W. L. (1987). *Applied behavior analysis.* Columbus, OH: Merrill.

Cooper, L. J., Peck, S., Wacker, D. P., & Millard, T. (1993). Functional assessment for a student with a mild mental disability and persistent behavior problems. *Teaching Exceptional Children, 25,* 56–57.

Coopersmith, S. (1967). *The antecedents of self-esteem.* San Francisco: Freeman.

Costello, E. J., Edelbrock, C. S., & Costello, A. J. (1985). Validity of the NIMH diagnostic interview schedule for children: A comparison between psychiatric and pediatric referrals. *Journal of Abnormal and Child Psychology, 13,* 579–595.

Cowan, E., Pederson, A., & Babigian, H., Izzo, L., & Trost, M. (1973). Long term follow-up of early detected vulnerable children. *Journal of Consulting and Clinical Psychology, 41,* 438–446.

Crick, N. R., & Ladd, G. W. (1990). Children's perceptions of the outcomes of social strategies: Do the ends justify being mean? *Developmental Psychology, 26,* 612–620.

Crombie, G. (1988). Gender differences: Implications for social skills assessment and training. *Journal of Clinical Child Psychology, 17,* 116–120.

Csapo, M. (1972). Peer models reverse the "one bad apple spoils the barrel" theory. *Teaching Exceptional Children, 4,* 20–24.

Curwin, R. L., & Curwin, G. (1974). *Developing individual values in the classroom.* Palo Alto, CA: Education Today Company, Inc.

D'Zurilla, T. J., & Goldfried, M. R. (1971). Problem solving and behavior modification. *Journal of Abnormal Psychology, 78,* 107–126.

Dadson, S., & Horner, R. H. (1993). Manipulating setting events to decrease problem behaviors: A case study. *Teaching Exceptional Children, 25,* 53–55.

Dardig, J. C., & Heward, W. L. (1980). *Sign here: A contracting book for children and their parents.* Columbus, OH: Merrill.

DeRisi, W. J., & Butz, G. (1975). *Writing behavioral contracts: A case simulation practice manual.* Champaign, IL: Research Press.

DeVries, D. L., & Slavin, R. E. (1978). Teams-Games-Tournament (TGT): Review of ten classroom experiments. *Journal of Research and Development in Education, 12,* 28–38.

Dickerson, E. A., & Creedon, C. F. (1981). Self-selection of standards by children: The relative effectiveness of pupil-selected and teacher-selected standards of performance. *Journal of Applied Behavior Analysis, 14,* 425–433.

Dinkmeyer, D. (1982). *Developing understanding of self and others (DUSO Program).* Circle Pines, MN: American Guidance Service, Inc.

Dodge, K. A. (1986). A social information processing model of social competence in children. In M. Perlmutter (Ed.), *Cognitive Perspectives on Children's Social and Behavioral Development: The Minnesota Symposia on Child Psychology, 18,* 77–125. Hillsdale, NJ: Erlbaum.

———. (1993). Social-cognitive mechanisms in the development of conduct disorder and depression. In L. W. Porter & M. R. Rosenzweig (Eds.), *Annual Review of Psychology, 44,* 559–584. Palo Alto, CA: Annual Reviews, Inc.

Dodge, K. A., McClaskey, C. L., & Feldman, E. (1985). Situational approach to the assessment of social competence in children. *Journal of Consulting and Clinical Psychology, 53,* 344–353.

Dodge, K. A., Schlundt, D. C., Schocken, I., & Delugach, J. D. (1983). Social competence and children's sociometric status: The role of peer group entry strategies. *Merrill-Palmer Quarterly, 29,* 309–336.

Dupont, H., Gardner, O., & Brody, D. (1974). *Toward affective development.* Circle Pines, MN: American Guidance Service, Inc.

Durand, V. M. (1990). *Severe behavior problems: A functional communication training approach.* New York: Guilford Press.

Durand, V. M., & Carr, E. G. (1987). Social influences on "self-stimulatory" behavior: Analysis and treatment application. *Journal of Applied Behavior Analysis, 20,* 119–132.

———. (1991). Functional communication training to reduce challenging behavior: Maintenance and application in new settings. *Journal of Applied Behavior Analysis, 24,* 251–264.

Durlak, J. A. (1985). Primary prevention of school maladjustment. *Journal of Consulting and Clinical Psychology, 33,* 623–630.

Durlak, J. A., Fuhrman, T., & Lampman, C. (1991). Effectiveness of cognitive-behavior therapy for maladapting children: A meta-analysis. *Psychological Bulletin, 110,* 204–214.

Dygdon, J., Conger, A. J., Conger, J. C., Wallanda, J. L., & Keane, S. P. (1980, September). *Behavioral correlates of social competence and dysfunction in early childhood.* Paper presented at the Conference of the American Psychological Association, Montreal.

Edelbrock, C. (1988). Informant reports. In E. S. Shapiro & T. R. Kratochwill (Eds.), *Behavioral assessment in schools* (pp. 351–383). New York: Guilford Press.

Edleson, J. L., & Cole-Kelly, K. (1978). *A behavioral roleplay test for assessing children's social skills: Scoring manual.* Unpublished manual, University of Wisconsin–Madison.

Edleson, J. L., & Rose, S. D. (1978). *A behavioral roleplay test for assessing children's social skills.* Paper presented at the Annual Convention of the Association for the Advancement of Behavior Therapy, Chicago.

———. (1981). Investigations into the efficacy of short-term group social skills training for socially isolated children. *Child Behavior Therapy, 3,* 1–16.

Edmonson, B., DeJung, J., Leland, H., & Leach, E. M. (1974). *The test of social inference.* Freeport, NY: Educational Activities, Inc.

Eisenberg, N., & Harris, J. D. (1984). Social competence: A developmental perspective. *School Psychology Review, 13,* 267–277.

Eisenberg, N., & Miller, P. A. (1987). The relation of empathy to prosocial and related behaviors. *Psychological Bulletin, 101,* 91–119.

Eisenberg-Berg, N., & Lennon, R. (1980). Altruism and the assessment of empathy in the preschool years. *Child Development, 51,* 552–557.

Eisler, R. M. (1976). Behavioral assessment of social skills. In M. Hersen & A. A. Bellack (Eds.), *Behavioral assessment: A practical handbook.* Elmsford, NY: Pergamon Press.

Eisler, R. M., & Frederiksen, L. W. (1980). *Perfecting social skills.* New York: Plenum Press.

Eisley, M. E., & Merrill, P. F. (1984, April). *Effects of context vs. substance in stories portraying moral behavior.* Paper presented at the Annual Convention of the American Educational Research Association, New Orleans.

Elardo, P. T., & Caldwell, B. M. (1979). The effects of an experimental social development program on children in the middle childhood period. *Psychology in the Schools, 16,* 93–100.

Elias, M. J., & Branden, L. R. (1988). Primary prevention of behavioral and emotional problems in school-aged populations. *School Psychology Review, 17,* 581–592.

Elias, M. J., Gara, M. A., Schuyler, T. F., Branden-Muller, L. R., & Sayette, M. A. (1991). The promotion of social competence: Longitudinal study of a preventive school-based program. *American Journal of Orthopsychiatry, 61,* 409–417.

Ellis, A. (1962). *Reason and emotion in psychotherapy.* New York: Lyle Stuart Press.

————. (1977). The basic clinical theory of rational-emotive therapy. In A. Ellis & R. Grieger (Eds.), *Handbook of rational-emotive therapy* (pp. 3–34). New York: Springer.

Enright, R. D., & Lapsley, D. K. (1980). Social role-taking: A review of the constructs, measures, and measurement properties. *Review of Educational Research, 50,* 647–675.

Erikson, E. (1963). *Childhood and society.* New York: Norton.

Etscheidt, S. (1991). Reducing aggressive behavior and improving self-control: A cognitive-behavioral training program for behaviorally disordered adolescents. *Behavioral Disorders, 16,* 107–115.

Evans, I., & Nelson, R. (1977). Assessment of child behavior problems. In A. R. Ciminero, K. S. Calhoun & H. E. Adams (Eds.), *Handbook of behavioral assessment* (pp. 603–681). New York: Wiley.

Fabes, R. A., & Eisenberg, N. (1992). Young children's coping with interpersonal anger. *Child Development, 63,* 116–128.

Fagen, S. A., Long, J. J., & Stevens, D. J. (1975). *Teaching children self-control.* Columbus, OH: Merrill.

Fantuzzo, J. W., & Clement, P. W. (1981). Generalization of the effects of teacher and self-administered token reinforcers to nontreated students. *Journal of Applied Behavior Analysis, 14,* 435–447.

Favell, J. E., & Reid, D. H. (1988). Generalizing and maintaining improvement in problem behavior. In R. Horner, G. Dunlap, & R. Koegel (Eds.), *Generalization and maintenance* (pp. 171–196). Baltimore: Paul H. Brookes.

Feffer, M., & Gourevitch, V. (1960). Cognitive aspects of role-taking in children. *Journal of Personality, 29,* 384–396.

Feldhusen, J., Houtz, J., & Ringenbach, S. (1972). The Purdue Elementary Problem-Solving Inventory. *Psychological Reports, 31,* 891–901.

Felixbrod, J. J., & O'Leary, K. D. (1973). Effects of reinforcement on children's academic behavior as a function of self-determined and externally imposed contingencies. *Journal of Applied Behavior Analysis, 6,* 241–250.

Feshbach, N. D. (1982). Sex differences in empathy and social behavior in children. In N. Eisenberg-Berg (Ed.), *The development of prosocial behavior* (pp. 315–338). New York: Academic Press.

Feshbach, N. D., Feshbach, S., Fauvre, M., & Ballard-Campbell, M. (1983). *Learning to care.* Glenview, IL: Scott, Foresman and Company.

Feshbach, N. D., & Roe, K. (1968). Empathy in six- and seven-year olds. *Child Development, 39,* 133–145.

Fiechtl, B. J., Innocenti, M., & Rule, S. (1987). *Skills for school success.* Logan, UT: Utah State University, Developmental Center for Handicapped Persons, Outreach Division.

Finch, A. J., Jr., Deardorff, P. A., & Montgomery, L. E. (1974). Individually tailored behavioral rating scales: A possible alternative. *Journal of Abnormal Child Psychology, 2,* 209–216.

Fishback, L. (1992). *Teaching a social skill: Making complimentary statements.* Unpublished manuscript.

Fixen, D. L., Phillips, E. L., & Wolf, M. M. (1972). Achievement place: The reliability of self-reporting and peer-reporting and their effects on behavior. *Journal of Applied Behavior Analysis, 5,* 19–30.

Flavell, J., Botkin, P., Fry, C., Wright, J., & Jarvis, P. (1968). *The development of note taking and communication skills in children.* New York: Wiley.

Foster, S. L., Bell-Dolan, D., & Berler, E. S. (1986). Methodological issues in the use of sociometrics for selecting children for social skills research and training. In R. J. Prinz (Ed.), *Advances in behavioral assessment of children and families* (Vol. 2). Greenwich, CT: JAI Press.

Foster, S. L., Delawyer, D. D., & Guevremont, D. C. (1986). A critical incidents analysis of liked and disliked peer behaviors and their situational parameters in childhood and adolescence. *Behavioral Assessment, 8,* 115–133.

Foster, S. L., & Ritchey, W. L. (1979). Issues in assessment of social competence in children. *Journal of Applied Behavior Analysis, 12,* 625–638.

Foster-Johnson, L., & Dunlap, G. (1993). Using functional assessment to develop effective, individualized interventions for challenging behaviors. *Teaching Exceptional Children, 25,* 44–50.

Fowler, S. (1988). The effects of peer-mediated interventions on establishing, maintaining, and generalizing children's behavior changes. In R. Horner, G. Dunlap, & R. Koegel (Eds.), *Generalization and maintenance* (pp. 143–170). Baltimore: Paul H. Brookes.

Fowler, S. A., & Baer, D. H. (1981). "Do I have to be good all day?" The timing of delayed reinforcement as a factor in generalization. *Journal of Applied Behavior Analysis, 14,* 13–24.

Foxx, R. M., & McMorrow, M. J. (1984). *Stacking the deck, a social skills game for retarded adults.* Champaign, IL: Research Press.

Foxx, R. M., McMorrow, M. J., & Mennemeier, M. (1984). Teaching social/vocational skills to retarded adults with a modified table game: An analysis of generalization. *Journal of Applied Behavior Analysis, 17,* 343–352.

Foxx, R. M., McMorrow, M. J., & Schloss, C. W. (1983). Stacking the deck: Teaching social skills to retarded adults with a modified table game. *Journal of Applied Behavior Analysis, 16,* 157–170.

Franks, C. M., & Wilson, T. (1978). *Annual review of behavior therapy: Theory and practice* (Vol. 6). New York: Brunner/Mazel.

Freud, S. (1961). *The standard edition of the complete psychological works of Sigmund Freud.* London: Hogarth Press.

Furman, W. (1980). Promoting social development: Developmental implications for treatment. In B. B. Lahey & A. E. Kazdin (Eds.), *Advances in clinical child psychology.* New York: Plenum Press.

Gaffney, L. R., & McFall, R. M. (1981). A comparison of social skills in delinquent and nondelinquent adolescent girls using a behavioral role-playing inventory. *Journal of Consulting and Clinical Psychology, 49,* 959–967.

Gambrill, E. D. (1977). *Behavior modification.* San Francisco: Jossey-Bass.

Gardner, W. I., & Cole, C. L. (1988). Self-monitoring procedures. In E. S. Shapiro & T. R. Kratochwill (Eds.), *Behavioral assessment in schools* (pp. 206–247). New York: Guilford Press.

Gaylord-Ross, R., & Haring, T. (1987). Social interaction research for adolescents with severe handicaps. *Behavioral Disorders, 12,* 264–275.

Gelfand, D. M., & Hartmann, D. P. (1975). *Child behavior analysis and therapy.* Elmsford, NY: Pergamon Press, Inc.

———. (1984). *Child behavior analysis and therapy* (2nd ed.). New York: Pergamon Press.

Gerber, P. J. & Zinkgraf, S. A. (1982). A comparative study of social-perceptual ability in learning disabled and non-handicapped students. *Learning Disability Quarterly, 5,* 374–378.

Glazier, R. (1970). *How to design educational games.* Cambridge, MA: Abt Associates.

Glennon, B., & Weisz, J. R. (1978). An observational approach to the assessment of anxiety in young children. *Journal of Counseling and Clinical Psychology, 46,* 1246–1257.

Glenwick, D. S., & Jason, L. A. (1984). Locus of intervention in child cognitive behavior therapy. In A. W. Meyers & W. E. Craighead (Eds.), *Cognitive behavior therapy with children* (pp. 129–162). New York: Plenum Press.

Goldfried, M., & D'Zurilla, T. (1969). A behavioral-analytic model for assessing competence. In C. D. Spielberger (Ed.), *Current topics in clinical and community psychology,* Vol. 1 (pp. 151–196). New York: Academic Press.

Goldfried, M. R., & Goldfried, A. P. (1975). Cognitive change methods. In F. H. Kanfer & A. P. Goldstein (Eds.), *Helping people change* (pp. 97–130). Elmsford, NY: Pergamon Press.

Goldman, J., L'Engle Stein, C., & Guerry, S. (1983). *Psychological methods of child assessment.* New York: Brunner/Mazel, Inc.

Goldstein, A. P. (1988a). *The prepare curriculum: Teaching prosocial competencies.* Champaign, IL: Research Press.

———. (1988b). *The skillstreaming video* [Videotape]. Champaign, IL.: Research Press.

Goldstein, A. P., Carr, E. G., Davidson, W. S., & Wehr, P. (1981). *In response to aggression.* Elmsford, NY: Pergamon Press.

Goldstein, A. P., & Michaels, G. Y. (1985). *Empathy.* Hillsdale, NJ: Lawrence Erlbaum Associates, Inc.

Goldstein, A. P., Sprafkin, R. P., & Gershaw, N. J. (1976). *Skill training for community living: Applying structured learning therapy.* Elmsford, NY: Pergamon Press.

Goodwin, S. E., & Mahoney, M. J. (1975). Modification of aggression through modeling: An experimental probe. *Journal of Behavior Therapy and Experimental Psychiatry, 6,* 200–202.

Gordon, A. K. (1972). *Games for growth.* Chicago: Science Research Associates.

Gottman, J. (1977). Toward a definition of social isolation in children. *Child Development, 48,* 513–517.

Gottman, J., Gonso, J., & Rasmussen, B. (1975). Social interaction, social competence and friendship in children. *Child Development, 46,* 709–718.

Graham, S., Harris, K. R., & Reid, R. (1992). Developing self-regulated learners. *Focus on Exceptional Children, 24,* 1–16.

Greenspan, S. (1981). Social competence and handicapped individuals: Practical implications of a proposed model. In B. K. Keogh (Ed.), *Advances in special education: Socialization influences on exceptionality* (pp. 41–82). Greenwich, CT: JAI Press.

Greenwood, C. R., & Hops, H. (1981). Group-oriented contingencies and peer behavior change. In P. S. Strain (Ed.), *The utilization of classroom peers as behavior change agents* (pp. 189–259). New York: Plenum Press.

Greenwood, C. R., Walker, H. M., & Hops, H. (1977). Some issues in social interaction/withdrawal assessment. *Exceptional Children, 43,* 490–499.

Greenwood, C. R., Walker, H. M., Todd, N. M., & Hops, H. (1979). Selecting a cost effective screening device for the assessment of preschool social withdrawal. *Journal of Applied Behavioral Analysis, 12,* 639–652.

Gresham, F. M. (1985). Utility of cognitive-behavioral procedures for social skills training with children: A critical review. *Journal of Abnormal Child Psychology, 13,* 411–423.

———. (1986). Conceptual and definitional issues in the assessment of children's social skills: Implications for classification and training. *Journal of Clinical Child Psychology, 15,* 3–15.

———. (1992). Social skills and learning disabilities: Causal, concomitant, or correlational? *School Psychology Review, 21,* 348–360.

Gresham, F. M., & Davis, C. J. (1988). Behavioral interviews with teachers and parents. In E. S. Shapiro & T. R. Kratochwill (Eds.), *Behavioral assessment in schools* (pp. 455–493). New York: Guilford Press.

Gresham, F. M., & Elliott, S. N. (1984). Assessment and classification of children's social skills: A review of methods and issues. *School Psychology Review, 13,* 292–301.

———. (1988). Teacher's social validity ratings of social skills: Comparisons between mildly handicapped and nonhandicapped children. *Journal of Psychoeducational Assessment, 6,* 225–234.

———. (1989). Social skills deficits as a primary learning disability. *Journal of Learning Disabilities, 22,* 120–124.

———. (1990). *Social skills rating system (SSRS).* Circle Pines, MN: American Guidance Service.

Gresham, F. M., Elliott, S. N., & Black, F. L. (1987). Teacher-rated social skills of mainstreamed mildly handicapped and nonhandicapped children. *School Psychology Review, 16,* 78–88.

Gresham, F. M., & Little, S. G. (1993). Peer-referenced assessment strategies. In T. H. Ollendick & M. Hersen (Eds.), *Handbook of child and adolescent assessment* (pp. 165–179). Boston: Allyn and Bacon.

Gresham, F. M., & Stuart, D. (1992). Stability of sociometric assessment: Implications for uses as selection and outcome measures in social skills training. *Journal of School Psychology, 30,* 223–231.

Gross, A. M., & Wojnilower, D. A. (1984). Self-directed behavior change in children: Is it self-directed? *Behavior Therapy, 15,* 501–514.

Guevremont, D. C., Osnes, P. G., & Stokes, T. F. (1988). Preschoolers' goal setting with contracting to facilitate maintenance. *Behavior Modification, 12,* 404–423.

Gunter, P., Fox, J. J., Brady, M.P., Shores, R. E., & Cavanaugh, K. (1988). Nonhandicapped peers as multiple exemplars: A generalization tactic for promoting autistic students' social skills. *Behavioral Disorders, 13,* 116–126.

Hansen, M. (1983). *A re-examination of the relationship between cognitive role taking and social competence in children.* Paper presented at Convention of the American Psychological Association, Anaheim, CA.

Haring, T., Roger, B., Lee, M., Breen, C., & Gaylord-Ross, R. (1986). Teaching social language to moderately handicapped students. *Journal of Applied Behavior Analysis, 19,* 159–171.

Harris, K. A. (1986). Self-monitoring of attentional behavior versus self-monitoring of productivity: Effects on on-task behavior and academic response rate among learning disabled children. *Journal of Applied Behavior Analysis, 19,* 417–423.

Harris, P. L. (1989). *Children and emotion.* New York: Basil Blackwell Inc.

Harris, W. J. (1984). The making better choices program. *Pointer, 29*, 16–19.

Harter, S. (1978). *The perceived competence scale for children: A new measure.* Unpublished manuscript.

———. (1982). The perceived competence scale for children. *Child Development, 53*, 87–97.

Hartup, W. W. (1970). Peer interaction and social organization. In P. H. Mussen (Ed.), *Carmichael's manual of child psychology*, Vol. 2 (pp. 361–456). New York: Wiley.

Hawkins, R. P. (1991). Is social validity what we are interested in? Argument for a functional approach. *Journal of Applied Behavior Analysis, 24,* 205–213.

Hawley, R., & Hawley, I. (1975). *Human values in the classroom: A handbook for teachers.* New York: Hart.

Hayvren, M., & Hymel, S. (1984). Ethical issues in sociometric testing: Impact of sociometric measures on interaction behavior. *Developmental Psychology, 20*, 849–884.

Hazel, J. S., Schumaker, J. B., Sherman, J. A., & Sheldon-Wildgen, J. (1982). Group training for social skills: A program for court-adjudicated, probationary youths. *Criminal Justice and Behavior, 9,* 35–53.

Heitzmann, W. R. (1974). *Educational games and simulations.* Washington, DC: National Education Association.

Hersen, M. (1973). Self assessment of fear. *Behavior Therapy, 4,* 241–257.

———. (1979). Limitations and problems in the clinical application of behavioral techniques in psychiatric settings. *Behavior Therapy, 10,* 65–80.

Hersen, M., & Bellack, A. S. (1977). Assessment of social skills. In A. R. Ciminero, K. S. Calhoun, & H. D. Adams (Eds.), *Handbook for behavior assessment* (pp. 509–554). New York: Wiley.

Hoier, T. S., & Cone, J. D. (1980). *Inductive idiographic assessment of social skills in children.* Paper presented at the Convention of the Association for Advancement of Behavior Therapy, New York.

———. (1987). Target selection of social skills for children: The template-matching procedure. *Behavior Modification, 11,* 137–163.

Homme, L., Csanyi, A. P., Gonzales, M. A., & Rechs, J. R. (1969). *How to use contingency contracting in the classroom.* Champaign, IL: Research Press.

Hopper, R. B., & Kirschenbaum, D. S. (1979, September). *Social problem-solving skills and social competence in preadolescent children.* Paper presented at the Convention of the American Psychological Association, New York, NY.

Hops, H. (1983). Children's social competence and skill: Current research practices and future directions. *Behavior Therapy, 14,* 3–18.

Hops, H., & Cobb, J. A. (1973). Survival behaviors in the educational setting: Their implications for research and intervention. In L. A. Hammerlynk, L. C. Handy, & E. J. Mash (Eds.), *Behavior change* (pp. 193–208). Champaign, IL: Research Press.

Hops, H., Fleischman, D. H., Guild, J., Paine, S., Street, A., Walker, H. M., & Greenwood, C. R. (1978). *Program for establishing effective relationship skills (PEERS): Consultant manual.* Eugene: University of Oregon, Center at Oregon for Research in the Behavioral Education of the Handicapped.

Hops, H., & Lewin, L. (1984). Peer sociometric forms. In T. H. Ollendick & M. Hersen (Eds.), *Child behavioral assessment* (pp. 124–147). New York: Pergamon Press.

Howe, L., & Howe, M. M. (1975). *Personalizing education: Values clarification and beyond.* New York: Hart.

Howell, K. W. (1985). A task-analytical approach to social behavior. *Remedial and Special Education, 6(2),* 24–30.

Hughes, C. A., Ruhl, K. L., & Misra, A. (1989). Self-management with behaviorally disordered students in school settings: A promise unfulfilled? *Behavioral Disorders, 14,* 250–262.

Hughes, J. N. (1986). Methods of skill selection in social skills training: A review. *Professional School Psychology, 1,* 235–248.

Hughes, J. N., Boodoo, G., Alcala, J., Maggio, M., Moore, L., & Villapando, R. (1989). Validation of a role-play measure of children's social skills. *Journal of Abnormal Psychology, 17,* 633–646.

Hughes, J. N., & Hall, D. M. (1985). Performance of disturbed and nondisturbed boys on a role play test of social competence. *Behavioral Disorders, 11,* 24–29.

Humphreys, L. E., & Ciminero, A. R. (1979). Parent report measures of child behavior: A review. *Journal of Clinical Child Psychology, 8,* 56–63.

Hymel, S. (1983). Preschool children's peer relations: Issues in sociometric assessment. *Merrill-Palmer Quarterly, 29,* 237–260.

Hymel, S., & Asher, S. (1977, March). *Assessment and training of isolated children's social skills.* Bethesda, MD: National Institute of Child Health and Human Development (NIH).

Hymel, S., Rubin, K. H., Rowden, L., & LeMare, L. (1990). Children's peer relationships: Longitudinal prediction of internalizing and externalizing problems from middle to late childhood. *Child Development, 61,* 2004–2021.

Hymel, S., Wagner, E., & Butler, L. J. (1990). Reputational bias: View from the peer group. In S. R. Asher & J. D. Coie (Eds.), *Peer rejection in childhood* (pp. 156–186). New York: Cambridge University Press.

Inhelder, B., & Piaget, J. (1964). *The early growth of logic in the child, classification and seriation.* New York: Harper & Row.

Irvin, L. K., Walker, H. M., Noell, J., Singer, G. H. S., Irvine, A. B., Marquez, K., & Britz, B. (1992). Measuring children's social skills using microcomputer-based videodisc assessment. *Behavior Modification, 16*(4), 475–503.

Izard, E. E. (1977). *Human emotions.* New York: Plenum Press.

Jackson, N. F., Jackson, D. A., & Monroe, C. (1983). *Getting along with others.* Champaign, IL: Research Press.

Jewett, J. F., & Clark, H. B. (1976, December). *Training preschoolers to use appropriate dinner time conversation: An analysis of generalization from school to home.* Paper presented at the Convention of the Association for the Advancement of Behavior Therapy, New York.

Johnson, D. W., & Johnson, R. T. (1987). *Learning together and alone: Cooperative, competitive, and individualistic learning.* Englewood Cliffs, NJ: Prentice-Hall.

———. (1989). Cooperative learning: What special education teachers need to know. *The Pointer, 33,* 5–10.

Jones, K. T., & Evans, H. L. (1980). Self-reinforcement: A continuum of external cues. *Journal of Educational Psychology, 72,* 625–635.

Jones, T. R., Nelson, R. E., & Kazdin, A. (1977). The role of external variables in self-reinforcement. *Behavior Modification, 1,* 147–178.

Kagan, J., & Kogan, N. (1970). Individual variation in cognitive processes. In P. H. Mussen (Ed.), *Carmichael's manual of child psychology, Vol. 1* (3d Ed.) (pp. 1273–1365). New York: Wiley.

Kanfer, F. H. (1975). Self-management methods. In F. H. Kanfer & A. P. Goldstein (Eds.), *Helping people change* (pp. 309–355). Elmsford, NY: Pergamon Press.

Katz, R. C., & Vinceguerra, P. (1980, November). *Interactions between informational context and reinforcement schedules in the maintenance of behavior change.* Paper presented at the 14th Annual Convention of the Association for Advancement of Behavior Therapy, New York.

Kazdin, A. E. (1985). Selection of target behaviors: The relationship of the treatment focus to clinical dysfunction. *Behavioral Assessment, 7,* 33–47.

Keller, H. R. (1988). Children's adaptive behaviors: Measure and source generalizability. *Journal of Psychoeducational Assessment, 6,* 371–389.

Kendall, P. C. (1978, November). *Self-instructions with children: An analysis of the inconsistent evidence for treatment generalization.* Paper presented at the Convention of the Association for the Advancement of Behavior Therapy, Chicago.

———. (1981). Cognitive-behavioral interventions with children. In B. B. Lahey & A. E. Kazdin (Eds.), *Advances in clinical child psychology,* Vol. 4 (pp. 53–90). New York: Plenum Press.

Kendall, P. C., & Braswell, L. (1985). *Cognitive-behavioral therapy for impulsive children.* New York: The Guilford Press.

Kendall, P. C., & Fischler, G. L. (1984). Behavioral and adjustment correlates of problem solving: Validation analyses of interpersonal cognitive problem-solving measures. *Child Development, 55,* 879–892.

Kendall, P. C., Lerner, R. M., & Craighead, W. E. (1984). Human development and intervention in childhood pathology. *Child Development, 55,* 71-82.

Kendall, P. C., & Morison, P. (1984). Integrating cognitive and behavioral procedures for the treatment of socially isolated children. In A. W. Meyers & W. E. Craighead (Eds.), *Cognitive behavior therapy with children* (pp. 261–288), New York: Plenum Press.

Kent, R. N., & Foster, S. L. (1977). Direct observation procedures: Methodological issues in naturalistic settings. In A. R. Ciminero, K. S. Calhoun, & H. E. Adams (Eds.), *Handbook of behavioral assessment.* New York: Wiley.

Kern-Dunlap, L., Dunlap, G., Clarke, S., Childs, K. E., White, R. L., & Stewart, M. P. (1992). Effects of a videotape feedback package on the peer interactions of children with serious behavioral and emotional challenges. *Journal of Applied Behavior Analysis, 25,* 355–364.

Kiburz, C. S., Miller, S. R., & Morrow, L. W. (1984). Structured learning using self-monitoring to promote maintenance and generalization of social skills across settings for a behaviorally disordered adolescent. *Behavioral Disorders, 10,* 47–55.

King, C. A., & Kirschenbaum, D. S. (1992). *Helping young children develop social skills.* Belmont, CA: Brooks/Cole.

Kirby, K. C., & Bickel, W. K. (1988). Toward an explicit analysis of generalization: A stimulus control interpretation. *The Behavior Analyst, 11,* 115–129.

Knapczyk, D. (1988). Reducing aggressive behaviors in special and regular class settings by training alternative social responses. *Behavioral Disorders, 14,* 27–39.

Knaus, W. J. (1974). *Rational emotive education.* New York: Institute for Rational Living.

Kohlberg, L. (1969). Stage and sequence: The cognitive-developmental approach to socialization. In D. A. Goslin (Ed.), *Handbook of socialization theory and research* (pp. 347–480). Chicago: Rand McNally.

Kohler, F. W., & Fowler, S. A. (1985). Training prosocial behaviors to young children: An analysis of reciprocity with untrained peers. *Journal of Applied Behavior Analysis, 18,* 187–200.

Kohler, F. W., & Greenwood, C. R. (1986). Toward a technology of generalization: The identification of natural contingencies of reinforcement. *The Behavior Analyst, 9,* 19–26.

Kohler, F. W., Greenwood, C. R., & Baer, D. M. (1985). *Assessing the peer tutoring process: The identification of natural communities of social reinforcement.* Paper presented at the Convention of the Association for Behavior Analysis, Columbus, OH.

Kovacs, M. (1992). *Children's depression inventory (CDI).* Los Angeles, CA: Western Psychological Services.

Krasnor, L. R., & Rubin, K. H. (1981). The assessment of social problem-solving skills in young children. In T. V. Merluzzi, C. R. Glass, & M. Genest (Eds.), *Cognitive assessment.* (pp. 452–476). New York: Guilford Press.

Krathwohl, D., Bloom, B., & Masia, B. (1956). *Taxonomy of educational objectives.* New York: David McKay.

Kratochwill, T. R. (1985). Selection of target behaviors in behavioral consultation. *Behavioral Assessment, 7,* 49–61.

Ladd, G. W. (1981). Effectiveness of a social learning method for enhancing children's social interactions and peer acceptance. *Child Development, 52,* 171–178.

Ladd, G. W., & Mize, J. (1983). A cognitive-social learning model of social skill training. *Psychological Review, 10,* 127–157.

LaGreca, A. M. (1992, August). *Children's social skills training: Where do we go from here?* Paper presented at the Convention of the American Psychological Association, Washington, DC.

LaGreca, A. M., & Mesibov, G. V. (1979). Social skills intervention with learning disabled children: Selecting skills and implementing training. *Journal of Clinical Child Psychology, 8,* 234–241.

LaGreca, A. M., & Santogrossi, D. A. (1980). Social skills training with elementary school students: A behavioral group approach. *Journal of Consulting and Clinical Psychology, 48,* 220–227.

Lambert, N. M., Windmiller, M., Cole, L., & Tharinger, D. (1974). *AAMD adaptive behavior scale—School edition.* Austin, Texas: PRO-ED.

Landau, S., & Moore, L. A. (1991). Social skill deficits in children with attention-deficit hyperactivity disorder. *School Psychology Review, 20,* 235–251.

Landrum, T. J., & Lloyd, J. W. (1992). Generalization in social behavior research with children and youth who have emotional or behavioral disorders. *Behavior Modification, 16,* 593–616.

Lang, M., & Tisher, M. (1978). *Children's depression scale.* Melbourne: Australian Council for Education Research.

Laski, K. E., Charlop, M. H., & Schreibman, L. (1988). Training parents to use the natural language paradigm to increase their autistic children's speech. *Journal of Applied Behavior Analysis, 21,* 391–400.

Lefkowitz, M. M., & Tesiny, E. P. (1980). Assessment of childhood depression. *Journal of Counseling and Clinical Psychology, 48,* 43–50.

Lew, M., & Mesch, D. (1984). *Isolated students in secondary schools: Cooperative group contingencies and social skills training.* Paper presented at the Conference of the American Psychological Association, Toronto.

Lewis, M., & Michalson, L. (1983). *Children's emotions and moods.* New York: Plenum Press.

Libet, J., & Lewinsohn, P. M. (1973). The concept of social skill with special references to the behavior of depressed persons. *Journal of Consulting and Clinical Psychology, 40,* 304–312.

Lionni, L. (1963). *Swimmy.* New York: Alfred A. Knopf.

Lloyd, J. W., Bateman, D. F., Landrum, T. J., & Hallahan, D. P. (1989). Self-recording of attention versus productivity. *Journal of Applied Behavior Analysis, 22,* 315–323.

Lochman, J. E., Burch, P. R., Curry, J. F., & Lampron, L. B. (1984). Treatment and generalization effects of cognitive-behavioral and goalsetting interventions with aggressive boys. *Journal of Consulting and Clinical Psychology, 52,* 915–916.

Lochman, J. E., & Curry, J. F. (1986). Effects of social problem-solving training and self-instruction training with aggressive boys. *Journal of Clinical Child Psychology, 15,* 159–164.

Lochman, J. E., Nelson, W. M., III, & Sims, J. P. (1981). A cognitive behavioral program for use with aggressive children. *Journal of Clinical Child Psychology, 10,* 146–148.

Luria, A. (1961). *The role of speech in the regulation of normal and abnormal behaviors.* New York: Liveright.

Luthar, S. S. (1991). Vulnerability and resilience: A study of high-risk adolescents. *Child Development, 62,* 600–616.

Luthar, S. S., & Doernberger, C. H. (1992, August). Resilience among inner-city teenagers: Further empirical insights. Paper presented at the Convention of the American Psychological Association, Washington, DC.

Maag, J. W. (1989). Assessment in social skills training: Methodological and conceptual issues for research and practice. *Remedial and Special Education, 10,* 6–17.

Maag, J. W., Parks, B. T., & Rutherford, R. B. (1988). Generalization and behavior covariation of aggression in children receiving stress inoculation therapy. *Child & Family Behavior Therapy, 10*(2/3), 29–47.

Mager, R. (1972). *Goal analysis.* Belmont, CA: Fearon.

Mager, R. G., & Pipe, P. (1970). *Analyzing performance problems.* Belmont, CA: Fearon.

Maheady, L., Maitland, G. E., & Sainato, D. M. (1982). *Interpretation of social interactions by learning disabled, socially/emotionally disturbed, educable mentally retarded, and non-disabled children.* Unpublished manuscript.

Mann, R. A. (1976). *Assessment of behavioral excess in children.* In M. Hersen & A. A. Bellack (Eds.), *Behavioral assessment: A practical handbook* (pp. 459–491). Elmsford, NY: Pergamon Press.

Marsh, H. W., & Gouvernet, P. J. (1989). Multidimensional self-concepts and perceptions of control: Construct validation of responses by children. *Journal of Educational Psychology, 81,* 57–69.

Mathur, S. R., & Rutherford, R. B. (1991). Peer-mediated interventions promoting social skills of children and youth with behavioral disorders. *Education and Treatment of Children, 14,* 227–242.

Matson, J. L., Esveldt-Dawson, K., & Kazdin, A. E. (1983). Validation of methods for assessing social skills in children. *Journal of Clinical Child Psychology, 12,* 174–180.

Matson, J. L., Rotatori, A. F., & Helsel, W. J. (1983). Development of a rating scale to measure social skills in children: The Matson evaluation of social skills with youngsters (MESSY). *Behavior Research and Therapy, 21,* 335–340.

McConaughy, S. H. (1993). Evaluating behavioral and emotional disorders with the CBCL, TFR, and YSR cross-informant scales. *Journal of Emotional and Behavioral Disorders, 1*(1), 40–52.

McConnell, S. R. (1987). Entrapment effects and the generalization and maintenance of social skills training for elementary school students with behavior disorders. *Behavioral Disorders, 12,* 252–263.

McConnell, S. R., & Odom, S. L. (1986). Sociometrics: Peer-referenced measures and the assessment of social competence. In P. S. Strain, M. J. Guralnick, & H. M. Walker (Eds.), *Children's social behavior* (pp. 215–284). Orlando, FL: Academic Press, Inc.

McConnell, S. R., Sisson, L. A., Cort, C. A., & Strain, P. S. (1991). Effects of social skills training and contingency management on reciprocal interaction of preschool children with behavioral handicaps. *The Journal of Special Education, 24,* 473–495.

McEvoy, M., & Odom, S. (1987). Social interaction training for preschool children with behavioral disorders, *Behavioral Disorders, 12,* 242–251.

McFall, R. M. (1977). Analogue methods in behavioral assessment: Issues and prospects. In J. D. Cone & R. P. Hawkins (Eds.), *Behavioral assessment.* New York: Brunner/Mazel, Inc.

———. (1982). A review and reformulation of the concept of social skills. *Behavioral Assessment, 4,* 1–33.

McFall, R. M., & Lillesand, D. B. (1971). Behavior rehearsal with modeling and coaching in assertion training. *Journal of Abnormal Psychology, 77,* 313–323.

McGinnis, E., & Goldstein, A. P. (1984). *Skillstreaming the elementary school child.* Champaign, IL: Research Press.

McKinnie, D. M., & Elliott, S. N. (1991, August). *The relationship among social skills, problem behaviors, and academic competence in learning.* Paper presented at the Convention of the American Psychological Association, San Francisco.

McLaughlin, T. F., Krappman, V. F., & Welsh, J. M. (1985). The effects of self-recording for the on-task behavior of behaviorally disordered special education students. *Remedial and Special Education, 6,* 42–45.

McLean, D. L. (1992). Test review: Social skills rating system (SSRS). *Journal of Psychoeducational Assessment, 10,* 196–205.

Meadows, N., Neel, R. S., Parker, G., & Timo, K. (1991). A validation of social skills for students with behavioral disorders. *Behavioral Disorders, 16,* 200–210.

Mehrabian, A., & Epstein, N. A. (1972). A measure of emotional empathy. *Journal of Personality, 40,* 525–543.

Meichenbaum, D. (1975). Self instructional methods. In R. H. Kanfer & A. P. Goldstein (Eds.), *Helping people change: A textbook of methods* (pp. 357–391). Elmsford, NY: Pergamon Press.

———. (1976). A cognitive behavior modification approach to assessment. In M. Hersen & A. S. Bellack (Eds.), *Behavioral assessment: A practical handbook* (pp. 143–171). Elmsford, NY: Pergamon Press.

———. (1977). *Cognitive-behavior modification: An integrative approach.* New York: Plenum Press.

Meichenbaum, D., & Goodman, J. (1971). Training impulsive children to talk to themselves: A means of developing self-control. *Journal of Abnormal Psychology, 77,* 115–126.

Meisel, C. J. (1989). Interpersonal problem solving and children's social competence: Are current measures valid? *Psychology in the Schools, 26,* 37–46.

Merluzzi, T. V., & Biever, J. (1987). Role-playing procedures for the behavioral assessment of social skill: A validity study. *Behavioral Assessment, 9,* 361–377.

Michelson, L., & DiLorenzo, T. M. (1981). Behavioral assessment of peer interaction and social functioning in institutional and structured settings. *Journal of Clinical Psychology, 87,* 499–504.

Michelson, L., Foster, S. L., & Ritchey, W. L. (1981). Social skills assessment of children. In B. B. Lahey & A. E. Kazdin (Eds.), *Advances in clinical child psychology* (pp. 119–165). New York: Plenum Press.

Michelson, L., Sugai, D. P., Wood, R. P., & Kazdin, A. E. (1983). *Social skill assessment and training with children.* New York: Plenum Press.

Michelson, L., & Wood, R. (1982). Development and psychometric properties of the Children's Assertive Behavior Scale. *Journal of Behavioral Assessment, 4,* 3–14.

Milburn, J. F. (1974). *Special education and regular class teacher attitudes regarding social behaviors of children: Steps toward the development of a social skills curriculum.* Unpublished doctoral dissertation, The Ohio State University, Columbus.

Milburn, J. F., & Cartledge, G. (1979). Build you own social skills curriculum. *Exceptional Teacher, 1,* 1–8.

Milich, R., & Landau, S. (1984). A comparison of the social status and social behavior of aggressive and aggressive/withdrawn boys. *Journal of Abnormal Child Psychology, 12,* 277–288.

Miller, D. C. (1977). *Handbook of research design and social measurement.* New York: David McKay.

Miller, L. C., Barrett, C., Hampe, E., & Noble, H. (1974). *Louisville fear survey scale for children*. Unpublished manuscript. Louisville, KY: Child Psychology Research Center, Bulletin No. 1.

Miller, P. M., Danaher, D. L., & Forbes, D. (1986). Sex-related strategies for coping with interpersonal conflict in children aged five and seven. *Developmental Psychology, 22*, 543–548.

Minskoff, E. H. (1980a). Teaching approach for developing nonverbal communication skills in students with social perception deficits. Part 1. *Journal of Learning Disabilities, 13*, 118–124.

———. (1980b). Teaching approach for developing nonverbal communication skills in students with social perception deficits. Part II. *Journal of Learning Disabilities, 13*, 203–208.

Misra, A. (1992). Generalization of social skills through self-monitoring by adults with mild mental retardation. *Exceptional Children, 58*, 495–507.

Moore, S., & Updegraff, R. (1964). Sociometric status of preschool children related to age, sex, nurturance-giving and dependency. *Child Development, 33*, 519–524.

Morales, D. (1992). Social skill instruction for students with behavior disabilities. Unpublished manuscript, The Ohio State University, Columbus.

Morgan, R. G. T. (1980). Analysis of social skills: The behavior analysis approach. In W. T. Singleton, P. Spurgeon, & R. B. Stammers (Eds.), *The analysis of social skill* (pp. 103–130). New York: Plenum Press.

Morrison, R. L., & Bellack, A. S. (1981). The role of social perception in social skill. *Behavior Therapy, 12*, 69–79.

Moyer, D. M. (1974). *The development of children's ability to recognize and express facially posed emotion*. Unpublished doctoral dissertation, The Ohio State University, Columbus.

Murdock, J. Y., Garcia, E. E., & Hardman, M. L. (1977). Generalizing articulation training with trainable mentally retarded subjects. *Journal of Applied Behavior Analysis, 10*, 717–733.

Naglieri, J., LeBuffe, P., & Pfeiffer, S. (1992). *The Devereux behavior rating scale—School form*. San Antonio: The Psychological Corporation.

Nay, W. (1977). Analogue measures. In A. R. Ciminero, K. S. Calhoun, & H. E. Adams (Eds.), *Handbook of behavioral assessment* (pp. 233–277). New York: Wiley.

Neel, R. S., Jenkins, Z. N., & Meadows, N. (1990). Social problem-solving behaviors and aggression in young children: A descriptive observational study. *Behavioral Disorders, 16*, 39–51.

Nelson, J. R., Smith, D. J., Young, R. K., & Dodd, J. M. (1991). A review of self-management outcome research conducted with students who exhibit behavioral disorders. *Behavioral Disorders, 16*, 169–179.

Nelson, R. O., & Hayes, S. C. (1981). Theoretical explanations for reactivity in self monitoring. *Behavior Modification, 5*, 3–14.

Newcomb, A. F., & Bukowski, N. M. (1983). Social impact and social preference as determinants of children's peer group status. *Developmental Psychology, 19*, 856–867.

Nihira, K., Lambert, N., & Leland, H. (1993). *AAMR adaptive behavior scale—school edition*, 2d ed. Austin, TX: PRO-ED.

Ninness, H. A. C., Fuerst, J., Rutherford, R. D., & Glenn, S. S. (1991). Effects of self-management training and reinforcement on the transfer of improved conduct in the absence of supervision. *Journal of Applied Behavior Analysis, 24*(3), 499–508.

Novaco, R. (1975). *Anger control: The development and evaluation of an experimental treatment*. Lexington, MA: Lexington Books.

O'Connor, R. D. (1973). Relative efficacy of modeling, shaping and combined procedures for modification of social withdrawal. In C. M. Franks & G. T. Wilson (Eds.), *Annual review of Behavior therapy and practice*, Vol. I (pp. 159–173). New York: Brunner/Mazel.

Oden, S. (1986). Developing social skills instruction for peer interaction and relationships. In G. Cartledge & J. F. Milburn (Eds.), *Teaching social skills to children*, 2d ed. (pp. 246–269). New York: Pergamon Press.

Odom, S. L., Chandler, L. K., Ostrosky, M., McConnell, S. R., & Reaney, S. (1992). Fading teacher prompts from peer-initiation interventions for young children with disabilities. *Journal of Applied Behavior Analysis, 25*, 307–317.

O'Leary, S. G., & Dubey, D. R. (1979). Applications of self-control procedures by children: A review. *Journal of Applied Behavioral Analysis, 12*, 449-465.

Olexa, D. F., & Forman, S. G. (1984). Effects of social problem-solving training on classroom behavior of urban disadvantaged students. *Journal of School Psychology, 22*, 165–175.

Ollendick, T. H. (1983). Reliability and validity of the revised fear survey schedule for children (FSSC-R). *Behavior Research Therapy, 21*, 685–692.

Ollendick, T. H., & Hersen, M. (1984). *Child behavior assessment*. Elmsford, NY: Pergamon Press.

Orlick, T. (1982). *The second cooperative sports and game book*. New York: Pantheon Books.

Osborne, S. S., Kiburz, C. S., & Miller, S. R. (1986). Treatment of self-injurious behavior using self-control techniques with a severe behaviorally disordered adolescent. *Behavioral Disorders, 12,* 60–67.

Paget, K. D. (1984). The structured assessment interview: A psychometric review. *Journal of School Psychology, 22,* 415–427.

Palkes, H., Steward, M., & Kahana, B. (1968). Porteus maze performance after training in self-directed verbal commands. *Child Development, 39,* 817–826.

Park, H., & Gaylord-Ross, R. (1989). A problem-solving approach to social skills training in employment settings with mentally retarded youth. *Journal of Applied Behavior Analysis, 22,* 373–380.

Parker, J. G., & Asher, S. R. (1987). Peer relations and later personal adjustment: Are low-accepted children at risk? *Psychological Bulletin, 102,* 357–389.

Pellegrini, D. S. (1985). Social cognition and competence in middle childhood. *Child Development, 56,* 253–264.

Pellegrini, D. S., & Urbain, E. S. (1985). An evaluation of interpersonal cognitive problem solving training with children. *Journal of Child Psychology & Psychiatry, 26,* 17–41.

Peterson, C. A,. & McConnell, S. R. (1993). Factors affecting the impact of social interaction skills interventions in early childhood special education. *Teaching Early Childhood Special Education, 13*, 38–56.

Petri, A.E., Mungin, C., & Emerson, B. (1992, April). *More precious than gold: African-American male mentors*. Paper presented at the 70th Council for Exceptional Children Annual Convention, Baltimore, MD.

Phillips, E. (1978). *The social skills basis of psychopathology: Alternatives to abnormal psychology*. New York: Grune & Stratton.

Piaget, J. (1965). *The moral judgment of the child*. New York: Free Press.

Piers, E. V. (1984). *The Piers-Harris children's self concept scale (The way I feel about myself)*, 1984 ed. Los Angeles: Western Psychological Services.

Platt, B. (1991). *The effects of self-monitoring on the academic performance and the on-task behavior of elementary school children with severe behavior handicaps*. Unpublished master's thesis, The Ohio State University, Columbus.

Polifka, J. A., Weissberg, R. P., Gesten, E. L., Flores De Apodaca, R., & Piccoli, L. (1981). *The open middle interview (OMI): Manual*. Rochester, NY: Center for Community Study.

Pray, B. D., Jr., Hall, C. W., & Markley, R. P. (1992). Social skills training: An analysis of social behaviors selected for individualized education programs. *Remedial and Special Education, 13*, 43–49.

Premack, D. (1959). Toward empirical behavior laws, part 1: Positive reinforcement. *Psychological Review, 66*, 219–233.

Prinz, R. J., Swan, G., Liebert, D., Weintraub, S., & Neal, J. M. (1978). Assess: Adjustment scales for sociometric evaluation of secondary-school students. *Journal of Abnormal Child Psychology, 6*, 493–501.

Prothrow-Stith, D. (1991). *Deadly consequences.* New York: HarperCollins.

Putallaz, M., & Wasserman, A. (1990). Children's entry behavior. In S. R. Asher & J. D. Coie (Eds.), *Peer rejection in childhood* (pp. 60–89). New York: Cambridge University Press.

Quay, H. C., & Peterson, D. R. (1987). *Manual for the revised behavior problem checklist.* Coral Gables, FL: Quay publisher.

Quiggle, N. L., Garber, J., Panak, W. F., & Dodge, K. A. (1992). Social information processing in aggressive and depressed children. *Child Development, 63*, 1305–1320.

Rathjen, D. P. (1984). Social skills training for children: Innovations and consumer guidelines. *School Psychology Review, 13*, 302–310.

Reardon, R. C., Hersen, M., Bellack, A. S., & Foley, J. M. (1979). Measuring social skill in grade school boys. *Journal of Behavioral Assessment, 1*, 87–105.

Redmond, N. B., Bennett, C., Wiggert, J., & McLean, B. (1993). Using functional assessment to support a student with severe disabilities in the community. *Teaching Exceptional Children, 25*, 51–52.

Renshaw, P. D., & Asher, S. R. (1983). Children's goals and strategies for social interaction. *Merrill-Palmer Quarterly, 29*, 353–374.

Reppucci, N. D., & Saunders, J. T. (1974). Social psychology of behavior modification: Problems of implementation in natural settings. *American Psychologist, 29*, 649–660.

Reynolds, C. R., & Richmond, B. A. (1978). Factor structure and construct validity of "what I think and feel," the revised children's manifest anxiety scale. *Journal of Personality Assessment, 33*, 281–283.

Reynolds, C. R., & Richmond, B. O. (1985). *Revised children's manifest anxiety scale (RCMAS).* Los Angeles: Western Psychological Services.

Reynolds, W. M. (1989). *Reynolds child depression scale.* Odessa, FL: Psychological Assessment Resources.

———. (1993). Self-report methodology. In T. H. Ollendick & M. Hersen (Eds.), *Handbook of child and adolescent assessment* (pp. 98–123). Boston: Allyn and Bacon.

Rhode, G., Morgan, D. P., & Young, K. R. (1983). Generalization and maintenance of treatment gains of behaviorally handicapped students from resource rooms to regular classrooms using self-evaluation procedures. *Journal of Applied Behavior Analysis, 16*, 171–188.

Richard, B. A., & Dodge, K. A. (1982). Social maladjustment and problem-solving in school-aged children. *Journal of Consulting and Clinical Psychology, 50*, 226–233.

Rie, E. D., & Friedman, D. P. (1978). *A survey of behavior rating scales for children.* Columbus, OH: Office of Program Evaluation and Research. Division of Mental Health, Ohio Department of Mental Health and Mental Retardation.

Riley, S. (1978). *Afraid.* Elgin, IL: Child's World.

———. (1978). *Angry.* Elgin, IL: Child's World.

———. (1978). *I'm Sorry.* Elgin, IL: Child's World.

Rincover, A., & Koegel, R. L. (1975). Setting generality and stimulus control in autistic children. *Journal of Applied Behavior Analysis, 8*, 235–246.

Roberts, N., & Nelson, R. O. (1984). Assessment issues and strategies. In A. W. Meyers

& W. E. Craighead (Eds.), *Cognitive behavior therapy with children* (pp. 99–128). New York: Plenum Press.

Robertson, R. J., Simon, S. J., Pachman, J. S., & Drabman, R. S. (1979). Self-control and generalization procedures in a classroom of disruptive retarded children. *Child Behavior Therapy, 1,* 347–362.

Roff, M., Sells, S. B., & Golden, M. (1972). *Social adjustment and personality development in children.* Minneapolis: University of Minnesota Press.

Rose, S. D. (1972). *Testing children in groups.* San Francisco: Jossey-Bass.

Rosenhan, D., & White, G. M. (1967). Observation and rehearsal as determinants of prosocial behavior. *Journal of Personality and Social Psychology, 5,* 424–431.

Rothenberg, B. (1970). Children's social sensitivity and the relationship to interpersonal competence, intrapersonal comfort, and intellectual level. *Developmental Psychology, 2,* 335–350.

Roush, D. W. (1984). Rational-emotive therapy and youth: Some new techniques for counselors. *Personnel and Guidance Journal, 62,* 414–417.

Rubin, K. H. (1982). Social and social-cognitive developmental characteristics of children. In K. H. Rubin & H. S. Ross (Eds.), *Peer relationships and social skills in childhood* (pp. 353–374). New York: Springer-Verlag.

Rubin, K. H., Daniels-Beirness, T., & Bream, L. (1984). Social isolation and social problem solving: A longitudinal study. *Journal of Consulting and Clinical Psychology, 52,* 17–25.

Rubin, K. H., & Krasnor, L. R. (1986). Social-cognitive and social behavioral perspectives on problem solving. In M. Perlmutter (Ed.), *Cognitive perspectives on children's social and behavioral development* (pp. 1–68). Hillsdale, NJ: Lawrence Erlbaum Associates.

Rule, S., Fiechtl, B. J., & Innocenti, M. S. (1990). Preparation for transition to mainstreamed post-preschool environments: Development of a survival skills curriculum. *Teaching Early Childhood Special Education, 9,* 78–90.

Sagotsky, G., Patterson, C. J., & Lepper, M. R. (1978). Training children's self control: A field experiment in self monitoring and goal setting in the classroom. *Journal of Experimental Child Psychology, 25,* 242–253.

Sainato, D. M., Strain, P. S., Lefebvre, D. & Rapp, N. (1990). Effects of self-evaluation on the independent work skills of preschool children with disabilities. *Exceptional Children, 56,* 540–549.

Salend, S. J., Whittaker, C. R., & Reeder, E. (1992). Group evaluation: A collaborative, peer-mediated behavior management system. *Exceptional Children, 59,* 203–209.

Santogrossi, D. A., O'Leary, K. D., Romanczyk, R. G., & Kaufman, K. F. (1973). Self-evaluation by adolescents in a psychiatric hospital school token program. *Journal of Applied Behavior Analysis, 6,* 277–287.

Sapon-Shevin, M. (1986). Teaching cooperation. In G. Cartledge & J. F. Milburn (Eds.), *Teaching social skills to children,* 2d ed. (pp. 270–302). New York: Pergamon Press.

Sarason, S. B., Davidson, K. F., Lighthall, F. F., Waite, R. R., & Ruebush, B. K. (1960). *Anxiety in elementary school children.* New York: Wiley.

Sasso, G., Melloy, K. J., & Kavale, K. A. (1990). Generalization, maintenance, & behavioral covariation associated with social skills training through structured learning. *Behavioral Disorders, 16,* 9–22.

Schaeffer, A. L., Zigmond, N., Kerr, M. M., & Farra, H. E. (1990). Helping teenagers develop school survival skills. *Teaching Exceptional Children, 23,* 6–9.

Scherer, M. W., & Nakamura, C. Y. (1968). A fear survey schedule for children (FSS-FC): A factor analytic comparison with manifest anxiety (CMAS). *Behavior Research and Therapy, 6,* 173–182.

Schirtzinger, M. A. (1990). *Effects of social skill instruction on friend-maintaining and classroom discussion behaviors of seventh-grade students with learning disabilities.* Master's thesis, The Ohio State University, Columbus.

Schloss, P. J., Schloss, C. N., Wood, C. E., & Kiehl, W. S. (1986). A critical review of social skills research with behaviorally disordered students. *Behavioral Disorders, 12,* 1–14.

Schneider, M., & Yoshida, R. K. (1988). Interpersonal problem-solving skills and classroom behavioral adjustment in learning-disabled adolescents and comparison peers. *Journal of School Psychology, 26,* 25–34.

Schofield, J. W., & Whitley, B. E. (1983). Peer nomination vs. rating scale measurement of children's peer preference. *Social Psychology Quarterly, 46,* 242–251.

Schonert-Reichl, K. A. (1993). Empathy and social relationships in adolescents with behavioral disorders. *Behavioral Disorders, 18,* 189–204.

Schreibman, L. (1988). Parent training as a means of facilitating generalization in autistic children. In R. Horner, G. Dunlap, & R. Koegel (Eds.), *Generalization and maintenance* (pp. 21-66). Baltimore: Paul H. Brookes.

Schwartz, I. S. & Baer, D. M. (1991). Social validity assessments: Is current practice state of the art? *Journal of Applied Behavior Analysis, 24,* 189-204.

Selman, R. L., & Byrne, D. F. (1974). A structural-developmental analysis of levels of role taking in middle childhood. *Child Development, 45,* 803-806.

Selman, R. L., Schorin, M. Z., Stone, C. R., & Phelps, E. (1983). A naturalistic study of children's social understanding. *Developmental Psychology, 19,* 82-102.

Seymour, F. W., & Stokes, T. F. (1976). Self- recording in training girls to increase work and evoke staff praise in an institution for offenders. *Journal of Applied Behavior Analysis, 9,* 41-54.

Shapiro, E. S. (1984). Self monitoring procedures. In T. H. Ollendick & M. Hersen (Eds.), *Child behavioral assessment* (pp. 148–165). Elmsford, NY: Pergamon Press.

Shapiro, E. S., & Cole, C. L. (1993). Self monitoring. In T. H. Ollendick & M. Hersen (Eds.) *Handbook of child and adolescent assessment* (pp. 124-139). Boston: Allyn and Bacon.

Shapiro, E. S., Gilbert, D., Friedman, J., & Steiner, S. (1985, November). *Concurrent validity of role-play and contrived tests in assessing social skills in disruptive adolescents.* Paper presented at the Annual Convention of the Association for the Advancement of Behavior Therapy, Houston, TX.

Shapiro, E. S., & Kratochwill, T. R. (1988). Analogue assessment: Methods for assessing emotional and behavioral problems. In E. S. Shapiro & T. R. Kratochwill (Eds.) *Behavioral assessment in schools* (pp. 290-321). New York: Guilford Press.

Shapiro, E. S., Stover, J. E., & Ifkovits, G. A. (1983, November). *Predictive and concurrent validity of role-play and naturalistic assessment of social skills in kindergarten children.* Paper presented at the Annual Convention of the Association for the Advancement of Behavior Therapy, Washington, DC.

Shneidman, E. S. (1952). *Make a picture story (MAPS).* New York: The Psychological Corporation.

Shores, R. E. (1987). Overview of research on social interaction: A historical and personal perspective. *Behavioral Disorders, 12,* 233–241.

Shure, M. B. (1992). *I can problem solve: An interpersonal cognitive problem-solving program for children.* Champaign, IL: Research Press.

Shure, M. B., & Spivack, G. (1978). *Problem-solving techniques in childrearing.* San Francisco: Jossey-Bass.

Simon, S., Howe, L., & Kirschenbaum, H. (1972). *Values clarification: A handbook of practical strategies for teachers and students.* New York: Hart.

Simpson, R. G. (1991). Agreement among teachers of secondary students in using the revised behavior problem checklist to identify deviant behavior. *Behavioral Disorders, 17,* 66-71.

Slavin, R. E. (1978). Student teams and achievement divisions. *Journal of Research and Development in Education, 12,* 39–49.

Slavin, R. E. (1990). Research on cooperative learning: Consensus and controversy. *Educational Leadership, 47,* 52–54.

Slavin, R. E., Leavey, M., & Madden, N. A. (1982). *Effects of student teams and individualized instruction on student mathematics achievement, attitudes, and behaviors.* Paper presented at the Annual Convention of the American Education Research Association, New York, NY.

Smith, D., Young, K. R., West, R. P., Morgan, D. P., & Rhode, G. (1988). Reducing the disruptive behavior of junior high school students: A classroom self-management procedure. *Behavioral Disorders, 13,* 231–239.

Smith, M. (1977). *A practical guide to values clarification.* La Jolla, CA: University Associates.

Sobel, J. (1983). *Everybody wins: Non-competitive games for young children.* New York: Walker and Co.

Spence, S. H., & Liddle, B. (1990). Self-report measures of social competence for children: An evaluation of the Matson evaluation of social skills for youngsters and the list of social situation problems. *Behavioral Assessment, 12,* 317–336.

Spielberger, C. D. (1973). *State-trait anxiety inventory for children.* Palo Alto, CA: Consulting Psychologist Press.

Spitzer, A. (1991). *A social skills project.* Unpublished manuscript.

Spivack, G., Platt, J. J., & Shure, M. (1976). *The problem-solving approach to adjustment.* San Francisco: Jossey-Bass.

Spivack, G., & Shure, M. B. (1974). *Social adjustment of young children. A cognitive approach to solving real-life problems.* San Francisco: Jossey-Bass.

Spivack, G., & Swift, M. (1967). *Devereux elementary school behavior rating scale.* Devon, PA: Devereux Foundation.

Stahmer, A. C., & Schreibman, L. (1992). Teaching children with autism appropriate play in unsupervised environments using a self-management treatment package. *Journal of Applied Behavior Analysis, 25,* 447–459.

Star, T. Z. (1986). Group social skills training: A comparison of two coaching programs. *Techniques: A Journal for Remedial Education and Counseling, 2,* 24–38.

Stephens, T. M. (1977). *Teaching skills to children with learning and behavior disorders.* Columbus, OH: Merrill.

———. (1978). *Social skills in the classroom.* Columbus, OH: Cedars Press.

———. (1986). Foreword. In G. Cartledge & J. F. Milburn (Eds.), *Teaching social skills to children,* 2d ed. (pp. ix-xii). New York: Pergamon Press.

———. (1992). *Social skills in the classroom.* Odessa, FL: Psychological Assessment Resources, Inc.

Stephens, T. M., & Arnold, K. D. (1992). *Social behavior assessment inventory: Examiner's manual.* Odessa, FL: Psychological Assessment Resources, Inc.

Stevenson, H. C., & Fantuzzo, J. W. (1984). Application of the "generalization map" to a self-control intervention with school-aged children. *Journal of Applied Behavior Analysis, 17,* 203–212.

Stokes, T. F., & Baer, D. M. (1977). An implicit technology of generalization. *Journal of Applied Behavior Analysis, 10,* 349–367.

Stokes, T. F., Baer, D. M., & Jackson, R. L. (1974). Programming the generalization of a greeting response in four retarded children. *Journal of Applied Behavior Analysis, 7,* 599–610.

Stokes, T., & Osnes, P. (1986). Generalizing children's social behavior. In P. Strain, M. Guralnick, & H. Walker (Eds.), *Children's social behavior* (pp. 407–443). Orlando, FL: Academic Press.

———. (1988). The developing applied technology of generalization and maintenance. In R. Horner, G. Dunlap, & R. Koegel (Eds.), *Generalization and maintenance* (pp. 5–19). Baltimore: Paul H. Brookes.

———. (1989). An operant pursuit of generalization. *Behavior Therapy, 20,* 337–355.

Strain, P. S., Kerr, M. M., & Ragland, E. U. (1981). The use of peer social initiations in the treatment of social withdrawal. In P. S. Strain (Ed.), *The utilization of classroom peers as behavior change agents* (pp. 101–128). New York: Plenum Press.

Strain, P. S., Odom, S. L. & McConnell, S. (1984). Promoting social reciprocity of exceptional children: Identification, target behavior selection, and intervention. *Remedial and Special Education, 5,* 21–28.

Strauss, C. C., Lahey, B. B., Frick, P., Frame, C. L., & Hynd, G. W. (1988). Peer social status of children with anxiety disorders. *Journal of Consulting and Clinical Psychology, 56,* 137–141.

Strayer, J. (1980). A naturalistic study of empathetic behaviors and their relation to affective states and perspective taking skills in preschool children. *Child Development, 51,* 815–822.

Stroman, C. A. (1991). Television's role in the socialization of African-American children and adolescents. *Journal of Negro Education, 60,* 314–327.

Sullivan, M. A., & O'Leary, S. G. (1990). Maintenance following reward and cost token programs. *Behavior Therapy, 21,* 139–149.

Thapanadilok, V. (1992, August). Social skills of educationally handicapped children. Paper presented at the Conference of the American Psychological Association, Washington, DC.

Tisher, M., & Lang, M. (1983). The children's depression scale: Review and further developments. In D. P. Cantwell & G. A. Carlson (Eds.), *Affective disorders in childhood and adolescence.* New York: SP Medical and Scientific Books.

Trower, P. (1980). Situational analysis of the components and processes of behavior of socially skilled and unskilled patients. *Journal of Consulting and Clinical Psychology, 3,* 327–339.

U.S. Bureau of the Census. *Statistical Abstract of the United States: 1986.* Washington, DC: U.S. Government Printing Office.

Van Hasselt, V. B., Hersen, M., & Bellack, A. S. (1981). The validity of role play tests for assessing social skills in children. *Behavior Therapy, 12,* 202–216.

Van Houten, R. (1980). *How to motivate others through feedback.* Lawrence, KS: H&H Enterprises, Inc.

Vaughn, B. E., & Langlois, J. H. (1983). Physical attractiveness as a correlate of peer status and social competence in preschool children. *Developmental Psychology, 19,* 516–567.

Vygotsky, L. (1962). *Thought and language.* New York: Wiley.

Wahler, R. G. (1969). Setting generality: Some specific and general effects of child behavior therapy. *Journal of Applied Behavior Analysis, 2,* 239–246.

Walker, H. M. (1983). *Problem behavior identification checklist.* Revised. Los Angeles: Western Psychological Services.

Walker, H. M., & Buckley, N. K. (1974). *Token reinforcement techniques.* Eugene, OR: E-B Press.

Walker, H. M., & McConnell, S. R. (1988). *Walker-McConnell scale of social competence and school adjustment.* Austin, TX: PRO-ED.

Walker, H. M., McConnell, S., Holmes, D., Todis, B., Walker, J., & Golden, N. (1983). *The Walker Social Skills Curriculum*. Austin, TX: PRO-ED.

Walker, H. M., Severson, H., Stiller, B., Williams, G., Haring, N., Shinn, M., & Todis, B. (1988). Systematic screening of pupils in the elementary age range at risk for behavior disorders: Development and trial testing of multiple gating model. *RASE, 9*, 8–14.

Walker, H. M., Street, A., Garrett, B., Crossen, J., Hops, H., & Greenwood, C. R. (1978). *Reprogramming environmental contingencies for effective social skills (RECESS): Consultant manual*. Eugene: University of Oregon, Center at Oregon for Research in the Behavioral Education of the Handicapped.

Walker, H. M., Todis, B., Holmes, D., & Horton, G. (1983). *The ACCESS Program: Adolescent curriculum for communication and effective social skills*. Austin, TX: PRO-ED.

Walls, R. T., Werner, T. J., Bacon, A., & Zane, T. (1977). Behavior checklists. In J. D. Cone & R. H. Hawkins (Eds.), *Behavioral assessment*. New York: Brunner/Mazel, Inc.

Waters, E., & Sroufe, L. A. (1983). Social competence as a developmental construct. *Developmental Review, 3*, 79–97.

Weiss, B., & Dodge, K. A. (1992). Some consequences of early harsh discipline: Child aggression and a maladaptive social information processing style. *Child Development, 63*, 132l–1335.

Weissberg, R. P., & Gesten, E. L. (1982). Considerations for developing effective school-based social problem solving (SPS) training programs. *School Psychology Review, 11*, 56–63.

Weissberg, R. P., Gesten, E. L., Liebenstein, N. L., Doherty-Schmid, K., & Hutton, H. (1980). *The Rochester social problem-solving (SPS) program. A training manual for teachers of 2nd–4th grade*. Rochester, NY: University of Rochester.

Weissberg, R. P., Gesten, E. L., Rapkin, B. D., Cowen, E. L., Davidson, E., Flores de Apodaca, R., & McKim, G. J. (1981). Evaluation of a social-problem-solving training program for suburban and inner-city third-grade children. *Journal of Consulting and Clinical Psychology, 49*, 251–261.

Weist, M. D. & Ollendick, T. H. (1991). Toward empirically valid target selection: The case of assertiveness in children. *Behavior Modification, 15*, 213–227.

Weist, M. D., Ollendick, T. H., & Finney, J. W. (1991). Toward the empirical validation of treatment targets in children. *Clinical Psychology Review, 11*, 515–538.

Wiig, E. (1982). *Let's talk: Developing prosocial communications skills*. Columbus, OH: Merrill.

Wiig, E. H., & Bray, C. M. (1983). *Let's talk for children*. Columbus, OH: Merrill.

Wiig, E. H., & Semel, E. M. (1976). *Language disabilities in children*. Columbus, OH: Merrill.

Wildman, B. G., & Erickson, M. T. (1977). Methodological problems in behavioral observation. In J. D. Cone, & R. P. Hawkins (Eds.), *Behavioral assessment* (pp. 255–273). New York: Brunner/Mazel, Inc.

Williams, S. L., Walker, H. M., Holmes, D., Todis, B., & Fabré, T. R. (1989). Social validation of adolescent social skills by teachers and students. *Remedial and Special Education, 10*, 18–28.

Witt, J. C., Cavell, T. A., Heffer, R. W., Carey, M. P., & Martens, B. K. (1988). Child self-report: Interviewing techniques and rating scales. In E. S. Shapiro & T. R. Kratochwill (Eds.), *Behavioral assessment in schools* (pp. 384–454). New York: Guilford Press.

Witt, J. C., & Martens, B. K. (1983). Assessing the acceptability of behavioral interventions. *Psychology in the Schools, 20*, 510–517.

Witt, J. C., Martens, B. K., & Elliott, S. N. (1984). Factors affecting teachers' judgments of the acceptability of behavioral interventions: Time involvement, behavior problem severity, and type of intervention. *Behavior Therapy, 15*, 204–209.

Wolf, M. M. (1978). Social validity: The case for subjective measurement or how applied behavior analysis is finding its heart. *Journal of Applied Behavior Analysis, 11*, 203–214.

Wood, M. M. (1975). *Developmental therapy.* Baltimore: University Park Press.

———. (1986). *Developmental therapy in the classroom.* Second Edition. Austin, TX: PRO-ED.

Wood, R., & Flynn, J. M. (1978). A self-evaluation token system *vs.* an external evaluation token system alone in a residential setting with predelinquent youth. *Journal of Applied Behavior Analysis, 11*, 503–512.

Wood, R., & Michelson, L. (1978). *Children's assertive behavior scales.* Unpublished manuscript.

Wood, R., Michelson, L., & Flynn, J. (1978, November). *Assessment of assertive behavior in elementary school children.* Paper presented at the Annual Convention of the Association for the Advancement of Behavior Therapy, Chicago.

Workman, E. A. (1982). *Teaching behavioral self-control to students.* Austin, TX: PRO-ED.

Yeats, K. O., & Selman, A. L. (1989). Social competence in the schools: Toward an integrative developmental model for intervention. *Developmental Review, 9*, 64–100.

Yeats, K. O., Schultz, L. H., & Selman, A. L. (1991). The development of interpersonal negotiation strategies in thought and action: A social-cognitive link to behavioral adjustment and social status. *Merrill-Palmer Quarterly, 37*, 369–406.

Yu, P., Harris, G. E., Solovitz, B. L., & Franklin, J. L. (1986). A social problem-solving intervention for children at high risk for later psychopathology. *Journal of Clinical Child Psychology, 15*, 30–40.

Zaragoza, N., Vaughn, S., & McIntosh, R. (1991). Social skills intervention and children with behavior problems: A review. *Behavioral Disorders, 16*, 260–275.

Zigmond, N., Kerr, M. M., Schaeffer, A. L., Brown, G., & Farra, H. E. (1986). *School survival skills curriculum.* Pittsburgh, PA: University of Pittsburgh.

Zimmerman, B. J., & Pike, E. O. (1972). Effects of modeling and reinforcement on the acquisition and generalization of question-asking behavior. *Child Development, 43*, 892–907.

Part 2

Special Applications of Social Skills Teaching

Chapter 6

Cognitive-Affective Approaches: Enhancing Competence in Aggressive Children

JAN N. HUGHES   TIMOTHY A. CAVELL

Not only is aggression one of the most common problems in school-aged children, but it is increasing dramatically (Loeber, 1990). Children with aggressive and antisocial behaviors comprise between one-third and one-half of all child referrals for psychological services (Achenbach & Edelbrock, 1978; Robins, 1979). Furthermore, costs to the aggressive child, the child's family, society, and the child's victim are tremendous and include special education placement, outpatient and inpatient services, juvenile probation, physical harm, property destruction, disrupted learning experiences for the child's classmates, and psychological harm. Because childhood aggression is highly stable and predicts adult criminality (Olweus, 1979; Robins, 1979; Stattin & Magnusson, 1989), its costs, ultimately, include a more violent society with all the associated psychological, social, and economic consequences.

Given the magnitude of the problem, it is not surprising that tremendous amounts of money and effort have been devoted both to determining the causes of aggression and to developing interventions that reduce childhood aggression and prevent its long-term consequences. These research efforts demonstrate that childhood aggression is a result of multiple, interactive factors and that effective interventions must have several components and occur over extended time periods (i.e., months or years) (Lochman, 1992). This chapter describes and critically reviews school-based intervention approaches with children that attempt to enhance their social competence and decrease their disruptive and aggressive behavior.

Aggression describes a variety of acting-out behaviors that have in common an intrusive demand and an aversive effect on others (Olweus, 1979). Aggressive acts include physically and verbally aggressive behaviors—threatening others, purposefully disturbing others, being verbally combative, making derogatory remarks, hitting, shoving—as well as destruction of property. Aggressive children are described by teachers as "starting fights," "mean," "argumentative," "teasing others," and "rebellious." The aggressive behavior disrupts classroom activities and places excessive demands on teachers' time and resources.

Short-term and Long-term Consequences of Aggression

Childhood aggression frequently is associated with concurrent and future learning problems. Rutter, Tizard, and Whitmore (1970) found that one quarter of slow readers showed antisocial behavior and one third of conduct-disordered children were reading disabled. Aggressive children lack skills that are necessary for effective learning such as paying attention and remaining seated (Krehbiel, 1984; Shinn, Ramsey, Walker, O'Neill, & Stieber, 1987).

Perhaps the most consistent correlate of childhood aggression is peer rejection (Wass, 1987). It is not surprising that negative, aversive social behaviors lead to peer rejection. Peer rejection and aggression are each predictive of serious long-term negative consequences. Recently researchers have attempted to determine the relative contribution of peer rejection and aggression to later maladjustment (Kupersmidt, Coie, & Dodge, 1990). These studies show that aggression in elementary school is the stronger predictor of criminality, whereas peer rejection is the stronger predictor of academic difficulties, including dropping out of school (Parker & Asher, 1987). The child who is both aggressive and peer-rejected is at greatest risk of multiple negative outcomes. Peer rejection has other consequences as well, including lack of a social support system, loneliness, and low self-esteem. The consequences of sustained peer rejection also can include changes in reactions to peers and by peers that maintain the rejected child's hostility and isolation.

Long-term consequences of early aggression include alcoholism, drug abuse, sexual promiscuity, dropping out of school, and unemployment (Robins, 1979; West & Farrington, 1977). However, the strongest associations are between childhood aggression and subsequent delinquency or adult criminality, associations that hold for both girls and boys (Stattin & Magnusson, 1989). This relationship also is found in racially diverse populations and holds when social class and level of intelligence are statistically controlled (Conger & Miller, 1966; Roff & Wirt, 1984; Stattin & Magnusson, 1989).

Distal Factors Associated with Childhood Aggression

In the past five to ten years, research on childhood aggression has rapidly expanded our knowledge about its stability, precursors, concomitants, and amenability to intervention. The studies emphasize multiple and interactive determinants in the development and maintenance of aggression. The variables most often implicated as determinants of aggression fall into the following categories:

- Biological,
- Family,
- Peer,
- Academic,
- School and community.

The following sections review current findings on the relationship between these variables and aggression and other conduct-disordered behaviors.

Biological Factors

Genetic factors (e.g., temperament), perinatal events (e.g., low birth weight), and other biological mechanisms (e.g., lead poisoning) may predispose children to react to their environment in negative ways. For example, persistent demands from the temperamentally difficult child can precipitate a cycle of interaction where a parent's attempts to gain control over the child's behavior leads to even more intense oppositional reactions. Other biological factors that contribute to childhood aggression include (1) a lack of autonomic nervous system responsiveness to punishing stimuli, (2) the action of certain biochemicals such as testosterone, and (3) the presence of symptoms commonly associated with attention deficit hyperactivity disorder (ADHD) (Loeber, 1990; Lytton, 1990).

Family Factors

Several family demographic variables have been implicated in the search for causes of childhood aggression. These include: level of economic deprivation, single parent status, family size, and ethnicity. These factors are often strongly correlated with one another, making it difficult to separate the effects of each (Cohn, Patterson, & Christopoulos, 1991). Socioeconomic status factors have shown the strongest and most consistent links to antisocial behavior (Loeber, 1990). Economic deprivation and other demographic risk factors, however, are thought to operate primarily through the disruption of essential parenting practices.

One of the most important findings is the significant role that parents play in the development of aggressive behavior (Eron, 1987; Loeber, 1990; Maccoby & Martin, 1983; Patterson, 1986). Many parenting variables have been examined. These include:

- Parents' effectiveness as disciplinarians,
- Their reliance on overly punitive forms of discipline,
- The extent to which they emotionally reject their children,
- Their level of warmth and positive involvement,
- The extent to which they monitor their child's whereabouts and supervise their activities, and
- The level of stability and organization they create in their homes.

Although it is often difficult to separate parent effects (e.g., overly punitive discipline) from child effects (e.g., difficult temperament), most researchers conclude that these two factors operate in a transactional manner to produce the aggressively behaving child (Lytton, 1990).

Perhaps the most influential model detailing the relation between parenting practices and children's conduct problems is that put forth by Patterson and his colleagues (Forgatch, 1991; Patterson, 1986; Patterson, Capaldi, & Bank, 1991; Patterson, Reid, & Dishion, *in press*). The cornerstone of Patterson's social learning model is the premise that parents inadvertently train children to engage in aggression by mismanaging early misbehaviors. For Patterson, inept discipline and ineffective monitoring constitute the "basic training" of antisocial children. Although modeling and positive reinforcement are involved, the training of aggressive behavior relies heavily on negative reinforcement or escape conditioning. Children who successfully use coercive behavior to escape their parents' attempts to exert control are likely to repeat such acts. Empirically, Patterson's *coercion model* has proven to be quite robust (Patterson, 1986); conceptually, it has had a tremendous impact on how researchers and practitioners understand parents and their aggressive children (Cavell, 1992).

Patterson's model emphasizes parents' failure to control their children's behavior, but also acknowledges the damaging effects of overly harsh and explosive discipline. This aspect of parenting has also been cast as parental rejection or the lack of warmth, nurturance, or positive parental involvement. As is true for parental control, parenting low in warmth also contributes to the development of childhood aggression (e.g., Eron, 1987; Greenberg & Speltz, 1988; Loeber, 1990; Parke & Slaby, 1983).

Another key aspect is family stability or organization: parents' ability to maintain a sense of order and predictability in the home (Radke-Yarrow, Richters, & Wilson, 1988), as well as their use of appropriate generational boundaries (Minuchin, 1974; Sroufe & Fleeson, 1988). Parents who are not seen as being in a position of authority and whose homes are marked by frequent chaos generally will find the strength of other aspects of parenting (e.g., discipline, emotionally positive interactions) to be greatly diminished (Maccoby & Martin, 1983).

Peer Factors

Social rejection—as measured primarily by negative peer nominations—has been shown to be a robust predictor of children's later adjustment, particularly the likelihood of school dropout (Parker & Asher, 1987). Because of this, many researchers have investigated the causes and correlates of peer rejection. Perhaps the most consistent finding is that aggressive behavior leads directly and rather quickly to rejected peer status (Coie & Kupersmidt, 1983; Dodge, 1983). In fact, researchers estimate that nearly half of all rejected children also are behaviorally aggressive (Coie, 1990). But what proportion of aggressive children are rejected by their peers? Although far less data exist on this issue, some studies indicate that only about one third of all aggressive children escape peer rejection (Bierman & Smoot, 1991; Coie, Underwood, & Lochman, 1991).

Children who behave in a hostile, aggressive manner invite aggressive responses from peers, in addition to social isolation and rejection (Price & Dodge, 1989). Moreover, to the extent aggressive behavior leads to peer rejection, a child's subsequent interactions with peers—even if predominantly prosocial in nature—will likely be perceived in a way that maintains a negative reputation (Hymel, 1986). Prosocial acts are often seen as uncharacteristic and due to external factors, or they may be overlooked entirely. Also, mild and very infrequent displays of aggression will be enough to maintain a child's negative reputation. The net effect is that aggressive-rejected children may perceive little incentive for changing their aggressive behavior or their own negatively biased perceptions, and thus create a powerful cycle of negative interaction (Price & Dodge, 1989).

Academic Factors

Aggression and poor academic performance often occur together. A lively and ongoing debate surrounds the question of whether aggression is a cause or a consequence of academic difficulties. Some studies suggest that aggression and associated conduct problems are best predicted by earlier cognitive deficits (Schonfeld, Shaffer, O'Connor, & Portnoy, 1988). Other investigations, however, indicate that aggressive and antisocial behavior precede school failure (e.g., Dishion, Patterson, Stoolmiller, & Skinner, 1991; Patterson et al., 1991). Still others view aggressive, externalizing behaviors *and* academic deficiencies as the result of a common set of underlying factors such as attentional difficulties and neurodevelopmental delay (Hinshaw, 1992). For our purposes, it is sufficient to recognize that academic difficulty is a frequent concomitant of childhood aggression that can quickly lead to peer rejection and possible school dropout.

School and Community Factors

Reactions from individual teachers can be an important factor in understanding a child's aggression. Although little research has addressed this issue, teachers—like parents—can vary widely in their ability to discipline firmly and relate warmly to aggressive children. Moreover, children's social judgments about peers often are based on how teachers respond to acts of misbehavior and poor academic performance (Morrison, Forness, & MacMillan, 1983; Retish, 1973). Not only do teachers differ in their response to aggressive children, but schools also vary in their strategies for dealing with aggressive children.

In some situations, a child's aggression may be an adaptive response to her or his environment. In some communities, extreme acts of violence are a common occurrence and thus physical and verbal aggression may be construed as necessary for one's survival (Richters & Martinez, 1991). Indeed, exchanging verbal insults and threats, a type of verbal repartee, may even serve to establish a cohesive peer group (Prinz & Miller, 1991). The instructor must decide whether to regard the aggression as a "natural manifestation of normal peer group socialization in specific cultural groups or as problem behaviors with adverse consequences" (Prinz & Miller, 1991, p. 380). Indications that intervention is needed are: (1) physical (versus verbal) aggression, (2) behaviors that bring the child into contact with juvenile authorities, and (3) uncontrolled, reactive aggressive behaviors that lead to peer rejection within the child's peer group.

Summary

Aggression, then, is not only quite stable, but is also a factor in the emergence of other problem behaviors (e.g., academic failure, peer rejection) many of which have several risks associated with them. Loeber (1990) refers to this phenomenon as the *stacking* of problematic behaviors, one atop the other. As Stattin and Magnusson (1989) note:

> It is rare to find a highly aggressive boy who is not educationally or socially handicapped in many ways. They often are restless and exhibit concentration difficulties, they show low school motivation and underachieve, and they tend to have poor peer relations (p. 717).

Unfortunately, as aggression becomes intertwined with other facets of a child's life, incentives for the continued use of aggression are often much stronger than incentives to desist.

Cognitive and Behavioral Characteristics of Aggressive Children

This section summarizes studies investigating the behavioral and cognitive skills of aggressive children to provide a basis for reviewing skill training approaches. Some presume that aggressive behaviors are the result of social skills deficits. Social skills training programs attempt to teach these children the social behaviors necessary for satisfactory peer interaction. Yet many children who engage in high rates of socially aversive and aggressive behavior do not exhibit deficiencies in prosocial behaviors. When researchers have measured both prosocial behaviors and aggression in the same group of children, they have found no correlation (or small positive or negative correlations) between aggression and prosocial behaviors (Radke-Yarrow, Zahn-Waxler, & Chapman, 1983; Strayer, 1984). Because there is considerable variability in prosocial behaviors among aggressive children, an individual assessment of prosocial behaviors should precede any effort to train prosocial skills. Given the independence of aggressive and prosocial behavior, interventions that focus only on prosocial skills are unlikely to result in decreased aggression (Bierman, Miller, & Stabb, 1987; Coie & Koeppl, 1990).

Research on social-cognitive deficits in aggressive children shows that they do exhibit social-cognitive deficits and distorted thinking that mediate their aggressive behavior (Akhtar & Bradley, 1991). Chandler (1973) documents differences in role-taking skills between delinquent and nondelinquent youths. Spivack, Shure, and their colleagues (Shure & Spivack, 1978) report a series of studies showing that specific social problem-solving skills are associated with adjustment outcomes in children. These early studies stimulated research interest in social-cognitive correlates of maladjustment. Some of the most productive research on the role of social-cognitive processes in childhood psychopathology has been conducted with aggressive and rejected children. Although a critical review of this field of research is beyond the scope of this chapter, selected studies that illustrate the importance of social-cognitive mediators in childhood aggression will be examined.

This review follows the stages in social-cognitive information processing proposed by Dodge (1986). According to his model, socially competent behavior involves the exercise of specific skills at five sequential stages: (1) encoding, (2) interpretation, (3) response search, (4) response decision, and (5) enactment. Socially competent responses require an individual to recognize relevant aspects of the social situation, accurately interpret social cues, generate appropriate social responses, select a response, and effectively implement the selected response in the situation. These stages are interdependent—performance at earlier stages affects performance at later stages. An aggressive response, then, is the outcome of the social information processing that precedes it. Recently, researchers have expanded this skill-based approach by addressing the role of general beliefs, motivations, and goals.

Encoding

Aggressive children often selectively attend to and recall aggressive cues (Dodge & Newman, 1981; Dodge & Frame, 1982; Gouze, 1987). Specifically, aggressive children and adolescents respond too quickly to social situations, without taking advantage of all the available social cues; they focus on the hostile cues. Indeed, when aggressive children take time to pay attention to more cues in a situation, they are no more likely to infer hostile intent than are nonaggressive children (Dodge & Newman, 1981).

Interpretation

Several researchers have found that aggressive children demonstrate a systematic bias to infer hostile intent in ambiguous social situations (Asarnow & Callan, 1985; Dodge, Murphy, & Birchsbaum, 1984; Steinberg & Dodge, 1983). Steinberg and Dodge had pairs of same-sex children compete in a block-building task. Each subject discovered that some of her or his blocks had fallen before the prize was awarded. The cause of the blocks falling was ambiguous. Aggressive subjects were more likely to attribute their misfortune to the hostile behavior of peers than were nonaggressive subjects. Children's perceptions of intent are also an important determinant of their behavioral response (Dodge et al., 1984). These attributional biases are the result of a preexisting expectancy that others will respond to them with hostile intent (Guerra & Slaby, 1989). Such generalized beliefs often affect what aspects of a situation are attended to and how information is interpreted.

Aggressive children also misinterpret peers' intent in prosocial situations. Hughes,

Robinson, and Moore (1991) found that aggressive/rejected children were unlikely to attribute prosocial intent when an unspecified classmate decided to give them a small prize for their participation. The failure to accurately read prosocial overtures from peers contributes to aggressive children's low levels of reciprocated positive peer interactions (Konstantareas & Homatidis, 1984).

Although interpretation of intent has dominated research on cognitive deficits and distortions, aggressive children exhibit other difficulties in accurately "reading" social cues. Greenspan (1981) refers to these aspects of social competence as *social insight*—the ability to understand the underpinnings or nuances of particular social situations. For example, aggressive children exhibit deficits in social *perspective taking*—the ability to take the point of view of another person (Chandler, 1973; Cohen, Kershner, & Wehrspann, 1985). It is important to note that deficits in perspective-taking ability are not specific to aggressive children but are also found in other groups of socially deviant children (Cohen et al., 1985).

Deficits in perspective taking may explain why aggressive children have difficulties assessing their relative power in peer groups. In normal peer groups, stable power hierarchies are established quickly, and children of lesser power rarely challenge or attack peers of a higher status. Stable dominance hierarchies are established more slowly among groups of aggressive children (Konstantareas & Homatidis, 1984; Strayer, 1984), and instances of attacks or challenges between individuals of differing power status are more frequent than in peer groups of nonaggressive children.

Finally, aggressive children tend to minimize their aggression level and overestimate the aggressiveness of their nonaggressive peer partners (Lochman, 1987). They are also likely to minimize the impact of their aggression on others (Slaby & Guerra, 1988).

Response Generation and Response Decision

Aggressive children and adolescents exhibit deficiencies in generating effective, nonaggressive solutions to conflict situations. It is the content of the solutions generated, rather than the number of solutions, that consistently differentiates aggressive and nonaggressive children: Aggressive children generate less effective and more aggressive solutions to interpersonal problems (Richard & Dodge, 1982; Slaby & Guerra, 1988; Guerra & Slaby, 1989). Interestingly, aggressive and nonaggressive children's first solutions to social problems tend not to differ, whereas subsequent solutions by aggressive children are less effective, even when controlling for differences in verbal reasoning ability (Evans & Short, 1991).

The response decision step involves generating consequences of different solutions and prioritizing solutions based on their anticipated consequences. Aggressive youth not only generate fewer consequences for aggressive solutions, but they also evaluate these solutions more positively. They believe that aggression will produce tangible rewards and reduce aversive treatment by others (Perry, Perry, & Rasmussen, 1986). They believe it will increase self-esteem and help avoid a negative image, all without causing excessive suffering by others (Slaby & Guerra, 1988; Guerra & Slaby, 1989). Furthermore, aggressive children report finding it easier to perform aggressive acts and more difficult to inhibit aggressive impulses (Perry et al., 1986). Such organized systems of beliefs may guide information processing at each step. That is, these children's beliefs that aggression is a legitimate solution that leads to positive outcomes with minimal negative costs, plus their confidence in executing aggressive solutions, may influence encoding of hostile cues, interpretation of social situations, and generation and selection of responses.

Enactment

Most research on the behavioral social skills of aggressive children has involved behavioral role-play (Bornstein, Bellack, & Hersen, 1980; Feldman & Dodge, 1987) rather than naturalistic observation. Evidence exists, however, suggesting that performance in role-plays may not be predictive of naturalistic behaviors (e.g., Kazdin, Esveldt-Dawson, & Matson, 1983). Furthermore, when researchers control for group differences in intelligence level, children who are popular, rejected, average, and neglected do not differ in their performance in social situation role-plays (Hughes, Boodoo, Alcala, Maggio, Moore, & Villapando, 1989).

Differences between aggressive and nonaggressive children in the enactment of social skills may result from differences in behavioral social skills or differences in the social reasoning that precedes the behavioral response. Furthermore, a child's failure to respond competently in a social situation may result from a lack of ability to perform competently or a lack of motivation to perform the competent response. If motivational factors are responsible for the child's failure to respond competently, skill training approaches would not be expected to lead to behavioral improvement (Cavell, 1990).

Aggressive children may be less bothered by the negative effect their aggressive behavior has on others. Aggressive adolescents minimize the amount of suffering experienced by victims of aggression (Slaby & Guerra, 1988), perhaps because they are deficient in their ability to vicariously experience the emotional reactions of others (Miller & Eisenberg, 1988). Aggressive children also tend to evaluate their own affective reaction to self-generated consequences of aggression as "wouldn't care" or not as "unhappy," even when they experience negative consequences (e.g., being suspended from school) (Guerra & Slaby, 1989).

Summary

Aggressive children tend to have deficiencies at several information-processing steps and possess general beliefs about aggression's legitimacy and efficacy that contribute to high levels of aggression. Because the cumulative effect of these social-cognitive factors is substantial (Guerra & Slaby, 1989), multiple interventions are required to produce socially consequential decreases in aggression.

Linking Assessment and Intervention Planning

Enhancing the social competence of aggressive children is a formidable task. Successful interventions must build on a comprehensive assessment of (1) aggressive behavior, (2) variables that maintain aggression, and (3) factors likely to alter a child's risk trajectory (Coie & Koeppl, 1990; Loeber, 1990). Assessment should be guided by a thorough understanding of childhood aggression. Indeed, practitioners equipped with a clear understanding of aggression and its development are better prepared to conduct assessments than those outfitted with a battery of ill-conceived tests. Simple, prepackaged approaches to assessing and treating aggressive children are doomed to fail. The number of areas that need to be addressed is too great and our ability to affect change in many areas is too limited.

In discussing childhood aggression assessment, one must consider both proximal and distal factors. *Proximal factors* are the behavioral, cognitive, and emotional aspects of aggression itself. *Distal factors* also are associated with aggression but are chronologically or causally distant from a child's aggressive act. To link assessment activities and intervention planning, assessment should proceed as follows. First, determine the presence and magnitude of the problem as perceived by others. Peer ratings and teacher ratings (see Chapter 2) provide information on the child's impact on others and the situations that provoke aggression. These measures also provide an index of the extent to which an intervention results in socially consequential outcomes.

In the second assessment stage, behaviors and cognitions associated with aggression are evaluated using the methods discussed in Chapter 2. The more distal variables that create the context for both the development and the maintenance of aggressive behavior are also assessed at this stage. Underlying the assessment are two questions:

1. To what extent is this factor contributing to the problem?
2. To what extent is this factor amenable to change?

Answering these questions helps identify contextual variables to target for intervention.

Assessment of Biological Factors

Perhaps the most important biological factor to consider is the presence of an attentional disorder, mainly *attention-deficit hyperactivity disorder* (ADHD)—a biologically based disorder; its core symptoms are impulsivity, inattentiveness, and overactivity (*Diagnostic and Statistical Manual III-R,* American Psychiatric Association, 1987). Aggression and attention problems frequently occur together, and most teacher rating scales do not distinguish between aggression and ADHD (Barkley, 1990). Many aggressive children are hyperactive, which may result, at least in part, from their impulsivity and inattention.

When problems with attention, impulsivity, and hyperactivity are suspected, the child should be evaluated for ADHD and considered for adjunctive medication therapy. Recent studies indicate that methylphenidate (Ritalin) can reduce aggressiveness and enhance the social behaviors of ADHD children (Hinshaw, Henker, Whalen, Erhardt, & Dunnington, 1989), while also improving their peer status (Whalen, Henker, Buhrmeister, Hinshaw, Huber, & Laski, 1989). Aggressive children with ADHD probably would benefit the most from combined medication therapy and skill enhancement approaches.

Assessment of Family Factors

Most of the information one needs to assess family factors can be obtained through sensitive interviewing and the observation of parent–child interactions (Hughes & Baker, 1990; McMahon & Forehand, 1988). (See McMahon and Forehand's, 1988, detailed discussion on the assessment of children's conduct problems for other information-gathering approaches.) Perhaps the two most important family factors to assess are parents' use of discipline and their ability to interact warmly with their children. Though some parents have trouble only with discipline (overly permissive) and others have trouble only with nurturance (overly authoritarian), most parents of aggressive children have difficulty in both areas (Maccoby & Martin, 1983; Patterson, 1986).

Assessment of Peer Factors

Children identified as aggressive (1) are often rejected by peers, (2) have reputations among peers and elicit reactions from peers that are often negative, (3) tend to associate with equally aggressive peers, and (4) have friendships that appear to be of poor quality.

Several methods are available for assessing these factors. Information obtained directly from peers (e.g., peer ratings or nominations) is perhaps most helpful, although often it is difficult to obtain. Child, parent, and teacher estimates of peer status and peer interactions can be used in lieu of peer reports, along with observations conducted in the classroom or on the playground. Information is needed about the number, duration, and quality of children's friendships, and the extent to which a child's friends are engaged in deviant, antisocial activity. Generally speaking, assessing these factors is easier for younger children than for older children. With adolescents, significant peer interactions often occur outside of the purview of adults. Thus, information provided by parents or teachers or obtained through direct observation is less accurate.

Assessment of Academic Factors

School failure and the associated frustration and threat to self-esteem may contribute to aggression. The high correlation between aggression and school learning problems does not establish a causal link between the two (Hinshaw, 1992); however, it does direct attention to the multiple problems aggressive children may experience and their diminished opportunities to feel competent and worthwhile.

Academic difficulties, combined with peer rejection, increase the risk of early school withdrawal and identification with deviant peer groups. Although its effectiveness has not been directly tested, Coie & Krehbiel (1984) found that academic tutoring improved the peer status and classroom behavior of socially rejected children.

Assessment of Teacher/School and Community Factors

As noted earlier, the way a teacher responds to an aggressive child seems an important though poorly understood piece of the overall picture for the school-based practitioner. Flanders and Havumaki (1960) found that teachers' patterns of public positive reinforcement had a significant impact on students' level of peer acceptance. These patterns, however, may be too narrow a perspective for understanding teachers' level of influence. For example, how do teachers deal emotionally with disquieting acts of aggression, and what are the emotional costs of containing and relating positively to aggressive children? One would suspect that teachers who can counter a child's aggression while maintaining a warm and supportive relationship would have the greatest success with these children. In fact, such a relationship may be especially powerful for resource teachers who have a greater opportunity to work one-on-one with aggressive children.

Both a school's and a community's culture, including norms for aggression, should be considered when assessing the aggressive child (Olweus, 1991; Richters & Martinez, 1991). Olweus (1991), for example, describes the effectiveness of a school-based program designed to reduce problems with bullies' aggression. The program has as its major components:

- A 32-page booklet for school personnel with information about and suggestions for dealing with bully/victim problems,
- A four-page folder about bully/victim issues distributed to parents of all school-age children,
- A 25-minute videotape showing episodes from the everyday lives of two bullied children, and
- A short self-report questionnaire that asks about the frequency of bully/victim problems and the readiness with which teachers and other students would intercede in these problems.

The questionnaires provide school administrators with a starting point for active interventions in their school (Olweus, 1991); they also serve to create a set of explicit and highly shared norms about what is inappropriate behavior. Although this intervention program has not been tested experimentally, Olweus (1991) presents results from quasi-experimental field trials that suggest it is highly effective in reducing bullying, being bullied, and general antisocial behavior.

Interventions for Aggressive Children

The model of aggression presented here emphasizes the importance of multifaceted interventions based on an individual assessment of problematic behaviors and their determinants. Consistent with the skills enhancement approach of this book, the following sections review interventions that directly enhance skills, or support skill enhancement programs, as well as ecological interventions that support skill-training approaches.

Skill Training Approaches

Social Skills Training

Social skills training (SST) programs use a combination of instruction, coaching, modeling, behavioral rehearsal, and feedback to teach low-accepted children prosocial skills such as helping, sharing, and asking questions (Ladd, 1981; Oden & Asher, 1977). SST with aggressive children is based on the view that these children lack the social skills necessary for successful peer interaction. During the 1970s and 1980s, several social skills-training programs for aggressive children and adolescents were promoted, despite research showing its limited benefits with aggressive children.

Although aggressive children improve in their ability to enact specific skills they have been taught (Bornstein et al., 1980; Greenleaf, 1982), they do not improve on measures of social interaction or disruptiveness outside the treatment setting (Ollendick & Hersen, 1979; Spence & Marzillier, 1981). These disappointing results are not surprising, given the fact that aggression encompasses a broad constellation of behaviors that are the result of multiple and interactive determinants. Furthermore, the assumption on which SST is based—aggressive children lack prosocial skills—is simply not true for a significant percentage of aggressive children who engage in high rates of both positive and negative social behaviors and who are both disliked and liked (Price & Dodge, 1989).

SST is effective in teaching prosocial skills and improving the peer acceptance of low-accepted children who engage in low levels of the prosocial skills taught in the program (Bierman & Furman, 1984). It also may be an effective component of more comprehensive treatment with those aggressive children who are also socially withdrawn (Ledingham, 1981).

Indeed, Bierman et al. (1987) demonstrate the effectiveness of combining social skills training in prosocial skills (helping, sharing, making conversation) with mild punishment for disruptive behavior (response cost) in improving the peer interactions and sociometric ratings of rejected/disruptive boys in grades 1 to 3. In the SST condition, modeled on Ladd (1981), the adult coach began each session with a brief discussion of the target skill and elicited behavioral examples from the group. After discussion of the target skills, children were instructed to practice the skill in a cooperative play activity. The coach led postplay reviews of performing the target skill. In a departure from Ladd's program, the therapist both praised skillful performance of the target skill and rewarded it during the play activity with tokens. In the prohibition/reinforcement condition, children were presented with rules for the sessions (e.g., no fighting or yelling) and lost tokens when they violated a rule. The coach provided nonspecific praise and tokens on a random basis when children were not involved in rule breaking.

Boys were randomly assigned to the SST condition, prohibition condition, or a combined SST plus prohibition condition, or to a no-treatment control. Boys in both the prohibition conditions decreased negative behaviors immediately after treatment and received more positive responses from other boys, but only boys receiving SST also increased their positive behaviors.

Results suggest SST and response cost for aggression have a differential impact on positive and negative behaviors. Observations at six weeks after treatment revealed that boys in all three treatment conditions initiated fewer negative behaviors, but only boys receiving SST increased their positive behaviors. Despite these positive changes in behavior, the rejected/disruptive children did not gain greater peer acceptance in the classroom or improved teacher ratings immediately after treatment or at the six-week or one-year follow-up. One exception was a decrease in being disliked on the part of classmates who served as partners in the play session for boys in the combined treatment condition. Apparently, unless a child's classmates have opportunities to work cooperatively with a disliked child, they are unlikely to change their feelings about that peer.

The difficulty in changing peers' acceptance for rejected/disruptive children indicates that children continue to view a child according to his or her reputation instead of according to current behavior. The length of the intervention (six weeks) was too short for classmates to change their perceptions of and reactions to the rejected, socially aversive children.

Problem-solving Skills Training

Problem-solving Skills Training (PSST) is based on the finding that aggressive children are deficient in problem-solving and other social-cognitive skills. Typically, problem-solving skills training is combined with instruction in anger-control techniques (Lochman & Curry, 1986). Children are first taught to "stop and think" in anger-provoking situations and then to apply problem-solving skills—defining the problem, setting a goal, generating alternatives, evaluating consequences of different alternatives, selecting a response, and evaluating its effectiveness. Discussions and role-plays of hypothetical social situations are used to teach self-control and problem-solving skills. Thus, PSST incorporates training in behavioral/social skills, anger-coping skills, and social-cognitive skills. The following sections describe four different research teams' efforts to develop and empirically evaluate the use of PSST with aggressive children.

Lochman. The first approach, Lochman's 18-session anger coping program (Lochman & Curry, 1986), focuses on:

- Building a sense of group purpose and cohesion and establishing group rules,
- Teaching perspective-taking skills,

- Helping children recognize the relationship between different types of self-talk and feelings of anger
- Teaching children to engage in self-talk that helps them reduce anger arousal and increase self-control,
- Identifying physiological cues of anger,
- Teaching children to use anger-coping self-talk when they experience anger,
- Identifying problem situations,
- Generating alternatives to anger-provoking situations, and
- Identifying and evaluating consequences of different alternatives.

Hypothetical stories and role-plays are used to model these skills. Children practice the skills in role-plays of actual anger-arousing situations they experience and in making a videotape in which they demonstrate using the complete set of self-control and problem-solving skills. To enhance generalization to the classroom setting, children identify goals for improving their classroom behavior that teachers monitor. The children are responsible for bringing their goal-monitoring sheets to the group, and receive reinforcement for achieving their classroom goals.

Lochman's anger-control groups comprise five or six children identified by teachers and peers as aggressive. The weekly sessions, each between 45 and 60 minutes in duration, are led by two co-leaders who follow an intervention manual (Lochman, Lampron, Gemmer, & Harris, 1987). The following are a few activities from the manual to illustrate the program's training goals and methods.

A *verbal taunting game* teaches children the difference between anger-coping and anger-building self-talk. Each child takes a turn having his or her puppet receive and respond to verbal taunts from the other children for 20 to 30 seconds. The leader asks the child what the puppet was feeling, what the puppet said to itself, whether what the puppet said helped it control angry feelings, and what the puppet might do next. Next, the leader's puppet receives taunts, and the leader models anger-controlling self-statements (e.g., "I'm not going to let them get me mad!"). The leader discusses how self-talk affects angry feelings and angry actions. Finally, the children's puppets each receive taunts a second time and the children practice anger-coping self-statements. The leader discusses the difference anger-coping statements make on the puppet's feelings and actions with each child.

To develop perspective-taking, children discuss *stimulus pictures* depicting problem situations. The leader asks each child questions like: "What is the problem?" "What is happening?" "What are the people thinking and feeling?" The leader points out the differences in how various people view a situation. Children also role-play problem situations until the leader gives the cue to stop the action. A child assumes the role of "roving reporter" and interviews the different actors in the role-play about their perceptions of the problem—what happened, what people were thinking and feeling, and what people were going to do next. The leader discusses the fact that there is more than one way to view a situation.

To help children integrate the problem-solving steps taught in the program, they *practice* the steps using problems they experienced during the preceding week. The leader guides the children through these problem-solving steps: (1) What is the problem? (2) What are my feelings? (3) What are my choices? (4) What will happen?

The outcomes of problem-solving training were positive. Treated children decreased disruptive/aggressive classroom behavior, improved on parent-completed measures of aggression, and reported increased self-esteem relative to controls (Lochman & Curry, 1986). More important, the effectiveness of the treatment was evident three years later when treated boys were in junior high school (Lochman, 1992); they displayed lower levels of substance use than untreated control boys. The evidence indicates that the lower level of substance use was a result of treated boys' higher self-esteem and social problem-solving skills. The researchers conclude that "the cognitive-behavioral intervention appears to have prepared the treated aggressive boys to make more careful, less impulsive decisions about alcohol and drug use, and their higher levels of self-esteem may have reduced their motivation to become involved with drugs" (p. 431).

In a series of studies, Lochman demonstrates that extending training from 12 to 18 weeks results in greater gains and that a greater emphasis on social problem-solving skills is more effective in reducing aggressive/disruptive behavior than a divided focus on self-control skills and social problem-solving skills (Lochman & Curry, 1986). Furthermore, children who are the most deficient in social problem-solving skills make the most behavioral gains in treatment (Lochman, Lampron, Burch, & Curry, 1985). Finally, adding "booster sessions" the year following PSST and including parent training enhances the effectiveness of PSST (Lochman, 1992). Lochman's systematic examination of intervention components and child characteristics that predict positive treatment outcomes is commendable and critical to efforts to increase the potency of interventions.

Guerra and Slaby (1990) developed and evaluated a social-cognitive intervention with severely aggressive adolescents based on the view that beliefs serve as "stable and organizing factors underlying aggression" and that "changes in these cognitive mediators should lead to relatively enduring patterns of behavior change" (p. 269). Their 12-week program involves weekly one-hour group sessions focusing on both social-cognitive skills (e.g., selective attention to hostile cues, attributional biases, generating nonaggressive responses) and beliefs (e.g., aggression is a legitimate and effective response to frustrating situations and victims of aggression do not suffer) implicated in aggression. In a departure from other problem-solving skills-training programs, they relied on group discussion of hypothetical and real problem situations, rather than on behavior role-plays, to teach the targeted skills and beliefs.

In their study, training resulted in improvements in the targeted skills and beliefs and, more important, in behavioral adjustment in the correctional facility. However, the program did not significantly reduce the incidence of recidivism (i.e., the likelihood of reincarceration). They also demonstrated that decreases in subjects' tendency to define problems in terms of a hostilely motivated adversary, and changes in their belief that aggression is a legitimate response to problems, predicted the amount of behavioral improvement, even after controlling for subjects' level of pretest aggression.

Arbuthnot and Gordon. Interventions that focus on values and moral reasoning may be especially effective with aggressive/disruptive adolescents. They (1986) designed an intervention to enhance the moral reasoning and "sociomoral world-view" of these youths. Each session discussed moral dilemmas such as the following:

> Sharon and her best friend, Jill, are shopping in a boutique. Jill finds a blouse she wants but cannot afford. She takes it into a fitting room and puts it on underneath her jacket. She shows it to Sharon and, despite Sharon's protest, leaves the store. Sharon is stopped by a security guard. The manager searches Sharon's bag, but finding nothing, concludes that Jill shoplifted the blouse. The manager asks Sharon for Jill's name, threatening to call both Sharon's parents and the police if she doesn't tell. Sharon's dilemma is whether or not to tell on her best friend (p. 210).

Through these discussions, the adolescents examined role obligations, conflicting obligations, and values, and then practiced perspective taking and problem solving. Treatment was school-based and involved 45-minute sessions held weekly for 16 to 20 weeks.

Treated adolescents demonstrated advances in moral reasoning and improvements in behavioral measures, compared with adolescents in a no-treatment control group. For the most part, these effects were maintained for one year. Evidence that behavioral improvement was mediated by advances in moral reasoning was supported by a significant relationship between advances in moral reasoning and behavioral improvement. That is, students who improved the most on behavioral measures also improved the most on measures of moral reasoning. Although the youth in this study were selected on the basis of behavior problems, not all the subjects were aggressive, and results might differ with severely aggressive adolescents.

Kazdin and his colleagues (Kazdin, Esveldt-Dawson, French, & Unis, 1987; Kazdin, Bass, Siegel, & Thomas, 1989) evaluated a PSST intervention with seriously aggressive children. They demonstrated that PSST results in significant behavioral improvement that lasts up to one year after treatment. These studies compared the effectiveness of training in interpersonal problem-solving skills and relationship therapy in the treatment of severely aggressive children age 7 to 13 years. The subjects were inpatients of a psychiatric facility where children are hospitalized for 2 to 3 months for acute disorders, including highly aggressive and destructive behavior. Parent and teacher ratings of aggressive behavior were collected when the child was admitted to the hospital and at follow-up assessments up to one year after discharge.

The problem-solving training was administered individually in 20 sessions, each lasting 45 minutes, two or three times per week. Interpersonal problem-solving skills were taught to the child through the application of verbal instruction, modeling, discussion of hypothetical problem situations, enactment of skills in role-plays, corrective feedback, and social reinforcement. Token reinforcement for completion of homework and response-cost procedures for errors in carrying out the problem-solving approach were used during the treatment sessions. The relationship therapy program also involved 20 individual sessions that focused on building a close relationship with the child and providing empathy, unconditional positive regard, and warmth.

The problem-solving program significantly improved behavior at school and at home and was superior to relationship therapy. Furthermore, treatment effects in the children's home schools were maintained up to one year after treatment. The researchers conclude that the "results suggest that cognitive behavior problem-solving skills training can effect changes in a seriously disturbed clinical population, that the changes are evident in community-based measures, and that changes are sustained at least up to 1 year" (Kazdin et al., 1987, p. 84). Despite these gains, a majority of the treated children continued to exhibit clinically significant levels of aggressive/disruptive behavior (Kazdin et al., 1989). This finding argues for more comprehensive treatments or for treatments that target both problem-solving skills and belief systems that influence social problem solving and motivation for aggressive responses.

The STAR Program

Hughes developed a PSST program that is currently undergoing experimental investigation with the support of a grant from the Hogg Foundation for Mental Health. The *Students Taking Assertive and Responsible Action* (STAR) program (Hughes, 1992) is an extension and modification of Lochman's *Anger Coping Program*. In addition to teaching children to apply self-control and problem-solving skills to situations in which they experience anger, the STAR program addresses aggressive children's tendency to define problems in terms of a hostilely motivated adversary (Guerra & Slaby, 1989). Whether children define a problem as a call for retaliation or as an opportunity to achieve some instrumental goal will guide their problem solving. How a problem is framed will determine what cues they encode, how they interpret cues, what strategies they generate, and how they evaluate the consequences of different strategies. Guerra and Slaby (1990) demonstrate that children who show the most behavioral improvement following a problem-solving intervention are those children who show the most change in how they define problems and in their beliefs about the legitimacy of aggression.

The STAR program is also unique in its inclusion of many relationship-enhancement and self-esteem-building activities. The attention given in the program to building a warm, caring relationship with the student is based on the finding that relationship-enhancement therapy increases the benefits of problem-solving skills training (Kendall, Reber, McLeer, Epps, & Ronan, 1990). It is also based on the belief that a high degree of leader warmth, positiveness, and responsiveness is critical to the success of skill-training programs, especially with aggressive children. Children who have participated in a supportive therapeutic relationship containing strong emotion and who feel accepted and valued by the leader are likely to: (1) be motivated to learn the skills taught; (2) develop increased self-esteem; and (3) enjoy a more positive, less angry mood. Thus, they may be better able to tolerate frustration that arises when old habits are being replaced with new skills.

Format of STAR

Groups of four to five children in second and third grade, who are nominated and rated by their teachers as aggressive and for whom parental permission is obtained, meet twice weekly for 12 weeks with a leader and co-leader for 45-minute sessions. The leaders follow a detailed manual. After the first three sessions, the format remains the same. First, the leaders ask each child to name something that happened to them since the last meeting that increased or decreased their self-esteem. Initially, the leader uses a balloon to illustrate self-esteem, telling children that some things "give you real good feelings and make you proud" or "make you want to stick out your chest and stand tall." These things make your balloon go up. Other things happen that give you sad or mad feelings. These things make your balloon go down.

During the "checking-in" time that begins each session, children tell something that made their balloon go up or go down. The leader listens empathically, letting the child know the leader understands and accepts the child's feelings. Although the leader does not engage the child in attempts to solve problems brought up during the check-in time, problem situations may be the subject of discussions or role-plays that occur later in the session. Second, the leader introduces the target skill or concept for that day. Table 6-1 presents an outline of the skills and concepts targeted in each session.

The Reinforcement Contingencies

During the first session, the leaders guide the children in developing a list of group rules, which are posted and include both "do" and "don't" rules. The *do* rules are: listening and paying attention, keeping your body to yourself, joining in, helping, controlling your temper by ignoring bugging, staying on the topic, and obeying the "stop-and-freeze" signal. The stop-and-freeze signal is selected by the group and means that everyone "freezes" and is quiet. The *don't* rules include physical aggression, verbal put-downs, and disrupting the group (horseplay). The leader models each rule as it is discussed, providing examples of following the rule and of not following the rule, and discussing how that rule helps everyone have a good time and get along together.

Children earn points on individual cards for following the "do" rules. Children receive a warning for violating a "don't" rule, and if the child continues to violate the rule, he or she loses a point. Physical aggression or destruction of property results immediately in a lost point (no warning) plus time out, if necessary. The session is divided into three reinforcement phases, and the child can earn up to three individual points during each phase, for a total of 15 points. One rule is that the children do not discuss the points, and the co-leader keeps track of the points earned and lost. At the

TABLE 6-1 Skills Taught in STAR Session

Session	Skills/Concept
1	People are different
	Rules/Reinforcement/Response cost
2	Giving compliments
3	Identifying feelings
4	Recognizing angry feelings
5	Anger-taming self-talk
6	Problem definition: Paying attention to all the evidence
7	Problem definition—Three steps:
	• Someone has upset feelings.
	• Problems happen between people.
	• Problems must be solved
8	Problem-solving Step 1—Define the problem:
	• Decide if you have an upset feeling.
	• Stop to think before acting.
	• Say exactly what the problem is.
	• Decide on your goal.
9	Using anger-taming self-talk when you have upset feelings
10	Recognizing anger-taming and anger-building self-talk
11	Setting goals
12	Problem-solving Step 2—Think of different ways you could solve the problem
13	More on Step 2
14	Problem-solving Step 3—Think ahead to what might happen next
15	Problem-solving Step 4—Do it
16	Problem-solving Step 5—Evaluate how you did
17	Cue detection skills (figuring out why people do what they do, paying attention to all the cues)
18–23	Integration and application of five problem-solving steps
24	Expressing feelings about the group

end of each session, points are totaled. Once a week, points are either exchanged for small prizes or recorded for future spending.

In addition to the individual point system, a group contingency is employed. The group members' total individual points are recorded on a chart that shows progress toward group rewards (e.g., ice cream or pizza). Up to five "bonus" points can be added to the group's total, based on how well they work together.

Enhancing Feelings Identification

Several activities and exercises help children recognize their own and others' feelings. Children develop a "feelings dictionary," use a feelings thermometer to show how angry they feel about different things, try to guess the feeling an actor in a role-play is expressing, and identify feelings in pictures. In one activity, a child recites a familiar poem (e.g., "Mary Had a Little Lamb") or the alphabet using voices that convey different feelings. The other children try to guess the feeling portrayed. During the checking-in time, the leader helps children label feelings they experienced in the situations that made their balloon go up or go down (affected their self-esteem).

Problem Definition/Cue Detection

The "detective game" is one of the activities designed to help children pay attention to cues inconsistent with hostile intent. In this game, children are detectives and look for clues about why people do what they do. The leader presents a scenario like the one below, and tells the children to decide if the protagonist acted "on purpose to be mean" or "by accident." Each child is given a card with "on purpose to be mean" and a card with "by accident" and is instructed to turn over one of the cards whenever she or he is sure about why the character did something? Although children can listen to as few or as many of the clues as they wish, once a card is turned over, the child can not change her or his mind.

The following is a sample detective game scenario:

Imagine that you painted a special picture in art class today. You wanted to take it home, but it was wet, so you left it on a table at the back of the classroom to dry while you went out to P.E. After you get back from P.E., you notice that your picture has been destroyed. All the paint has run together and your picture is ruined. Chris stayed in the classroom during recess, and you have to decide if he ruined your picture on purpose or whether it was an accident.

Next, the leader reads the following clues in order:

1. Chris sometimes does mean things so that other kids will think he's cool.
2. Chris and you got into an argument this morning because you both wanted to use the earphones in the listening center, and the teacher let you use them first.
3. Chris has paint on his fingers.
4. You heard Chris say something mean about you to another kid.
5. Chris stayed in at P.E. because he needed to finish his painting for art class.
6. When Chris saw you notice your ruined picture, he said, "Gee. That's too bad."
7. The teacher tells you that she asked Chris to move your picture because she needed the table.
8. Another child tells you that your teacher told him he had to move his picture, too. When he tried to pick it up, the paint ran and ruined your picture.
9. Chris likes to try to help other kids. Yesterday he offered to help you with some math problems that were really hard.

Another activity designed to help children accurately interpret social situations involves watching a videotape of social interactions in which a provocation occurs and the intention of the protagonist is ambiguous. For example, one scenario depicts a boy bumping into another boy in the lunchroom. The lunchroom is crowded and the boy was not looking where he was going when he bumped into the other boy, causing the second boy to drop his tray. The leader asks the children why the first boy bumped into the other one, making certain that several reasons are suggested—he can't see well with his thick glasses, he was trying to find a place to sit, he did it on purpose to be mean, he wanted to make the kids laugh. The leader asks the children what clues they use to decide on the boy's intention (surprised expression on his face, the crowded lunchroom). The leader then asks the children how the bumped boy might feel if he thought the boy bumped him by accident or on purpose, and what the bumped boy would do in each case. The leader asks the children how the bumped boy could find out why he was bumped.

Anger-taming Self-talk

Cartoon drawings are used to help children understand the relationship between self-talk and angry feelings. The leader presents a cartoon drawing depicting a problem situation such as someone stepping on a child's paper airplane. The character in the cartoon has an empty thought bubble. The leader describes what happened in the cartoon, how the child felt (e.g., real mad), and what the child did (e.g., pushed the other child). Then the leader asks the children what the child was thinking that made him or her so mad. These anger-building statements are written in the thought bubble. Next, the leader presents a duplicate of the picture and describes what happened in an identical manner but portrays the child as feeling a little angry and as responding assertively (e.g., asking the other child to be more careful). The leader asks the children what the child said that helped him to keep his cool. These anger-taming self-statements are written in the bubble. Anger-taming self-talk is also practiced in role-plays and illustrated in stories and puppet play.

Problem-solving Skills

Children are taught first how to recognize they have a problem. Children are told that problems make people feel upset, problems usually are between people, and that problems need to be solved. Stories, puppet play, videotaped role-plays, and live role-plays are used to teach children to recognize problems and to follow problem-solving steps. One of the hardest steps for children is defining the problem and stating a goal (the first step of problem solving). To help children with this step, problem definition cards are posted:

- Decide if you have upset feelings.
- Stop and think before acting.
- Decide what your problem is.
- Decide what your goal is.

At first the leader is the main actor—the one who has the problem—in the role-play and models the steps in defining the problem. For example, if the problem involved someone grabbing the scissors when the main actor had been waiting for them, the leader would act out the situation, saying something like the following:

1. I'm feeling angry.
2. I'm going to stop and think before acting.
3. My problem is that it is my turn to use the scissors but Jody grabbed them.
4. My goal is to get them back.

The remaining steps in problem solving are taught in a similar manner, with the leader first describing the step, giving examples of the step, explaining why that step is important, and demonstrating that step in a role-play. Next, the children practice the skill in role-plays and receive feedback from the leader and peers on their performance. Beginning in session 18 and continuing through session 23, the children create a videotape of their role-plays, which is shown to their teachers at the end of the training.

Goal Setting

The goal setting intervention—patterned on Lochman, Burch, Curry, & Lampron (1984)—involves having each child select a behavior to increase or decrease in his or her classroom. The teacher must approve the behavioral goal and record the child's goal accomplishment each week. The child is responsible for bringing the goal card to class. Goal accomplishment is rewarded with additional points and with leader praise. Failure to achieve the goal results in a problem-solving discussion.

Preliminary Results of STAR

The initial evaluation of the STAR program involved 41 second- and third-grade children nominated by their teachers as aggressive and scoring at least one standard deviation above the mean on the aggressive subscale of the *School Behavior Checklist* (Miller, 1977). The children were ethnically diverse, and 80 percent were male. Children were randomly assigned to the STAR program or to a comparison intervention—teacher consultation. Children assigned to the teacher consultation condition did not receive direct services. Instead, a psychologist met individually with the child's teacher for four sessions to develop classroom-based, teacher-directed interventions to reduce aggression.

At the time of this writing, posttreatment analyses had been completed. Dependent measures, administered pre- and posttreatment, included peer sociometrics, classroom observations, parent ratings, teacher ratings, measures of social-cognitive skills, and self-concept. Both treatments resulted in pretreatment to posttreatment improvements on teacher ratings of aggression, peer ratings of social competence, parent ratings of aggression, and classroom observations of on-task behavior. Furthermore, children in the STAR program who improved the most on measures of social problem solving displayed the greatest behavioral improvement. This finding supports the mediating role of problem-solving skills on behavioral adjustment.

Without a wait-list or no-treatment control condition, one cannot determine definitively that the improvements shown by children in both groups were a result of the interventions. However, several researchers demonstrate that without intervention, teacher-identified aggressive children increase rather than decrease their aggressive and disruptive behavior (Bierman et al., 1987; Kazdin et al., 1987). Nevertheless, the fact that the more intensive STAR program did not produce improvements above that obtained with the less intensive teacher consultation raises questions about the cost-effectiveness of the STAR program.

Identifying children who are most likely to benefit from these programs is one way to increase intervention effectiveness and cost-effectiveness. Some children may benefit from a brief intervention, whereas other children may require a more intensive, multifaceted intervention. Hughes, Grossman, and Hart (1993) predicted that children in the STAR or consultation program whose parents reported less positive attachment histories (less closeness and warmth) would be least likely to benefit from the interventions, because neither intervention focuses on parental determinants of aggression. Indeed, a measure of parents' attachment histories (reported parental acceptance and rejection) significantly predicted children's behavioral improvement from pretreatment to posttreatment in both interventions. Specifically, mothers with more negative attachment histories in both intervention groups had children who responded less favorably to treatment, based on teacher ratings.

One explanation of this finding is that mothers develop mental representations, or internal working models, of the parent–child relationship that will to some extent determine the quality of the child-rearing environment they provide for their children. Consistent with the model of aggression presented in this chapter, children of mothers who experienced more harsh and less accepting parental behavior during their own childhoods may require a more comprehensive intervention that addresses the parent–child relationship as well as problem-solving and behavioral-skill deficits.

Implementation Issues

Our experience providing school-based PSST taught us the importance of successfully addressing several practical implementation issues. The leader must select group members who are able to function within the group and benefit from it, work with teachers and principals to schedule group sessions, and arrange for an appropriate room and materials.

The optimal group size is between four and six, with two co-leaders. One leader provides instruction and directs discussions, role-plays, and other learning activities. The other leader monitors the reinforcement system, addresses behavioral problems in the group, and supervises students whose behavior requires a "time out" from the group. Early in the program, children are likely to test the limits, and it is important to be able to remove a disruptive student from the group temporarily. A student is removed if he or she loses all his or her points during one of the fifteen-minute periods or engages in seriously aggressive behavior. Students are unable to earn points during the time they are in "time out."

When assigning children to groups, pay attention to ethnic and gender balance. It is best to avoid having only one girl in a group. Additionally, the presence of one member of an ethnic group may place that child at risk for receiving racial insults or other forms of mistreatment by the majority group members.

Some aggressive children are unlikely to benefit from PSST. Children who are extremely hyperactive and impulsive not only are unlikely to benefit from the training, but also are a highly disruptive influence on the group. Aggressive children diagnosed with ADHD and whose symptoms respond positively to medication are good candidates for PSST. Children with extreme levels of aggression are not selected for this secondary prevention intervention. They require a different and more intensive treatment.

Children experiencing extreme environmental stress, such as domestic violence or parental alcoholism, also require a more individualized and intensive intervention that includes assistance to the family. Children with cognitive delays may not be able to grasp such concepts as self-talk and attributional biases and experience difficulty applying the problem-solving steps.

Scheduling one or two 45- to 60-minute periods a week during the schoolday requires flexibility on the part of teachers and leaders. Because aggressive children often experience learning problems, it is important to schedule meetings so that children do not miss instruction in academic areas. Alternating meeting times between a daily music/art period and a daily physical education period so that children miss one period of music/art and one period of physical education during a week is ideal.

Most important, leaders need to communicate regularly with teachers, the principal, and other school professionals to identify problems that may be developing early on. The leaders must recognize that schools have multiple priorities and complex scheduling demands and be willing to work around scheduling conflicts.

The room in which sessions are held needs to be large enough to allow considerable movement during videotaping. Children sit in a circle on pillows or a carpet for a good part of each session, which promotes a sense of group cohesion and inclusion. Younger children often enjoy sitting on the leaders' laps or just very close. The STAR manual includes several discussion pictures and describes any special materials required for a session. Most of the required materials are easily made or purchased. The large discussion pictures from the Dinkmeyer (1973) guidance program, *Developing Understanding of Self and Others* (DUSO), are helpful. A videocamera, VCR, and monitor are necessary.

Designing Effective Social-Cognitive Training Programs

Recent social-cognitive training programs for use with aggressive children and adolescents have yielded promising results and point the way to design more effective interventions. Several conclusions about how to design and implement skill-training programs follow.

1. Programs should target multiple social-cognitive factors, including social-cognitive skills (e.g., attending to nonhostile cues, selecting nonhostile goals, accurately interpreting social cues that indicate different intentions, generating nonaggressive alternatives to social problems, anticipating and evaluating consequences of alternatives) and altering beliefs (e.g., that aggression is a legitimate response to frustration, that aggression enhances self-esteem, and that victims of aggression do not suffer). Through role-plays and discussion of social problem situations, children should be taught how to integrate skills, beliefs, and affective reactions.

2. Teaching children to inhibit aggressive impulses through investigative self-statements (e.g., "Stop and think. What is my problem?") is not as helpful as teaching children specific self-statements that mediate aggression in anger-arousing situations (e.g., "Stay cool and think it through so I won't get in trouble."). Self-control training may be helpful when it is practiced in the context of anger-arousing situations and followed with social problem-solving training. In this case, its purpose may be to inhibit a child's automatic reaction to provocation, allowing the child to think rather than to react.

3. Skill-training programs should provide a high level of acceptance and warmth to the child. Unless the child is motivated to learn and practice the skills taught, training is likely to be unsuccessful. If the child feels accepted and valued by the therapist, the child is more likely to want to learn from him or her. The experience of being accepted and valued by the therapist may provide the child with improved self-esteem that allows her or him to respond with less angry, reactive aggression to provocations. Although this hypothesis has not been subjected to empirical scrutiny, there is indirect support for it. First, Kazdin's successful problem-solving training was conducted in individual sessions. It is likely that the relationship with the therapist provided motivation to learn the skills and improved the child's self-esteem. Second, when social-cognitive skill training follows relationship-enhancement therapy, children improve more on measures of social competence than when skill training precedes relationship therapy (Kendall et al., 1990). Finally, in at least two studies comparing skill-training programs with relationship-enhancement therapy, skill training was less successful than relationship-enhancement therapy in decreasing aggression and increasing prosocial skills (Camp & Bash, 1981; Dubow, Huesman, & Eron, 1987).

4. Training needs to be of sufficient length to permit children to master the skills and change their beliefs about aggression. At a minimum, sessions should continue four months and occur at least weekly for a minimum of 45 minutes. Multiyear programs, which can involve booster sessions in the years following the more intensive treatment, are most likely to produce durable decreases in aggression (Lochman, 1992).

5. Behavioral contingencies should be a part of skill-training interventions. Response-cost procedures are necessary to reduce aggressive behavior in the training sessions. Providing reinforcement for acceptable classroom behavior will motivate children to practice the skills taught.

6. Children should be assessed and found deficient on the skills taught before they are placed in a skills-training program. Some children may exhibit high levels of aggression because they expect aggression to lead to tangible rewards, not because they are deficient in social skills.

7. Teachers need to be included in the intervention. Minimally, teachers should be given a full explanation of the program at the beginning and provided weekly progress reports on the child's participation. Teachers can help children practice skills in the classroom if they know which ones have been introduced in training. Teachers can provide feedback to group leaders on the child's attainment of goals, and the leaders can provide rewards for goal attainment.

8. Problem-solving training probably achieves its greatest success when integrated with parenting intervention. Parenting skills and the quality of the parent–child relationship are strong correlates of childhood aggression and should be the focus of an integrated skill-building intervention.

Parent Training

As noted earlier, many causal processes explain the link between parenting practices and childhood aggression (Cohn et al., 1991; Putallaz & Heflin, 1990). Parent training can be used effectively to reduce children's aggressive behavior. For example, Patterson (1986) found that newly learned parenting techniques have a direct effect on the frequency of aggressive behavior by changing the consequences that maintain it. Less direct mechanisms are also possible. Training enables parents to model for their children the effective use of prosocial behaviors. Instigation of aggressive—counter-controlling behavior—in children also is decreased when parents learn to avoid highly punitive forms of discipline (Eron, 1987). Finally, parent training targeting enhanced parent–child interactions leads to children's increased ability to regulate their affect and to more adaptive "internal working models" of close relationships (Greenberg & Speltz, 1988).

Nearly all parent-training programs designed to reduce the incidence of childhood aggression fit a behavior management model (Cavell, 1992). The use of behavior management parent training (BMPT) with the families of aggressive children began 25 years ago. The goal of BMPT is to eliminate coercive chains of behavior in families with aggressive children (Patterson, 1982). Originally, it was thought that training parents to extinguish inappropriate behavior and reinforce desirable behavior was sufficient to meet this objective. Researchers soon discovered, however, that punishment techniques such as "time out" were critical to the success of BMPT (Patterson & Fleischman, 1979). As these programs have evolved, teaching parents how to make their children more compliant has taken on increasing importance (Forehand & McMahon, 1981). Also, some researchers suggest that the focus on the control aspects of parenting has been overemphasized (Cavell, 1992; Eyberg, 1988; Greenberg & Speltz, 1988). They argue that parental warmth and nurturance are just as important to children's social development, particularly during those years when "basic training" for aggressive behavior is in its early stages (Patterson, 1982).

Most BMPT programs follow a common format of initial instruction in techniques to increase desirable behaviors, followed by instruction in techniques to decrease undesirable behaviors (Hanf, 1969). For example, in Forehand and McMahon's (1981) widely disseminated BMPT program, parents participate in a differential attention phase (Phase I) followed by a compliance training phase (Phase II). Phase I training teaches parents to attend to their child's appropriate behavior in a positive manner by describing it in a way that is free of questions, commands, and criticism. Play sessions are often the context for this type of parent–child interaction.

The primary goal of Phase I is for "the parent to learn to be a more effective reinforcing agent" (McMahon & Forehand, 1984, p. 300), although most BMPT programs recognize the value these play sessions have for promoting positive interactions between parents and children. Parents also learn to issue verbal praise and physical rewards for specific behaviors they wish to increase (e.g., "I like the way you put your clothes in the hamper") and to ignore minor negative behaviors they wish to decrease. Parents are instructed to rehearse these skills at home in daily 10-minute practice sessions. In Phase II, parents learn to give direct, concise commands and to praise their child if compliance occurs within five seconds. If the child does not comply, parents are taught to place the child in "time out" for three minutes.

The manner in which these skills are taught can vary from group didactic instruction to intense, closely supervised individual training. The parents in Forehand and McMahon's (1981) program learned their skills through didactic instruction, modeling, role-playing, clinic rehearsal and feedback, and home rehearsal. These parents also are trained individually in clinic settings equipped with one-way observation mirrors and bug-in-the-ear coaching devices. The rather costly and time-consuming nature of this approach led Webster-Stratton (1981, 1987) to develop her own program based entirely on videotaped modeling and instruction. The videotape series contains approximately 250 vignettes that can be part of a parent training group or can be self-administered by individual parents. The skills modeled in these tapes parallel those in the Forehand and McMahon (1981) protocol, although a recent version of the tapes includes additional emphasis on parent–child play and coping with parental stressors (Webster-Stratton, 1987).

Most reviews of the BMPT outcome literature (e.g., Kazdin, 1987; Miller & Prinz, 1990; Patterson, 1985) begin by noting that early single-case studies offer clear support for programs that train parents in these techniques (e.g., Patterson & Brodsky, 1966). Impressive initial results soon gave way, however, to findings from group outcome studies that both supported (e.g., Patterson, Chamberlain, & Reid, 1982) and failed to support (e.g., Bernal, Klinnert, & Schultz, 1980) the short-term efficacy of BMPT. Follow-up studies, ranging from one to seven years in duration, are fairly consistent in reporting favorable findings (e.g., Baum & Forehand, 1981; Forehand & Long, 1991; Patterson & Fleischman, 1979; Webster-Stratton, 1990). However, these studies also found that many children do not respond to BMPT. Webster-Stratton (1990), in comparing the findings of her three-year follow-up study with those of other BMPT researchers, concludes that the "results are similar to other parent training studies, which have suggested that 30% to 50% of treated families fail to maintain clinically significant improvements" (p. 148).

Patterson (1985) and others, including Forgatch (1991), suggest that negative findings reported in some parent-training studies were due to treatment formats that were too brief (e.g., 8–10 weeks) or to the use of therapists who were inexperienced or poorly trained. They argue that parent trainers should be experienced clinicians who have the ability to blend parent training with traditional clinical skills—skills essential when dealing with parents who are resistant to change (Patterson, 1985).

The difficulty therapists face when trying to modify parents' disciplinary style is illustrated in a recent study (Forgatch, 1991) that focuses on parents' use of discipline and monitoring. Few parents were able to improve their actual use of these skills. Adopting a criterion of a 30 percent increase above baseline to define improvement, Forgatch (1991) found that, out of 50 families, only 25 (50 percent) improved their discipline, only 8 (16 percent) improved their monitoring, and only 5 (10 percent) improved both their discipline and their monitoring. When these data are considered in light of the propensity for parents of aggressive children to experience emotional distress, marital conflict, and extra-familial stress, one can appreciate the difficult challenge that awaits those therapists who use available models of parent training (Cavell, 1992). In fact, some researchers question whether parent training by itself is adequate to meet the needs of families with aggressive children (Miller & Prinz, 1990; Patterson, 1985; Webster-Stratton, 1990).

More recently, researchers suggest that parent-training programs for aggressive children may achieve greater success if they are used in conjunction with the more child-focused, social skills-training programs (Coie et al., 1991; Patterson, DeBaryshe, & Ramsey, 1989). For example, a 12-year, multisite study is currently in progress in which parent training and social skills training are to be combined into a single intervention package for first-grade children identified by teachers as aggressive (McMahon & The Behavior Disorders Prevention Group, 1991). Intervention will begin in first grade and last for approximately 22 weeks, followed by an additional year of treatment when the child is in second grade. Another aspect of this very comprehensive program—borrowing from the work of Coie and Krehbiel (1984)—is the use of tutoring for children with academic delays.

Peer-Based Interventions

Because negative reactions from peers (e.g., hostile punishment, a lack of social reinforcement, negative perceptions, social rejection) can actually function to maintain a child's aggressive behavior, a number of researchers propose the use of peer-based interventions in conjunction with social skills-training programs. Unfortunately, our understanding of the process by which aggressive children become stably identified as rejected has vastly outpaced our capacity to alter this predicament. Nevertheless, peer-based interventions are often recommended because changes in children's social skills (increased use of prosocial acts, decreased use of antisocial acts) are often insufficient to change negative peer status (Hymel, 1986; Bierman & Furman, 1984). The most frequently recommended peer-based interventions are those involving shared activities, particularly those with an overarching group benefit. These activities are thought to create opportunities for children to challenge negative stereotypes held by peers (Price & Dodge, 1989).

Several sobering conclusions result from reviewing the literature on peer-based interventions for aggressive children. First, a great many of the approaches—peer-initiated contact, peer reinforcement, peer modeling—described in the literature have been evaluated primarily with isolated and withdrawn children, not with children who are rejected or aggressive (Furman & Gavin, 1989; Price & Dodge, 1989). Eliciting the aid of peers to draw out a shy child is very different from trying to promote sustained positive interchanges between peers and an aggressive child.

Second, despite a number of investigations exploring the academic and social benefits of peer-based interventions—peer tutoring, cooperative learning, peer collaboration—commonly used in school settings, few researchers have used these approaches with behaviorally disordered children, especially those manifesting high rates of aggression (Damon & Phelps, 1989; Furman & Gavin, 1989; Scruggs, Mastropieri, & Richter, 1985). Thus, the academic gains and improvements in self-esteem found in nondisordered samples may not generalize to children whose social (and possibly academic) behavior lead to a more negative reputation among peers. Also, the nature of these tasks may be too demanding for many aggressive children:

1. Peer tutoring requires an acknowledgment by the tutee of the tutor's authority and appropriate use of that authority by the tutor.
2. Cooperative learning tasks (e.g., jigsaw teaching, group investigation, student teams/achievement divisions) rely on group contingencies and pressure from peers to motivate children to master various academic topics.
3. Peer collaboration is loosely structured and supervised, requiring children to behave in a way that promotes a positive, supportive atmosphere.

In reviewing empirical studies that tested the benefits of peer tutoring with behaviorally disordered students, many of whom were not aggressive, Scruggs et al. (1985) conclude that "sociometric measures and teacher surveys have generally failed to document improvement in social functioning . . . [and] tutoring interventions cannot generally be expected to effect general social functioning" (p. 292).

Bierman and Furman (1984) developed one of the few peer-based interventions that has shown some promise. Their study examines the benefits of peer involvement in a social skills intervention for low-accepted fifth- and sixth-grade children. These children, who also demonstrated poor conversational skills, were assigned to one of four treatment conditions: (1) individual coaching in social skills, (2) group experience, (3) group experience with coaching, and (4) no treatment.

Children in the group experience conditions were to work together to make a friendly interaction video for the university. Each subject was paired with two classmates who were randomly chosen from among students receiving adequate sociometric ratings. Treatment consisted of 10 half-hour sessions spread over a six-week period. A follow-up assessment was conducted one year later. Results indicate that children who received skills training evidenced improved conversational skills at both posttreatment and at follow-up. Skills training also contributed to increased naturalistic interactions with peers.

A different set of benefits followed children's participation in the group experiences. Compared to subjects in other conditions, children involved with peer groups enjoyed greater gains in self-perceived competence and in peer acceptance ratings. However, these gains were not apparent at follow-up, except that children in the group experience condition earned significantly higher acceptance ratings from their treatment partners. This finding did not extend to more general acceptance by classroom peers. Bierman and Furman (1984) thus demonstrate that both social skills training and peer-based exercises are needed if one hopes to make lasting and generalized gains in both social behavior and peer acceptance.

Promises and Constraints of Treating Aggressive Children

Interventions for aggressive children must teach not only skills for successful social interaction and self-regulation but also must promote contexts supportive of competence. The most effective skill enhancement interventions for aggressive children, then, incorporate parents and peers as well as teachers and other school personnel. Furthermore, interventions must be given sufficient time to work. Brief exposure to social skills instruction will have little impact on an aggressive children's patterns of thinking, feeling, and behaving.

Schools provide the best opportunity to implement multiyear, ecologically-oriented skill enhancement programs. The majority of a child's peer interactions occur during the schoolday under teachers' supervision. For example, ecologically valid interventions, such as interdependent learning and peer tutoring, though in need of greater testing with aggressive children, may help improve both tutors' and tutees' attitudes toward school, their peer relationships, and their academic performance (Hightower & Avery, 1986).

Intensive programs of academic tutoring also may help alleviate academic problems, which might preempt associated problems with low school motivation, school withdrawal, and the drift toward deviant peer groups. Interestingly, the consistency and emotional quality of the adult tutor–student relationship may be as important as the quantity and quality of academic instruction received. Further studies are needed to separate these overlapping components.

School psychologists can also serve as consultants to individual teachers, assisting in efforts to implement classroom-based interventions with aggressive children. These interventions might include: (1) response-cost procedures; (2) modeling, prompting, and rewarding of prosocial skills; and (3) teachers' use of interactional skills to enhance the emotional quality of the teacher–child relationship. Once again, the benefits of these procedures, particularly attempts to improve teachers' affective relationships with aggressive children, have not been empirically established.

Schools have access to parents too. Because schools are part of the community, parents are often more willing to attend school-sponsored programs than clinic-based programs. Nevertheless, for various reasons many parents are reluctant or unable to attend parent-training programs. They may view teachers and other school personnel as "experts" who will criticize their parenting practices, or at least not understand or affirm them. Parents, particularly single parents with more than one child, have limited time; their lives may be too disorganized and too focused on just surviving to allow time for parent training. Practical problems, such as transportation and babysitting, also make it difficult to attend programs. Some parents believe that teachers are biased against their child or do not understand or appreciate the child or his or her culture. Finally, other parents do not perceive a problem with their child or else believe the problem is one that occurs only at school. Identifying these kinds of obstacles and attempting to overcome them is the first step in implementing intervention programs for parents of aggressive children.

To the extent that skill training programs for aggressive children are coordinated with other systemwide interventions, the likelihood of success is increased. School-based personnel often are in the best position to perform these coordinating functions. Teachers, counselors, and other school professionals also play a vital role in identifying young children at risk for continued aggressive behavior. When well-planned and broad-based interventions are used to target children for whom aggression is still an option and not a rule, the potential to change the lives of these children in a profound way exists. It is our hope that this chapter offers guidance to professionals in a position to intervene and make the best of their brief window of opportunity.

References

Achenbach, T. M., & Edelbrock, C. S. (1978). The classification of child psychopathology: A review and analysis of empirical efforts. *Psychological Bulletin, 85,* 1275–1301.

Akhtar, N., & Bradley, E. J. (1991). Social information processing deficits of aggressive children. Present findings and implications for social skills training. *Clinical Psychology Review, 11,* 621–644.

American Psychiatric Association. (1987). *Diagnostic and Statistical Manual III—Revised (III-R).* Washington, DC: APA.

Arbuthnot, J., & Gordon, D. A. (1986). Behavioral and cognitive effects of a moral reasoning development intervention for high-risk behavior-disordered adolescents. *Journal of Consulting and Clinical Psychology, 54,* 208–216.

Asarnow, J. R., & Callan, J. W. (1985). Boys with peer adjustment problems: Social cognitive processes. *Journal of Consulting and Clinical Psychology, 53,* 80–87.

Barkley, R. A. (1990). *Attention deficit hyperactivity disorder: A handbook for diagnosis and treatment.* New York: Guilford Press.

Baum, C. G., & Forehand, R. (1981). Long term follow-up assessment of parent training by use of multiple outcome measures. *Behavior Therapy, 12,* 643–652.

Bernal, M. E., Klinnert, M. D., & Schultz, L. A. (1980). Outcome evaluations of behavioral parent training and client centered parent counseling for children with conduct problems. *Journal of Applied Behavioral Analysis, 13,* 677–691.

Bierman, K. L., & Furman, W. (1984). The effects of social skills training and peer involvement on the social adjustment of preadolescents. *Child Development, 55,* 151–162.

Bierman, K. L., Miller, C. L., & Stabb, S. D. (1987). Improving the social behavior and peer acceptance of rejected boys: Effect of social skill training with instructions and prohibitions. *Journal of Consulting and Clinical Psychology, 55,* 194–200.

Bierman, K. L., & Smoot, D. L. (1991). Linking family characteristics with poor peer relations: The mediating role of conduct problems. *Journal of Abnormal Child Psychology, 19,* 341–356.

Bornstein, M., Bellack, A. S., & Hersen, M. (1980). Social skills training for highly aggressive children. *Behavior Modification, 4,* 173–186.

Camp, B. W., & Bash, M. A. (1981). *Think aloud: Increasing social and cognitive skills: A problem-solving program for children (primary level)*. Champaign, IL: Research Press.

Cavell, T. A. (1990). Social adjustment, social performance, and social skills: A tri-component model of social competence. *Journal of Clinical Child Psychology, 19,* 111–122.

———. (1992). *Divergent models of parent training: The first 25 years*. Manuscript under review.

Chandler, M. J. (1973). Egocentrism and antisocial behavior: The assessment and training of social perspective-taking skills. *Developmental Psychology, 9,* 326–332.

Cohen, N. J., Kershner, J., & Wehrspann, W. (1985). Characteristics of social cognition in children with different symptom patterns. *Journal of Applied Developmental Psychology, 6,* 227–290.

Cohn, D. A., Patterson, C. J., & Christopoulos, C. (1991). The family and children's peer relations. *Journal of Social and Personal Relationships, 8,* 315–346.

Coie, J. D. (1990). Toward a theory of peer rejection. In S. R. Asher & J. D. Coie (Eds.), *Peer rejection in childhood* (pp. 365–401). New York: Cambridge University Press.

Coie, J. D., & Koeppl, K. G. (1990). Adapting intervention to the problems of aggressive and disruptive rejected children. In S. R. Asher & J. D. Coie (Eds.), *Peer rejection in childhood* (pp. 309–337). New York: Cambridge University Press.

Coie, J. D., & Krehbiel, G. (1984). Effects of academic tutoring on the social status of low-achieving, socially rejected children. *Child Development, 55,* 1465–1478.

Coie, J. D., & Kupersmidt, J. B. (1983). A behavioral analysis of emerging social status in boys' groups. *Child Development, 54,* 1400–1416.

Coie, J. D., Underwood, M., & Lochman, J. E. (1991). Programmatic intervention with aggressive children in the school setting. In D. J. Pepler & K. H. Rubin (Eds.), *The development and treatment of childhood aggression* (pp. 389–410). Hillsdale, NJ: Erlbaum.

Conger, J. J., & Miller, W. C. (1966). *Personality, social class, and delinquency*. New York: Wiley.

Damon, W., & Phelps, E. (1989). Strategic uses of peer learning in children's education. In T. J. Berndt & G. W. Ladd (Eds.), *Peer relationships in child development* (pp. 135–157). New York: John Wiley & Sons.

Dinkmeyer, P. (1973). *Developing Understanding of Self and Others* (DUSO). Circle Pines, MN: American Guidance Service.

Dishion, T. J., Patterson, G. R., Stoolmiller, M., & Skinner, M. L. (1991). Family, school, and behavioral antecedents to early adolescent involvement with antisocial peers. *Developmental Psychology, 27,* 172–180.

Dodge, K. A. (1983). Behavioral antecedents of peer social status. *Child Development, 54,* 1386–1399.

———. (1986). A social information processing model of social competence in children. In M. Perlmutter (Ed.), *Cognitive perspective on children's social and behavioral development* (pp. 77–125). Hillsdale, NJ: Erlbaum.

Dodge, K. A., & Frame, C. L. (1982). Social cognitive biases and deficits in aggressive boys. *Child Development, 53,* 620–635.

Dodge, K. A., Murphy, R. R., & Birchsbaum, K. C. (1984). The assessment of intention-cue detection skills in children: Implications for developmental psychology. *Child Development, 55,* 163–173.

Dodge, K. A., & Newman, J. P. (1981). Biased decision-making processes in aggressive boys. *Journal of Abnormal Psychology, 90,* 375–379.

Dubow, E., Huesman, R., & Eron, L. D. (1987). Mitigating aggression and promoting prosocial behavior in aggressive elementary school boys. *Behavior Research and Therapy, 25,* 527–531.

Eron, L. (1987). The development of aggressive behavior from the perspective of a developing behaviorism. *American Psychologist, 42,* 435–442.

Evans, S. W., & Short, E. J. (1991). A qualitative and serial analysis of social problem solving in aggressive boys. *Journal of Abnormal Child Psychology, 19,* 331–340.

Eyberg, S. (1988). Parent-Child Interaction Therapy: Integration of traditional and behavioral concerns. *Child and Family Behavior Therapy, 10,* 33–45.

Feldman, E., & Dodge, K. A. (1987). Social information processing and sociometric status: Sex, age, and situational effects. *Journal of Abnormal Child Psychology, 15,* 211–227.

Flanders, N. A., & Havumaki, S. (1960). The effect of teacher-pupil contacts involving praise on the sociometric choices of students. *Journal of Educational Psychology, 57,* 65–68.

Forehand, R., L., & Long, N. (1991). Prevention of aggression and other behavior problems in the early adolescent years. In D. J. Pepler & K. H. Rubin (Eds.), *The development and treatment of childhood aggression* (pp. 317–330). Hillsdale, NJ: Erlbaum.

Forehand, R. L., & McMahon, R. J. (1981). *Helping the noncompliant child: A clinician's guide to present training.* New York: Guilford Press.

Forgatch, M. S. (1991). The clinical science vortex: A developing theory of antisocial behavior. In D. J. Pepler and K. H. Rubin (Eds.), *The development and treatment of childhood aggression* (pp. 291–315). Hillsdale, NJ: Erlbaum.

Furman, W., & Gavin, L. A. (1989). Peers' influence on adjustment and development: A view from the intervention literature. In T. J. Berndt & G. W. Ladd (Eds.), *Peer relationships in child development* (pp. 319–340). New York: John Wiley & Sons.

Gouze, K. R. (1987). Attention and social problem solving as correlates of aggression in preschool males. *Journal of Abnormal Child Psychology, 15,* 181–197.

Greenberg, M. T., & Speltz, M. L. (1988). Attachment and the ontogeny of conduct problems. In J. Belsky & T. Nezworski (Eds.), *Clinical implications of attachment* (pp. 177–218). Hillsdale, NJ: Erlbaum.

Greenleaf, D. O. (1982). The use of structured learning therapy and transfer programming with disruptive adolescents in a school setting. *Journal of School Psychology, 20,* 122–130.

Greenspan, S. (1981). Defining childhood social competence: A proposed working model. In B. K. Keogh (Ed.), *Advances in special education: Socialization influences on exceptionality* (pp. 1–40). Greenwich, CT: JAI.

Guerra, N. J., Slaby, R. G. (1989). Evaluative factors in social problem solving by aggressive boys. *Journal of Abnormal Child Psychology, 17,* 277–289.

———. (1990). Cognitive mediators of aggression in adolescent offenders. 2. Intervention. *Developmental Psychology, 26,* 269–277.

Hanf, C. (1969). *A two-stage program for modifying maternal controlling during mother-child interaction.* Paper presented at the meeting of the Western Psychological Association, Vancouver, BC.

Hightower, A. P., & Avery, R. R. (1986, August). *The study buddy program.* Paper presented at the 96th Annual Convention of the American Psychological Association, Washington, DC.

Hinshaw, S. P. (1992). Academic under-achievement, attention deficits, and aggression: Comorbidity and implications for intervention. *Journal of Consulting and Clinical Psychology, 60,* 893–903.

Hinshaw, S. P., Henker, B., Whalen, C. K., Erhardt, D., & Dunnington, R. E. (1989). Aggressive prosocial and nonsocial behavior in hyperactive boys: Dose effects of methylphenidate in naturalistic settings. *Journal of Consulting and Clinical Psychology, 57,* 636–643.

Hughes, J. N. (1992). *The STAR Program Manual.* Available from author, Texas A&M University, College Station, TX 77843-4225.

Hughes, J. N., & Baker, D. (1990). *The clinical child interview.* New York: Guilford Press.

Hughes, J. N., Boodoo, G., Alcala, J., Maggio, M., Moore, L., & Villapando, R. (1989). Validation of a role play measure of children's social skills. *Journal of Abnormal Child Psychology, 17,* 633–646.

Hughes, J. N., Grossman, P. B., & Hart, M. T. (1993, August). *Effectiveness of problem-solving training and teacher consultation with aggressive children.* Paper presented at the Annual Convention of the American Psychological Association, Toronto.

Hughes, J. N., Robinson, M. S., & Moore, L. A. (1991). Children's attributions for peers' positive behaviors: Social status differences. *Journal of Abnormal Child Psychology, 19,* 645–657.

Hymel, S. (1986). Interpretations of peer behavior: Affective bias in childhood and adolescence. *Child Development, 57,* 431–445.

Kazdin, A. E. (1987). Treatment of antisocial behavior in children: Current status and future directions. *Psychology Bulletin, 102,* 187–203.

Kazdin, A. E., Bass, D., Siegel, T., & Thomas, C. (1989). Cognitive-behavioral therapy and relationship therapy in the treatment of children referred for antisocial behavior. *Journal of Consulting and Clinical Psychology, 57,* 522–535.

Kazdin, A. E., Esveldt-Dawson, K., French, N. H., & Unis, A. S. (1987). Problem-solving skills training and relationship therapy in the treatment of antisocial child behavior. *Journal of Consulting and Clinical Psychology, 55,* 76–85.

Kendall, P. C., Reber, M., McLeer, S., Epps, J., & Ronan, K. (1990). Cognitive-behavioral treatment of conduct-disordered children. *Cognitive Therapy and Research, 14,* 279–297.

Konstantareas, M. M., & Homatidis, S. (1984). Aggressive and prosocial behaviors before and after treatment in conduct-disordered children and in matched controls. *Journal of Child Psychology and Psychiatry, 25,* 607–620.

Krehbiel, G .G. (1984). *Sociometric status and achievement based differences in behavior and peer assessed reputation.* Unpublished doctoral dissertation. Durham, NC: Duke University.

Kupersmidt, J. B., Coie, J. D., & Dodge, K. A. (1990). The role of poor peer relationships in the development of disorder. In S. R. Asher & J. D. Coie (Eds.), *Peer rejection in childhood* (pp. 274–305). New York: Cambridge University Press.

Ladd, G. W. (1981). Effectiveness of a social learning model for enhancing children's social interaction and peer acceptance. *Child Development, 52,* 171–178.

Ledingham, J. E. (1981). Developmental patterns of aggressive and withdrawn behavior in childhood: A possible method for identifying pre-schizophrenics. *Journal of Abnormal Child Psychology, 9,* 1–22.

Lochman, J. E. (1992). Cognitive-behavioral intervention with aggressive boys: Three-year follow-up and preventive effects. *Journal of Consulting and Clinical Psychology, 60,* 426–432.

Lochman, J. E., Burch, P. R., Curry, J. F., & Lampron, L. B. (1984). Treatment and generalization effects of cognitive behavioral and goal setting interventions with aggressive boys. *Journal of Consulting and Clinical Psychology, 52,* 915–916.

Lochman, J. E., & Curry, J. F. (1986). Effects of social problem-solving training and self-instructional training with aggressive boys. *Journal of Clinical Child Psychology, 15,* 159–164.

Lochman, J. E., Lampron, L. B., Burch, P. R., & Curry, J. F. (1985). Client characteristics associated with behavior change for treated and untreated aggressive boys. *Journal of Abnormal Child Psychology, 13,* 527–538.

Lochman, J. E., Lampron, L. B., Gemmer, T. C., & Harris, S. R. (1987). Anger coping intervention with aggressive children: A guide to implementation in school settings. In P. Keller & S. Heyman (Eds.), *Innovations in Clinical Practice: A Source Book,* Vol. 6 (pp. 339–356). Sarasota, FL: Professional Resource Exchange.

Loeber, R. (1990). Development and risk factors of juvenile antisocial behavior and delinquency. *Clinical Psychology Review, 10,* 1–42.

Lytton, H. (1990). Child and parent effects in boys' conduct disorder: A reinterpretation. *Developmental Psychology, 26,* 683–697.

Maccoby, E. E., & Martin, J. (1983). Socialization in the context of the family: Parent–child interaction. In E. M. Hetherington (Ed.), P. H. Mussen (Series Ed.), *Handbook of child psychology: Vol. 4. Socialization, personality, and social development* (pp. 1–101). New York: Wiley.

McMahon, R. J., & Forehand, R. (1984). Parent training for the noncompliant child: Treatment outcome, generalization, and adjunctive therapy procedures. In R. F. Dangel & R. A. Polster (Eds.), *Parent training: Foundations of research and practice* (pp. 298–328). New York: Guilford.

———. (1988). Conduct disorders. In E. J. Mash & L. G. Terdal (Eds.), *Behavioral assessment of childhood disorders,* 2d ed. (pp. 105–153). New York: Guilford.

McMahon, R. J., & The Conduct Problems Prevention Research Group (1991, August). Parent training as an intervention component in preventing conduct disorders. In T. A. Cavell (Chair), *New directions in parent training research and practice.* Symposium conducted at the meeting of the American Psychological Association, San Francisco.

Miller, G. E., & Prinz, R. J. (1990). Enhancement of social learning family interventions for childhood conduct disorder. *Psychological Bulletin, 108,* 291–307.

Miller, L. C. (1972). School behavior checklist: An inventory of deviant behavior for elementary school children. *Journal of Consulting and Clinical Psychology, 38,* 134–144.

Miller, P. A., & Eisenberg, N. (1988). The relation of empathy to aggressive and externalizing antisocial behavior. *Psychological Bulletin, 103,* 324–344.

Minuchin, S. (1974). *Families and family therapy.* Cambridge, MA: Harvard University Press.

Morrison, G. M., Forness, S. R., & MacMillan, D. L. (1983). Influences on the sociometric ratings of mildly handicapped children: A path analysis. *Journal of Educational Psychology, 75,* 63–74.

Oden, S., & Asher, S. (1977). Coaching children in skills for friendship making. *Child Development, 48,* 495–506.

Ollendick, T., & Hersen, J. (1979). Social skills training for juvenile delinquents. *Behavior Research and Therapy, 17,* 547–554.

Olweus, D. (1979). Stability of aggressive behavior patterns in males: A review. *Psychological Bulletin, 86,* 852–875.

———. (1991). Bully/victim problems among schoolchildren: Basic facts and effects of a school based intervention program. In D. J. Pepler & K. H. Rubin (Eds.), *The development and treatment of childhood aggression* (pp. 139–168). Hillsdale, NJ: Erlbaum.

Parke, R. D., & Slaby, R. G. (1983). The development of aggression. In E. M. Hetherington

(Ed.), *Handbook of child psychology: Vol. 4. Socialization, personality, and social development* (pp. 547–641). New York: Wiley.

Parker, J. G., & Asher, S. R. (1987). Peer relations and later personal adjustment: Are low-accepted children at risk? *Psychological Bulletin, 102,* 357–389.

Patterson, G. R. (1982). *Coercive family process,* Vol. 3. Eugene, OR: Castalia.

———. (1985). Beyond technology: The next stage in developing an empirical base for parent training. In L. L'Abate (Ed.), *Handbook of family psychology,* Vol. 2 (pp. 1344–1379). Homewood, IL: Dorsey.

———. (1986). Performance models for antisocial boys. *American Psychologist, 41,* 432–444.

Patterson, G. R., & Brodsky, G. (1966). A behavior modification program for a child with multiple problem behaviors. *Journal of Child Psychology and Psychiatry, 7,* 277–295.

Patterson, G. R., Capaldi, D. M. & Bank, L. (1991). An early starter model for predicting delinquency. In D. J. Pepler & K. H. Rubin (Eds.), *The development and treatment of childhood aggression* (pp. 139–168). Hillsdale, NJ: Erlbaum.

Patterson, G. R., Chamberlain, P., & Reid, J. B. (1982). A comparative evaluation of a parent-training program. *Behavior Therapy, 13,* 638–650.

Patterson, G. R., DeBaryshe, B. D., & Ramsey, E. (1989). A developmental perspective on antisocial behavior. *American Psychologist, 44,* 329–335.

Patterson, G. R. & Fleischman, M. J. (1979). Maintenance of treatment effects: Some considerations concerning family systems and follow-up data. *Behavior Therapy, 10,* 168–185.

Patterson, G. R., Reid, J. B., & Dishion, T. J. (1992). *Antisocial boys.* Eugene, OR: Castalia.

Perry, P. G., Perry, L. C., & Rasmussen, P. (1986). Cognitive social learning mediators of aggression. *Child Development, 57,* 700–711.

Price, J. M., & Dodge, K. A. (1989). Peers' contributions to children's social maladjustment: Description and intervention. In T. J. Berndt & G. W. Ladd (Eds.), *Peer relationships in child development* (pp. 341–370). New York: John Wiley & Sons.

Prinz, R. J., & Miller, G. E. (1991). Issues in understanding and treating childhood conduct problems in disadvantaged populations. *Journal of Clinical Child Psychology, 20,* 379–385.

Putallaz, M., & Heflin, A. H. (1990). Parent–child interaction. In S. R. Asher & J. D. Coie (Eds.), *Peer rejection in childhood* (pp. 189–216). New York: Cambridge University Press.

Radke-Yarrow, M., Richters, J., & Wilson, W. E. (1988). Child development in a network of relationships. In R. A. Hinde & J. Stevenson-Hinde (Eds.). *Relationships within families: Mutual influences* (pp. 48–67). New York: Oxford Press.

Radke-Yarrow, M., Zahn-Waxler, C., & Chapman, M. (1983). Children's prosocial dispositions and behavior. In P. H. Mussen (Ed.), *Handbook of child psychology,* Vol. 4, 4th ed. (pp. 469–545). New York: Wiley.

Retish, P. (1973). Changing the status of poorly-esteemed students through teacher reinforcement. *Journal of Applied Behavior Analysis, 9,* 44–50.

Richard, B. A., & Dodge, K. A. (1982). Social maladjustment and problem solving in school-aged children. *Journal of Consulting and Clinical Psychology, 50,* 226–233.

Richters, J. E. & Martinez, P. (1991, April). *Children living in violent communities: An epidemiological analysis.* Paper presented at the Biennial Meeting of the Society for Research in Child Development, Seattle.

Robins, L. N. (1979). Follow-up studies. In H. C. Quay & J. S. Werry (Eds.), *Psychopathological disorders of childhood* (pp. 483–513). New York: John Wiley & Sons.

Roff, J. D., & Wirt, R. D. (1984). Childhood aggression and social adjustment as antecedents of delinquency. *Journal of Abnormal Child Psychology, 12,* 111–126.

Rutter, M., Tizzard, J., & Whitmore, K. (Eds.). (1970). *Education, health, and behavior.* London: Longmans.

Schonfeld, I. S., Shaffer, D., O'Connor, P., & Portnoy, S. (1988). Conduct disorder and cognitive functioning: Testing three causal hypotheses. *Child Development, 59,* 993–1007.

Scruggs, T. E., Mastropieri, M. A., & Richter, L. (1985). Peer tutoring with behavioral disordered students: Social and academic benefits. *Behavioral Disorders, 10,* 283–298.

Shinn, M. R., Ramsey, E., Walker, H. M., O'Neill, R. E., & Stieber, S. (1987). Antisocial behavior in school settings: Initial differences in an at-risk and normal population. *Journal of Special Education, 21,* 69–84.

Shure, M. B., & Spivack, G. (1978). *Problem-solving techniques in childrearing.* San Francisco: Jossey-Bass.

Slaby, R. G., & Guerra, N. G. (1988). Cognitive mediators of aggression in adolescent offenders I. Assessment. *Developmental Psychology, 24,* 580–588.

Spence, S. H., & Marzillier, J. S. (1981). Social skills training with adolescent male offenders II. Short-term and generalized effects. *Behavior Research and Therapy, 19,* 349–368.

Sroufe, L. A., & Fleeson, J. (1988). The coherence of family relationships. In R. A. Hinde & J. Stevenson-Hinde (Eds.), *Relationships within families: Mutual influences* (pp. 27–47). New York: Oxford Press.

Stattin, H., & Magnusson, D. (1989). The role of early aggressive behavior in the frequency, seriousness, and types of later crimes. *Journal of Consulting and Clinical Psychology, 57,* 710–718.

Steinberg, M. D., & Dodge, K. A. (1983). Attributional bias in aggressive adolescent boys and girls. *Journal of Social and Clinical Psychology, 1,* 312–321.

Strayer, J. (1984). Social behaviors, social cognitive skills, and clinicians' judgements of children referred for aggression. *Journal of Clinical Child Psychology, 13,* 24–32.

Wass, G. A. (1987). Aggressive rejected children: Implications for school psychologists. *Journal of School Psychology, 25,* 383–388.

Webster-Stratton, C. (1981). Videotape modeling: A method of parent education. *Journal of Clinical Child Psychology,* 93–97.

———. (1987). *The parents and children series.* Eugene, OR: Castalia.

———. (1990). Long-term follow-up of families with young conduct problem children: From preschool to grade school. *Journal of Clinical Child Psychology, 19,* 144–149.

West, D. J., & Farrington, D. P. (1977). *The delinquent way of life.* London: Heinemann.

Whalen, C. K., Henker, B., Buhrmester, D., Hinshaw, S. P., Huber, A., & Laski, K. (1989). Does stimulant medication improve the peer status of hyperactive children? *Journal of Consulting and Clinical Psychology, 57,* 545–549.

Chapter 7

Coaching Preschool Children in Social Skills: A Cognitive-Social Learning Curriculum

JACQUELYN MIZE

Research documenting the concurrent and long-term negative consequences of poor peer relationships during childhood (e.g., Cassidy & Asher, 1992; Parker & Asher, 1987) has prompted development of social skills training programs for school-age children. A group of these, often termed social skills *coaching* programs, has been particularly successful in improving children's peer-related behavior and acceptance by age-mates (Oden, 1986). Social skills coaching curricula are based on research evidence that peer rejection is largely the result of inappropriate and/or unskilled social behavior (for reviews, see Coie, Dodge, & Kupersmidt, 1990; Ladd, Price, & Hart, 1990). Coaching programs are designed to teach children the behaviors associated with peer acceptance, through techniques such as discussion, rehearsal, and feedback from the instructor (Asher, 1985). Perhaps because it is peer rejection during middle childhood that has been most closely linked to dysfunction, the majority of these coaching efforts have targeted low-status elementary and preadolescent children.

Fewer research efforts have focused on developing social skills coaching interventions for preschoolers. This is surprising because one of the most frequent requests made by parents when they enroll their children in preschool programs is that the children learn to get along well with peers (Hendrick, 1990). In fact, fostering young children's social competence traditionally has been a priority for both parents of young children and early childhood professionals. The importance teachers attach to developing young children's social skills springs, to some extent, from a justifiable concern about the effects that a disruptive or isolated child can have on classroom atmosphere, disciplinary encounters, and curriculum decisions (Mize, 1987). It also reflects a sense that developing peer friendships and relationship skills are critical tasks during the preschool years (Hendrick, 1992). Moreover, the goals and curriculum structure of many preschool programs make them amenable to the inclusion of social skills training activities.

Research evidence, especially over the past decade, confirms early childhood professionals' beliefs that peer relationships are important for children well before they enter primary school. Young children value friendships with age-mates (Gottman, 1986) and many of these friendships persist over longer periods than previously thought (Howes, 1988). Moreover, individual differences in children's relationship styles begin to stabilize by the preschool years (Howes, 1988) and children who experience trouble with peer interaction during preschool are at increased risk for academic difficulties and peer rejection or neglect in elementary school. For instance, the range, stability, and quality of preschool peer relationships are associated with concurrent and subsequent adjustment (Ladd, Price, & Hart, 1988; Ladd & Price, 1987; Van Alstnyne & Hattwick, 1939), including their accommodation to kindergarten and their eventual acceptance by classmates in this new setting (Ladd & Price, 1987). Early peer relationship problems may be exacerbated through the elementary school years if children are excluded from peer interaction contexts and deprived of opportunities to learn ever-more sophisticated and subtle skills (cf., Eisenberg, Cameron, Tryon, & Dodez, 1981).

The critical role good peer relationships play in young children's development suggests that the preschool years are an ideal time to provide social skills interventions for children experiencing interaction difficulties. Moreover, features of preschool classrooms and peer group dynamics make this an especially suitable context for intervention. By the middle-school years, group dynamics, such as reputational biases (Hymel, Wagner, Butler, 1990), may make it more difficult for children to improve their standing in the peer group even if they succeed in changing their behavior (see Bierman & Furman, 1984). Peer alliances are more fluid and reputational biases less rigid in preschool groups, so efforts to improve peer acceptance may be more successful among younger children.

This chapter describes a cognitive-social learning (CSL) approach to social skills training for young children that is appropriate for use in typical nursery school, day care, and kindergarten classrooms. This chapter will focus on an empirical investigation carried out with preschool children who were experiencing peer relationship difficulties.

The CSL curriculum may be used as a universal intervention with all children in a classroom, not just those experiencing problems. Its goals are similar to those of social skills coaching programs shown to be effective with elementary-age children (e.g., Ladd, 1985; Oden & Asher, 1977). The intervention is designed to change children's behavior by addressing potential deficits in (1) their knowledge of social skills, (2) their ability to translate knowledge of strategies into proficient behavioral performance, and (3) their ability to accurately monitor and evaluate social interaction and adjust performance accordingly (Ladd & Mize, 1983a). This program differs from skill training efforts with older children, however, in the specific social skills taught and the instructional techniques used. Social skills associated with good quality peer relationships among preschool children were identified and used to develop effective, developmentally appropriate instructional procedures for three- to five-year-old children.

Children who participated in the intervention increased the frequency with which they used the targeted social skills with peers and showed some gains in peer friendships. The success of the CSL program is attributable, in part, to the selection of target skills and the use of theoretically-derived teaching goals. Because understanding these foundations is likely to be crucial to adaptation of the CSL model, each will be reviewed prior to describing how the skills training program was implemented.

Socially Competent Behavior

Although much remains to be learned about what constitutes peer social skills among preschool children, some progress has been made during the past decade (Gottman & Parker, 1986). As researchers, such as Gottman (1983), have noted, it is imperative to learn what social processes and behaviors are natural for young children to avoid teaching children to behave in ways that are inappropriate, or even dysfunctional, in their peer groups.

Careful observation of children from preschool to the middle childhood years suggests that, although the discrete behaviors used to initiate and maintain peer play change both with development and as a function of the child's gender and ethnic or cultural group, some features of socially competent interaction appear to be universal. Whether the participants are preschool peers, a mother and child, or two middle-school-age best friends, the interactions of socially competent individuals tend to be positive, situationally appropriate or circumspect, and well-synchronized or meshed with the behavior of interactive partners. Because the ultimate success of social skills intervention is limited by the appropriateness of the target behaviors children learn, the next two sections of this chapter further describe the universal features of successful interaction and differentiate the discrete behaviors used by socially skilled preschool children.

Universal Features of Competent Human Interaction: The Secrets of Success

Consider the following interaction that occurred in a classroom of four-year-old children:

> Wendy is busily setting a table in the housekeeping corner when Angela approaches. Looking up, Wendy says, "You can play; you be the baby. I have to go to work now." Angela responds, petulantly, "I don't want to be a baby—I want to be the mommy." "I know; you can be the other mommy and we have coffee at work," Wendy counters

affably. Angela appears to accept this suggestion and Wendy rummages through a pile of dress-up clothes to find a pair of high heels, which Angela puts on. Angela clomps to the toy typewriter and bangs on the keys. "Yea," Wendy exclaims exuberantly, "we gotta get our work done fast!"

In what ways can the qualities of Wendy's interaction with Angela be described? Are there similarities between her behavioral "style" and that of socially competent elementary-age children? That is, are there qualities of competent social interaction that can be said to "cut across all ages?"

Although the specific, discrete behaviors Wendy uses to turn this episode into an exciting adventure in play are, for the most part, unique to preschool children, Wendy's style can be described in terms universal to all competent human interactions.

First, Wendy can be described as *positive and agreeable.* That is, she is friendly and enthusiastic, even when faced with the peer's negative affect. Through her goodwill she manages to turn a potentially unpleasant episode into a positive one. A long history of research confirms that general positivity characterizes social orientations of well-liked, competent individuals from preschool age through adulthood (e.g., see Coie, Dodge, and Kupersmidt (1990) for a review of relevant research on children). Moreover, the positivity of children's interactions with peers and the extent of these positive interactions not only indicate current peer acceptance, but also predict subsequent acceptance in the same setting (Ladd, Price, & Hart, 1988) and across transitions such as from preschool to kindergarten (Ladd & Price, 1987).

Second, Wendy is *circumspect* in using appropriate contextual and social cues to guide her behavior (Pettit & Harrist, in press). For instance, her offer of a pair of high heels to Angela is highly relevant to Angela's interest at that moment in being "the other mommy." A growing body of research suggests that competent children of all ages are "tuned-in" to social and environmental cues and are able to adjust their behavior to that of the group's. In a study by Putallaz (1983) in which kindergarten boys attempted to enter an ongoing play dyad, boys whose behavior was more relevant to the behavior and interests of the group were better accepted in first grade. In contrast, rejected children's play efforts often are characterized by disruptive, contextually inappropriate behavior (Dodge, Schlundt, Schocken, & Degulach, 1983). Hazen and Black (1989) found that, even in preschool, well-liked children are more able to adapt their behavior and communication to different peer interaction contexts (such as group entry and ongoing play) than are disliked children.

Finally, Wendy is *positively synchronous:* She sensitively and responsively "meshes" her behavior with that of the other child (Pettit & Harrist, in press). The fact that Wendy immediately noticed and responded to Angela's presence, and her later comment, "We gotta get our work done fast" in response to Angela's attack of the typewriter, suggest that Wendy is sensitive to her interactive partner. Children as young as age two show responsivity during conversation by making relevant comments and smiling at appropriate times (Miller, Lechner, & Rugs, 1985).

Positively synchronous play in toddlers between ages one and two often takes the form of complimentary, reciprocal interactive games such as run-and-chase or offer-and-receive (Howes, 1988). By preschool, bouts of positively synchronous behaviors, such as matching and reflecting the actions of peers, are characteristic of socially competent children (Dodge, Pettit, McClaskey, & Brown, 1986). For instance, well-liked preschoolers are more likely to acknowledge and respond contingently to others, and to reinitiate or offer an alternative when they reject a play suggestion, than are their disliked peers. Moreover, this generally responsive style is bestowed on all peers in the group, not just a favored few (Hazen & Black, 1989).

Disliked children, in contrast, more often are disengaged, disconnected, or "tuned-out" (termed *asynchrony* by Pettit & Harrist, in press). They are able to achieve behavioral reciprocity only through negatively synchronous interaction sequences (Pettit & Harrist, in press) such as arguing (Dodge et al., 1986). These "out-of-step" and antagonistic behaviors usually are disruptive of peers' activities and frequently will be ignored or rebuffed (Pettit & Harrist, in press). The ability to participate in positively responsive and contingent behavioral exchanges with others appears to be a fairly stable individual difference. Howes (1988) indicates that positively synchronous play during the early toddler period predicts joint cooperative play during the preschool years.

Social competence in children, then, is not simply a matter of limiting aggression and behaving in generally positive ways; rather, even among preschool children, interpersonally competent behavior reflects an appreciation of social contexts and a responsiveness and sensitivity to others. This interactional style may indicate an ability and proclivity to attend to and accurately interpret social cues (Pettit & Mize, in press). A later section considers the underlying social cognitive abilities that make successful behavior possible; next, however, we examine molecular behaviors used by competent preschool children.

Discrete Social Skills Used by Preschool-Age Children: But What Do You Say?

It is, of course, specific, discrete behaviors that form the fabric of social interaction. There are a number of discrete skills that socially competent children use to initiate, maintain, and elaborate play. These skills—prosocial leading, asking questions, commenting, and offering support—are the discrete behaviors targeted by the CSL for social skills training. Early childhood professionals, however, may be able to identify other skills frequently used by socially competent children in groups with which they are working. Teachers and social skills coaches should encourage preschool-age children to use specific verbal behaviors described in this section, as well as those identified through observation, during peer interaction.

Prosocial *leading*, or making positive play suggestions, is a particularly useful skill for young children as they attempt to initiate and elaborate joint play themes (Parker, 1986). Because the ability to escalate the level and excitement of play is an important element of successful interaction among young children, it is not surprising that leading behavior is associated with measures of peer competence in preschool groups (Scarlett, 1980). Skilled use of leading by preschoolers may appear somewhat directive by adult standards (Scarlett, 1980), but it is not bossy or unpleasant.

Leading may be used to change the theme of ongoing play such as when a girl shouted during relatively calm housekeeping play, "Quick, get the fire hose! This house is on fire!" Suggestions that enlist others in the pursuit of a goal also are considered leads such as when a boy who was trying to push a large tire alone called out to two other boys playing quietly nearby, "Help, you guys! We gotta get this to the Enterprise." However, a command offered in a unpleasantly bossy or aggressive tone, or that is disruptive or irrelevant to peers' activities, is likely to be rejected or ignored. One such incident occurred when a child approached a pair of girls who were thoroughly engrossed in "driving" (with packed suitcases) to their "vacation." The third child suggested that the two girls join her at the art table. The vacationing pair immediately replied that the other child was "not our friend." Although even the best-framed leads often will be rejected or ignored (see Corsaro, 1981), leading behavior is more likely to be well-received by peers, and ultimately more effective in escalating the pleasure of play when it is used in positive, circumspect, and synchronous ways.

The second skill, asking *questions* in friendly or neutral ways, likewise is associated with social competence in preschool-age children (White & Watt, 1973). Questions frequently are used by preschoolers to seek help or information from peers, as when one child asks another, "How are we supposed to do this, anyway?" or "Would you let me have the red one?" Tag questions are used at the end of a statement to establish commonalities with a peer, or to seek confirmation or a response (Parker, 1986). For instance, the question, "We're very strong, right?" seeks both to establish common ground between the peers and elicit a response. Play suggestions or commands (leads) may be phrased in the form of questions, presumably as a way of softening the directive and ensuring a response, especially early in an interaction sequence. "Do you wanna build this really tall, so tall?" is likely to meet with a positive response, or at least be countered with an alternative suggestion, if it is contextually and socially relevant.

Commenting on play is included as a target skill because informal classroom observations indicate that competent preschoolers frequently make statements about joint play (Mize & Ladd, 1990b). These comments are descriptive of ongoing activity and may seem unsophisticated or obvious to adults. For young children, however, commenting appears to keep peers apprised of the play theme, establishes commonalities, and contributes to dyadic or group cohesion. The comment made by a group of four-year-olds as they pretended to hose down a tower of blocks, "We're putting out the fire!" not only attracted other children to the play area, but ensured that all interactants were aware of the common theme and goal (Mize & Ladd, 1990b). Of course, comments are unlikely to be well-received or effective if they are irrelevant, out of synch with peers, or disruptive.

Supporting—making explicitly positive statements to peers or performing prosocial acts—is the fourth behavior included as a target skill in the CSL intervention (Moore & Updegraff, 1964). Spontaneous prosocial acts (as opposed to prosocial behavior performed at the request of another) may be particularly important because preschoolers who more often engage in spontaneous helping have more frequent peer contacts (Eisenberg, Cameron, Tryon, & Dodez, 1981). Although adults often focus on prosocial acts as a crucial part of social skill, supporting behaviors occur rather infrequently among preschoolers and do not seem to be as important in discriminating between well-liked and disliked children as the other three social skills described (Mize & Ladd, 1990a).

Use of these social skills in socially and contextually appropriate ways requires a great deal of knowledge, awareness of social norms, and sensitivity to others. As illustrated in the literature, children vary in their ability to coordinate social interaction on these multiple levels. What enables some children to negotiate the social world so well, while others manage less capably and frequently alienate peers? We address this question next.

A Cognitive-Social Learning Model of Social Skillfulness

Peer play provides the most exciting, but also the most challenging, interactional context young children are likely to encounter. What cognitive, perceptual, and behavioral competencies are necessary to coordinate interaction and use the specific social skills described earlier in positive, circumspect, and synchronous ways?

Children need to know the discrete behaviors normative for their peer group and be able to perform them with skill. However, they also must be sensitively attuned to social situations and read social cues accurately to know when and how to use the behaviors. It is not enough to know that one way of initiating peer interaction is to suggest a fantasy play theme; the suggestion should be circumspect, synchronous with peers' interests, and positively framed. That is, the play suggestion is more likely to be met favorably if it is made in an appropriate context (e.g., during free play rather than at story time); if it is well-timed and meshed with peer's interests (e.g., when it would fit in with or amplify the peers' interests, rather than disrupt ongoing play); and if it is made in a positive, friendly way instead of being overly bossy or aggressive.

Success in peer relations, then, requires coordination and integration of a sophisticated array of cognitive, perceptual, and behavioral abilities. These underlying components of social competence include: (1) knowledge of social goals and interaction strategies appropriate for the peer group, (2) ability to translate one's perceptions and knowledge into skilled behavior, and (3) ability to "read" social situations and social cues accurately (Ladd & Mize, 1983a). Children who lack competence in one or more of these areas are likely to behave in ways that are nonnormative or inappropriate. Each of these components has implications for teaching appropriate social skills to children with peer relationship difficulties.

Component 1: Social Knowledge

Children who lack knowledge of culturally approved social goals and strategies risk behaving in ways deemed inappropriate by peers. For instance, if a child's goal in playing a game is to win at all costs, or to always be the center of attention, he or she ultimately is likely to experience rejection from other players. Well-liked children, in contrast, are more likely to have prosocial goals such as maintaining friendships or ensuring that all players have fun (Taylor & Asher, 1984). Of course, in addition to holding socially appropriate goals, children must know positive ways to achieve those goals.

Studies in which children are presented with hypothetical peer dilemmas and asked to provide solutions indicate that well-liked children have a repertoire of normative and friendly strategies. Children who are disliked or aggressive, on the other hand, more often suggest solutions that are nonnormative, vague, or aggressive and unfriendly (Mize & Ladd, 1988). For instance, when presented with a scenario in which two peers refuse to allow a child to play because there "are only two farm animals," one popular child said that she would get a small doll to be the farmer so she could join the others (Ladd & Mize, 1983b). Unpopular children, in contrast, often reported that they would grab the farm animals, or just go away and play alone.

For the most part, children's selection of social goals and strategies are more script-based and automatic than reflective or thoughtful. That is, when faced with a common social situation, rather than generating a list of alternative solutions and picking one, young children generally enact a strategy they have used before or seen (Mize & Ladd, 1988). Because young children's social interaction often is guided by relatively unreflective, spontaneous accessing of scripts, teaching children new goals and strategies requires replacing old, maladaptive scripts with more appropriate ones. Scripts are learned through repeated participation in, and/or observation of, interaction sequences (Nelson, 1978; 1981). Therefore, during social skills training, new scripted knowledge should be modeled for children and re-hearsed by them until they easily and automatically access it during interaction (Mize & Ladd, 1988).

Component 2: Performance Proficiency

Knowledge of appropriate strategies must translate into skilled behavioral perform-ance. Children who hold appropriate social goals and know positive strategies to achieve those goals still may behave inappropriately, perhaps because they cannot, or will not, act on the strategies. For instance, a child may be able to describe a good strategy for group entry to a researcher or teacher but may not be able to carry it out in practice. One four-year-old with whom the author worked seemed to have appropriate social goals (i.e., he wanted to play with other children) and he could generate ideas for initiating interaction. When he attempted the strategies with peers, however, he often spoke so rapidly and with such enthusiasm that peers were baffled. This failure to translate knowledge into action may result from ineptness, anxiety, or lack of practice. Therefore, in social skills training, children need opportunities to practice new strategies until they can be performed with poise and confidence.

Moreover, because training often occurs in relatively sheltered contexts in which children have the support and prompting of an adult coach, it usually is necessary to plan for skill generalization to other contexts. A child may learn to use a new behavior in skills training session, but fail to realize that the skill would be useful in the classroom, or feel too timid to try it out there. To help children generalize skills to natural contexts, the coach may arrange to have several different peers come to skills training sessions, or prompt the child to use the skill in classroom play, and then monitor and encourage performance in that context.

Component 3: Monitoring and Self-evaluation

Circumspect and socially relevant behavior requires accurate reading of social contexts and social cues. Monitoring and self-evaluation describe the propensity to attend to important contextual and interpersonal signals and interpret them realistically and constructively. Individuals deficient in this ability often appear to lack good social judgment because they

- Overlook important social barometers such as an interactive partner looking bored or offended,
- Attend exclusively to one type of signal—signs of hostility or rejection, or
- Interpret behavior incorrectly such as when a child assumes another intended harm when he or she is accidentally bumped in line.

For the purposes of this chapter, three aspects of monitoring social interaction will be identified: attending to social and contextual cues, observing the reactions of others to one's behavior, and interpreting others' behavior in nonbiased, constructive ways.

It is, in large part, the ability to attend to and encode social cues that allows children to behave in socially circumspect and responsive ways. Research with low-accepted children and children who frequently exhibit inappropriate social behavior shows that many are inattentive to relevant social cues or focus too much attention on particular types of cues. Aggressive behavior in preschoolers correlates with less ability to direct attention away from aggressive stimuli (Gouze, 1987). Observational studies of peer group behavior provide further evidence that attention to social cues is a critical component of social competence. Low-status preschool children are less able than their better-accepted peers to adapt their behavior to different social contexts—group entry versus ongoing play (Hazen & Black, 1989); their actions are likely to be inappropriate to the situation. Rejected elementary-school children often make social initiations while other children are engaged in schoolwork (Coie, Dodge, & Kupersmidt, 1990).

In a study by Putallaz (1983), first-grade boys who made more statements relevant to what a group was doing and accurately perceived the group members' behavior were better liked four months later. These studies imply that an important goal of social skills training should be to teach children to scan the social context for relevant information to guide their behavior.

A second aspect of monitoring is the ability to observe one's own behavior and others' reactions to it. Even when children learn new social skills, if they are unable to accurately judge others' reactions to them, the new skills are unlikely to be maintained. Some children appear to be unaware that their behavior is important in determining others' responses. After several training sessions, one child in a social skills training study conducted by Sherri Oden asked, "You mean, what I do affects whether kids like me or not?" (cited in Asher & Renshaw, 1981). During social skills training, children should be encouraged to notice the reactions of others and to try to adjust their performance accordingly.

Attention to the reactions of others does not mean that children should feel defeated or permanently rejected when they experience social failure. For some children, however, this sort of self-defeating, biased interpretation of social cues causes significant difficulties. Goetz and Dweck (1980) found that, when presented with hypothetical instances of social rejection for which no explanation was readily apparent (e.g., a new girl in the neighborhood does not want to play with you), some children believed the rejection was the result of their own social incompetence. Other children were more likely to attribute the hypothetical rejection to mismatches in personality, the bad mood of the rejector, or to a misunderstanding. Moreover, this bias in attributing rejection to one's unlikability (or inability to make friends) had repercussions for the child's behavior. When faced with actual rejection (exclusion from a pen-pal club), children who attributed the hypothetical rejection to their incompetence (e.g., "I'm not very good at making friends") were less likely to make renewed attempts to gain acceptance and attempted to withdraw from the situation. Children who tended to attribute rejection to causes other than their incompetence were more willing to make additional, prosocial attempts to gain acceptance.

Assuming that every rejection is evidence of one's incompetence, then, causes some children to withdraw from peer interaction. A more adaptive interpretation is that rejection can be the result of many factors, some of which may be ameliorated by using prosocial skills. Thus, although children obviously need to know their behavior influences the extent to which others accept them, they also should be encouraged to adapt a constructive, resilient attitude that allows them to adjust their behavior in light of social feedback.

Other children assume that negative outcomes are the fault of others. Crick and Ladd (in press) found that rejected children were more likely than popular children to assign blame for negative relationship outcomes (e.g., not being friends) to a peer (e.g., "The other kid does not like very many people"). Similarly, some aggressive children assume, especially in ambiguous situations, that others intentionally cause them harm. For instance, if bumped accidentally by a peer, children identified as aggressive are more likely to jump to the conclusion that the peer acted with hostility (Dodge, 1980). In social skills training, children should be encouraged to attend to social cues and interpret the behavior of others in constructive ways.

To summarize, competent behavior appears to depend on the coordination of a set of social-cognitive abilities. Because these abilities are critical for skilled interaction, they are the basis around which the CSL approach to skills training is organized. That is, the CSL curriculum improves the social interaction skills of young children by teaching them new social concepts, helping them translate their new strategy knowledge into proficient performance, and helping them more accurately monitor and evaluate social interaction.

Social Skills Instruction

The second half of this chapter explains how the CSL approach to social skills training was used to improve the peer relationship skills of unpopular preschool children in an experimental study. Adaptations of this model in typical classrooms may require considerable flexibility, but should be guided by knowledge of the theoretical and empirical basis of the curriculum. In addition to descriptions of the experimental intervention, this chapter provides explanations of how the curriculum was adapted during less formal, consultant work.

The CSL program's underlying philosophy and instructional goals are similar to other social skills coaching curricula. In the CSL model, as in other coaching programs, the coach avoids stigmatizing children with labels or descriptions of them as lacking in skills. Instead, children are told that the adults need help in identifying ways children can have the most fun together playing with the toys they have brought. Children, then, are made to feel that they are valued consultants who can provide important information to the adult. In addition, like other social skills coaching curricula, instruction, rehearsal, and feedback are used to help children learn social concepts, encourage performance, and monitor and evaluate interactions with others.

In a program Oden and Asher (1977) developed for elementary children, the social skills coach introduced concepts of positive social goals, such as having fun with another person, and strategies, such as cooperation, through discussion and verbal instruction. They elicited examples of specific behaviors from children, encouraged behavioral rehearsal of the concept, and encouraged children to monitor and evaluate their interactions with others. The following excerpts are from Oden (1986, pp. 264–265):

> *ADULT:* Okay, I have some ideas about what makes a game fun to play with another person. There are a couple of things that are important to do. You should *cooperate* with the other person. Do you know what *cooperation* is? Can you tell me in your own words?
>
> *CHILD:* Ahhh . . . sharing.
>
> *ADULT:* Yes, sharing. (If child gives an inaccurate example, say, "I was thinking of something like sharing.") . . . Okay, let's say you and I are playing the game you played last time . . . tell me what would be an example of sharing when playing the picture drawing game?
>
> *CHILD:* I'd let you use some pens, too.
>
> *ADULT:* Right . . . Would sharing the pens with me make the game fun to play for both you and the other person? . . .

ADULT: Okay, I'd like you to try out some of these ideas when you play   (game)   with   (child)   . . . .

ADULT: (Later, after children have played together for a few minutes): Did you get a chance to try out some of the ideas we talked about to see how they worked? Let's see, did you cooperate by sharing and taking turns? How did that work?

Although the underlying conceptual framework of the CSL program is similar to social skills coaching programs for older children, the instructional techniques and materials were adapted specifically for preschoolers. Perhaps the most salient modification was that instruction was based primarily on modeling and role-playing (often with puppets), as opposed to heavy reliance on verbal instruction and discussion common in older children's programs. This decision was based on research evidence that young children learn better through active and enactive means (Siegler, 1983) and that their social knowledge often is script-based (Mize & Ladd, 1988). Thus, many variations of each social concept (for instance, suggesting a joint play idea relevant to the interests of the peer) were modeled with puppets, and children role-played the skills in many different contexts.

Modeled scenarios and practice sessions were conducted using sociodramatic play themes, instead of organized games often used with older children, because being a skilled sociodramatic player seems to be an important aspect of social competence for preschoolers (Scarlett, 1980); and the extent to which toddlers engage in cooperative social pretend play predicts their acceptance by peers in preschool (Howes, 1988). Finally, specific behaviors associated with peer acceptance among preschool children were identified. Children were taught to use the skills *Leads, Comments, Questions* and *Supports* to obtain positive social goals.

Experimental Design

In the experimental study of CSL's effectiveness in social skills training, preschool children, who were not well-liked by peers and who also were aggressive or infrequently used the targeted social skills during peer interaction, were identified. For a description of the specific selection criteria, see Mize and Ladd (1990a). These criteria provided reasonable assurance that the children selected for the study were unpopular as a result of inappropriate behavior rather than because they were new to school, because of a different cultural or racial background from the majority, or because of other reasons not related to social skills.

Twenty-nine preschool children from a sample of 123 in six classrooms qualified for the study and were randomly assigned to either a skills-training condition or to an attention-control condition. Children in both conditions spent the same amount of time with the adult coach and with peers and played with the same toys. The only difference between the two groups was that instruction in the control condition focused on nonsocial aspects of play, such as how to make constructions from Lego blocks, whereas instruction in the skills-training condition focused on social skills and the underlying components of social competence. Social interaction was not discouraged between control group children, however, and child–child conflicts were handled in appropriate ways in both conditions.

To evaluate the effectiveness of the intervention, sociometric assessments of children's social acceptance by peers, observations of children's appropriate use of the targeted social skills in classroom interactions, and social strategy knowledge interviews were conducted at pre- and posttest. A behavior, such as *Leads,* was counted as an appropriate use of a social skill only if it was positively toned, was contextually appropriate (i.e., circumspect), and was used in a way synchronous with peers' behavior. In addition, about one month after the study was completed, a third sociometric interview was conducted to provide follow-up data on children's peer acceptance.

Low-status children in both the training and control conditions participated in pairs for eight half-hour sessions over a period of about two months. In consultant work, the number of sessions was both increased and decreased. Variations on the pairing of two low-status children also have been used—for instance, we have worked with dyads and triads consisting of one or two low-status children and one or two high-status children. This arrangement works particularly well when the low-status child is extremely deficient in social skills and the high-status children are especially sensitive and cooperative. Pairing of high- and low-status children provides a good model of social skills use for the skill-deficient child and the skilled child(ren) can sometimes help the less-skilled make the transition to larger group contexts.

Overview of Social Skills Training Curriculum

Because active and interactive images are more likely to capture the attention of young children and are more easily remembered by them than is didactically presented information, we used puppets to present new social knowledge to children. Human hand puppets[1] (described as children, two of which were named Sandy and Mandy, after Chittenden, 1942), and a dog hand puppet (Fluffy) modeled and described both appropriate and inappropriate behavior and their consequences. Training was done in sociodramatic and constructive play settings because these are critical contexts for the use of social skills and development of peer relationships during preschool years. Props for the training scenes included a Sesame Street Railroad, stuffed animals, toy medical equipment (for a veterinary role-play), Tinker Toys, Lego blocks, toy trucks and cars, and plastic farm animals—a variety of other toys would be equally appropriate.

A critical consideration when working with young children is the style the coach uses to interact with and guide them. Training done in a dry, lecture style is likely to be ignored (Oden, 1986). To maintain the interest and cooperation of preschool children, the coach must be enthusiastic, sensitive, and warm, and he or she should

---

[1]For this study we used several puppets hand-sewn from brown-, tan-, or cream-colored felt with a variety of hair colors and styles. Directions for making similar puppets can be found in many preschool curriculum guides. Pairs of puppets that resembled the two children being trained were selected to represent Sandy and Mandy during each session. Any type of appealing human puppets that can be handled easily by children and with whom children can identify work just as well.

avoid taking on the role of a judge or disciplinarian (Oden, 1986). Rather, the coach, while placing limits on inappropriate behavior when necessary, should engage children as equal participants in a problem-solving process as much as possible.

The concept of the "zone of proximal development" (Campione, Brown, Ferrara, & Bryant, 1984) is useful as a guide for adapting training to the needs of individual children. Working within this zone, the adult provides support so that the child can perform at a slightly higher level than he or she could independently. The child's skill determines the pace of instruction. Skills training is likely to be more successful if the adult thus begins at the child's developmental level and works with the child to achieve more advanced understanding and performance (Mize & Ladd, 1990b).

In this experimental study, each skills training session followed a similar format and had similar goals: Each session was designed to help children learn new social concepts (social knowledge), to provide opportunities for children to translate knowledge of new skills into proficient behavior, and to encourage accurate monitoring and evaluation of social interaction. For each session, the coach brought children to a room near the classroom in pairs. In some cases, a quiet area of the classroom was used for consultant work. The children were greeted with enthusiasm by the hand puppets (Fluffy, Sandy, and Mandy) and were told that their help was needed to make videotapes of how children have fun playing together. For consultant work, in which videotaping was not done, children were told that their help was needed so Sandy and Mandy could learn to have fun together.

In each session children practiced the skills by role-playing with the puppets, then in play together, and finally with two additional children who were brought to the training room. Children were encouraged to recall and evaluate attempts at skill use following each play session and to generalize the newly learned social skills to other contexts. A more detailed description of these instructional techniques is provided in later sections.

Sessions during the experimental study varied, however, in the target skills taught (one per session during early sessions, multiple skills during later sessions). Sessions also varied in the contexts (e.g., block play, sociodramatic play), and in the social problem scenarios on which training focused (e.g., attempts at group entry, handling a peer's aggression). As a coach develops an awareness of the types of situations that are problematic for individual children, he or she can create scenarios that depict similar contexts. When working with a child who frequently uses aggression to obtain desired objects, the coach can portray many scenarios with the puppets in which one child uses prosocial strategies to gain access to an attractive toy while including others in joint play. However, the coach should take care to avoid making the child feel that he or she is being singled out or that his or her behavior is being portrayed or discussed.

Teaching Social Concepts

The instructional procedures the CSL model used to teach children new ideas about social behaviors were taken from guidelines proposed by Ladd and Mize (1983a) and included:

- Establishing an *intent (or desire) to learn* the concept,
- *Defining the concept* or skill,
- Providing *examples and counter-examples* (i.e., positive and negative) *exemplars* of the skill,
- Getting the child to recall and *rehearse* the skill concept, and
- Helping the child *refine the concept*, by thinking of other situations in which the skill could be used.

To encourage the development of positive social goals and an intent to learn, Fluffy welcomed the two children enthusiastically at the beginning of each session, saying that he liked to see children playing together and having fun but that seeing children playing alone or fighting made him feel sad. Fluffy explained that the children should help Sandy and Mandy find ways to play and have fun together. (Fluffy also was used to direct and encourage children's attention to relevant aspects of the ensuing vignettes.)

A social dilemma was enacted in which Sandy or Mandy (and other hand puppets if necessary) used an ineffective strategy and experienced an unsatisfactory outcome—for instance, Sandy wants to play with Mandy but just stands to the side watching. Thus, a negative exemplar of the skill was provided initially: hovering (as just described), trying to take a toy, or intruding in an inappropriate way. The children were first asked to evaluate the consequences of the strategy ("Are they having fun now?"). The children's response, if correct, was reinforced, and one or more of the human hand puppets continued by explicitly identifying the consequences of the ineffective strategy ("It makes both children feel sad to fight"), expressing dissatisfaction with the outcome ("We're not both having fun") and asking Fluffy and the children for help. Fluffy suggested and defined a social skill strategy—Leading, Supporting, Questioning, or Commenting).

An attempt was made to define goals and skills in terms meaningful for preschool children. For example, the identified social goal the children were asked to help achieve was finding "ways for everybody to have fun playing together," as opposed to more abstract social goals such as being "nice" or "cooperative".

Specific social skills also were defined concretely. *Leading* was defined as "having a fun idea about something both kids can do so they have fun playing together." *Supporting* was described as "doing something 'really nice' that would make the other kid feel good or be happy." *Questioning* was defined as "asking the other kid a question so they can tell you something (or answer you)." *Commenting* was described as "just talking about what you and the other kid are doing." In all cases, modeled social skills were used in positive, circumspect, and responsive ways.

Some teachers who work with young children argue against modeling of negative exemplars such as aggression. We believe, however, that because young children are less skilled than older children in identifying causes and consequences of behavior (Shantz, 1983), it is critical that the negative consequences of inappropriate behavior be highlighted. Because many of the children in the study had problems with inappropriate behavior, such as aggression and taking toys from peers, it was especially important to depict these negative acts and their unsatisfactory consequences with this population.

The manner in which negative social behavior is portrayed, however, is critical. Negative behavior always was enacted in an understated way because many young children are attracted to very active behavior and imitate it with enthusiasm. An act of aggression, therefore, might consist of one puppet gently taking a toy from another. This was followed by a quiet explanation of the unhappy consequences of this act (one child feels sad, neither has fun, and so on). Children in this study did not laugh at or try to imitate the examples of negative social behavior. In contrast, when teachers depict aggression with puppets in animated, humorous ways, it usually results in children's excited imitation of the aggression.

The following illustration shows how these instructional techniques were used to enhance children's social knowledge.

FLUFFY: Hi, (child 1) ! Hi, (child 2) ! I'm so glad you came back. Do you remember what makes me happy? . . . That's right, seeing children playing together and having fun makes me happy. And what makes me feel sad? . . . That's right, I feel sad when children play by themselves or when they fight (take toys, etc.)".

COACH: Let's watch Sandy and Mandy and see if we can help them have fun together. (Sandy is playing with a desirable train engine, while Mandy watches from the sidelines. Some toy farm animals lie nearby.)

MANDY: I want to have some fun with that train, too! Maybe if I take the train I'll get to play. (Mandy gently takes train from Sandy).

SANDY: Hey, I was playing with that! (Sounds sad.)

FLUFFY: Are both Sandy and Mandy having fun? No, and they aren't playing together, are they? How do you think Sandy felt when Mandy took the train? Do you think she was happy or sad?

SANDY: I'm sad 'cause you took my train.

FLUFFY: And how do you think Mandy feels now that she has the train all alone?

MANDY: I still don't have anybody to play with. This isn't much fun. What can we do Fluffy? (Turning to the children) What can we do (child 1 and child 2) ?

FLUFFY: Maybe you could have a "fun idea" about how to play together. A fun idea is a way both kids can play and have more fun together. What would be a fun idea? Let's see, one fun idea might be for you and Mandy to take the farm animals in the train. Try that—you could say, "Hey, Sandy, I have a fun idea. We could have these farm animals ride in the train."

MANDY: Sandy, here are my horses and cows. I have a fun idea—let's take them to town in your train.

SANDY: Okay! Load 'er in here, we have to hurry. . . . (Sandy and Mandy play for a few more seconds, saying several times that they are having fun playing together.)

FLUFFY: (With excitement to children) Hey, was that a fun idea? What was the fun idea that Mandy had? . . . What did Sandy do when Mandy had the fun idea? Are Sandy and Mandy having fun together now?

Depending on the children's attentiveness and understanding, other positive and negative exemplars of skills sometimes were presented in a similar manner.

To encourage *rehearsal* of the new skill concepts, the coach next encouraged the children to "use the puppets" (one child played Sandy, the other Mandy) to demonstrate the prosocial solution.

COACH: Okay, (children's names) . You use Sandy and Mandy to show how they can have fun ideas and play together. (Children were helped to put on the puppets and prompted, if necessary, to role play the previously enacted scenario.) (child 1) , can you show how Sandy was playing with the train? Okay, (child 2) , what fun idea did Mandy have so (s)he could get to play?

CHILD 2: I don't know.

FLUFFY: (Whispers to child 2): Did Mandy think that his (her) horse could ride in Sandy's train? Can you try that now? Can you say, "Hey, I have a fun idea—my horse could ride in the train."

CHILD 2: Hey, I have a fun idea—my horse can ride in the train.

FLUFFY: (To child 1): That sounds like fun, doesn't it? What can you say?. . .

As children better understood the concepts, they often were able to come up with additional prosocial solutions that were different from the one that had been demonstrated.

Moreover, at the beginning of each session, after the first one, children were asked to recall what made playing fun (playing with other children, having fun ideas, and so on). Early in training children rarely could recall concepts from previous sessions. By the end of training, however, most children could report at least one social skill they had learned earlier.

As children became more familiar with the skills, their concepts were *refined* by asking them to apply them to new situations presented with the hand puppets. In addition, the coach and children together looked at pictures of toys typically found in preschool classrooms but that were not used in training. The coach asked the children to think of ways to use the skills to have fun with other children playing with the toys.

COACH: What is this, (child 1) ? (a toy stove and some cookware) Do you have these in your school? Can you think of a "fun idea" about how to play with these toys with some other kids?

CHILD 1: Yea, I have a fun idea. I can cook the coffee and then we'll go to school.

As the following dialogue illustrates, children are not consistently cooperative. They do not always agree that a particular joint activity qualifies as "fun." In cases like this, the coach should rely on empirically based descriptions of the behavior of socially competent preschool children and model responses consistent with this literature. For example, when one child rejects the peer's play idea, the coach encourages child 2 to offer an alternative suggestion (Hazen & Black, 1989).

CHILD 1: I have a fun idea! Let's get dressed up to go to McDonald's.

COACH: Oh, does that sound like fun, __(child 2)__ ?

CHILD 2: I wouldn't want to, 'cause I don't like to play with dress up.

COACH: Well, what could you say, then? Is there some other idea that would be more fun?

CHILD 2: I'd want to play with that car.

COACH: Okay, __(child 2)__ . Let's think of a fun idea with the car that you two could do together. Maybe she needs a taxi to McDonald's. Would that be fun, to drive her there? . . .

Encouraging Performance of Social Skills

Next, to promote proficient behavioral performance, children were asked to "try out" the skills themselves as they played with the toys so that a videotape could be made of "how children can have fun playing with toys together." Especially during early sessions, Fluffy often was used to prompt children to try the social skills. If one child was playing with toy animals while the other played with cars and trucks, Fluffy might "whisper" to one that a "fun idea" would be to see if the peer would like to carry the animals in his or her truck to go to the veterinarian, and then encourage the child to try this strategy. Fluffy also was used to provide encouragement and feedback to the children about their performance.

FLUFFY: Okay, now let's make a movie of how you two have fun playing with these Tinker Toys together. I'm going to be watching to see if you guys have any fun ideas about how to play together and to see if you ask any questions. Then when we watch the movie, we'll see you two having fun. (The coach turns on the videocamera and Fluffy "watches" the children. If the children do not use the skills appropriately, Fluffy intervenes, usually by whispering ideas to one or both children.)

In consultant work, of course, reference to videotaping was not made. Instead, children were asked to "see if having fun ideas makes it fun to play together," or to "show how you can have fun ideas to have fun playing with these toys."

Encouraging Accurate Monitoring and Generalization of Skills

To encourage children to better monitor and evaluate peer interaction, and make accurate attributions for peers' reactions, each peer play session was reviewed. First the coach asked the children whether either had used any of the social skills and what the peer's response had been. During early sessions children rarely could recall any use of social skills or the peer's responses, in which case Fluffy or the coach reminded children of skill use, but by the end of training most children could accurately describe at least one use of social skills and the results. Children also were asked to recall instances of other significant behaviors, such as aggression, and to evaluate the consequences. The following is an example of one such review:

FLUFFY: I was watching you guys playing together. Did anybody have a fun idea?

CHILDREN: I don't know.

FLUFFY: Let's remember.   (Child 1) , when you saw   (child 2)   playing with that kitty cat, what did you say?

CHILD 1: That he was sick and we gotta take him for a shot.

FLUFFY: (Child 1) , what did   (child 2)   do?

CHILD 1: Got the boat.

FLUFFY: Yea, you guys took him to the vet in that boat, didn't you? Was that a fun idea? . . . And what happened when   (child 1)   grabbed that car? How did you feel? Did that make playing together fun? Can you tell him (her) what a good way to get to play with the car would be? (Fluffy and children identify strategies.)

Following the verbal review, the coach asked children to watch a replay of the videotaped play session to find any instances of skill use and identify the peer's response. Review of the videotape was useful in encouraging children to be more sensitive interpreters of the peer's behavior and in encouraging accurate attributions for outcomes as well. In one session, a four-year-old boy was particularly boisterous, laughing gleefully as he flung toys toward his play partner. The play partner, meanwhile, repeatedly asked him to "stop it," but the boy apparently misinterpreted her protestations as part of the game. While reviewing the video, the coach asked the boy to notice what his play partner said and to watch her facial expressions. The play partner, in turn, was asked to tell the boy what she meant by her statements. She said, "I meant I wanted you to stop." The boy decided that his play partner had not been having fun, and he did not engage in one-sided boisterous behavior again during a skills training session (Mize & Ladd, 1990b).

Several procedures were used to help children generalize their newly learned skills to other contexts. Over the course of each session, rehearsal became less sheltered and more closely approximated real-life settings. Specifically, after moving from role-play with puppets to real play, two more children were brought to the skills training session to participate in four-child play. (Usually the coach and the subjects briefly returned to the classroom together to select the two children.)

Between the sixth and eighth sessions, the coach spent about 20 minutes with each subject in his or her classroom to encourage skill use in this context; these are known as in-class generalization sessions. While there, the coach watched for opportunities for the child to use one of the social skills and quietly suggested that the child try the idea. During one visit, a subject was playing at a sand table near other children but not interacting. The coach whispered to the subject that the two children could fill up a bucket together. The subject turned to the peer and said, "I have a fun idea—let's fill up this bucket."

In consultant work, generalizing skills to other contexts was accomplished by accompanying the target child back to the classroom after a training session and prompting her or him to try the new skill. Socially competent training partners can be particularly helpful in this context, sometimes by identifying opportunities for the target child to use a skill, and often by willingly accepting the child as a play partner after he or she makes an overture. In one case, a four-year-old boy, with whom the author worked rarely, spoke to other children and typically acquired toys by force (e.g., pushing another child off a tricycle or biting a child until a toy was relinquished).

For several months prior to beginning CSL training, classroom teachers had used a system of rewards (for being near or talking to peers) and punishments (especially for biting) with little effect other than a somewhat decreased frequency of peer- and teacher-directed aggression. Immediately after each CSL training session the coach and a skilled peer, who had been paired with the child in the training session, accompanied this child into the classroom and helped him identify an activity in which he was interested. It was then necessary to enlist the cooperation of the peers involved in the activity, provide this child with the exact words he could use to join the peers' play or ask for a toy, prompt him to say the words, coach him as to how to respond to the peers' answer, and help him become involved in play. Eventually this child was able to think of strategies for joining play and by the end of the schoolyear was an active participant in many peer group activities.

Results of the Experimental Study

Sociometric interviews, observations of children's behavior with peers in their classrooms, and child interviews were conducted to evaluate the effectiveness of the CSL approach to skills training. Behavioral observations indicated that children who participated in the training condition more than doubled the frequency with which they used the target skills with peers from pretest to posttest. Children in the control condition showed a slight decrease in their use of the social skills. Most improvement was seen in the skills Commenting and Leading, although small improvements were seen in the Questioning and Supporting skills as well. This was not a function of simple increases in rates of interaction; rather, there was a disproportionate increase in the trained skills.

It is interesting to speculate why greater improvement was seen in the skills Commenting and Leading than in the other two. One possibility is that these two skills were operationally defined so preschoolers could understand them. In fact, from early in training children seemed to understand the concept of Leading and often used the phrase, "I have a fun idea!" Another possibility is that Leading and Commenting are more developmentally appropriate and relevant skills for pre-schoolers than are Questioning and Supporting.

Perhaps Leading and Commenting are especially important skills for initiating and elaborating play themes and are useful for making play more exciting. Sup-porting and Questioning, on the other hand, may be salient for adults, but infrequent (in the case of Supporting) or relatively unimportant (in the case of Questioning) for young children. The differential rates of increase in the four target skills underscores the need for further research on the social skills critical for success in different age groups.

Interviews were conducted with children at pre- and posttest to assess their knowledge of social concepts. Children's responses to three hypothetical social dilemmas (Mize & Ladd, 1988; 1990a) were recorded and rated for their friendliness and assertiveness—aggression was considered highly assertive in this rating system. There was a significant tendency for children in the skills-training condition to suggest strategies that were friendlier and less assertive at posttest than they had suggested at pretest, whereas the opposite trend was found for control-group children.

These findings suggest that social knowledge is an important underlying compo-nent of social competence and that the CSL intervention was successful in teaching children new social skills concepts. Even more convincing was a positive correlation between pre- to posttest changes in social knowledge friendliness ratings and changes in rates of peer interaction. In other words, children who improved more in the friendliness of their responses to the social knowledge interview showed greater increases in their use of social skills in classroom interaction with peers. These data indicate that improvements in children's social knowledge were partially responsible for increased social skills use.

Positive changes also were seen in children's peer friendships. Although signifi-cant improvements in peer group acceptance were not seen immediately at posttest after training, by follow-up testing one month later, skills training children showed increases in friendship nominations (measured by positive sociometric nominations) and a trend toward greater overall group acceptance (measured by sociometric ratings). Children in the control group showed declines in both measures of group acceptance at follow-up testing. These results are consistent with previously observed patterns in skills training research (Ladd, 1981) and suggest that, although children may learn new skills fairly quickly, it may take time before these changes are noted by peers.

Summary

The results of this study and the author's experiences during consultant work suggest that the CSL approach to social skills training can improve the social knowledge, social interaction skills, and peer relationships of low-status, low-skilled preschool children. Success is, at least partially, attributable to the focus on training empirically validated social skills and social interaction styles. Equally important, however, is the fact that the CSL program is designed to address potential deficits in social knowledge, the ability to translate knowledge of social goals and strategies into skilled behavior, and the ability and propensity to read social cues and evaluate interaction constructively. Additional research is needed to more thoroughly assess these underlying components of social competence and the process of skill learning.

An unanswered question in the field of social skills training is the optimal timing for intervention. Strong arguments have been made here for skills training during the preschool years, and a case also can be made for offering intervention when children are in elementary school. Specifically, some children may begin having interactional difficulties in preschool but, for others, problems emerge only later. By elementary school, children's relationship styles are established more firmly. Social skills instruction at this level can be used to reinforce previous learnings as well as treat problems that may surface during this period. Social skills training can be beneficial at many times during childhood. Although intervention with preschoolers may prevent or reduce later problems for children who are already having difficulties, social skills training of the type described in this chapter is most appropriate as a regular part of preschool curricula for all children.

References

Asher, S. R. (1985). An evolving paradigm in social skill training research with children. In B. H. Schneider, K. H. Rubin, & J. E. Ledingham (Eds.), *Children's peer relations: Issues in assessment and intervention* (pp. 157–171). New York: Springer-Verlag.

Asher, S. R., & Renshaw, P. D. (1981). Children without friends: Social knowledge and social skill training. In S. R. Asher & J. M. Gottman (Eds.), *The development of children's friendships* (pp. 273–296). New York: Cambridge University Press.

Bierman, K. L., & Furman, W. (1984). The effects of social skills training and peer involvement on the social adjustment of preadolescents. *Child Development, 55*, 151–162.

Campione, J. C., Brown, A. L., Ferrara, R. A., & Bryant, N. R. (1984). The zone of proximal development: Implications for individual differences and learning. In B. Rogoff & J. V. Wertsch (Eds.), *Children's learning in the zone of proximal development* (pp. 77–91). San Francisco: Jossey-Bass.

Cassidy, J., & Asher, S. R. (1992). Loneliness and peer relations in young children. *Child Development, 63*, 350–365.

Chittenden, C. E. (1942). An experimental study in measuring and modifying assertive behavior in young children. *Monographs of the Society for Research in Child Development, 7*(1, Serial No. 31).

Coie, J. D., Dodge, K. A., & Kupersmidt, J. B. (1990). Peer group behavior and social status.

In S. R. Asher & J. D. Coie (Eds.), *Peer rejection in childhood* (pp. 17–59). New York: Cambridge University Press.

Corsaro, W. A. (1981). Friendship in the nursery school: Social organization in a peer environment. In S. R. Asher & J. M. Gottman (Eds.), *The development of children's friendships* (pp. 207–241). New York: Cambridge University Press.

Crick, N. R. & Ladd, G. W. (in press). Children's perceptions of their peer experiences: Attributions, loneliness, social anxiety, and social avoidance. *Developmental Psychology.*

Dodge, K. A. (1980). Social cognition and children's aggressive behavior. *Child Development, 51,* 162–170.

Dodge, K. A. & Frame, C. L. (1982). Social cognitive biases and deficits in aggressive boys. *Child Development, 53,* 620–635.

Dodge, K. A., Pettit, G. S. McClaskey, C. L., & Brown, M. M. (1986). Social competence in children. *Monographs of the Society for Research in Child Development, 51*(1, Serial No. 213).

Dodge, K. A., Schlundt, D. G., Schocken, I., & Degulach, J. D. (1983). Social competence and children's sociometric status: The role of peer group entry strategies. *Merrill-Palmer Quarterly, 29,* 309–336.

Eisenberg, N., Cameron, E., Tryon, K., & Dodez, R. (1981). Socialization of prosocial behavior in the preschool classroom. *Developmental Psychology, 17,* 773–782.

Goetz, T. E., & Dweck, C. S. (1980). Learned helplessness in social situations. *Journal of Personality and Social Psychology, 39,* 246–255.

Gottman, J. M. (1983). How children become friends. *Monographs of the Society for Research in Child Development, 48*(3, Serial No. 201).

———. (1986). The world of coordinated play: Same- and cross-sex friendship in young children. In J. M. Gottman & J. G. Parker (Eds.), *Conversations of friends: Speculations on affective development* (pp. 139–191). New York: Cambridge University Press.

Gottman, J. M., & Parker, J. G. (1986). *Conversations of friends: Speculations on affective development.* New York: Cambridge University Press.

Gouze, K. R. (1987). Attention and social problem solving as correlates of aggression in preschool males. *Journal of Abnormal Child Psychology, 15,* 181–197.

Hazen, N. L., & Black, B. (1989). Preschool peer communication skills: The role of social status and interaction context. *Child Development, 60,* 867–876.

Hendrick, J. (1990). *Total learning: Developmental curriculum for the young child.* New York: Merrill.

———. (1992). *The whole child: Developmental education for the early years.* New York: Merrill.

Howes, C. (1988). Peer interaction of young children. *Monographs of the Society for Research in Child Development, 53*(1, Serial No. 217).

Hymel, S., Wagner, E., & Butler, L. J. (1990). Reputational biases: View from the peer group. In S. R. Asher & J. D. Coie (Eds.), *Peer rejection in childhood* (pp. 156–186). New York: Cambridge University Press.

Ladd, G. W. (1981). Effectiveness of a social learning method for enhancing children's social interaction and peer acceptance. *Child Development, 52,* 71–82.

———. (1985). Documenting the effects of social skill training with children: Process and outcome assessment. In B. H. Schneider, K. H. Rubin, & J. E. Ledingham (Eds.), *Children's peer relations: Issues in assessment and intervention* (pp. 243–269). New York: Springer-Verlag.

Ladd, G. W., & Asher, S. R. (1985). Social skill training and children's peer relations. In L. L'Abate & M. A. Milan (Eds.), *Handbook of social skills training and research* (pp. 219–244). New York: Wiley.

Ladd, G. W., & Mize, J. (1983a). A cognitive-social learning model of social skill training. *Psychological Review, 90,* 127–157.

———. (1983b). Social skills training with children: A cognitive-social learning approach. *Child and Youth Services, 5,* 61–74.

Ladd, G. W., & Price, J. M. (1987). Predicting children's social and school adjustment following the transition from preschool to kindergarten. *Child Development, 58,* 1168–1189.

Ladd, G. W., Price, J. M., & Hart, C. H. (1988). Predicting preschoolers' peer status from their playground behaviors and peer contacts. *Child Development, 59,* 986–992.

———. (1990). Preschoolers' behavioral orientations and patterns of peer contact: Predictive of peer status? In S. R. Asher & J. D. Coie (Eds.), *Peer rejection in childhood.* New York: Cambridge University Press.

Miller, L. C., Lechner, R. E., & Rugs, D. (1985). Development of conversational responsiveness: Preschoolers' use of responsive listener cues and relevant comments. *Developmental Psychology, 21,* 473–480.

Mize, J. (1987). Fostering preschool children's social interaction skills: An effective classroom management tool. *Dimensions, 15,* 21–24.

Mize, J., & Ladd, G. W. (1988). Predicting preschoolers' peer behavior and status from their interpersonal strategies: A comparison of hypothetical reflective and hypothetical enactive assessments. *Developmental Psychology, 24,* 782–788.

———. (1990a). A cognitive-social learning approach to social skill training with low-status preschool children. *Developmental Psychology, 26*(3), 388–397.

———. (1990b). Toward the development of successful social skills training for preschool children. In S. R. Asher & J. D. Coie (Eds.), *Peer rejection in childhood* (pp. 338–361). New York: Cambridge University Press.

Moore, S., & Updegraff, R. (1964). Sociometric status of preschool children related to age, sex, nurturance-giving, and dependency. *Child Development, 35,* 519–524.

Nelson, K. (1978). How children represent knowledge of their world in and out of language: A preliminary report. In R. S. Siegler (Ed.), *Children's thinking: What develops?* (pp. 255–273). Hillsdale, NJ: Erlbaum.

———. (1981). Social cognition in a script framework. In J. H. Flavell & L. Ross (Eds.), *Social cognitive development* (pp. 97–118). New York: Cambridge University Press.

Oden, S. (1986). Developing social skills instruction for peer interaction and relationships. In G. Cartledge & J. F. Milburn (Eds.), *Teaching social skills to children* (pp. 246–269). New York: Pergamon Press.

Oden, S., & Asher, S. R. (1977). Coaching children in social skills for friendship making. *Child Development, 48,* 495–506.

Parker, J. (1986). Becoming friends: conversational skills for friendship formation in young children. In J. M. Gottman & J. G. Parker (Eds.), *Conversations of friends: Speculations on affective development* (pp. 103–138). New York: Cambridge University Press.

Parker, J. G., & Asher, S. R. (1987). Peer relations and later personal adjustment: Are low-accepted children at risk? *Psychological Bulletin, 102,* 357–389.

Pettit, G. S., & Harrist, A. W. (1993). Children's aggressive and socially unskilled playground behavior with peers: Origins in early family relations. In C. H. Hart (Ed.), *Children on playgrounds: Research perspectives and applications* (pp. 240–270). Albany, NY: State University of New York Press.

Pettit, G. S., & Mize, J. (1993). Substance and style: Understanding the ways in which parents teach children about social relationships. In S. Duck (Ed.), *Understanding relationship processes. Vol 2: Learning about relationships* (pp. 118–151). Newbury Park, CA: Sage.

Putallaz, M. (1983). Predicting children's sociometric status from their behavior. *Child Development, 54,* 1417–1426.

Scarlett, W. G. (1980). Social isolation from agemates among nursery school children. *Journal of Child Psychology and Psychiatry, 21,* 231–240.

Shantz, C. U. (1983). Social cognition. In J. H. Flavell & E. M. Markman (Eds.), *Handbook of child psychology: Vol. 3 Cognitive development* (pp. 495–555). New York: John Wiley.

Siegler, R. S. (1983). Information processing approaches to development. In W. Kessen (Ed.), *Handbook of child psychology: Vol. 1. History, theory, and methods* (pp. 129–212). New York: John Wiley.

Taylor, A. R., & Asher, S. R. (1984). Children's goals and social competence: Individual differences in a game-playing context. In T. Field, J. L. Roopnarine, & M. Segal (Eds.), *Friendships in normal and handicapped children* (pp. 53-78). Norwood, NJ: Ablex.

Van Alstnyne, D., & Hattwick, L. A. (1939). A follow-up study of the behavior of nursery school children. *Child Development, 10,* 43–72.

White, B. L., & Watt, J. C. (1973). *Experience and environment.* Englewood Cliffs, NJ: Prentice-Hall.

Chapter **8**

Teaching Severely Handicapped Children: Social Skills Development Through Leisure Skills Programming

STUART J. SCHLEIEN   LINDA A. HEYNE
JOHN DATTILO

The purpose of this chapter is to discuss assessment techniques, instructional procedures, and intervention strategies in leisure skills programming that can be used to facilitate social skills development in children with severe disabilities. Individualized programs in four recreational program areas—toy play, games, hobbies, and sports—are presented in the latter part of the chapter to assist in the acquisition of leisure and social skills. The task analyses presented are not meant to be comprehensive; instead, they are representative of socially oriented leisure skills children can master through systematic instruction.

A Rationale for Leisure Education

Abundance of Leisure Time

Appropriate use of free time has become a vital aspect of healthy, normal living. For children with severe disabilities, learning leisure skills can facilitate the development of social skills, interpersonal relationships, and friends. Yet all too often, children with severe disabilities have not developed the necessary skills to use their free time creatively or constructively. They will participate in an educational program for a portion of their day, then have nothing to do during the remaining hours at home. Constructive recreational activities can be offered to fill this void. The development of nonwork and nonschool-related skills must be encouraged and systematically programmed; unoccupied time must cease to be dominant in the child's lifestyle. The child's attitude toward and use of free time may determine the degree of success she or he will experience through educational efforts.

Recreation as a Means of Teaching Social Skills

Luckey and Shapiro (1974) summarize the role of recreation as a mediator of social development by:

> Games with increasingly complex rules and social demands further enhance children's social adaption as they grow older, and participation in clubs and organizations takes on increasing social importance during the school years. . . . [O]rganized sports additionally provide young adults opportunities for personal achievement, while teaching rules of competition and the controlled expression of aggression (p. 33).

These social traits are mandatory for successful adjustment to the community. The benefits to children with severe disabilities of participating in games, recreational activities, and sports are becoming increasingly clear. Successful recreational experiences are helpful in establishing appropriate social behavior patterns and in providing opportunities for positive learning experiences (Wehman & Schleien, 1981). The development of cooperative play behavior and participation in leisure activities usually leads to making friends; getting along with others; and learning to share, compete, cooperate, and take turns. Generally, it leads to a more satisfactory social adjustment, which is required for successful daily living, including time on the job, in the community, and with friends and family.

In a national survey of families with children with disabilities, Brewer and Kakalik (1979) report that only a small portion of the children, those with hearing impairments, had used at least one recreational service. Of the families that did use recreational services, the parents favorably regarded leisure as an end in itself—the parents were most satisfied that their children learned independent living skills and made new friends. This study provides just one example of the interplay between participation in recreation and socialization. A major reason for inappropriate play behavior by children with disabilities is their limited cooperative play skills and lack of social interaction among peers (Wehman & Schleien, 1981). Paloutzian, Hasazi, Streifel, and Edgard (1971) also note an inordinate amount of isolated play among young children with severe disabilities, reinforcing this association.

Independent, or solitary, play is a lower stage of social development than cooperative play. Effective feedback cannot be obtained without social interactions between children. In fact, children fail to develop higher level social behaviors when they have little peer interaction during play (Wehman, 1979). As a child becomes more proficient at playing with others, he or she acquires social skills (Paloutzian et al., 1971). Sharing, taking turns, and teamwork are aspects of this social interaction (Knapczyk & Yoppi, 1975; Schleien, Rynders, Mustonen, & Fox, 1990).

In her rationale for leisure education as a process rather than a specific service in education, Collard (1981) identifies the many roles leisure education can play in the development of needed social skills. Children who are disabled can learn valuable and critical skills to facilitate independent functioning in school, on the job, and in the community. Zigmond (1978) indicates that children with disabilities must be socially competent to attain maximum benefit from classroom instruction in all curriculum areas. Others cite the importance of proficient socialization to perform successfully on the job (President's Committee on Mental Retardation, 1974; Wehman, 1979) and within the community (Novak & Heal, 1980; Rynders & Schleien, 1988; Schleien & Ray, 1988).

A publication of the Alcohol, Drug Abuse, and Mental Health Administration of the U.S. Department of Health and Human Services (1979) outlines how play teaches children to relate to other people and helps them learn how to live in a particular place in the way the culture expects. Social rules and morals are learned in this manner. Practicing principles of give and take, sharing similar space, and exchanging information with other children through play assists in preparation for adult life.

Three recent studies by Schleien, Rynders, and their associates document further the value of recreation to teach social behaviors for children with developmental disabilities. Schleien, Fahnestock, Green, and Rynders (1990) describe a case study involving a child with severe and multiple developmental disabilities. The study demonstrates successful implementation of sociometry, circle of friends, and cooperative learning techniques as strategies to integrate children with severe developmental disabilities into community recreation programs.

Using a quasi-experimental design, Rynders, Schleien, and Mustonen (1990) implemented an intervention that included social reinforcement of appropriate behavior on the part of three campers with developmental disabilities, and contingent reinforcement of social interactions of their peers without disabilities. Results indicate an increase in social interaction bids and perceptions of friendship by campers without disabilities, skill acquisition by campers with disabilities, and positive ratings of staff members who participated in the integrated camping experience. Similarly, Schleien, Cameron, Rynders, and Slick (1988) taught three age-appropriate leisure skills to two children with severe developmental disabilities while facilitating social interactions and cooperative play behaviors within a public school's integrated leisure skills program. Improvements in social interaction, cooperative play, and appropriate play illustrate the benefits of integrating children with developmental disabilities into recreation programs that include children without disabilities.

Systematic Instruction Required for Appropriate Leisure Activity

Without systematic instruction in leisure skills programming, children with severe disabilities often do not learn to play and socialize appropriately. Even after the child has acquired a skill, maintenance, generalization, or initiation of the skill may not occur without continuous systematic instruction. Besides activities that build on the present capabilities of the child and prevent further disability, instruction must be provided to foster engagement in appropriate recreation activities. This may include assessing the leisure competencies of the individual; careful selection of materials and skills for instruction; and specific training methods to assist in acquisition, maintenance, and generalization of skills.

Reduction of Inappropriate Social Behaviors

Children with severe disabilities often engage in seemingly inappropriate, unacceptable social behavior (e.g., self-stimulatory behavior, self-injurious behavior, social withdrawal). Children who are constructively using their free time do not exhibit these behaviors. Schleien, Kiernan, and Wehman (1981) conducted a leisure skills training program in a group home for six residents with moderate mental retardation. An inverse relationship was found between high-quality (goal-directed, age-appropriate) leisure behaviors and inappropriate (stereotypic or age-inappropriate) behaviors. The training program provided leisure counseling, applied reinforcement, and made recreational materials available. In another study, three children with severe disabilities were prompted and given positive physical reinforcement for appropriate toy play (Flavell, 1973). These two factors were correlated with an increase in appropriate play and a decrease in stereotypic behaviors.

Wuerch and Voeltz (1982) found increased frequencies of positive behaviors when individuals were systematically trained in recreation activities. They measured the effects of leisure instruction on the behaviors of four adolescents with severe disabilities attending a private special education school. Two students exhibited increased constructive, exploratory, and attending behavior during downtime as a result of the training. A third student decreased self-stimulation when using the materials, but increased it when she had no objects to manipulate. These results offer cautious support for associating play training with positive collateral effects.

Another study explored the effects of four social levels of play—isolate, dyadic, group, and team—on the appropriate play behavior of children with autism in an integrated leisure education/physical education program (Schleien, Rynders, Mustonen, & Fox, 1990). Recreation activities representing the four levels were implemented during ten-minute periods on a randomized basis within a multielement design. Same-age peers without disabilities, who were trained to participate in integrated activities, were present during all four conditions. Not only did the type of play activity significantly influence the frequency of appropriate play behavior exhibited by the children, but they consistently played more appropriately in the more developmentally advanced (i.e., team, group, dyadic) play activities than in isolate play activities. Based on these findings, the authors suggest furthering the development of recreation and play curricula to serve individuals with autism in integrated settings.

Acceptance in Community and Reduction of Institutionalization

One of the major goals of any recreation program for children with severe disabilities is to contribute to the individual's ability to function independently in the community. By fostering the child's capability for independent living (e.g., through communication, transportation, self-help skills), the need for institutionalization is significantly reduced. Unfortunately, many of these children are isolated from their peers and the community in general because of untidy appearance, unacceptable social behavior, limited leisure repertoires, and negative attitudes of community members. It is nearly impossible for them to develop social relationships, and they are typically excluded from normal contacts. In some way, each leisure experience makes a contribution to social skills development and community living. One of the more effective ways to reduce the attitudinal barriers prevalent in the mainstream of community living is for children with disabilities to play with nondisabled peers, allowing all to notice the similarities, not the differences, between them as they play (Rynders & Schleien, 1991).

Play Skill Variables for Initial Assessment

Once a commitment to leisure education has been made, teachers and other practitioners are faced with the question, Which leisure skills should be selected for instruction? With the large number of leisure skills available (games, toys to manipulate, sports, hobbies), and the leisure skill deficits characteristic of most children with severe disabilities, assessment of the individuals' leisure skill strengths and weaknesses is critical to efficient instruction.

Initial assessment helps determine which skills the child can perform independently and which skills require verbal, gestural, or physical assistance. Fortunately, in the last 15 years, several criterion-referenced recreation curriculum guides, sensitive to the unique needs and problems of children with severe disabilities, have been developed (Bender & Valletutti, 1976; Dattilo & Murphy, 1991; Musselwhite, 1986; Rynders & Schleien, 1991; Wehman & Schleien, 1981; Wuerch & Voeltz, 1982). These curricula use strategies, such as task analyses, activity modifications, and other behavioral procedures, to promote recreation and social skills development. They also describe leisure skill inventories, activity checklists, and assessment techniques to assist the instructor with activity selection and IEP development. The variables examined below highlight some of the important leisure skill areas for functional assessment.

Proficiency of Leisure Skill: Task Analytic Assessment

Although a number of skill areas can be assessed in any play environment, an initial consideration must be whether the child knows how to interact with the materials.

Stated another way, when given leisure skills materials, can the child use them appropriately? If not, systematic instruction is required.

Task analytic assessment is required for evaluating leisure skill proficiency (Wehman & Schleien, 1981). A step-by-step description (task analysis) that specifies exactly what is to be done throughout every aspect of the activity or program must be prepared. The task analysis can be modified either to avoid problem areas or to overcome problems identified in the overall program plan (Rynders & Schleien, 1988). A performance objective also must be written for each activity, reflecting the specific skill for the child to learn. Table 8-1 shows an example of a 13-step task analytic assessment for playing with a *Simon* game. For the first five days of assessment (baseline), the child performs a total of three, three, two, four, and four steps of the game independently. This indicates that instruction should probably begin at step four ("Take game out of box and place on table top.") of the task analysis.

There are many advantages of task analysis observational assessment. First, as shown, the information collected about the child on this particular play skill helps pinpoint the exact step at which instruction should begin. In this way, the child does not receive instruction on previously acquired skills. Second, task analysis facilitates step-by-step individualized instruction for children with complex learning problems.

TABLE 8-1 Task Analytic Assessment for Playing with a *Simon* Game

		M	T	W	Th	F
1.	Locate *Simon* game.	+	+	+	+	+
2.	Bring *Simon* game to play area.	+	+	+	+	+
3.	Locate second player to play game with.	+	+	−	+	+
4.	Take game out of box and place on table top.	−	−	−	+	+
5.	Slide the on/off switch to "on" position.	−	−	−	−	−
6.	Slide the game-selector switch to "1" position.	−	−	−	−	−
7.	Slide the skill-level switch to "1" position.	−	−	−	−	−
8.	Press start button.	−	−	−	−	−
9.	Look at lighted panel and/or listen to its sound.	−	−	−	−	−
10.	Press lighted panel within 5 seconds. If matching error occurs, wait for next turn while attending to partner. If correct panel is selected, wait turn while attending to partner.	−	−	−	−	−
11.	Slide the on/off switch to "off" position.	−	−	−	−	−
12.	Place game back into box.	−	−	−	−	−
13.	Return game to original location.	−	−	−	−	−

Evaluation of the child's proficiency in recreation activities over an extended period of time also will be more objective, precise, and less subject to instructor bias.

Duration of Activity

Reid, Willis, Jarman, and Brown (1978) suggest that if the individual has some proficiency with leisure materials, the length of time the child engages in the activity should be recorded. Because this may be an extremely time-consuming measure to use with several children, the teacher may observe only half the participants on one day and the other half the next, or record activity involvement only twice a week instead of daily.

The duration of independent recreation activity is particularly important to assess because of its relevance to most home situations, where parents cannot continuously engage their child in activities. A request frequently heard from parents is to teach the child to play independently to relieve the family of the need to constantly supervise. Careful assessment of the child's duration of recreation activity before instruction provides valuable information when developing leisure goals for the child. It also is a valuable indication of the child's preferred recreational activities. Figure 8-1 presents a sample duration data collection form.

Appropriate Versus Inappropriate Object Manipulation

Another assessment issue is differentiating between appropriate actions with toys versus actions that would not be considered appropriate. Behaviors typically considered inappropriate are harmful or destructive to the child, peers, or materials. However, many children with severe to profound mental retardation or autism exhibit high rates of repetitive, self-stimulated behavior with toys (e.g., banging, pounding, slamming) that are not necessarily harmful or destructive, yet are still inappropriate. The problem is compounded because, with certain objects, banging or slamming actions may actually be appropriate. Many children will do unusual things with toys that might be considered appropriate by other observers.

Hence, instructors are faced with how to assess the *qualitative* nature of toy play. One way to cope with this difficulty is to use more than one observer periodically and have each observer rate the appropriateness of the action. Objective judging provides a check-and-balance system for the instructor. A second method is to identify the principle actions a peer without disabilities might exhibit with each object. These actions serve as assessment guidelines.

Yet another method is to generate a fine-motor classification system instructors can use as a basis for recording children's actions. Tilton and Ottinger (1964) provide nine self-explanatory categories that were identified after extensive observational analysis of children without disabilities, as well as of children with developmental disabilities:

1. Repetitive manual manipulation
2. Oral contacts

3. Pounding
4. Throwing
5. Pushing or pulling
6. Personalized toy use
7. Manipulation of movable parts
8. Separation of parts of toys
9. Combinational uses of toys

Leisure Preference Evaluation

One goal for children with severe disabilities should be to provide them with the skills and opportunities to participate in chosen leisure experiences. According to Ficker-Terrill and Rowitz (1991), practitioners must become familiar with best-practice strategies, such as self-advocacy procedures and communication techniques, that facilitate informed choices. Demonstration of choice through selection encourages spontaneous initiation of recreation activities, engagement with the environment (including other people), and the assertion of a degree of control over one's surroundings (Dattilo & Barnett, 1985). Because choice-making skills are within the capabilities of children with the most severe disabilities (Kishi, Teelucksingh, Zollers, Park-Lee, & Meyer, 1988), professionals must attempt to secure personal autonomy, freedom, and choice for these individuals.

There is a strong positive relationship between having opportunities to engage in preferred activities and the development of social skills. Koegel, Dyer, and Bell (1987) show that when children were able to choose to participate in desired activities,

Leisure Skill Object	Minutes/Seconds Engaged with Object	Type of Action (e.g., appropriate/ inappropriate)
1. Waterpaints		
2. Record player		
3. Plants		
4. Autoharp		
5. Multipurpose ball		
6. Dominoes		
7. Target game with bean bags		
8. Lincoln Logs		
9. Viewmaster		
10. Pinball machine		

FIGURE 8-1   Initial Object and Duration Assessment

they were more socially responsive than when participating in activities they did not choose. Providing choice and preferences for persons with disabilities also can increase spontaneous communication and subsequent social skills (Dyer, 1987; Peck, 1985). Likewise, Koegel, O'Dell, and Koegel (1987) suggest that if activities are modified to allow a person shared control, improvements in speech and other areas (e.g., leisure, social skills) can occur. Perhaps shared control results in higher motivation to approach learning situations.

Several research studies have been successful in facilitating choice-making behavior with individuals with severe disabilities. Lanagan and Dattilo (1989) report that by the end of a leisure education program, using a democratic leadership style to encourage people with disabilities to make leisure choices, most participants began to demonstrate preference by asking for recreation activities. Similarly, Wetherby and Prutting (1984) found that children with disabilities frequently initiated communication with an adult in a free-play setting if the adult was not directive and allowed the child to engage in preferred activities rather than in activities arbitrarily chosen by the adult. These studies provide encouragement for practitioners to respond to the preferences of children with disabilities.

Limited response repertoires of children with severe disabilities often result in unreliable assumptions about their preferences for various items. If practitioners are to provide opportunities for these children to demonstrate leisure preferences, they must develop strategies to recognize choices made through unconventional means (Houghton, Bronicki, & Guess, 1987). Nietupski et al. (1986) recommend providing frequent opportunities for choice in a structured fashion, rather than assuming individuals with severe disabilities lack self-initiation skills.

Dattilo (1984) originally describe the following techniques to assess leisure preferences:

- *Frequency:* Count the number of times children choose an activity, manipulate a toy, or smile while participating in an activity.
- *Rate:* Record the number of times a behavior (e.g., vocalizations) occurs within a specified time period such as within the first five minutes a toy, activity, or person is presented.
- *Duration:* Record the length of time children participate in an activity or play with another child.
- *Latency:* Record the time it takes for children to respond to different activities or materials such as turning their head toward music or touching a person's outreached hand.

Recording the latency of responses was employed by McCall (1974), who measured the length of time that elapsed before infants acted on a variety of objects.

Some researchers have used technology (e.g., microswitches, computers, environmental control devices) to determine preferences (Brown, Cavalier, Mineo, & Buckley, 1988; Dattilo & Mirenda, 1987; Wacker, Wiggins, Fowler, & Berg, 1988). In a series of investigations, Dattilo (1986; 1987; 1988) demonstrates that the preferences of children with severe disabilities can be assessed systematically with computers, resulting in unique leisure profiles for each participant. Once assessment occurs, children with severe disabilities can experience enjoyment through participation in preferred social activities during time formerly characterized by boredom and solitary, passive observation.

Individual control in a social context also is an important variable in successful leisure programs. Smith (1985) states that individuals strive for a level of independence in social situations that allows them to feel in control. Recreation activities provide opportunities for children with disabilities to experience this sense of control by showing them that their social responses have an effect on others.

Frequency of Interactions

Most children without disabilities participate in social interactions daily, ranging from explicit verbal statements ("I'm proud of your work") to subtle facial expressions or body language (a smile to indicate pleasure or acceptance to another). However, many individuals with developmental disabilities demonstrate minimal social interactions (Schleien & Wehman, 1986). More critically social interactions often are not included in instructional programs for these children (Certo & Schleien, 1982). Many of them also are not provided with frequent opportunities to interact socially (Certo & Kohl, 1984).

For many children with severe disabilities, an important instructional goal is to initiate and sustain more frequent interactions with peers. These children commonly play in isolation during free play time (Green & Schleien, 1991). When this occurs, the potential benefits of social interaction are not accrued.

One way to assess social interaction is a simple count of the number of times one child (1) initiates an interaction, (2) receives an interaction, and (3) terminates an interaction. Duration assessment can measure the interaction time between peers or between the child and adults in the room. Coding of specific types of interactions is a second means of gathering information. Carney and associates (1977) detail the following social interaction skills:

1. Receives Interaction
   - Receives hug
   - Returns smile
   - Gives object to other who has requested it
   - Returns greeting
   - "Receives" cooperative play
   - Answers questions
   - Recognizes peers, teacher by name
   - Shows approval
   - Discriminates appropriate time, place, situation before receiving interaction

2. Initiates Interaction
   - Greets another person
   - Requests objects from another person

- Initiates cooperative play
- Seeks approval
- Seeks affiliation with familiar person
- Helps one who has difficulty manipulating environment
- Initiates conversation

3. Sustaining Interactions

- Attends to ongoing cooperative activity
- Sustains conversation

4. Terminates Interactions

- Terminates cooperative play activity
- Terminates conversation

In addition to providing sequence, these skills may be task analyzed and the child's proficiency on selected behaviors may be assessed. The four categories can be used to code the qualitative nature of the interaction.

Direction of Interaction

Analyzing to whom interactions are directed also may be helpful in assessing which individuals in the play environment are reinforcing to the child. As Beveridge, Spencer, and Miller (1978) and Green and Schleien (1991), observe, child–teacher interactions occur more frequently than child–child interactions, especially among children with severe disabilities. Structured intervention by an adult usually is required initially to increase child–child interactions (Rynders & Schleien, 1991).

When the child is playing with siblings or peers, observe the direction of interactions with children who are severely disabled as well as with nondisabled peers. This type of behavioral analysis can be revealing because most children without disabilities do not include those with disabilities in play unless prompted and reinforced by adults (Apolloni & Cooke, 1978).

The checklist in Table 8-2 might be used to code a number of interactions. This form, however, does not allow for analyzing the *direction* of interactions. The

TABLE 8-2   Checklist for Conducting a Behavioral Assessment of Social Interactions

Name	Initiated Interaction	Received Interaction
Jason		
Jenna		
Leigh		
David		

TABLE 8-3 Checklist for Interactions

	Jason	Jenna	Leigh	David	Instructor
Jason	X				
Jenna		X			
Leigh			X		
David				X	

checklist in Table 8-3 facilitates assessing with which peers or adults the child interacted.

Free Play Assessment

In some instances, there may be little interest or time to collect the specific types of information discussed previously. Some instructors may want to use a simpler method of assessing the level of free play at which the child is functioning. One such strategy makes use of Parten's (1932) developmental sequence: autistic-unoccupied-independent-observing-attempt-associative-cooperative interaction. With this strategy, the instructor clearly defines the types of behaviors characteristic of the different developmental levels of play. For example, in the autistic play stage, characteristic behaviors could include not touching or physically acting on any toys during free-play periods, or nonfunctional repetitive actions for prolonged periods of time. Independent play may be considered as any appropriate play behaviors exhibited alone or away from other peers. Cooperative or social play could be another skill level added to the basic developmental sequence and could include skills such as physical or verbal interaction with peers and instructors.

This assessment strategy is convenient and economical in terms of time expended, and can facilitate collecting fairly accurate information, provided the categories are clearly defined and, therefore, easy to discriminate. It does not, however, capture many of the collateral abilities clearly associated with play skill development such as fine and gross motor skills, changes in affect, social behavior, and friendship development.

Schleien (1982) demonstrates the use of this approach with children with severe learning disabilities. The study attempted to determine whether an individualized leisure education instructional program could produce significant gains in cooperative play during free time in the classroom. Leisure skill competencies, repertoires, and activity/material preferences were assessed for 23 students across two classrooms. Four categories of developmental levels of play—inappropriate, isolate, parallel, cooperative—were derived from the Social Interaction Rating Scale, an eight-point scale used to measure the level of social behavior of young children with severe mental retardation in a free-play setting (Paloutzian et al., 1971). (Paloutzian's levels were adapted from those used by Parten and Newhall [1943] for children with average intelligence.) The operational definitions of the modified developmental levels of play (adapted by Schleien, 1982) are:

1. *Inappropriate Play:* Percentage of time child plays or uses free time inappropriately; manipulates or uses toys, objects, or recreation materials incorrectly; engages in socially inappropriate behavior (e.g., verbal/physical abuse of others); manipulates chronological age-inappropriate toys, objects, or recreation materials (determined by manufacturer's age-level recommendation); engages in nongoal–directed, nonfunctional, purposeless behavior; stereotypic behavior (e.g., self-stimulation).

2. *Isolate Play:* Percentage of time child plays with or manipulates toys, objects, or recreation materials appropriately but in a solitary manner (at least five feet from a peer).

3. *Parallel Play:* Percentage of time child plays with or manipulates toys, objects, or recreation materials appropriately, in the presence of a peer, but not cooperatively: although peers are within five feet, child does not interact with them (makes no attempt to communicate with, hand toy to, touch, and so on).

4. *Cooperative Play:* Percentage of time child plays with or manipulates toys, objects, or recreation materials in an appropriate and cooperative fashion (interacts socially with peers; plays with another and joins in a cooperative, give-and-take manner; does not hit or yell at others; shares toys/objects/game).

The leisure instructional program, including exposure to cooperative games and materials, and instruction using various behavioral methods, such as modeling and social reinforcement, was an effective means of facilitating cooperative and socially appropriate play. Inappropriate social behaviors also were reduced in all of the students. These results indicate that children with severe disabilities can acquire a more diverse repertoire of social and cooperative play skills than had been demonstrated previously in the literature.

Cooperative Play

There have been numerous studies since the 1970s describing the development of cooperative play among children with severe disabilities. However, these efforts often fall far short of the sustained cooperative play documented by early childhood researchers such as Parten and Newhall (1943) and Barnes (1971).

Whitman, Mercurio, and Caponigri (1970), for example, taught two children with severe mental retardation to roll a ball back and forth. Extensive physical guidance and modeling were required before the children performed the skill under the trainer's verbal cues. Generalization was achieved by gradually bringing in two other peers and having them enter into the ball rolling game. A similar study (but with a greater emphasis on comparing the effects of a higher functioning peer model versus an adult model) has been conducted with a young child who was extremely withdrawn and profoundly mentally retarded (Morris & Dolker, 1974). Ball rolling again was the skill being trained. No significant differences were found between models. Extensive behavior shaping (e.g., physical guidance) was required, in addition to modeling, for the social play behavior to develop.

Knapczyk and Peterson (1975) integrated children without disabilities into the playroom of younger children with moderate mental retardation and encouraged them to interact through cooperative play. Substantially increased rates of cooperative play occurred with the models without disabilities. A second study conducted by the same investigators (Knapczyk & Peterson, 1975) was equally revealing. Introduction of preschool children of equivalent mental ages but younger chronological ages (three- and four-year-olds) without disabilities led to few changes in cooperative play levels of the students with moderate mental retardation. Knapczyk and Peterson interpret these findings as an indication that the younger children without disabilities were not effective models and that competence in models, when viewed by less competent observers, influences the likelihood of social play behavior being imitated.

In a program conducted by Strain (1975), the use of sociodramatic activities increased the amount of social play a group of preschool children with severe mental retardation engaged in. The instructor read a story and assigned each student a role. During the reading, the teacher encouraged students to perform two of the character's verbal and/or motor behaviors. The amount of social play among children increased as a result of the sociodramatic storytelling. Children who had little or no social play behaviors prior to the sociodramatic activities increased their degree of social play, but not to the extent of the children who already possessed appropriate interpersonal skills. This type of activity may be beneficial as a supplemental activity to promote social play following the training of primary social interactions. It also may facilitate generalization.

Paloutzian et al. (1971) successfully used prompting and reinforcement with 10 children with severe mental retardation to imitate novel social behaviors (passing a bean bag, walking up to another student and gently stroking his or her face, pushing a child in a swing, pulling a peer in a wagon, rocking another peer in a rocking chair or hobby horse). In the first phase, children imitated modeled responses that were not social in nature. After the participant reached criterion for this phase, phase two taught them social behaviors with two trainers and two participants working together. The first trainer offered the cue and modeled the correct response for the first student. This student performed the behavior with or without prompting (as necessary) and received food and social attention as reinforcement. The roles of the students and trainers were then reversed to train the second student. There were significant increases from pre- to posttest scores in the levels of social behaviors in participants trained using the prompting and reinforcement methods. Adults and peer models were used, providing a method of training complex social responses to a large number of children with a small number of staff.

One of the more comprehensive efforts at analyzing the instructional components of social interaction training can be found in Williams's (1975) work with students with moderate mental retardation. Williams analyzed four components of social interactions: initiates interaction, receives interaction, sustains interaction, and terminates interaction. Peer functioning level, task availability, and training across environmental settings were major points considered when arranging an appropriate environment for social interaction. Several task analyses for recreational activities (e.g., use of a Viewmaster, playing Old Maid) also were presented. The explicit instructional direction given for conducting the program made it unique.

The goal of cooperative play and social interaction between two or more peers can be attained through numerous strategies. Wehman and Schleien (1981) describe several of them:

1. A child can be paired with an instructor and trained in different play situations.
2. A child can be paired with a higher functioning peer who is also disabled and engages in socially appropriate play.
3. A child can be paired with a nondisabled peer who engages in socially appropriate play.
4. Two equivalent (low functioning) peers can be paired and trained by one or more instructors.
5. A group of children with severe disabilities can be integrated with nondisabled peers.
6. Any of the previous combinations can be used and different types of reinforcements provided such as points, edibles, or praise for instances of cooperative play.
7. Environmental arrangements preceding the onset of play sessions may be manipulated through activity selection, room size, or background music.

Many strategies have yet to be exhaustively examined by programmers or researchers. Because verbal language is not required for cooperative play, nonverbal language can be an efficient means of communication for children with severe disabilities. Toys and other play materials are excellent vehicles for communication with peers and adults. Individuals who were institutionalized have little desire to communicate after years in a dismal and apathetic living environment, but stimulating play materials associated with positively reinforcing play sessions can alter this limited incentive to communicate.

Leisure Curriculum Facilitating Social Interaction

The rest of this chapter provides a sampling of individualized, task-analyzed programs that can facilitate social skills development and cooperative play among children with and without severe disabilities. These programs have been adapted from work on leisure skills curriculum development (Rynders & Schleien, 1991; Wehman & Schleien, 1981) and emphasize leisure skills that facilitate social interaction and friendship. The activities depicted are representative of the four program areas—toy play, games, hobbies, and sports/dance. Within each program area, two representative activities are offered, one for the preschool (0 to 6 years) and the other for the school-age (7 to 15 years) child (see Figures 8-2–8-9). The programs are examples of recreational activities that can take place in multiple environments to encourage generalization across home, school, and community settings.

Guidelines for Instructional Cues and Correction Procedures

To promote the appropriate use of play materials and skill acquisition, instructional cues and correction procedures should be individualized to each child's needs and abilities. The guidelines below may be applied to each of the eight, task-analyzed activities that follow, as appropriate to program goals:

1. Instructor gives verbal cue to participant; if participant responds correctly, instructor provides reinforcement immediately.
2. If participant does not respond correctly, instructor repeats verbal cue and models correct response.
3. If participant still does not respond correctly, instructor repeats verbal cue and physically guides participant through correct response.
4. Repeat the first three steps several times in each training session with participant, as needed.

Guidelines for Instructors to Promote Social Interaction

Activity instructors play a key role in promoting social interaction among participants. Rynders and Schleien (1991) offer these tips to instructors that encourage sensitivity to individual needs, grouping arrangements, and cooperation among participants:

1. Make sure materials and tools are laid out for safe and easy access. Arrange supplies in one small area rather than scattered around the room to help keep group members involved with each other.
2. Seat participants in small integrated groups. Check that the position of each person with a disability is close to his/her partner.
3. If a person with a disability has a behavior problem, have him/her join a larger group of participants without disabilities. Rotate the interaction responsibilities of nondisabled members.
4. Adapt the activity for the age and ability levels of the participants.
5. Emphasize the importance of enjoying an activity with another person rather than the speed and/or accuracy with which it is done.
6. Develop directions for the activity in such a way that they require an interdependent (cooperative) effort, rather than a competitive effort.
7. Redirect when someone is off task, and step in if a situation is deteriorating.

8. Prompt cooperative interactions when they are not occurring. Reward cooperative interactions when they are occurring.

Guidelines for Nondisabled Companions to Promote Social Interaction

Rynders and Schleien (1991) also provide suggestions that instructors can give nondisabled peer companions to encourage social interaction, cooperation, and friendship development in recreational activities. While some nondisabled children have a natural willingness and aptitude for interacting with and offering assistance to children with disabilities, most nondisabled children can benefit from the concrete examples of interactional behaviors these tips provide:

1. Welcome your partner and stay close to him/her during the activity.
2. Smile, talk pleasantly, and look at your partner when talking.
3. Divide up tasks to encourage your partner to be involved.
4. Make the activity enjoyable and let your partner know you are having a good time.
5. Take turns.
6. Share materials and responsibilities.
7. Help your partner do things as independently as possible. Don't help too much or too soon. If s/he appears to be confused, losing interest, or frustrated, step in. To assist, describe (pleasantly) how to perform the task, then invite him/her to do it. If that doesn't work, show him/her how to do the task as you continue to explain how to do it. Invite him/her to do it like you did it. If that doesn't work, guide him/her through the task by gently nudging his/her arm toward it, or by actually moving his/her hand to perform the task while continuing to explain how to do it. Then invite him/her to do it.
8. Encourage your partner.
9. End the activity by saying and/or doing something pleasant.

Toy Play

Toy play involves a child's interaction with an inanimate object, either as an individual or as a member of a group. When two or more children are involved, toy play can stimulate social and cooperative activity, allowing them to express themselves creatively and develop progressively higher skilled competencies. Because rules generally do not exist during toy play, children have the freedom to design activities to fit their own individual needs and interests.

Games

Games are perhaps the purest form of recreation, with sheer pleasure being the primary motivating factor. Children engage in games because they enjoy the activity and appreciate the company of other players. Games follow definite rules and may involve a wide range of functioning competencies, ranging from simple to complex

---

Name of Activity: Racing Remote Control Vehicles

Program Area:	Toy Play
Age Group:	Preschool
Materials:	Remote control vehicle for each participant

Instructional Objective:	Given a remote control vehicle, the participant will manipulate the controls to move the vehicle forward toward the finish line.

Task Analysis	Correction Procedures/Activity Guidelines/Special Adaptations
1. Using dominant hand, slide power switch located under vehicle to "on."	1. Refer to "Guidelines for Instructional Cues and Correction Procedures" section in this chapter.
2. Place vehicle on ground behind starting line.	2. Refer to "Guidelines for Instructors to Promote Social Interaction" section in this chapter.
3. With the dominant hand, pick up hand control.	3. Refer to "Guidelines for Nondisabled Companions to Promote Social Interaction" section in this chapter.
4. At the command, "Go!" press button on hand control to forward position to move vehicle toward finish line.	4. Adapt the length of the track to meet individual abilities.
5. Continue to press button in forward position until vehicle has moved straight ahead and crossed finish line.	5. The instructor may need to explain the meaning of the action verb, "go," before the race begins. Subsequently, the participant should be able to follow the command independently.
6. Release the button to stop vehicle.	6. Once the forward movement of the vehicle is mastered, the participant may be taught how to reverse and turn the vehicle.
7. Slide the power switch to "off."	7. For a challenging race, design an obstacle or "cross-country" course.

FIGURE 8-2 "Racing Remote Control Vehicles" Activity

levels of participation in cooperative and/or competitive interactions. Manipulation of an object or toy, taking turns, following rules, and the concept of winning and losing may all be learned through recreational games. Categories include board and table games, social (get acquainted) games, gross motor games, musical/rhythmical games, and card games.

Name of Activity: Catch Frisbee

Program Area:	Toy Play
Age Group:	School age
Materials:	Frisbee

Instructional Objective:	Given a Frisbee tossed by another person, the participant will catch the Frisbee from 5' away.

Task Analysis	**Correction Procedures/Activity Guidelines/Special Adaptations**
1. Stand 5' away from and facing other player, with feet parallel and shoulder's width apart.	1. Refer to "Guidelines for Instructional Cues and Correction Procedures" section in this chapter.
2. Extend both arms outward toward other person, palms faced outward, fingers extended.	2. Refer to "Guidelines for Instructors to Promote Social Interaction" section in this chapter.
3. Eye-track path of Frisbee through air.	3. Refer to "Guidelines for Nondisabled Companions to Promote Social Interaction" section in this chapter.
4. As Frisbee approaches, position palms directly parallel with Frisbee.	4. Participant may practice catching Frisbee as it is slid across floor; as proficiency develops, Frisbee may be thrown through air as the distance is gradually increased.
5. When Frisbee makes contact with palms, curl fingers inward toward palms until they are resting on top of Frisbee, thumbs resting on underside of Frisbee.	5. Frisbees come in several sizes and weights and should be selected according to individual preference and skill level.
6. Apply inward pressure between fingers and thumbs to grasp Frisbee firmly, catching Frisbee.	6. Initially a nerf Frisbee could be used to prevent injury and facilitate grasping.
	7. Several players may play this game to increase opportunity for social interaction.

FIGURE 8-3 "Catch Frisbee" Activity

Hobbies

Hobbies can contribute to the development of lifelong leisure skills. A child may pursue a hobby as a youngster and continue to excel in and use those skills with increasing degrees of sophistication throughout her or his lifetime. Participation in hobbies tends to be less active than in either sports or other physical games and may include activities such as playing a musical instrument in a home rhythm band and a wide variety of arts and crafts. Participation in a hobby is usually of a noncompetitive nature, without any losers. Although it is hoped that interest in

Name of Activity: Parachute Play

Program Area:	Games
Age Group:	Preschool
Materials:	Parachute
Instructional Objective:	Given 12 or more participants arranged in a circle and a parachute spread out on the ground inside the circle, the participant will help make a "mushroom" by raising the parachute over his or her head and then lowering it to waist level.

Task Analysis	Correction Procedures/Activity Guidelines/Special Adaptations
1. Stand facing inside of circle, with feet parallel and shoulder's with apart.	1. Refer to "Guidelines for Instructional Cues and Correction Procedures" section in this chapter.
2. Bend knees until body is in squatting position.	2. Refer to "Guidelines for Instructors to Promote Social Interaction" section in this chapter.
3. Extend both arms downward toward outer edge of parachute.	3. Refer to "Guidelines for Nondisabled Companions to Promote Social Interaction" section in this chapter.
4. Grasp parachute with both hands, using palmar grasp.	4. Parachutes may be purchased in many sizes, from 6' to 24' diameters. Select a size appropriate for the number of participants.
5. Straighten knees to standing position.	5. To facilitate grasping the edge of the parachute, rope, ribbon, or Velcro loops may be sewn onto the parachute edge.
6. Lift parachute to waist level by bending at elbows.	
7. Continue raising arms until parachute is above ahead and arms are fully extended.	6. To promote socialization and cooperation, two participants may cross underneath the "mushroom" together.
8. Bend at elbows to lower parachute to form "mushroom."	7. Many exercises and games may be played using a parachute: balls may be placed on top of the parachute for a game of "Popcorn"; participants may run underneath the parachute and attempt to get out before it lands; participants may form animals underneath the parachute for the others to guess; name games and circle games may be played.
	8. Emphasize the cooperation needed to raise and lower the parachute together. Assistants may need to be distributed evenly around the parachute to facilitate manipulating the parachute.

FIGURE 8-4 "Parachute Play" Activity

Name of Activity: Fooseball

Program Area:	Games
Age Group:	School age
Materials:	Fooseball Table
Instructional Objective:	Given a fooseball table and another player, the participant will manipulate the two rows of playing men to hit the ball into the opponent's goal to score 1 point (first player to score 7 points wins the game).

Task Analysis	**Correction Procedures/Activity Guidelines/Special Adaptations**
1. Stand facing levers on side of fooseball table.	1. Refer to "Guidelines for Instructional Cues and Correction Procedures" section in this chapter.
2. Grasp levers with both hands, using palmar grasps.	2. Refer to "Guidelines for Instructors to Promote Social Interaction" section in this chapter.
3. Eye-track path of ball across table.	
4. Position one row of playing men directly in path of ball by either extending arm or bending it at elbow, pushing or pulling appropriate level to move row of men laterally across table.	3. Refer to "Guidelines for Nondisabled Companions to Promote Social Interaction" section in this chapter.
	4. Levers may be enlarged with adhesive tape or sponge to facilitate grasping.
5. When ball makes contact with playing man and has been stopped, quickly rotate wrist to turn appropriate lever, causing playing man to make contact with ball, hitting ball forward toward opponent's goal.	5. For participants who use wheelchairs, table may be lowered to a comfortable level and the levers lengthened by attaching wooden dowels to them.
	6. A heavier ball, the same size as a standard fooseball, may be used to slow down the pace of the game.
6. Opponent attempts to block ball.	
7. Hit ball into goal, scoring 1 point.	7. Since each side of the table has four levers, with proficiency, two teams of two players each can compete against each other.
8. Continue playing until one player scores 7 points to win game.	

FIGURE 8-5 "Fooseball" Activity

Name of Activity: Papier-Mâché Balloons

Program Area:	Hobbies
Age Group:	Preschool
Materials:	1 pound all-purpose flour, large plastic bucket containing 2 gallons water, paint stick, 3" strips of newspaper, balloons

Instructional Objective: Given the necessary supplies, the participant will mix a paste of flour and water, and cover a balloon with papier-mâché.

Task Analysis	Correction Procedures/Activity Guidelines/Special Adaptations
1. Grasp sides of open bag of flour with both hands, using palmar grasp	1. Refer to "Guidelines for Instructional and Corection Procedures" section in this chapter.
2. Lift bag by bending at elbows.	
3. Position bag directly above bucket containing water.	2. Refer to "Guidelines for Instructors to Promote Social Interaction" section in this chapter
4. Pour flour into bucket by rotating both wrists outward, away from body.	3. Refer to "Guidelines for Nondisabled Companions to Promote Social Interaction" section in this chapter.
5. Grasp paint stick handle with dominant hand, using palmar grasp.	4. Strips of newspaper may be prepared in advance either by instructor or students.
6. Dip paint stick into flour and water by lowering elbow.	5. Nondisabled companions may assist participants with motor difficulties in opening bag.
7. Mix flour and water by rotating dominant arm and hand in circular motion.	6. The handle of the paint stick may be built up with tape and foam rubber to facilitate grasping.
8. Grasp strip of newspaper with dominant hand, using pincer grasp.	7. The amount of paste made may be varied as desired, using a proportion of 1 part flour to 2 parts water.
9. Dip newspaper into paste by lowering hand into bucket.	8. Depending on the shape and size of the balloons, faces, masks, animals, or other forms may be made by building up the surface of the balloon using the papier-mâché.
10. Raise newspaper out of bucket by lifting hand at elbow.	
11. Hold balloon gently, but firmly with nondominant hand.	
12. Apply newspaper to surface of balloon by extending fingers of dominant hand.	9. Once the balloon is covered with papier-mâché, allow it to dry thoroughly and paint it by using nontoxic tempera paints.
13. With fingertips of dominant hand, pat surface of paper till smooth.	
14. Continue dipping strips of newspaper into paste and applying them to balloon until entire surface of balloon is covered	

FIGURE 8-6 "Papier-mâché Balloons" Activity

Name of Activity: Watercolor Painting

Program Area:	Hobbies
Age Group:	School age
Materials:	Set of watercolors, paintbrush, jar of water, watercolor paper
Instructional Objective:	Given appropriate art supplies, the participant will paint a picture in watercolors

Task Analysis	Correction Procedures/Activity Guidelines/Special Adaptations
1. Grasp handle of paintbrush with dominant hand, using pincer grasp.	1. Refer to "Guidelines for Instructional Cues and Correction Procedures" section in this chapter.
2. Position brush directly above jar of water.	2. Refer to "Guidelines for Instructors to Promote Social Interaction" section in this chapter.
3. Dip brush into water by moving hand downward.	3. Refer to "Guidelines for Nondisabled Companions to Promote Social Interaction" section in this chapter.
4. Lift brush out of water by moving hand upward.	
5. Position brush directly over pad of colored paint in watercolor set.	4. Tape watercolor paper to surface of table or tray of wheelchair to prevent it from slipping.
6. Lower brush to pad of colored paint by moving hand downward.	5. The handle of the paintbrush may be built up with tape and foam rubber, or fastened to the hand with Velcro, to facilitate grasping.
7. Swirl brush in paint by rotating wrist in a circular motion (to mix paint and water and apply paint to brush).	6. Paint materials may be shared to promote social interaction.
8. Lift brush off paint by moving hand upward.	7. Participants may guess the subject of the pictures or give other feedback about designs to encourage interaction.
9. Position brush directly above paper.	
10 Lower brush to paper by moving hand downward.	8. All but the desired color in the paint set could be covered to make the desired color more accessible to the participant.
11. Apply paint to paper by moving brush across paper as desired.	9. Color recognition and discrimination can be taught in conjunction with this activity.
12. Lift brush off paper by moving hand upward.	
13. Rinse brush by dipping it in jar of water	
14. Continue to apply different colors of paint to paper as desired.	

FIGURE 8-7 "Watercolor Painting" Activity

Name of Activity: Shapes (Creative Movement)

Program Area:	Sports/Dance
Age Group:	Preschool
Materials:	Open area inside or outdoors
Instructional Objective:	Given instructions about a particular kind of shape to make with the body, the participant makes the shape with his or her body and then freezes in that position for a few moments until the next instruction is given.

Task Analysis	Correction Procedures/Activity Guidelines/Special Adaptations
1. Pair up participants with and without disabilities in an open space.	1. Refer to "Guidelines for Instructional Cues and Correction Procedures" section in this chapter.
2. Stand with feet parallel and shoulder's width apart.	2. Refer to "Guidelines for Instructors to Promote Social Interaction" section in this chapter.
3. At a command from the instructor to make a particular kind of shape ("tall," "crooked," "shakey," "shaped like an animal," "shape where you touch someone's elbow, foot, hair," etc.), move to form shape with body.	3. Refer to "Guidelines for Nondisabled Companions to Promote Social Interaction" section in this chapter.
	4. Participant may make their own suggestions for shapes to make.
4. When shape is formed, freeze motion so all participants can see each other's shapes.	5. Participants may make shapes for the other participants to guess.
5. When all have seen the shapes, continue to make other shapes as directed by instructor.	6. Participants may make shapes individually, in pairs, threes, etc., or in one large group. Large shapes might include an elephant, fire engine, rocket, factory, forest, etc.
	7. This activity may be performed to music, or the rhythm of a drum beat, stopping the music as a cue to "freeze."

FIGURE 8-8 "Shapes (Creative Movement)" Activity

many different leisure skills develop throughout a person's lifetime, the skills related to hobbies are typically most enduring for the individual.

Sports/Dance

The distinction between sports and games often is characterized by a timeline. Although activities in both categories employ a definite set of rules, sports tend to

Name of Activity: Volleyball, Underhand Serve

Program Area:	Sports/Dance
Age Group:	School age
Materials:	Volleyball, net
Instructional Objective:	Given a volleyball and a volleyball net, the participant will serve the ball over the net in an underhand fashion from 10' away.

Task Analysis	Correction Procedures/Activity Guidelines/Special Adaptations
1. Stand at back right corner of court behind end line, with feet parallel and shoulder's width apart, facing net 10' away.	1. Refer to "Guidelines for Instructional Cues and Correction Procedures" section in this chapter.
2. Grasp ball with one hand on each side of ball.	2. Refer to "Guidelines for Instructors to Promote Social Interaction" section in this chapter.
3. Rotate hands and ball counter-clockwise so that dominant hand is resting on top of ball and non-dominant hand is supporting ball on bottom.	3. Refer to "Guidelines for Nondisabled Companions to Promote Social Interaction" section in this chapter.
4. Release ball with dominant hand allowing ball to rest in palm of nondominant hand.	4. Underhand serve may be performed with a close-fisted hand or with an open hand (hitting ball with heel of palm). Ball will usually travel farther when fist is used.
5. Extend arm of nondominant arm, moving ball outward to front of body.	5. Initially, participant should serve ball a short distance from net to assure success. As skill develops, participant may gradually back up to end line.
6. Curl fingers of dominant hand to make a fist.	6. As lead-up activity to underhand serve, participant could throw ball required distance over net (as in "Newcomb" game that requires participants to throw balls over the net).
7. Extend dominant arm, bring-ing fist downward to side of body.	
8. Quickly flex elbow, raising fist upward toward lower half of ball.	7. To improve eye-hand coordination and simplify task, participant may practice serving balloon or beach ball instead of standard volleyball.
9. Continue to raise fist upward against ball, hitting it forward, serving ball 2'.	
10. Serve 4', 6', 8', then 10' over net.	

FIGURE 8-9 "Volleyball: Underhand Serve" Activity

contain greater sophistication in the rules and equipment used, with greater emphasis on competition. An individual's skill repertoire should include both individual and team sports, requiring various degrees of social and motor coordination. Children with severe disabilities are becoming more active in sports nationwide—as can be observed by the increased interest and participation in Special Olympics, wheelchair sports and games, and gross-motor activities in community recreation. Dance is also included here as a unique recreational activity that can improve physical fitness, coordination, flexibility, self-expression, self-awareness, cooperation, and teamwork and it can be performed in a variety of settings.

Summary

The purpose of this chapter has been to discuss the development of social and leisure skills in children with severe disabilities. With appropriate assessment techniques, skill selection, instructional strategies, and activity modifications, children will learn to play cooperatively and, as a result, develop socially. Several areas of leisure skill competency can be assessed: the *proficiency* with which toys, objects, or materials are used; the *duration* of self-initiated action; the materials *preferred* by students; and the frequency and direction of *social interactions*. When these assessment and intervention strategies are used with a logically sequenced recreation curriculum and instructional technology, the application of the systematic instructional process to leisure and social skills development is complete. There are several recreational programs that have been task analyzed and specially adapted for implementation with preschoolers and school-age children with and without severe disabilities. The ultimate goal of any such program is for the child to develop a leisure skill repertoire in order to be able to use free time appropriately, as well as to acquire the necessary social skills that can promote independent living and facilitate making friends at home and in school and community settings.

References

Apolloni, T., & Cooke, T. (1978). Integrated programming at the infant, toddler, and preschool levels. In M. Guralnick (Ed.), *Early intervention and the integration of handicapped and nonhandicapped children* (pp. 147–165). Baltimore: University Park Press.

Barnes, K. (1971). Preschool play, norms: A replication. *Developmental Psychology, 5,* 99–103.

Bender, M., & Valletutti, P. (1976). *Teaching the moderately and severely handicapped: Curriculum, objectives, strategies, and activities,* Vol. 2. Baltimore: University Park Press.

Beveridge, M., Spencer, J., & Miller, P. (1978). Language and social behavior in severely educationally subnormal children. *British Journal of Social and Clinical Psychology, 17,* 75–83.

Brewer, G., & Kakalik, J. (1979). *Handicapped children: Strategies for improving services.* New York: McGraw-Hill.

Brown, C., Cavalier, A., Mineo, B., & Buckley, R. (1988). Sound-to-speech translation and environmental control for people with mental retardation. *Augmentative and Alternative Communication, 4,* 172.

Carney, I., Clobuciar, A., Corley, E., Wilcox, B., Bigler, J., Fleisler, L., Pany, D., & Turner, P. (1977). Social interaction in severely handicapped students. In B. Wilcox (Ed.), *The severely and profoundly handicapped child* (pp. 62–93). Springfield, IL: State Department of Education.

Certo, N., & Kohl, F. (1984). A strategy for developing interpersonal interaction instructional content for severely handicapped students. In N. Certo, N. Haring, & R. York (Eds.), *Public school integration of severely handicapped students: Rational issues and progressive alternatives* (pp. 221–244). Baltimore: Paul H. Brookes.

Certo, N., & Schleien, S. (1982). Individualized leisure instruction. In P. Verhoven, S. Schleien, & M. Bender (Eds.), *Leisure education and the handicapped individual: An ecological perspective* (pp. 121–153). Washington, DC: Institute for Career and Leisure Development.

Collard, K. (1981). Leisure education in the schools: Why, who, and the need for advocacy. *Therapeutic Recreation Journal, 15,* 8–16.

Dattilo, J. (1984). Incorporating choice into therapeutic recreation programming for individuals with severe handicaps. In G. Hitzhusen (Ed.), *Expanding horizons in therapeutic recreation,* Vol. XII (pp. 62–83). Columbia, MO: Curators University of Missouri.

———. (1986). Computerized assessment of preferences for persons with severe handicaps. *Journal of Applied Behavior Analysis, 19 ,* 445–448.

———. (1987). Computerized assessment of leisure preferences: A replication. *Education and Training in Mental Retardation, 22*(2), 128–133.

———. (1988). Assessing music preferences of persons with severe disabilities. *Therapeutic Recreation Journal, 21*(2), 12–23.

Dattilo, J., & Barnett, L. (1985). Therapeutic recreation for individuals with severe handicaps: Implications of chosen participation. *Therapeutic Recreation Journal, 19,* 79–91.

Dattilo, J., & Mirenda, P. (1987). An application of a leisure preference assessment protocol for persons with severe disabilities. *Journal of the Association for Persons with Severe Disabilities, 12,* 306–311.

Dattilo, J., & Murphy, W. (1991). *Leisure education programming: A systematic approach.* State College, PA: Venture.

Dyer, K. (1987). The competition of autistic stereotyped behavior with usual and specially assessed reinforcers. *Research in Developmental Disabilities, 8,* 607–626.

Ficker-Terrill, C., & Rowitz, L. (1991). Choices. *Mental Retardation, 29,* 63–65.

Flavell, J. (1973). Reduction of stereotypes by reinforcement of toy play. *Mental Retardation, 11,* 21–23.

Green, F., & Schleien, S. (1991). Understanding friendship and recreation: A theoretical sampling. *Therapeutic Recreation Journal, 25*(4), 29–40.

Houghton, J., Bronicki, G., & Guess, D. (1987). Opportunities to express preferences and make choices among students with severe disabilities in classroom settings. *Journal of the Association for Persons with Severe Handicaps, 12*(1), 18–27.

Kishi, G., Teelucksingh, B., Zollers, N., Park-Lee, S., & Meyer, L. (1988). Daily decision-making in community residences: A social comparison of adults with and without mental retardation. *American Journal on Mental Retardation, 92,* 430–435.

Knapczyk, D., & Peterson, N. (1975). Task analytic assessment of severe learning problems. *Education of Mentally Retarded, 10,* 74–77.

Knapczyk, D., & Yoppi, J. (1975). Development of cooperative and competitive play responses in developmentally disabled children. *American Journal on Mental Deficiency, 80,* 245–255.

Koegel, R., Dyer, K., & Bell, L. (1987). The influence of child-preferred activities on autistic children's social behavior. *Journal of Applied Behavior Analysis, 20,* 243–252.

Koegel, R., O'Dell, M., & Koegel, L. (1987). A natural language teaching paradigm for nonverbal autistic children. *Journal of Autism and Developmental Disorders, 17,* 187–200.

Lanagan, D., & Dattilo, J. (1989). The effects of a leisure education program on individuals with mental retardation. *Therapeutic Recreation Journal, 23*(4), 62–72.

Luckey, R., & Shapiro, I. (1974). Recreation: An essential aspect of habilitative programming. *Mental Retardation, 12,* 33–36.

McCall, R. (1974). *Exploratory manipulation and play in the human infant.* Monograph of Society for Research on Child Development. Chicago: University of Chicago Press.

Morris, R., & Dolker, M. (1974). Developing cooperative play in socially withdrawn retarded children. *Mental Retardation, 12,* 24–27.

Musselwhite, C. (1986). *Adaptive play for special needs children: Strategies to enhance communication and learning.* San Diego: College Hill.

Nietupski, J., Hamre-Nietupski, S., Green, K., Varnum-Teeter, K., Twedt, B., LePera, D., Scebold, K., & Hanrahan, M. (1986). Self-initiated and sustained leisure activity participation by students with moderate/severe handicaps. *Education and Training of the Mentally Retarded, 21,* 259–264.

Novak, A., & Heal, L. (Eds.). (1980). *Integration of developmentally disabled individuals into the community.* Baltimore: Paul H. Brookes.

Paloutzian, R., Hasazi, J., Streifel, J., & Edgard, C. (1971). Promotion of positive social interactions in severely retarded young children. *American Journal of Mental Deficiency, 75,* 519–524.

Parten, M. (1932). Social play among school children. *Journal of Abnormal Psychology, 28,* 136–147.

Parten, M., & Newhall, S. (1943). Social behavior of preschool children. In R. Barker, J. Kovnin, & H. Wright (Eds.), *Child behavior and development* (pp. 509–525). New York: McGraw-Hill.

Peck, C. (1985). Increasing opportunities for social control by children with autism and severe handicaps: Effects on student behavior and perceived classroom climate. *Journal of the Association for Persons with Severe Handicaps, 10,* 183–193.

President's Committee on Mental Retardation. (1974). *America's needs in habilitation and employment of the mentally retarded.* Washington, DC: U.S. Government Printing Office.

Reid, D., Willis, B., Jarman, P., & Brown, K. (1978). Increasing leisure activity of physically disabled retarded persons through modifying resource availability. *AAESPH Review, 3,* 78–93.

Rynders, J., & Schleien, S. (1988). Recreation: A promising vehicle for promoting the community integration of young adults with Down syndrome. In C. Tingey (Ed.), *Down syndrome: A resource handbook* (pp. 181–198). Boston: College Hill.

———. (1991). *Together successfully: Creating recreational and educational programs that integrate people with and without disabilities.* Arlington, TX: Association for Retarded Citizens—United States, National 4-H, and the Institute on Community Integration, University of Minnesota.

Rynders, J., Schleien, S., & Mustonen, T. (1990). Integrating children with severe disabilities for intensified outdoor education: Focus on feasibility. *Mental Retardation, 28*(1), 7–14.

Schleien, S. (1982). Leisure education for the learning disabled student. *Learning Disabilities, 1,* 105–122.

Schleien, S., Cameron, J., Rynders, J., & Slick, C. (1988). Acquisition and generalization of leisure skills from school to the home and community by learners with multihandicaps. *Therapeutic Recreation Journal, 22*(3), 53–71.

Schleien, S., Fahnestock, M., Green, F. & Rynders, J., (1990). Building positive social networks through environmental interventions in integrated recreation programs. *Therapeutic Recreation Journal, 24*(4), 42–52.

Schleien, S., Kiernan, J., & Wehman, P. (1981). Evaluation of an age-appropriate leisure skills program for moderately retarded adults. *Education and Training of the Mentally Retarded, 16,* 13–19.

Schleien, S., & Ray, M. (1988). *Community recreation and persons with disabilities: Strategies for integration.* Baltimore: Paul H. Brookes.

Schleien, S., Rynders, J., Mustonen, T., & Fox, A. (1990). Effects of social play activities on the play behavior of children with autism. *Journal of Leisure Research, 22,* 317–328.

Schleien, S., & Wehman, P. (1986), Severely handicapped children: Social skills development through leisure skills programming. In G. Cartledge, & J. F. Milburn (Eds.), *Teaching social skills to children: Innovative approaches* (pp. 219–245). Elmsford, NY: Pergamon Press.

Smith, R. (1985). Barriers are more than architectural. *Parks and Recreation, 20*(10), 58–62.

Strain, P. (1975). Increasing social play of severely retarded preschoolers through socio-dramatic activities. *Mental Retardation, 13,* 7–9.

Tilton, J., & Ottinger, D. (1964). Comparison of toy play behavior of autistic, retarded and normal children. *Psychological Reports, 15,* 967–975.

U.S. Department of Health and Human Services. (1979). *Plain talk about children with learning disabilities.* Rockville, MD: Alcohol, Drug Abuse, and Mental Health Administration.

Wacker, D., Wiggins, B., Fowler, M., & Berg, W. (1988). Training students with profound or multiple handicaps to make requests via microswitches. *Journal of Applied Behavior Analysis, 21,* 331–343.

Wehman, P. (1979). *Recreation programming for developmentally disabled persons.* Austin, TX: PRO-ED.

Wehman, P., & Schleien, S. (1981). *Leisure programs for handicapped persons: Adaptations, techniques, and curriculum.* Austin, TX: PRO-ED.

Wetherby, A., & Prutting, C. (1984). Profiles of communicative and cognitive-social abilities in autistic children. *Journal of Speech and Hearing Research, 27,* 364–377.

Whitman, T., Mercurio, J., & Caponigri, V. (1970). Development of social responses in severely retarded children. *Journal of Applied Behavioral Responses, 3,* 133–138.

Williams, W. (1975). Procedures of task analysis as related to developing instructional programs for the severely handicapped. In L. Brown, T. Crowner, W. Williams, & R. York (Eds.), *Madison alternative to zero exclusion: A book of readings.* Madison, WI: Madison Public Schools.

Wuerch, B., & Voeltz, L. (1982). *Longitudinal leisure skills for severely handicapped learners: The Ho'onanea curriculum component.* Baltimore: Paul H. Brookes.

Zigmond, N. (1978). A prototype of comprehensive service for secondary students with learning disabilities: A preliminary report. *Learning Disabilities Quarterly, 1,* 39–49.

Acknowledgment: This chapter was partially supported by Grant Project No. H029F90067, funded by the Office of Special Education and Rehabilitative Services, and Cooperative Agreement No. H133B80048, funded by the National Institute on Disability and Rehabilitation Research, both of the U.S. Department of Education. The opinions expressed herein do not necessarily reflect the opinions of the U.S. Department of Education, and no official endorsement should be inferred.

Chapter 9

Teaching the Adolescent: Social Skills Training Through Skillstreaming

ARNOLD P. GOLDSTEIN   ROBERT P. SPRAFKIN

N. JANE GERSHAW

Skillstreaming—a skills training approach developed for use with certain adolescent and other skill-deficient populations—is the focus of this chapter. We will present the nature of our target adolescent populations—who they are, how they are optimally identified and classified, and how they have been dealt with in treatment and skill-remediation efforts in the past. Skillstreaming will then be presented in detail; its history, specific procedures, target skills, and research evaluation outcomes will each be described. In all, the effort is to familiarize the reader with the substance of this approach, highlight its strengths and weaknesses and, in doing so, encourage both its further application and continued examination through research.

The Social Skill-Deficient Adolescent

Many diverse attempts have been undertaken to develop classification systems to adequately describe children and adolescents exhibiting behavior disorders. Prior to 1966, 24 such systems had been proposed (Group for the Advancement of Psychiatry, 1966). Unfortunately, most lacked evidence of sufficient reliability, as well as evidence that the system recommended the best types of remedial treatment. The Group's

(1966) classification system made some beginning strides at dealing with these chronic deficiencies. But a truly useful system of classifying behavior disorders (perhaps because of technological necessity) awaited the development of multivariate statistical techniques. By means of these techniques, investigators, in recent years, have been able to bring together and simultaneously draw on diverse types of information on a broad range of behaviorally disordered adolescents. Quay, Peterson, and their colleagues have used observational behavior ratings by teachers, parents, clinic staff, and correctional workers; case history materials—the responses of adolescents themselves to personality testing; and other types of information. All of it has been obtained from and about adolescents in public schools, child guidance clinics, institutions for delinquents, and mental hospitals. In the research of these investigators, as well as several others (Achenbach, 1966; Achenbach & Edelbrock, 1978; Hewitt & Jenkins, 1946; Patterson & Anderson, 1964; Peterson, Quay, & Tiffany, 1961; and Ross, Lacey, & Parton, 1965), a three-category classification pattern has consistently emerged. The three categories—aggression, withdrawal, and immaturity—account for the majority of behaviors typically included under the term *behavior disorders*.

Aggression

Quay (1966, p. 9) comments:

> Almost without exception multivariate statistical studies of problem behaviors . . . reveal the presence of a pattern involving aggressive behavior, both verbal and physical, associated with poor interpersonal relationships with both adults and peers. This pattern has received a variety of labels: e.g., unsocialized aggressive (Hewitt & Jenkins, 1946); conduct problem (Peterson et al., 1961; Quay & Quay, 1965); aggressive (Patterson & Anderson, 1964); unsocialized psychopath (Quay, 1964); psychopathic delinquency (Peterson, Quay, & Cameron, 1959); antisocial aggressiveness and sadistic aggressiveness (Dreger et al., 1964); and externalizing (Achenbach, 1966).

This classification reflects specific behaviors such as fighting, disruptiveness, destructiveness, profanity, irritability, quarrelsomeness, defiance of authority, irresponsibility, high levels of attention seeking and low levels of guilt feelings. In Quay's (1966) research, youngsters in this category typically answer affirmatively to such questionnaire items as (pp. 10–11):

> I do what I want to whether anybody likes it or not.
> The only way to settle anything is to lick the guy.
> If you don't have enough to live on, it's OK to steal.
> It's dumb to trust other people.
> I'm too tough a guy to get along with most kids.

Quay observes that the essence of this pattern is an active antisocial aggressiveness almost inevitably resulting in conflict with parents, peers, and social institutions. Children and adolescents in this pattern seem likely to be in enough difficulty to be involved with the courts and institutions for delinquents.

Withdrawal

Other researchers also have consistently identified a behavior disorder pattern characterized by withdrawal and variously labeled it as *overinhibited* (Hewitt & Jenkins, 1946), *personality problem* (Peterson et al., 1961), *disturbed neurotic* (Quay, 1964), *internalizing* (Achenbach, 1966), and *withdrawn* (Patterson & Anderson, 1964; Ross et al., 1965). Quay (1966, p. 11) describes this pattern further:

> These behaviors, attitudes, and feelings clearly involve a different pattern of social interaction than do those comprising conduct disorder; they generally imply withdrawal instead of attack. In marked contrast to the characteristics of conduct disorder are such traits as feelings of distress, fear, anxiety, physical complaints, and open and expressed unhappiness. It is within this pattern that the child who is clinically labeled as an anxiety neurotic or as phobic will be found.

As the studies demonstrate, the behavior disorder pattern characterized centrally by withdrawal is also marked by depression, feelings of inferiority, self-consciousness, shyness, anxiety, hypersensitivity, seclusiveness, and timidity.

Immaturity

Immaturity frequently has emerged as a third prominent class of adolescent behavior disorder. It has been identified in samples of adolescents studied in public schools, child guidance clinics, and institutions for delinquents. Behaviors forming a significant component of the immaturity pattern include short attention span, clumsiness, preference for younger playmates, passivity, daydreaming, and incompetence. As Quay notes, this pattern represents a persistence of behaviors that largely were age appropriate earlier in the youngster's development, but that have become inappropriate in view of the chronological age of the adolescent and society's expectations of her or him.

Quay's (1966) reflections on the three patterns of behavior disorders most relevant to the skill deficiency focus are:

> The characteristics of the three . . . patterns may all be said to be clearly maladaptive either from the social or individual viewpoint. Extremes of such behaviors are at variance with either the expectations of self, parents, or educational and other social institutions. . . . Each of the previous patterns also involves interpersonal alienation with peers, attack in the case of conduct disorders, withdrawal in the case of personality disorder, or lack of engagement in the case of immaturity (pp. 13–14).

In describing the aggressive, withdrawn, or immature adolescent, we have focused on what each youngster is and does. But it is profitable from a skill-deficiency viewpoint to examine what each such youngster is not and does not do as well. Thus, the aggressive adolescent often is not only proficient in fighting, disruptiveness, destructiveness, and similar antisocial skills; he or she also is deficient in prosocial skills such as self-control, negotiating, asking permission, avoiding trouble with others, understanding feelings of others, and dealing with someone else's anger. The withdrawn youngster lacks proficiency in prosocial skills, such as having a conversation, joining in, dealing with fear, decision making, dealing with being left out, responding to persuasion, and dealing with contradictory messages, as well as expressing or receiving apologies, complaints, or instructions. The immature adolescent typically lacks competence in sharing, responding to teasing, responding to failure, dealing with group pressure, goal setting, and concentration. The prosocial skills enumerated here are a brief sampling of the skill-training targets that are Skillstreaming's major focus.

Developmental Hurdles

It is our belief that a treatment oriented toward explicit teaching of prosocial skills can be an optimal approach for the three types of behavior-disordered adolescents. Desirable, functional skills missing from their behavioral repertoires can be taught successfully. However, it is not only the aggressive, withdrawn, or immature youngster with whom we are concerned. Many other adolescents (those less likely to come to the attention of school, clinic, or institution personnel) are appropriate potential targets for skill-training efforts.

Manaster (1977), in his book *Adolescent Development and the Life Tasks*, describes the sequence of life tasks all adolescents must successfully master. In school, at work, in the community, and with peers, family, and authority figures, the developing adolescent meets and must cope with a wide and increasingly complex series of personal and interpersonal life tasks. In the realm of love, sex, and peer relationships, the skills demanded may include social skills (having a conversation, listening, joining in), skills for dealing with feelings (coping with fear, expressing affection, understanding the feelings of others), and skills useful for dealing with stress (coping with embarrassment, preparing for a stressful conversation, responding to failure).

School-related tasks demand proficiency at other skills, including planning (goal setting, gathering information, decision making). School settings also require daily success at tasks involving both peers (e.g., dealing with group pressure) and authority figures (e.g., following instructions). The work setting similarly is multifaceted in its task demands and, hence, in its requisite skills—planning and stress management competencies in particular. For many youngsters, whether in school, at work, or elsewhere, the skill demands placed on them frequently involve the ability to deal satisfactorily with aggression—either their own or someone else's. In these instances, skills to be mastered include self-control, negotiating, and dealing with group pressure.

The developmental sequences involved are rarely smooth, and efforts to aid their progression are a worthy goal. It is in this sense that the clinically "normal" adolescent who needs assistance over certain developmental hurdles is also a potential target for Skillstreaming.

Treatment Approaches

This section examines of the diverse treatment approaches in use for skill-deficient adolescents, placing the heaviest emphasis on efforts to remediate the aggressive youngster without slighting the withdrawn, the immature, or the normal adolescent. Techniques applied to these latter youngsters, and the effectiveness of these techniques, will be specifically examined. But in terms of its impact on society, altering the overt behavior of aggressive adolescents and reorienting it in more prosocial directions are goals of prime importance—and, thus, clearly deserve special attention.

A Prescriptive Viewpoint: What Works for Whom?

Diverse approaches exist for the training, treatment, and rehabilitation of aggressive, withdrawn, immature, and other seriously skill-deficient youngsters. These include:

- Putatively correctional, rehabilitative procedures such as incarceration and probation;
- Traditional types of individual and group psychotherapy;
- Less psychodynamic group-oriented approaches, such as positive peer culture or guided group interaction procedures;
- Newer behavioral techniques, mostly centering around efforts to alter overt maladaptive or antisocial behavior by the management of reinforcement contingencies; and
- Very recent psychoeducational therapies in which the treatment goal is usually to increase the adolescent's proficiency in prosocial skills and, by implication, decrease reliance on antisocial behaviors.

Each of these approaches has its proponents and opponents; for each there are testimonials, critics, and, in some instances, research supporting its value.

One view of these procedures is prescriptive: None of them may be viewed as good or bad or effective or ineffective in any absolute sense. Consider the recent history of psychotherapy. In the 1950s, when research on the effectiveness of psychotherapy was just beginning, investigators asked: "Does treatment A work?" "Is treatment A better than treatment B?" Answers to such questions, even when positive, proved nearly useless. Little or no information was provided about either how to improve the effectiveness of the particular treatment (because it was studied as a whole, with no attention to its separate components) or how to use the research findings to help any individual person (because only group effects were studied).

In response, clinicians and researchers now ask a new, more differential type of question: "Which type of patient, meeting with which type of therapist, for which type of treatment, will yield which outcome?" This customized, differential, or prescriptive view of the intervention:

- Avoids assigning of all types of patients to any given treatment;
- Acknowledges that a given psychotherapist or counselor may be therapeutic for one type of patient but may not be helpful or even could be psychonoxious for another; and
- Counteracts the patient, therapist, and treatment uniformity myths.

Above all, this view leads to positive efforts to match patients, therapists, and treatments to maximize the likelihood of a beneficial outcome. The prescriptive viewpoint is elaborated in considerable detail elsewhere (Goldstein, 1978; Goldstein & Stein, 1976).

In 1974, Martinson published an article titled "What Works?"—a review of efforts to alter the deviant behavior of juvenile offenders. His conclusion was unequivocal: "With few and isolated exceptions, the rehabilitative efforts that have been reported so far have had no appreciable effect on recidivism" (p. 25). However, Palmer (1976) shows that this singularly negative conclusion rests on Martinson's reliance on what is called the "one-true-light-assumption" (Goldstein & Stein, 1976). This assumption, the antithesis of a prescriptive viewpoint, holds that specific treatments are sufficiently powerful to override substantial individual differences and to aid heterogeneous groups of patients. Research in all fields of psychotherapy shows the one-true-light-assumption to be erroneous (Goldstein, 1978; Goldstein & Stein, 1976); and Palmer (1976) has shown it to be especially in error with regard to aggressive and delinquent adolescents.

Palmer returned to the data Martinson had examined and drawn his "nothing works" conclusion. In dozens of the studies, there were homogeneous subsamples of adolescents for whom the given interventions did work. Martinson's error was not responding to the fact that, when homogeneous subsamples are combined to form a heterogeneously composed full sample, positive, negative, and no-change treatment outcome effects of different subsamples cancel one another out. This makes the full sample appear no different in average change than an untreated control group. But (to repeat) when smaller, more homogeneous subsamples are examined separately, many treatments work. The task then, is not to continue futile pursuit of the one true light, the one intervention that works for all, but to discern which treatments, administered by which people, work for whom, and for whom they do not work.[1]

Incarceration

It is one thing to espouse a prescriptive clinical strategy for disturbed and disturbing adolescents, but quite another to implement such a strategy. The state of prescriptive

---

[1]The reader involved in elementary or secondary education will find the reasoning here to be familiar: what we have described as a growing orientation toward prescriptiveness in the practice and investigation of psychotherapy parallels a similar movement in the field of education. The work of Cronback and Snow (1977) on aptitude treatment interactions, Hunt's (1961) behavior–person–environment matching model, and Klausmeier, Rossmiller, and Saily's (1977) individually guided education are only three of several examples of growing attention to a prescriptive intervention strategy in educational theory and practice.

knowledge is primitive. Most investigators and correctional practitioners, for example, view incarceration as the least desirable alternative for juvenile offenders. "Locking them up" as a correctional treatment is seen to often lead to more, not less, eventual antisocial behavior. Yet, in almost every instance, holders of this anti-incarceration viewpoint acknowledge, directly or by implication, that there is a yet-to-be-specified subsample of offenders, probably characterized by a high prior rate of recidivism, for whom incarceration may well be the optimal intervention (Achenbach, 1974; Bailey, 1966; Empey, 1969; Kassenbaum, Ward, & Wilner, 1972; McClintock, 1961; Robinson & Smith, 1976).

Probation

Probation, too, has its champions as a differentially offered treatment. Evidence exists that probation may be an appropriate intervention for adolescent offenders who are neurotic (Empey, 1969); who display a reasonable level of prosocial behavior (Garrity, 1956) or social maturity (Sealy & Banks, 1971); or who are, in interpersonal (I-level) maturity terminology, Cultural Conformists (California Department of the Youth Authority, 1967). However, probation may well be a considerably less-than-optimal prescription when the youth is nonneurotic (Empey, 1969), manipulative (Garrity, 1956), or low in social maturity (Sealy & Banks, 1971).

Individual Psychotherapy

A clearly analogous differential position may be taken regarding the appropriateness of other treatment interventions for certain types of disturbed and disturbing adolescents. Individual psychotherapy, for example, has been shown to be effective with highly anxious adolescents (Adams, 1962); the socially withdrawn (Stein & Bogin, 1978); those displaying, at most, a moderate level of psychopathic behavior (Carney, 1966; Craft, Stephenson, & Granger, 1964); and youngsters displaying a set of characteristics summarized by Adams (1961) as "amenable." More blatantly psychopathic youngsters, low-anxious youngsters, or those "nonamenable" in Adam's (1961) terms, are viewed as prescriptively poor candidates for individual psychotherapy interventions.

Group Approaches

Many group approaches have been developed in attempts to aid aggressive, withdrawn, or immature adolescents. Some of the more popular have been activity group therapy (Slavson, 1964), guided group interaction (McCorkle, Elias, & Bixby, 1958), and positive peer culture (Vorrath & Brendtro, 1974). Research evidence demonstrates that such approaches are, indeed, useful for older, more sociable and person-oriented adolescents (Knight, 1969); those who tend to accept confrontations (Warren, 1972); and the more neurotic-conflicted (Harrison & Mueller, 1964), or acting-out neurotic (California Department of the Youth Authority, 1967). Youngsters who are younger, less sociable, or more delinquent (Knight, 1969), who avoid confrontations (Warren, 1972) or are psychopathic (Craft, 1964) are less likely to benefit from group interventions.

Behavior Modification

In recent years, a host of therapeutic procedures have been developed and proffered under the rubric *behavior modification*. Although withdrawn (O'Connor, 1972) and immature (Stumphauser, 1972) youngsters have been the recipients of some of these efforts, much research has focused on the aggressive, oppositional, or delinquent adolescent (Bernal, Duryec, Pruett, & Burns, 1968; Braukmann and Fixsen, 1976; Drabman, Spitalnik, & O'Leary, 1973; Patterson & Reid, 1973; Stumphauser, 1972; Wahler, 1969). As Braukmann and Fixsen (1976) note, the most effective behavior modification programs typically include (1) a teaching component (e.g., modeling, shaping) designed to add the desired behavior to the adolescent's repertoire, (2) an incentive component (e.g., token economy, behavioral contract) to motivate her or him, and (3) the actual delivery of reinforcement contingent on performance of the desired behavior. Dozens of specific techniques incorporate one or more of these components. Even though behavior modification has been the focus of much more experimental scrutiny than any other orientation, a great deal of evaluative research still must be done before the effectiveness of such interventions is firmly established. The outcomes of this research are more likely to be positive if the treatments are conceived, implemented, and evaluated prescriptively.

Summary

As shown in this brief prescriptive view, there is an array of interventions currently in use for adolescents—incarceration, probation, individual and group psychotherapy, other group approaches, and a number of behavior modification efforts. Bailey (1966), Martinson (1974), Vinter and Janowitz (1959), Kassenbaum et al. (1972), and others who have similarly reviewed the (especially aggressive) adolescent research literature and concluded, in essence, that "nothing works," are, in our view, simply wrong. They have succumbed to the joint influence of the one-true-light-assumption and the patient uniformity myth. It is not correct that "nothing works." Almost everything works but, in each instance, only for certain youngsters. To be sure, prescriptive sophistication for the treatment of adolescents is merely beginning. The few characteristics that can be pointed to in connection with each treatment clearly show the rudimentary level of prescriptive matching now possible. But it is, indeed, a beginning. The task is to develop and continuously refine treatment offerings, and to engage in research that enables us to make better matches of treaters, youngsters, and intervention approaches. Other books have considered how such research is optimally planned, executed, and evaluated (see Goldstein, 1978; and Goldstein & Stein, 1976).

The remainder of this chapter presents one prescriptive approach, Skillstreaming. It is a psychoeducational intervention specifically designed to enhance the prosocial, interpersonal, stress management, and planning skills of the aggressive, withdrawn, immature, and "normal" but developmentally lagging adolescent—all of whom are, by definition, skill deficient.

What Is Skillstreaming?

Skillstreaming[2] consists of four components—modeling, role-playing, feedback, and transfer training—each of which is a well-established behavioral change procedure. *Modeling* refers to providing small groups of trainees with a demonstration of the skill behaviors they are to learn. If the skill to be learned were negotiating, we would present youngsters with vivid, live, audiotaped, videotaped, or filmed displays (geared to maximize attention and motivation to learn) of adolescents who use the skill effectively. In the display, the skill of negotiating would be broken down into a series of behavioral steps, and each example presented or modeled would illustrate the use of the steps. Trainees would see and hear the models negotiating successfully in a variety of relevant settings: at home, at school, and with peer groups.

The next step is *role-playing*—behavioral rehearsal or practice for eventual real-life use of the skill. Individuals in the group are asked to think about times in their lives when they would benefit from using the behavior they have just seen modeled or demonstrated. In turn, each youth is given the opportunity to practice using steps that make up the skill as he or she might eventually use them in real life. Other group members, as well as the trainers, simulate the real-life situation. The teenager who wishes to practice negotiation with a friend about where to go after school might role-play the scene with another group member acting out the part of the friend.

Feedback, the third component in Skillstreaming, refers to giving the youngster an evaluation of the role-play rehearsal. Following each role-play, group members and trainers provide the role player with praise (and sometimes material rewards) as her or his behavior becomes more and more like that of the model. During this part of the group session, adolescents are given corrective instruction, which enables them to continue to improve their skill use.

The last element in Skillstreaming is *transfer of training*. Various methods are used to encourage transfer of the newly learned behaviors from the training setting to the real-life situation. Homework assignments, use of real or imaginary props to make role-playing realistic, and repeating role-play of a scene even after it is learned well (overlearning) are some of Skillstreaming's transfer-enhancing procedures. Goldstein and Kanfer (1979) describe additional means of training transfer. This is the most important, and often most difficult, aspect of Skillstreaming. If the newly learned behavior does not carry over to the real-life environment, a lasting and meaningful change in the youngster's behavior is unlikely to occur.

---

[2]A further examination of the background and content of this approach appears in Goldstein, Sprafkin, Gershaw, and Klein (1980). This source also contains a detailed presentation of Skillstreaming skills taught to adolescents and forms (Checklist, Grouping Chart, Homework) used to select and group trainees, as well as to record their skill-acquisition progress.

Organizing the Skillstreaming Group

Selecting Participants

Each Skillstreaming group should consist of adolescents clearly deficient in whatever skills are going to be taught. If possible, they also should be grouped according to the degree of their deficiency in the skill. Trainees who lack certain common clusters of behaviors, as assessed by the Skillstreaming Checklist, can be selected. Defining which skills to work on is the behavioral objective for those in the class. The optimal group size for effective Skillstreaming sessions is five to eight trainees plus two trainers.[3] Members need not be from the same class or even the same grade. However, because behavioral rehearsal or role-playing is most beneficial when it is as realistic as possible, it is useful to include adolescents whose social worlds (family, school, peer groups) have some elements of similarity.

There are times when it will not be possible to group according to shared skill deficits. Instead, the trainer may want to use naturally occurring units such as school classes, residential cottages, and so on. If the instructor decides to use these units, members will probably reflect a range of skill strengths and weaknesses. In this case, it will be helpful to fill out a skill checklist for each trainee to obtain a group profile. Starting skills should be those in which many show a deficiency. In such a potentially diverse group, one or two members may be proficient in the use of whatever behavior is taught on a given day. These more skillful youngsters can be used in helper roles such as co-actors or providers of useful feedback.

Number, Length, and Spacing of Sessions

The Skillstreaming modeling displays and associated procedures typically constitute a training program, which can be broken into segments matching part or all of the semesters of the school or other setting. Ideally, training should occur one or two times each week. Spacing is crucial. Most trainees learn well in the training setting. However, most fail to transfer this learning to where it counts—at home, in school, with friends, and in the community. To provide ample opportunity for students to try out in real life what they have learned in training, there must be ample time and opportunity for skill use between sessions.

Typically, each training session should focus on learning one skill. It needs to include one sequence of modeling, several role-plays, feedback, and assignment of homework. Each session should be scheduled for an hour. Actual length of session can be determined by a number of factors such as attention span, impulsivity, and

---

[3]We recognize that most schools' classes are much larger than is desirable for a Skillstreaming class. Often it is possible for two or more teachers to combine their classes for a period or two and have one teacher take the larger group while a smaller group of five to eight students participates in Skillstreaming. Goldstein et al. (1980) describe other means for organizing Skillstreaming groups in regular classes.

verbal ability. If most trainees in the group show particularly brief attention spans, the session can be as brief as 20 minutes (in such cases, more frequent sessions are advisable). Sessions longer than an hour are possible for trainees whose capacity for sustained attention is greater. Because Skillstreaming is intensive, a limit of one-and-one-half hours is recommended; learning efficiency tends to diminish beyond that length of time.

Trainer Preparation

The role-playing and feedback activities that make up most of each Skillstreaming session are a series of "action-reaction" sequences in which effective skill behaviors are first rehearsed (role-play) and then critiqued (feedback). As such, the instructor must both lead and observe. We have found that one trainer is hard pressed to do both of these tasks well at the same time; thus, we recommend strongly that each session be led by a team of two trainers.

Two types of skills appear necessary for successful Skillstreaming leadership. The first might best be described as *general trainer skills*—those requisite for success in almost any training or teaching effort. These include:

1. Oral communication and listening skills;
2. Flexibility and resourcefulness;
3. Enthusiasm;
4. Ability to work under pressure;
5. Interpersonal sensitivity; and
6. Broad knowledge of human behavior, adolescent development, and so on.

The second type is *specific trainer skills*—those germane to Skillstreaming in particular. These include:

1. Knowledge of Skillstreaming—its background, procedures, and goals;
2. Ability to orient both trainees and supporting staff to Skillstreaming;
3. Ability to initiate and sustain role playing;
4. Ability to present material in concrete, behavioral form;
5. Ability to deal with management problems effectively; and
6. Sensitivity in providing corrective feedback.

For both selection and development purposes, potential trainers should first participate in a series of Skillstreaming sessions led by two experienced trainers. After this experience, each beginner can co-lead a series of sessions with someone more experienced. In this way, potential instructors can be given several opportunities to practice what they have seen and also receive feedback about their performance. In effect, the Skillstreaming procedures of modeling, role-playing, and feedback are recommended to train Skillstreaming techniques appropriately.

Skillstreaming Sessions

Setting

The rule of identical elements is a major principle for encouraging transfer from the classroom or clinical situation to the real-life setting. This rule states that the more similar or identical the two settings (the greater number of physical and interpersonal qualities shared by them), the greater the transfer from one setting to the other. Skillstreaming should be conducted in the same general setting as the real-life environment of most participating youngsters and the training setting should be furnished to resemble or simulate the likely application settings. In a typical classroom, one can accomplish this, in part, through creative use of available furniture and supplies. Should a couch be needed for a role-play, several chairs can be pushed together to simulate the couch. Should a television set be an important part of the role-play, a box, a chair, or a drawing on the chalkboard can, in imagination, approximate the real object. If actual props are available (TV set, store counter, living room furniture), they certainly should be used in the role-play scenes.

A horseshoe seating arrangement is one good example of how furniture might be arranged in the training room. Participating trainees sit at desks or tables so that some writing space is provided. Role-playing takes place in the front of the room. Behind and to the side of one of the role-players should be a chalkboard displaying the behavioral steps of the skill being worked with at that time. In this way, the role-player can glance up at the steps during the role-play. If film strips or other visual modeling displays are used, the screen should be easily visible to all.

Premeeting Preparation of Trainees

Individual preparation of trainees may be helpful prior to the first meeting of the Skillstreaming class. This orientation, or structuring, should be tailored to the individual needs and maturity level of each person. It should be designed to provide each member with heightened motivation to attend to and participate in the group, as well as with accurate expectations of what the group activities will be like. Methods of preparation might include:

1. Mentioning what the purposes of the group will be, as they relate to the specific skill deficits of the youngster; for example, the trainer might say, "Remember when you got into a fight with Billy, and you wound up restricted for a week? Well, in this class you'll be able to learn how to stay out of that kind of trouble so you don't get restricted."

2. Mentioning briefly and generally what procedures will be used. The trainee must have an accurate picture of what to expect and not feel as if he or she has been tricked. The trainer might say, "To learn to handle (these kinds of) situations better, we're going to see and hear some examples of how different kids do it well, and then actually take turns trying some of these ways right here. Then we'll let you know how you did, and you'll have a chance to practice them on your own."

3. Mentioning the benefits to be gained from participation, stating that the group will help the trainee work on particular relevant issues such as getting along in school, at home, and with peers.

4. Mentioning the tangible or token (points, credits, etc.) rewards that trainees will receive for participation.

5. Using the trainer–trainee relationship to promote cooperation; for example, the instructor might ask the youngster to "Give it a try. I think you'll get something out of it."

6. Presenting the Skillstreaming class as a new part of the curriculum in which the student is expected to participate. Trainees also should understand that the group is not compulsory and that confidentiality will be respected. A verbal commitment from the youngster to "give it a try" is useful at this point.

7. Mentioning the particular skills the student is likely to identify as his or her major perceived deficiency, and how progress might be made on such skills.

Opening Session

The opening session is designed to create trainee interest in the group as well as to educate the members about Skillstreaming procedures. The trainers open the session by first introducing themselves and having each trainee do likewise. A brief familiarization period or warm-up follows, with the goal of helping the students become comfortable interacting with the instructors and with others in the group. Content for this initial phase should be interesting and nonthreatening. Next, trainers introduce the Skillstreaming program by providing trainees with a brief description of what skill training is about. Typically, this introduction covers topics such as the importance of interpersonal skills for effective and satisfying living, examples of behaviors that will be taught, and how these can be useful to trainees in their everyday lives. It is often helpful to expand on this discussion of practical skill use to emphasize the importance of the undertaking and its personal relevance to the participants. The specific training procedures (modeling, role-playing) are then described at a level the group can easily understand.

New trainers should note that, although this overview is intended to acquaint trainees with Skillstreaming procedures, frequently they will not grasp the concepts until they actually get involved in the training process. Because of this, we do not advise that instructors spend a great deal of time describing the procedures. Instead, talk about them briefly, as an introduction, with the expectation that students will experience and understand the training process more fully once they have actually started.

Modeling

As the first step, the trainer describes the skill to be taught and hands out cards (Skill Cards) on which the name of the skill and its behavioral steps are printed. The first live modeling display is then enacted. Trainees are told to watch and listen closely to the way the actors in each vignette portray the behavioral steps. The skills taught by Skillstreaming are listed in Table 9-1.

Modeling displays should begin with a narrator setting the scene and stating the name of the skill and its behavioral steps. The trainers then portray a series of vignettes in which each step is clearly enacted in sequence. Content should be varied and relevant to the lives of the trainees. See Goldstein, Sprafkin, and Gershaw (1976) for characteristics of modeling displays that usually enhance or diminish the degree of learning. Model characteristics are also discussed in Chapter 3.

Examples of Skillstreaming skills for adolescents, and the behavioral steps that constitute each skill, include those on the next page.

TABLE 9-1   Structured Learning Skills for Adolescents

Group I. Beginning Social Skills
1. Listening
2. Starting a conversation
3. Having a conversation
4. Asking a question
5. Saying thank you
6. Introducing yourself
7. Introducing other people
8. Giving a compliment

Group II. Advanced Social Skills
9. Asking for help
10. Joining in
11. Giving instructions
12. Following instructions
13. Apologizing
14. Convincing others

Group III. Skills for Dealing with Feelings
15. Knowing your feelings
16. Expressing your feelings
17. Understanding the feelings of others
18. Dealing with someone else's anger
19. Expressing affection
20. Dealing with fear
21. Rewarding yourself

Group IV. Skill Alternatives to Aggression
22. Asking permission
23. Sharing something
24. Helping others
25. Negotiating
26. Using self-control
27. Standing up for your rights
28. Responding to teasing
29. Avoiding trouble with others
30. Keeping out of fights

Group V. Skills for Dealing with Stress
31. Making a complaint
32. Answering a complaint
33. Sportsmanship after the game
34. Dealing with embarrassment
35. Dealing with being left out
36. Standing up for a friend
37. Responding to persuasion
38. Responding to failure
39. Dealing with contradictory messages
40. Dealing with an accusation
41. Getting ready for a difficult conversation
42. Dealing with group pressure

Group VI. Planning Skills
43. Deciding on something to do
44. Deciding what caused a problem
45. Setting a goal
46. Deciding on your abilities
47. Gathering information
48. Arranging problems by importance
49. Making a decision
50. Concentrating on a task

1. Starting a conversation:
  - Greet the other person.
  - Make small talk.
  - Decide if the other person is listening.
  - Bring up the main topic.

2. Giving instructions:
  - Decide what needs to be done.
  - Think about the different people who could do it and choose one.
  - Ask that person to do what you want done.
  - Ask the other person if he or she understands what to do. Change or repeat your instructions if necessary.

3. Understanding the feelings of others:
  - Watch the other person.
  - Listen to what he or she is saying.
  - Figure out what the other person might be feeling.
  - Think about ways to show you understand what he or she is feeling.
  - Decide on the best way and do it.

4. Negotiation:
  - Decide if you and the other person are having a difference of opinion.
  - Tell the other person what you think about the problem.
  - Ask the other person what he or she thinks about the problem.
  - Listen openly to his or her answer.
  - Think about why the other person might feel this way.
  - Suggest a compromise.

Role-Playing

The trainer should direct discussion next toward helping trainees relate the modeled skill to their own lives. Invite comments on the behavioral steps and how these steps might be useful in the real-life situations students encounter. Focus on specific current and future skill use by trainees rather than only on general issues involving the skill.

It is important to remember that Skillstreaming role-play is viewed as behavioral rehearsal or practice for future use of the skill. Trainers should be aware that role-playing past events that have little relevance for future situations is of limited value to trainees. However, discussion of past events involving skill use can stimulate students to think of times when a similar situation might occur in the future. In such a case, the hypothetical future situation rather than the past event should be role-played.

Once a trainee has described a situation in his or her life in which the skill might be helpful, that person is designated the main actor. He or she chooses a second student (co-actor) to play the role of the significant person (e.g., mother, peer) relevant to the skill problem in his or her life. The trainee should be urged to pick someone who resembles the real-life person as a co-actor in as many ways as possible. The trainer then elicits any additional information—a description of the physical setting, the events immediately preceding the role-play, or the co-actor's mood or manner—needed to set the stage for role-playing from the main actor.

It is crucial that the main actor enact the behavioral steps modeled. The trainer should go over each step as it applies to the role-play situation prior to the start of any actual role-play, to aid the primary actor in making a successful effort. The main actor is told to refer to the skill card on which the behavioral steps are printed. (As noted previously, the steps also should be written on a chalkboard visible to the actors during role-play.) The trainer then reminds all the participants of their roles: the main actor is told to follow the behavioral steps; the co-actor, to stay in the role of the other person; and the observers, to watch carefully for enactment of the steps. For the first several role-plays, it is helpful to coach observers about the kinds of cues to watch for—such as posture, tone of voice, and content of speech. This also sets a positive example for feedback from the observers.

Next, the trainer instructs the role-players to begin. It is the instructor's responsibility, at this point, to provide the main actor with any help or coaching needed to keep the role-play going according to the behavioral steps. The trainer urges those who "break role" and begin to explain or make comments to get back into role and explain later. If the role-play clearly is going astray from the behavioral steps, the trainer may stop the scene, provide needed instruction, and begin again. One instructor should be positioned near the chalkboard and point to each behavioral step, in turn, as the role-play unfolds, to help the main actor (as well as the other trainees) follow each step in order.

The role-playing should continue until all group members have had an opportunity to participate (in either role) and preferably until all have had a chance to be the primary actor. Sometimes this will require two or three sessions for a given skill; it is suggested that each session begin with two or three modeling vignettes for the skill, even if it is not new to the group. It is important to note that, while the framework (behavioral steps) of each role-play in the series remains the same, the actual content can and should change from vignette to vignette. The problem as it actually occurs, or could occur, in each youngster's real life should be the content of that person's role-play. When completed, each trainee will thus be better armed to act appropriately in a real situation requiring social skill use.

A few more procedures will increase the effectiveness of role-playing. Role reversal is often useful. A trainee role-playing a skill may have a difficult time perceiving his or her co-actor's viewpoint, and vice versa. Have them exchange roles and resume the role-play. The trainer also can assume the co-actor role, to expose youngsters to types of reactions not otherwise role-played during the session. (It is here that trainers' flexibility and creativity are essential.) For example, it may be crucial to have a difficult adult role realistically portrayed. This may be particularly helpful when dealing with less verbal or more hesitant trainees.

Feedback

A brief feedback period should follow each role-play. This helps the main actor find out how well he or she followed the behavioral steps and explore the psychological impact of his or her enactment on the co-actor. It also provides encouragement to try out the role-play behaviors in real life. The trainer should ask the primary actor to wait until he or she has heard everyone's comments before talking. The instructor asks the co-actor about his or her reactions first, then asks observers to comment on the behavioral steps and other aspects of the role-play. The trainers should comment in particular on how well the steps were followed and provide social reinforcement (praise, approval, encouragement) for close adherence. For effective reinforcement, use the guidelines listed in Table 9-2.

After the main actor hears all the feedback, the trainer invites him or her to make comments on the role-play and the comments of others. In this way, he or she can learn to evaluate the effectiveness of his or her skill enactment in light of evidence from others about its success or lack of success.

In all aspects of feedback, it is crucial that the instructors maintain the behavioral focus of Skillstreaming. Trainer comments must point to the presence or absence of specific, concrete behaviors, not take the form of general evaluative comments or broad generalities. Feedback, of course, may be positive or negative. Negative comments always should be followed by a constructive comment as to how a particular fault might be improved. At minimum, a "poor" performance (major departures from the behavioral steps) can be praised as "a good try" at the same time it is being criticized. Trainees should be given the opportunity to role-play the same behavioral steps again after receiving corrective feedback. At times, as a further feedback procedure, entire role-plays can be audiotaped or videotaped. Observing themselves on tape can be an effective aid to students' learning, enabling them to reflect on their behavior.

Because a primary goal of Skillstreaming is skill flexibility, role-play enactment

TABLE 9-2 Guidelines for Positive Reinforcement

1. Provide reinforcement at the earliest appropriate opportunity after role-plays that follow the behavioral steps.

2. Always provide reinforcement to the co-actor for being helpful, cooperative, and the like.

3. Provide reinforcement only after role-plays that follow the behavioral steps.

4. Vary the specific content of reinforcements offered; that is, praise particular aspects of the performance such as tone of voice, posture, or phrasing.

5. Provide enough role-play activity so that each group member has sufficient opportunity to be reinforced.

6. Provide reinforcement in an amount consistent with the quality of the specific role-play.

7. Provide no reinforcement when the role-play departs significantly from the behavioral steps (except praise for "trying" in the first session or two).

8. Provide reinforcement for an individual student's improvement over her or his previous performance.

that departs markedly from the behavioral steps may not be "wrong." That is, a different approach to the skill may in fact work in some situations. Trainers should stress that they are trying to teach effective alternatives, and that the students would do well to have the steps available to use when appropriate. After all role-play and discussion is complete, the instructors may enact one additional modeling vignette or replay portions of the modeling tape. This step summarizes the session and leaves trainees with a final review of the behavioral steps.

Transfer of Training

Several aspects of the training sessions are designed to augment the likelihood that learning in this setting will transfer to the youngster's real-life environment. However, even more forthright steps need to be taken to maximize transfer. When possible, use a homework technique that has been successful with most groups: Tell them first how important this transfer aspect is (the most important step of all) and instruct them how best to implement it. Trainees should be instructed to try, in their own life, the behaviors they have practiced during the session. The name of the person(s) with whom they will try it, the day, the place, and so on, are all discussed. The student is urged to take notes about his or her first transfer attempt on the Homework Report form provided by the trainers. This form requests detailed information about what happened—how well he or she followed the relevant behavioral steps, the trainee's evaluation of his or her performance, and thoughts about what the next assignment might appropriately be.

It is often useful to start with relatively simple homework behaviors and, as mastery is achieved, work up to more complex and demanding assignments. Make a first homework assignment something that can be done close by; that is, in the school, community center, or wherever the class is meeting. It may then be possible to forewarn and prepare the person(s) with whom the youngster is planning to try out the new skill to ensure a positive outcome. For example, a trainee's homework assignment might be to ask the gym teacher a particular question. The trainer might tell the gym teacher to expect the student's question so that she or he is prepared to answer in a positive way. However, breach of confidentiality can damage a teenager's trust in the trainer. If persons outside the group are to be informed of specific training activities, students should be told this, and their permission should be asked early in the group's life.

Experiences of success at beginning homework attempts are crucial to encourage the trainee to make further attempts at real-life skill use. The first part of each session is devoted to presenting and discussing these homework reports. When students make an effort to complete their assignments, the instructors should provide social reinforcement—praise, approval, encouragement. Trainers should meet trainee's failure to do their homework with some chagrin and expressed disappointment. It cannot be stressed too strongly that without these, or similar attempts to maximize transfer, the value of the entire training effort is in severe jeopardy.

External Support and Self-reward

Of the principles of transfer training for which research evidence exists, performance feedback is clearly most consequential. A youngster can learn very well in the training setting and do all his or her transfer homework, and yet the program can be a performance failure. "Learning" concerns the question: Can they do it? "Performance" is a matter of: Will they do it? Students will perform as trained if—and only if—there is some "payoff" for doing so. Stated simply, new behaviors persist if they are rewarded, but diminish if they are ignored or actively challenged.

Several supplemental programs outside the Skillstreaming training setting can help give the rewards or reinforcements trainees need to maintain their new behaviors. These programs provide for both external social reward (from people in the trainee's real life) and self-reward (from the student herself or himself).

Environmental or external support can be actively identified and developed by holding orientation meetings for school staff and for relatives and friends of youngsters—that is, the real-life givers of rewards and punishment. In such sessions, instructors should provide the students' significant others with an overview of Skillstreaming, much like the overview given to a new group of trainees. An accurate picture of what goes on in a Skillstreaming class—what procedures are typically used, and why—should be portrayed. Most important, participants should be informed about how they can help in the transfer effort, and why their contributions are so necessary to the success of the program. These potential reward-givers can be instructed on how to reinforce appropriate behaviors or the approximations of such behaviors. Tell them what specific responses on their part would be appropriate for the skills being covered in class. It is often worthwhile to engage them in role-playing the kinds of responses they might make, so they can have practice and provide feedback using these behaviors.

Frequently, environmental support is insufficient to maintain newly learned skills. In fact, many real-life environments in which youngsters work and live actually resist efforts at behavior change. For this reason, students need to learn to be their own rewarders—to use self-reinforcement or self-reward.

Once a new skill has been practiced through role-play, and the trainee has made his or her first homework effort and received group feedback, recommend that trainees continue to practice their new skill as frequently as possible. At this time self-reinforcement can and should be initiated. Students can be instructed in the nature of self-reinforcement and encouraged to "say something and do something nice for yourself" if they practice their new skill well. Self-rewards may be both things that one says to oneself and things that one does for oneself.

Teach the trainee to evaluate his or her own performance, even if efforts do not meet with the hoped-for response from others. For example, the youngster who follows all of the steps of a particular skill might reward himself or herself by saying something like, "I'll play basketball after school as a special reward." It is important that these self-rewards are indeed special—things that are not said or done routinely, but things done to acknowledge and reinforce special efforts. Trainees' notes can be collected by the trainer to keep abreast of independent progress, without consuming group time. Advance a student to this level of independent practice only when it is clear that he or she can successfully do what is being asked.

It is important to acknowledge the power of peer group pressure on the behaviors of adolescents. The natural peer leader often is far more influential in a youngster's life than any adult trainer could hope to be. It is sometimes possible to capitalize on the leadership qualities of some adolescents. The trainer may want to select and instruct a peer (adolescent) co-trainer to be used instead of a second adult. The peer selected, of course, must be proficient in the particular skill being taught.

Trainee Motivation

We believe that psychological skills training research and practice have not given sufficient attention to trainee motivation for skill competency development. It is as if, in the Hullian terms of several years ago, the focus has been almost exclusively on habit strength at the expense of drive. As Hull (1943) demonstrated, behavior was a multiplicative function of both. Future investigative efforts should seek to redress this imbalance and examine means to enhance skill competency motivation—a matter often of special relevance for aggressive adolescents. In addition to appropriate contingent reinforcement, which is well established in the skills training context, trainee motivation may be enhanced in conjunction with three different events that unfold sequentially during the skills training process: (1) the establishment of the trainer–trainee relationship, (2) the selection of appropriate target skills, and (3) the establishment of certain motivation-relevant group parameters.

Trainer–Trainee Relationship

It is a truism in such interpersonal influence contexts as psychotherapy, counseling, and education that client or student motivation to do "the work" of the process, in part, is "driven by the steam" of a positive relationship with the change agent involved. Ladd and Mize (1983) comment:

> As in any pedigogical undertaking, it is likely that the success of a social skill training program also depends on the quality of the relationship established between the child and the instructor. Even the most well-designed and all-inclusive training program may be rendered ineffective if it is conducted in an overly didactic, mechanical, and uninviting manner. Rarely, however, have previous social skill training investigators alluded to instructor characteristics or the instructor–child relationship as important aspects of the skill training process (p. 153).

It seems that we ought to conclude—consistent with the prevailing truism for other change endeavors—that a warm, close, personal, empathic, trainer–trainee relationship can potentiate skill acquisition in aggressive adolescent trainees. But all truisms are not necessarily true; in fact, by their very comprehensiveness they may deny or minimize the opportunity for a differentiated, prescriptive perspective. A host of clinicians have speculated that therapeutic progress with aggressive adolescents would, in fact, be advanced by a different kind of (especially initial) helper–helpee relationship–one of *low* empathy, *high* impersonality, and *careful* avoidance of emotional exploration (Dean, 1958; Goldstein, Heller, & Sechrest, 1966; Redl & Wineman, 1957; Schwitzgebel, 1967; Slack, 1960).

Edelman and Goldstein (1984) examined this proposition empirically, and found substantial support for the prescriptive utility in such pairings of low empathy (plus high genuineness) helper behavior. This indeed supports the generalization that trainee motivation and resulting skill acquisition likely are influenced by the quality of the trainer–trainee relationship. But precisely what kind(s) of relationships are optimal in this context remains very much an open question—with considerable speculation and some beginning evidence combining to indicate a relationship quite different from that sought in most other change endeavors.

Skill Selection

Which skills shall be taught, and who will select them? This is as much a motivational as a tactical question, for to the degree that students anticipate learning skill competencies *they* feel they need (discern as presently deficient but of likely utility in real-world relationships), their motivation is enhanced. Skillstreaming operational-izes this perspective by *negotiating the curriculum*. First, trainers avoid the option of serving as unilateral skill selector for the trainee. This decision concurs with Schinke (1981) who observes,

> Seldom recognized in interpersonal skills training with adolescents is how values influence client referral and problem definition. Decisions about desirable skills are weighted by personal preferences, moral judgments, and ethical constraints (p. 81).

Skillstreaming instructors similarly avoid a cafeterialike option: denying the potential value of skill-relevant expertise and knowledge and laying out the entire skill curriculum for the student simply to select those he or she wishes. Either unilateral approach is inadequate: The first delimits trainee motivation, the second denies trainer expertise. Instead, both parties actively participate. First, the trainer (if she or he knows the trainee well) and the trainee each *independently* complete versions of the Skillstreaming Skills Inventory (Goldstein et al., 1980). Then, much as an academic advisor and a student meet to juxtapose and reconcile their respective tentative course programs for the student's next semester, skills trainer and trainee mutually compare, contrast, examine, and select a program from their Skills Inventories. This combined program reflects both the instructor's beliefs about what the adolescent needs and the adolescent's beliefs about what are his or her deficiencies and desired competen-cies. Whether this applied procedure in fact enhances motivation is an investigative question worth careful examination.

Group Procedures

Optimizing trainee participation in the skill-selection process is an example of seeking to enhance his or her task-associated intrinsic motivation. Extrinsic task characteristics also may be profitably mobilized toward maximizing inducements for active, on-task participation. Although as yet there is little empirical evidence to support the following group procedure recommendations, they appear to be reliable extrinsic means to enhance trainee motivation.

Where are the group sessions held?

In schools and institutions, try to seek a special place, associated in the adolescent's thinking with particular privileges or opportunities (e.g., teacher's lounge, student center, recreation area). It should not be so removed in its characteristics from the typical skill application settings as to reduce the likelihood of skill transfer.

When will the group meet?

If not too great an academic sacrifice, attempt to schedule skills training sessions when what the youngsters will miss is an activity they do not especially enjoy (including certain academic subjects), rather than free play, lunch, gym, or the like.

Who will lead the group?

For initial, program-initiating groups in particular, try to utilize as trainers those teachers, cottage parents, members of the institutional staff, or others who seem to be most stimulating, most tuned in to the needs and behaviors of aggressive adolescents (but not the most overtly empathic, for the reasons described earlier), and in general, most able to capture and hold the attention of participating youngsters. The group leadership skills of the first trainers employed can have far-reaching motivational consequences: The impact of the initial group's first meeting(s) bears on not only the motivation and performance of trainees in that group, but also, rapidly, through the school or institution's grapevine, on the interest, motivation and, eventually, performance of youngsters in subsequently formed groups.

Which skill shall be taught first?

This is a crucial decision of special relevance to trainee motivation. In addition to reflecting the give-and-take of the negotiated skill curriculum, the first skill taught optimally is one likely to yield immediate, real-world reward for the trainee. It must "work"—it must pay off. Whereas some trainers prefer to begin with the simpler conversational skills, as a sort of warm up, we try to respond to both simplicity and reward potential. The trainee's "felt need" and perception of near-future value for a given skill, therefore, weighs heavily especially in initial skill selection decisions.

Research Evaluation

Several investigations have examined Skillstreaming's skill acquisition efficacy with adolescents. In most of these studies, the youngsters involved were aggressive, disruptive, or similarly antisocial. Research with Skillstreaming reveals successful training of adolescents in prosocial skills such as empathy (Berlin, 1976), negotiating (D. Fleming, 1976; L. Fleming, 1976), assertiveness (Raleigh, 1977; Wood, 1977), following instructions (Golden, 1975; Litwack, 1976), self-control (Greenleaf, 1977; Hummel, 1977; Swanstrom, 1977), perspective-taking (Trief, 1976), and interviewee behaviors (Jennings, 1975).

Fleming (1976), attempting to capitalize on adolescent responsiveness to peer influence, demonstrated that gains in negotiation skill are as great when the Skillstreaming group leader is a respected peer as when the leader is an adult. Litwack (1976), more concerned with the skill-enhancing effects of an adolescent who anticipates later serving as a peer leader, showed that such helper role expectation increases the degree of skill acquired—a finding clearly relevant to Reissman's helper therapy principle (1965). Trief (1976) demonstrated that successful use of Skillstreaming to increase the perspective-taking skill (seeing matters from other people's viewpoint) also leads to increases in cooperative behavior. The significant transfer effects both in this study and in the Golden (1975), Litwack (1976), and Raleigh (1977) investigations have been important in planning further research on Skillstreaming's transfer enhancement.

As in earlier efforts with adult trainees, we have begun to examine the value of teaching certain skill combinations. Aggression-prone adolescents often get into difficulty when they respond with overt aggression to authority figures with whom they disagree. Golden (1975), responding to this, successfully used Skillstreaming to teach such youngsters *resistance-reducing behavior,* defined as a combination of reflection of feeling (the authority figure's) and assertiveness (forthright but nonaggressive statement of the adolescent's own position).

Jennings (1975) successfully used Skillstreaming to train adolescents in several verbal skills necessary for satisfactory participation in more traditional, insight-oriented psychotherapy. Guzetta (1974) used Skillstreaming to teach empathic skills to parents, and helped close the gap between them and their adolescent children.

After these demonstrations of the skill acquisition efficacy of Skillstreaming, research evaluation took two significant directions. The first concerned the central issue of skill transfer. In a series of investigations, reported at length in the book *Psychological Skill Training* (1981), Goldstein presents evidence of the transfer-enhancing value of procedures such as overlearning, identical elements, general principles, and stimulus variability. This emerging technology is the *prime* research direction for future skills training studies.[4]

Aggression Replacement Training

The frequent failure of transfer or maintenance of training and therapeutic gains occurs not only in skills training approaches, but in interventions of any kind (Goldstein & Kanfer, 1979; Karoly & Steffan, 1980; Keeley, Shemberg, & Carbonell, 1976). This formed the primary motivation to expand training intervention beyond Skillstreaming to a more comprehensive program—Aggression Replacement Training. Many efforts designed to enhance transfer have turned outward—to parents,

---

[4]Two texts examining the full array of demonstrable and potential transfer-enhancing techniques are *Maximizing Treatment Gains: Transfer Enhancement in Psychotherapy* (Goldstein & Kanfer, 1979) and *Improving the Long-Term Effects of Psychotherapy* (Karoly & Steffan, 1980).

employers, teacher, siblings, or other benign and gain-reinforcing persons available in the trainee's real-world environment. The type of low-income client on whom most research work has focused—chronically aggressive youth—is rarely so fortunate. Far too often parents are indifferent or unavailable; peers are the original tutors of antisocial, not prosocial, behavior; employers are nonexistent or too busy; teachers have written off the youngsters years ago. To be sure, when and if one can mobilize the assistance of such persons, one should energetically do so. More often, however, a single transfer enhancement option—working with the target adolescent himself or herself—is left. If Skillstreaming alone fails to provide reliable transfer outcomes, its training intervention must be broadened, its coverage and potency increased, in a fuller effort to arm the trainee with whatever is needed to want to and be able to behave in constructive, nonaggressive, and still satisfying ways in her or his community. With this as the guiding philosophy, we constructed and evaluated Aggression Replacement Training—a three-component training intervention.

Course 1. Skillstreaming

As noted above, Skillstreaming is a systematic, psychoeducational intervention demonstrated in many investigations to reliably teach a fifty-skill curriculum of prosocial behaviors. In addition to other skills, it teaches youngsters behaviors they may use instead of aggression in response to provocation.

Course 2. Anger Control Training

This intervention was developed by Feindler and her research group (Feindler, Marriott, & Iwata, 1984), based in part on the earlier anger control and stress inoculation research, respectively, of Novaco (1975) and Meichenbaum (1977). Anger Control Training—in contrast to Skillstreaming's goal of prosocial skill facilitation—teaches the inhibition of anger, aggression, and, more generally, antisocial behavior.

By means of its constituent components (identification of the physiological cues of anger, its external and internal triggers or instigators, self-statement disputation training, refocusing anticipation of consequences, and so forth), chronically angry and aggressive youth are taught to respond to provocation less impulsively, more reflectively, and with less likelihood of acting-out behavior. In short, Anger Control Training teaches youngsters what *not to do in anger-instigating situations*.

Course 3. Moral Education

Armed with both the ability to respond to the real world prosocially, and the skills necessary to stifle or at least diminish impulsive anger and aggression, will the chronically acting-out adolescent in fact choose to use these abilities? To enhance the likelihood of this choice, one must enter into the realm of moral values. In a long and pioneering series of investigations, Kohlberg (1969, 1973) demonstrated that exposing youngsters to a series of moral dilemmas (in a discussion-group context that includes youngsters reasoning at differing levels of moral thinking) arouses cognitive conflict; its resolution frequently advances a youngster's moral reasoning to that of the higher level peers in the group.

Although such moral reasoning stage advancement is a reliable finding, as with other single interventions, efforts to utilize it by itself as a means of enhancing actual, overt moral behavior have yielded only mixed success (Arbuthnot & Golden, 1983; Zimmerman, 1984). Possibly this is because such youngsters did not have in their behavioral repertoires the actual skill behaviors either for acting prosocially or for successfully inhibiting the antisocial. Kohlbergian moral education has marked potential for providing constructive motivation toward prosocialness and away from antisocialness in youngsters armed with both Skillstreaming and Anger Control Training.

There has been a series of investigations to evaluate the efficacy of Aggression Replacement Training. The first two involved delinquent, low-income youth incarcerated at medium-secure or maximum-secure facilities for adjudicated delinquents (Goldstein & Glick, 1989). The third study was community-based, and the intervention was employed with chronically aggressive youths residing in either their own or group homes (Goldstein, Glick, Irwin, Pask, & Rubama, 1989). All three investigations yielded encouraging, positive outcomes—skills were learned, aggression reduced, and recidivism was positively impacted. Such evaluation outcomes are not only supportive of further use and evaluation of the intervention involved, but also of the philosophical underpinnings on which it rests. Thus, the almost 20-year positive clinical and research experience with both Skillstreaming and Aggression Replacement Training stands as concrete support for an intervention philosophy for low-income clients: a reformity prescription in spirit; psychoeducational and centered on skill remediation in broad procedure; and action-oriented, consequence-focused, and authoritatively administered in substance. Most recently research has gone beyond Aggression Replacement Training, to a new, more comprehensive, but as yet largely unevaluated expression of this intervention philosophy: the *Prepare* Curriculum (Goldstein, 1989).

Prepare *Curriculum*

Table 9-3 schematizes the progression of low-income client-oriented interventions developed since 1973. As can be seen, Skillstreaming grew into Aggression Replacement Training, which in turn grew into the *Prepare* curriculum. The latter's 10 constituent, course-length interventions appear in the last column. We have described the first three courses above; a description of the other seven follows.

Course 4. Problem-Solving Training

Aggressive adolescents and younger children are frequently deficient not only in knowledge of and ability to use prosocial competencies, such as the array of interpersonal skills and anger control techniques taught in Courses 1 and 2, but they also may be deficient in other ways crucial to the use of prosocial behavior. As Ladd & Mize (1983) point out, they may be deficient in such problem-solving factors as "(a) knowledge of appropriate *goals* for social interaction, (b) knowledge of appro-

TABLE 9-3   Intervention Progression

1973–1983	1984–1988	1988–Present
Skillstreaming	Aggression Replacement Training	The *Prepare* Curriculum
	1. Skillstreaming 2. Anger Control Training 3. Moral Reasoning Training	1. Skillstreaming 2. Anger Control Training 3. Moral Reasoning Training 4. Problem-solving Training 5. Empathy Training 6. Situational Perception Training 7. Stress Management 8. Cooperation Training 9. Recruiting Supportive Models 10. Understanding and Using Group Processes

priate *strategies* for reaching a social goal, and (c) knowledge of the *contexts* in which specific strategies may be appropriately applied" (p. 130).

Spivack, Platt, and Shure's (1976) research program on interpersonal problem solving produces an analogous conclusion. At early and middle childhood, as well as in adolescence, chronically aggressive youngsters were less able than others to function effectively in most problem-solving subskills such as identification of alternatives, consideration of consequences, determining causality, means–ends thinking, and perspective-taking.

Several programs have been developed already in an effort to remediate such deficiencies (Delange, Lanham, & Barton, 1981; Giebink, Stover, & Fahl, 1968; Sarason & Sarason, 1981). This represents a fine beginning, but problem-solving deficiency in such youth is substantial (Chandler, 1973; Selman, 1980; Spivack et al., 1976) and requires longer-term, more comprehensive interventions.

The course discussed here seeks to provide just such an effort. In an early pilot development, it is a long-term sequence of graduated problem-solving skills such as reflection, problem identification, information gathering, identification of alternatives, consideration of consequences, and decision making. Initial evaluation of this sequence with an aggressive adolescent population has yielded significant gains in problem-solving skills as defined, substantially encouraging further development of this course (Grant, 1986). These results are beginning to give substance to the earlier assertion that individuals can be systematically trained in problem-solving skills both to build general competence in meeting life's challenges and as a specific means of supplying one more reliable, prosocial alternative to aggression (Goldstein, 1981).

Course 5. Empathy Training

A course designed to enhance the participating youth's level of empathy is to be included in the *Prepare* curriculum for two reasons. Expression of empathic understanding can simultaneously serve as an inhibitor of negative interactions and facilitator of positive ones. Evidence clearly demonstrates (Goldstein & Michaels, (1985) that

> . . . responding to another individual in an empathic manner and assuming temporarily their perspective decreases or inhibits one's potential for acting aggressively toward the other (Feshbach, 1984; Feshbach & Feshbach, 1969). Stated otherwise, empathy and aggression are incompatible interpersonal responses, hence to be more skilled in the former serves as an aid to diminishing the latter. (p. 309)

The notion of empathy facilitating positive interpersonal relations stands on an even broader base of research evidence. A review of the hundreds of investigations on the interpersonal consequences of empathic responding reveals it to be a consistently potent promoter of interpersonal attraction, dyadic openness, conflict resolution, and individual growth (Goldstein & Michaels, 1985).

This same review led to defining empathy as a multistage process: perception of emotional cues, affective reverberation of the emotions perceived, their cognitive labeling, and communication. The *Prepare* curriculum's multistage training program teaches these four constituent components.

Course 6. Situational Perception Training

Once armed with interpersonal skills to respond prosocially to others (Course 1, 2, 3), the problem-solving strategies underlying skill selection and usage (Course 4), and a fuller, empathic sense of the other person's perspective (Course 5), the chronically aggressive youngster may still fail to behave prosocially because he or she "misreads" the context in which the behavior is to occur. In the past 15 years, psychology has emphasized the situation or setting, as perceived by the individual, and its importance in determining overt behavior. Morrison and Bellack (1981) comment, for example:

> . . . adequate social performance not only requires a repertoire of response skills, but knowledge about when and how these responses should be applied. Application of this knowledge, in turn, depends upon the ability to accurately 'read' the social environment: determine the particular norms and conventions operating at the moment, and to understand the messages being sent . . . and intentions guiding the behavior of the interpersonal partner (p. 70).

Dil (1972), Emery (1975), and Rothenberg (1970) show that emotionally disturbed youngsters, as well as those "socially maladjusted" in other ways, are characteristically deficient in such social perceptiveness. Furnham and Argyle (1981) observe:

> . . . it has been found that people who are socially inadequate are unable to read everyday situations and respond appropriately. They are unable to perform or interpret nonverbal signals, unaware of the rules of social behavior, mystified by ritualized routines and

conventions of self-presentation and self-disclosure, and are hence like foreigners in their own land (p. 37).

Argyle, Furnham, and Graham (1981) and Backman (1979) stress the same social-perceptual deficit in their work with aggressive individuals. Yet we believe the ability to "read" social situations accurately can be taught. To accomplish this goal, this course's contents are responsive to the valuable leads provided by Brown and Fraser (1979), who propose three salient dimensions of accurate social percep-tiveness: (1) the *setting* of the interaction and its associated rules and norms, (2) the *purpose* of the interaction and its goals, tasks, and topics, and (3) the *relationship* of the participants—their roles, responsibilities, expectations, and group member-ships.

Course 7. Stress Management

Each of the preceding course descriptions is oriented toward either directly enhanc-ing prosocial competency (e.g., Interpersonal Skills Training, Moral Reasoning, Social Perceptiveness), or reducing qualities that inhibit previously learned or newly acquired prosocial competency (e.g., Anger Control Training). This course is of the latter type. Arkowitz, Lichtenstein, McGovern, and Hines (1975) and Curran (1977) demonstrate that individuals may possess prosocial skills in their repertoires, but not employ them in particularly challenging or difficult situations because of anxiety. A youth may have learned the Interpersonal Skills Training skill, "Responding to Failure," well but embarrassment at a failing grade in front of a teacher or missing a foul shot in front of friends may engender a level of anxiety that inhibits proper use of this skill. A young man may possess the problem-solving competency to plan for a job interview, but perform poorly in the interview itself because anxiety "takes over." Anxiety-inhibition as a source of prosocially incompetent and unsat-isfying behavior may be especially prevalent in the highly peer-conscious adolescent years.

A series of self-managed procedures exists by which stress-induced anxiety may be substantially reduced. These procedures form the contents of the *Prepare* curriculum Stress Management course. Participating youngsters are taught systematic deep muscular relaxation (Benson, 1975; Jacobson, 1964), meditation techniques (Assagioli, 1973; Naranjo & Ornstein, 1971), environmental restructuring (Anderson, 1978), exercise (Walker, 1975), and related means for the management, control, and reduction of stress.

Course 8. Cooperation Training

Chronically aggressive youth display a personality trait pattern that is often high in egocentricity and competitiveness, and low in concern for others and cooperativeness (Pepitone, 1985; Slavin et al., 1985). We offer a course in Cooperation Training not only because enhanced cooperation among individuals is a valuable social goal, but also because of its valuable concomitants and consequences. An extended review of research on "cooperative learning" reveals outcomes of enhanced self-esteem, group cohesiveness, altruism and cooperation itself, as well as reduced egocentricity. As long ago as 1929, Maller commented:

> The frequent staging of contests, the constant emphasis upon the making and breaking of records, and the glorification of the heroic individual achievement . . . in our present educational system lead toward the acquisition of competitiveness. The child is trained to look at members of his group as constant competitors and urged to put forth a maximum effort to excel them. The lack of practice in group activities and community projects in which the child works with his fellows for a common goal precludes the formation of habits of cooperativeness . . . (p. 163).

It was many years before the educational establishment responded concretely to this Deweyian-like challenge, but when it did, it created a wide series of innovative, cooperation-enhancing methodologies, each of which deserves long and careful application and scrutiny both in general educational contexts and with particularly noncooperative youth. The cooperative learning methods include:

- Student Teams—Achievement Divisions (Slavin, 1980),
- Teams—Games—Tournaments (Slavin, 1980),
- Jigsaw Classrooms I (Aronson, 1978),
- Jigsaw Classrooms II (Slavin, 1980),
- Group-Investigation (Sharan & Hertz-Lazarowitz, 1980), and
- Co-op (Kagan, 1985).

Using shared materials, interdependent tasks, group rewards, and similar features, these methods (applied to any content area—mathematics, social studies, etc.) consistently yield the interpersonal, cooperation-enhancing, group and individual benefits noted previously.

In our course, we sorted through the existing methods, adding aspects of our own, and prescriptively tailored a cooperative learning course sequence for chronically aggressive youth. We made use not only of the valuable features of the approaches noted earlier but, in addition, responded to the physical action orientation typical of such youth by relying heavily on cooperative sports and games. Such athletic activity, while not popular in the United States, does exist elsewhere in both action and written document (Orlick, 1978a, 1978b, 1982; Fluegelman, 1981). Collective score basketball, no hitting football, cross-team rotational hockey, collective fastest-time track meets, and other sports restructured to be what cooperative gaming creators term "all touch," "all play," "all positions," "all shoot," and cooperative in other playing and scoring ways, may seem strange to the typical American youth, weaned on highly competitive, individualistic sports, but this appears to be a valuable channel toward the goal of cooperation enhancement among aggressive adolescents.

Course 9. Recruiting Supportive Models
Aggressive youth typically are exposed regularly to highly aggressive models in their interpersonal worlds. Parents, siblings, and peers each are often chronically aggressive individuals themselves (Knight & West, 1975; Loeber & Dishion, 1983; Osborn & West,

1979; Robins, West, & Herjanic, 1975). Simultaneously, there tend to be few prosocial models available to be observed and imitated. When they are, however, such models can make a tremendous difference in the daily lives and development of aggressive youth. This assertion is supported by community-provided examples of prosocial modeling such as Big Brothers, Police Athletic League, Boy Scouts, and the like. Laboratory research also consistently shows that rewarded prosocial behaviors (sharing, altruism, cooperation) are often imitated (Bryan & Test, 1967; Evers & Schwartz, 1973; Canale, 1977).

Werner and Smith (1982), in their impressive longitudinal study of aggressive and nonaggressive youth, *Vulnerable but Invincible,* clearly demonstrate that many youngsters growing up in a community characterized by high levels of crime, unemployment, high school drop out and aggressive models, developed into effective, satisfied, prosocially oriented individuals if they had had sustained exposure to at least one significant prosocial model—be it parent, relative or peer.

Because such models are often scarce in the real-world environments of the youth *Prepare* is intended to serve, efforts must be made to help these youth identify, encourage, attract, elicit, and at times perhaps even create sources and attachments to others who not only function as prosocial models themselves, but who can also serve as sustained sources of direct support for the youth's own prosocially oriented efforts.

Prepare's course contents for teaching identification, encouraging, attraction, elicitation, and creation abilities rely in large part on both the teaching procedures and some of the interpersonal skills that constitute the Skillstreaming training curricula for adolescents (Goldstein et al., 1980) and younger children (McGinnis & Goldstein, 1984).

Course 10. Understanding and Using Group Processes

Adolescent and preadolescent acute responsiveness to peer influences is often cited in both lay and professional literature on child development. It is a conclusion resting on a solid research foundation (Baumrind, 1975; Field, 1981; Guralnick, 1981; Manaster, 1977; Moriarty & Toussieng, 1976; Rosenberg, 1975). Thus, one of *Prepare's* segments gives special emphasis to group—especially peer—processes. Its title includes both "understanding" and "using" because both clearly are its goal. Participating youth will be helped to understand group forces and phenomena such as peer pressure, clique formation and dissolution, leaders and leadership, cohesiveness, initiation, reciprocity, in-group versus out-group relations, developmental phases, competition, and within-group communication and its failure.

For such understanding to have real-world value (the "using" component of the course title), the instructional format consists almost exclusively of group activities in which, *experientally,* participants can learn means for effectively resisting group pressure when they elect to do so, for seeking and enacting a group leadership role, for helping build and enjoy the fruits of group cohesiveness, and so forth. Specific examples of these activities include the following group simulations, structured experiences, and gaming (Pfeiffer & Jones, 1969; Thayer & Beeler, 1975):

"Assessment of Leadership Style,"
"Committee Meeting: Demonstrating Hidden Agendas,"
"Process Observation: A Guide,"
"Top Problems: A Consensus-Seeking Task,"
"Dealing with Shared Leadership,"
"Conflict Resolution: A Collection of Tasks,"
"Group on Group,"
"Line Up and Power Inversion,"
"Polarization: A Demonstration,"
"Not Listening: A Dyadic Role Play,"
"Towers: An Intergroup Competition," and
"Peer Perceptions: A Feedback Experience."

Summary

This chapter has presented a broad psychoeducational strategy oriented toward adolescents displaying various psychological skill deficits. The three increasingly complex, multipronged interventions described are sequential attempts to counteract the way newly learned competencies frequently fail to generalize. Evaluative research on their efficacy to date appears to encourage both their continued use and further scrutiny.

References

Achenbach, T. M. (1966). The classification of children's psychiatric symptoms: A factor-analytic study. *Psychological Monographs, 80* (Whole No. 615).

―――. (1974). *Developmental psychopathology.* New York: Ronald Press.

Achenbach, T. M., & Edelbrock, C. S. (1978). The classification of child psychopathology: A review and analysis of empirical efforts. *Psychological Bulletin, 85,* 1275–1301.

Adams, S. (1961). *Assessment of the psychiatric treatment program, phase I: Third interim report.* Research Report No. 21, California Youth Authority.

―――. (1962). The PICO project. In N. Johnson, L. Savits, & M. E. Wolfgang (Eds.), *The sociology of punishment and correction* (pp. 213–224). New York: Wiley.

Anderson, R. A. (1978). *Stress power.* New York: Human Sciences Press.

Arbuthnot, J., & Golden, D. A. (1983). Moral reasoning development in correctional intervention. *Journal of Correctional Education, 34,* 133–138.

Argyle, M., Furnham, A., & Graham, J. (1981). *Social situations.* Cambridge, UK: Cambridge University Press.

Arkowitz, H., Lichtenstein, E., McGovern, K., & Hines, P. (1975). The behavioral assessment of social competence in males. *Behavior Therapy, 6,* 3–13.

Aronson, E. (1978). *The jigsaw classroom.* Beverly Hills, CA: Sage.

Assagioli, R. (1973). *The act of will.* New York: Viking Press.

Backman, C. (1979). Epilogue: A new paradigm. In G. Ginsburg (Ed.), *Emerging strategies in social psychological research.* Chichester, UK: Wiley.

Bailey, W. (1966). *Correctional outcome: An evaluation of 100 reports.* Unpublished manuscript, University of California at Los Angeles.

Baumrind, D. (1975). Early socialization and adolescent competence. In S. E. Dragastin & G. H. Elder (Eds.), *Adolescence in the life cycle* (pp. 117–143). Washington, DC: Hemisphere Publishing Co.

Benson, H. (1975). *The relaxation response.* New York: Avon.

Bernal, M. E., Duryee, J. S., Pruett, H. L., & Burns, B. J. (1968). Behavior modification and the brat syndrome. *Journal of Consulting and Clinical Psychology, 32,* 447–456.

Braukmann, C. L., & Fixsen, D. L. (1976). Behavior modification with delinquents. In M. Herson, R. M. Eisler, & P. M. Miller (Eds.), *Progress in behavior modification,* Vol. 1 (pp. 191–231). New York: Academic Press.

Brown, P., & Fraser, C. (1979). Speech as a marker of situations. In K. Scherer and H. Giles (Eds.), *Social markers in speech* (pp. 33–62). Cambridge: Cambridge University Press.

Bryan, J. H., & Test, M. A. (1967). Models and helping: Naturalistic studies in aiding behavior. *Journal of Personality and Social Psychology, 6,* 400–407.

California Department of the Youth Authority (1967). James Marshall treatment program: Progress report.

Canale, J. R. (1977). The effect of modeling and length of ownership on sharing behavior of children. *Social Behavior and Personality, 5,* 187–191.

Carney, F. J. (1966). *Summary of studies on the derivation of base expectance categories for predicting recidivism of subjects released from institutions of the Massachusetts Department of Corrections.* Boston, MA: Department of Corrections.

Chandler, M. J. (1973). Egocentrism and anti-social behavior: The assessment and training of social perspective-taking skills. *Developmental Psychology, 9,* 326–332.

Craft, M., Stephenson, G., & Granger, C. (1964). A controlled trial of authoritarian and self-governing regimes with adolescent psychopaths. *American Journal of Orthopsychiatry, 34,* 543–554.

Cronbach, L. J., & Snow, R. E. (1977). *Aptitudes and instructional methods.* New York: Irvington.

Curran, J. P. (1977). Skills training as an approach to the treatment of heterosexual-social anxiety: A review. *Psychological Bulletin, 84,* 140–157.

Dean, S. I. (1958). Treatment of the reluctant client. *American Psychologist, 13,* 627–630.

DeLange, J. M., Lanham, S. L., & Barton, J. A. (1981). Social skills training for juvenile delinquents: Behavioral skill training and cognitive techniques. In D. Upper & S. Ross (Eds.), *Behavioral group therapy* (1981: An annual review). Champaign, IL: Research Press.

Dil, N. (1972). *Sensitivity of emotionally disturbed and emotionally nondisturbed elementary school children to emotional meanings of facial expressions.* Unpublished doctoral dissertation, Indiana University.

Drabman, R. S., Spitalnik, R., & O'Leary, K. D. (1973). Teaching self-control to disruptive children. *Journal of Abnormal Psychology, 82,* 10–16.

Dreger, R. M., Lewis, P. M., Rich, T. A., Miller, K. S., Reid, M. P., Overlade, D. C., Taffel, C., & Flemming, E. L. (1964). Behavioral classification project. *Journal of Consulting Psychology, 28,* 1–13.

Edelman, E., & Goldstein, A. P. (1984). Prescriptive relationship levels for juvenile delinquents in a psychotherapy analog. *Aggressive Behavior, 10,* 269–278.

Emery, J. E. (1975). *Social perception processes in normal and learning disabled children.* Unpublished doctoral dissertation, New York University.

Empey, L. T. (1969). Contemporary programs for convicted juvenile offenders: Problems of theory, practice and research. In D. J. Mulvihill & M. M. Tumin (Eds.), *Crimes of violence* (Vol. 13). Washington, DC: U.S. Government Printing Office.

Evers, W. L., & Schwartz, J. C. (1973). Modifying social withdrawal in preschoolers: The effects of filmed modeling and teacher praise. *Journal of Abnormal Psychology, 1,* 248–256.

Feindler, E. L., Marriott, S. A., & Iwata, M. (1984). Group anger control training for junior high school delinquents. *Cognitive Therapy and Research, 8,* 299–311.

Feshbach, N. D. (1984). Empathy, empathy training and the regulation of aggression in elementary school children. In R. M. Kaplan, V. J. Konecni, & R. Novaco (Eds.), *Aggression in children and youth* (pp. 192–208). The Hague, The Netherlands: Martinus Nojhoff Publishers.

Feshbach, N. D., & Feshbach, S. (1969). The relationship between empathy and aggression in two age groups. *Developmental Psychology, 1,* 102–107.

Field, T. (1981). Early peer relations. In P. S. Strain (Ed.), *The utilization of classroom peers as behavior change agents* (pp. 1–30). New York: Plenum Press.

Fleming, D. (1976). *Teaching negotiation skills to pre-adolescents.* Unpublished doctoral dissertation, Syracuse University.

Fluegelman, A. (1981). *More new games.* Garden City, NY: Dolphin Books.

Furnham, A., & Argyle, M. (1981). *The psychology of social situations.* New York: Pergamon Press.

Garrity, D. (1956). T*he effects of length of incarceration upon parole adjustment and estimation of optimum sentence. Washington State Correction Institution.* Unpublished doctoral dissertation, University of Washington.

Giebink, J. W., Stover, D. S., & Fahl, M. A. (1968). Teaching adaptive response to frustration to emotionally disturbed boys. *Journal of Consulting and Clinical Psychology, 32,* 336–368.

Golden, R. (1975). *Teaching resistance-reducing behavior to high school students.* Unpublished doctoral dissertation, Syracuse University.

Goldstein, A. P. (Ed.). (1978). *Prescriptions for child mental health and education.* Elmsford, NY: Pergamon Press.

———. (1981). *Psychological skill training.* Elmsford, NY: Pergamon Press.

———. (1989). *The prepare curriculum.* Champaign, IL: Research Press.

Goldstein, A. P., & Glick, B. (1989). *Aggression replacement training.* Champaign, IL: Research Press.

Goldstein, A. P., Glick, B., Irwin, M. J., Pask, C., & Rubama, I. (1989). *Reducing delinquency: Intervention in the community.* New York: Pergamon Press.

Goldstein, A. P., Heller, K., & Sechrest, L. B. (1966). *Psychotherapy and the psychology of behavior change.* New York: Wiley.

Goldstein, A. P., & Kanfer, F. H. (1979). *Maximizing treatment gains: Transfer enhancement in psychotherapy.* New York: Academic Press.

Goldstein, A. P., & Michaels, G. Y. (1985). *Empathy: Development, training and consequences.* Hillsdale, NJ: Erlbaum.

Goldstein, A. P., Sprafkin, R. P., & Gershaw, N. J. (1976). *Skill training for community living.* Elmsford, NY: Pergamon Press.

Goldstein, A. P., Sprafkin, R. P., Gershaw, N. J., & Klein, P. (1980). *Skillstreaming the adolescent: A structured learning approach to teaching prosocial behavior.* Champaign, IL: Research Press.

Goldstein, A. P., & Stein, N. (1976). *Prescriptive psychotherapies.* Elmsford, NY: Pergamon Press.

Grant, J. (1986). *An instructional training program for problem solving skill enhancement with delinquent youth.* Unpublished doctoral dissertation, Syracuse University.

Group for the Advancement of Psychiatry. (1966). *Psychopathological disorders in childhood: Theoretical considerations and a proposed classification.* GAP Report No. 62.

Guralnick, M. J. (1981). Peer influences on the development of communicative competence. In P. S. Strain (Ed.), *The utilization of classroom peers as behavior change agents.* New York: Plenum Press.

Guzetta, R. A. (1974). *Acquisition and transfer of empathy by the parents of early adolescents through structured learning training.* Unpublished doctoral dissertation, Syracuse University.

Harrison, R. M., & Mueller, P. (1964). Clue hunting about group counseling and parole outcome, Sacramento: California Department of Corrections.

Hewitt, L. E., & Jenkins, R. L. (1946). *Fundamental patterns of maladjustment: The dynamics of their origins.* Springfield, IL: State of Illinois.

Hull, C. L. (1943). *The principles of behavior.* New York: Appleton-Century-Crofts.

Hunt, D. E. (1961). Matching models in education. *The coordination of teaching methods with student characteristics.* Toronto: Ontario Institution of Studies in Education.

Jacobson, E. (1964). *Anxiety and tension control.* Philadelphia: Lippincott.

Jennings, R. I. (1975). *The use of structured learning techniques to teach attraction enhancing interviewee skills to residentially hospitalized, lower socioeconomic emotionally disturbed children and adolescents: A psychotherapy analogue investigation.* Unpublished doctoral dissertation, University of Iowa.

Kagan, S. (1985). Co-op Co-op: A flexible cooperative learning technique. In R. Slavin, S. Sharan, S. Kagan, R. Hertz-Lazarowitz, C. Webb, & R. Schmuck (Eds.), *Learning to cooperate, cooperating to learn* (pp. 437–462). New York: Plenum Press.

Karoly, P., & Steffan, J. (1980). *Improving the long-term effects of psychotherapy.* New York: Gardner Press.

Kassenbaum, G., Ward, D., & Wilner, D. (1972). *Prison treatment and its outcome.* New York: Wiley.

Keeley, S. M., Shemberg, K. M., & Carbonell, J. (1976). Operant clinical intervention: Behavior management or beyond? *Behavior Therapy, 7,* 292–305.

Klausmeier, H. J., Rossmiller, R. A., & Saily, M. (Eds.). (1977). *Individually guided elementary education.* New York: Academic Press.

Knight, B. J., & West, D. J. (1975). Temporary and continuing delinquency. *British Journal of Criminology, 15,* 43–50.

Knight, D. (1969). *The Marshall program: Assessment of a short-term institutional treatment program.* Research Report 56. Sacramento: Department of the Youth Authority.

Kohlberg, L. (1969). Stage and sequence: The cognitive-developmental approach to socialization. In D. Goslin (Ed.), *Handbook of socialization theory and research* (pp. 347–480). Chicago: Rand McNally.

———. (Ed.). (1973). *Collected papers on moral development and moral education.* Cambridge, MA: Center for Moral Education, Harvard University.

Ladd, G. W., & Mize, J. (1983). A cognitive-social learning model of social skill training. *Psychological Review, 90,* 127–157.

Litwack, S. E. (1976). *The use of the helper therapy principle to increase therapeutic effectiveness and reduce therapeutic resistance: Structured learning therapy with resistant adolescents.* Unpublished doctoral dissertation, Syracuse University.

Loeber, R., & Dishion, T. (1983). Early predictors of male delinquency: A review. *Psychological Bulletin, 94,* 68–99.

Maller, J. B. (1929). *Cooperation and competition: An experimental study in motivation.* New York: Teacher's Colleges, Columbia University.

Manaster, G. J. (1977). *Adolescent development and the life tasks.* Boston: Allyn and Bacon.

Martinson, R. (1974). What works? Questions and answers about prison reform. *The Public Interest,* 0, 22–54.

McClintock, F. (1961). *Attendance centres.* London: Macmillan.

McCorkle, L. W., Elias, A., & Bixby, F. (1958). *The Highfields story.* New York: Holt, Rinehart and Winston.

McGinnis, E., & Goldstein, A. P. (1984). *Skillstreaming the elementary school child.* Champaign, IL: Research Press.

Meichenbaum, D. (1977). *Cognitive behavior modification: An integrative approach.* New York: Plenum Press.

Moriarty, A. E., & Toussieng, P. W. (1976). *Adolescent coping.* New York: Grune & Stratton.

Morrison, R. L., & Bellack, A. S. (1981). The role of social perception in social skill. *Behavior Therapy, 12,* 69–79.

Naranjo, C., & Ornstein, R. E. (1971). *On the psychology of meditation.* New York: Viking Press.

Novaco, R. (1975). *Anger control: The development and evaluation of an experimental treatment.* Lexington, MA: D. C. Health.

O'Connor, R. D. (1972). Relative efficacy of modeling, shaping, and the combined procedures for modification of social withdrawal. *Journal of Abnormal Psychology, 79,* 327–334.

Orlick, T. (1978a). *Winning through cooperation.* Washington, DC: Acropolis Books, Ltd.

———. (1978b). *The cooperative sports and games book.* New York: Pantheon Books.

———. (1982). *The second cooperative sports and games book.* New York: Pantheon Books.

Osborn, S. G., & West, D. J. (1979). Conviction records of fathers and sons compared. *British Journal of Criminology, 19,* 120–133.

Palmer, T. (1976). *Final report to the California Community Treatment Project.* Sacramento: California Youth Authority.

Patterson, G. R., & Anderson, D. (1964). Peers as social reinforcers. *Child Development, 35,* 951–960.

Patterson, G. R., & Reid, J. B. (1973). Intervention for families of aggressive boys: A replication study. B*ehavior Research and Therapy, 11,* 383–394.

Pepitone, E. A. (1985). Children in cooperation and competition: antecedents and consequences of self-orientation. In R. Slavin (Ed.), *Learning to cooperate, cooperating to learn* (pp. 17–65). New York: Plenum Press.

Peterson, D. R., Quay, H. C., & Cameron, G. R. (1959). Personality and background factors in juvenile delinquency as inferred from questionnaire responses. *Journal of Consulting Psychology, 23,* 392–399.

Peterson, D. R., Quay, H. C., & Tiffany, T. L. (1961). Personality factors related to juvenile delinquency. *Child Development, 32,* 355–372.

Pfeiffer, J. W., & Jones, J. E. (1969). *A handbook of structured experiences for human relations training.* LaJolla, CA: University Associates.

Quay, H. C. (1964). Dimensions of personality in delinquent boys as inferred from the factor analysis of case history data. *Child Development, 35,* 479–484.

———. (1966). Patterns of aggression, withdrawal and immaturity. In H. C. Quay & J. S. Werry (Eds.), *Psychopathological disorders of childhood* (pp. 1–29). New York: Wiley.

Quay, H. C., & Quay, L. C. (1965). Behavior problems in early adolescence. *Child Development, 36,* 215–220.

Raleigh, R. (1977). *Individual vs. group structured learning therapy for assertiveness training with senior and junior high school students.* Unpublished doctoral dissertation, Syracuse University.

Redl, R., & Wineman, D. (1957). *The aggressive child.* New York: Free Press.

Reissman, F. (1965). *The culturally deprived child.* New York: Harper.

Robins, L. N., West, P. A., & Herjanic, B. L. (1975). Arrests and delinquency in two generations: A study of black urban families and their children. *Journal of Child Psychology and Psychiatry, 16,* 125–140.

Robinson, J., & Smith, G. (1976). The effectiveness of correctional programs. In R. Giallombardo (Eds.), *Juvenile delinquency* (pp. 585–597). New York: Wiley.

Rosenberg, M. (1975). The dissonant context and the adolescent self-concept. In S. E. Dragastin & G. H. Elder (Eds.), *Adolescence in the life cycle* (pp. 97–116). Washington, DC: Hemisphere Publishing Co.

Ross, A. O., Lacey, H. M., & Parton, D. A. (1965). The development of a behavior checklist for boys. *Child Development, 36,* 1013–1027.

Rothenberg, B. B. (1970). Children's social sensitivity and the relationship to interpersonal competence, interpersonal comfort, and intellectual level. *Developmental Psychology, 2,* 335–350.

Sarason, I. G., & Sarason, B. R. (1981). Teaching cognitive and social skills to high school students. *Journal of Consulting and Clinical Psychology, 49,* 908–918.

Schinke, S. P. (1981). Interpersonal-skills training with adolescents. In M. Hersen, R. M. Eisler, & P. M. Miller (Eds.), *Progress in Behavior Modification,* Vol. 11, (pp. 65–115). New York: Academic Press.

Schwitzgebel, R. L. (1967). Short-term operant conditioning of adolescent offenders on socially relevant variable. *Journal of Abnormal Psychology, 72,* 134–142.

Sealy, A., & Banks, C. (1971). Social maturity, training, experience, and recidivism amongst British borstal boys. *British Journal of Criminology, 11,* 245–264.

Selman, R. L. (1980). *The growth of interpersonal understanding: Developmental and clinical analyses.* New York: Academic Press.

Sharan, S., & Hertz-Lazarowitz, R. (1980). A group-investigation method of cooperative learning in the classroom. In S. Sharan, P. Hare, C. D. Webb, & R. Hertz-Lazarowitz (Eds.), *Cooperation in education* (pp. 14–46). Provo, UT: Brigham Young University.

Slack, C. W. (1960). Experimenter-subject psychotherapy: A new method of introducing intensive office treatment for unreachable cases. *Mental Hygiene, 44,* 238–256.

Slavin, R. E. (1980). Cooperative learning. *Review of Educational Research, 50,* 315–342.

Slavin, R., Sharan, S., Kagan, S., Hertz-Lazarowitz, R., Webb, C., & Schmuck, R. (1985). *Learning to cooperate, cooperating to learn.* New York: Plenum Press.

Slavson, S. R. (1964). *A textbook in analytic psychotherapy.* New York: International Universities Press.

Spivack, G., Platt, J. J., & Shure, M. B. (1976). *The problem-solving approach to adjustment: A guide to research and intervention.* San Francisco: Jossey-Bass.

Stein, N., & Bogin, D. (1978). Individual child psychotherapy. In A. P. Goldstein (Ed.), *Prescriptions for child mental health and education* (pp. 14–87). Elmsford, NY: Pergamon Press.

Stumphauser, J. S. (1972). Increased delay of gratification in young prison inmates through imitation of high-delay peer models. *Journal of Personality and Social Psychology, 21,* 10–17.

Thayer, L., & Beeler, K. D. (1975). *Activities and exercises for affective education.* Washington, DC: American Educational Research Association.

Trief, P. (1976). *The reduction of egocentrism in acting-out adolescents by structured learning therapy.* Unpublished doctoral dissertation, Syracuse University.

Vinter, R., & Janowitz, M. (1959). Effective institutions for juvenile delinquents: A research statement. *Social Service Review, 33,* 118–130.

Vorrath, H. H., & Brendtro, L. K. (1974). *Positive peer culture.* Chicago: Aldine.

Wahler, R. G. (1969). Setting generality: Some specific and general effects of child behavior therapy. *Journal of Applied Behavior Analysis, 2,* 239–246.

Walker, C. E. (1975). *Learn to relax.* Englewood Cliffs, NJ: Spectrum Books.

Warren, M. Q. (1972). *Classification for treatment.* Paper presented at Seminar on the Classification of Criminal Behavior. Washington, DC: National Institute of Law Enforcement and Criminal Justice.

Werner, E., & Smith, R. (1982). *Vulnerable but invincible: A study of resilient children.* New York: McGraw-Hill.

Zimmerman, D. (1984). *Enhancing perspective-taking and moral education with aggressive adolescents.* Unpublished master's thesis, Syracuse University.

Chapter 10

Cultural Diversity: Multicultural Factors in Teaching Social Skills

GWENDOLYN CARTLEDGE   JEANETTE W. LEE
HUA FENG

The early symbol of a melting pot to characterize the multiple backgrounds of the American people has been replaced with a national sentiment to recognize a mosaic. Public school classrooms are living laboratories for issues related to the culturally diverse population and integration. Unfortunately, based on the alarming dropout rates and poor adjustment reports, the current school environment has been less than successful in producing desired levels of academic and social competence in a significant portion of its minority population. A logical assumption examined by several researchers is that cultural differences appreciably determine the social patterns observed in the classroom (Arnold & Orozco, 1989; Fuentes, 1988; Kochman, 1981; Moore & Porter, 1988; Smith & Brewbaker, 1989; Sugai & Maheady, 1988; Swisher & Deyhle, 1989). These differences may cause minority students to respond to school environmental stimuli in nonproductive ways, or culturally based behaviors may be misperceived by mainstream peers and adults.

The social skills trainer is challenged to interpret the behaviors of learners from culturally diverse backgrounds accurately, to distinguish social skill differences from deficits, and to employ instructional strategies effective to help these learners maximize their schooling experiences and acquire the most productive interpersonal skills. While focus- ing on the unique patterns that are instructive for these purposes, it is imperative to remain cognizant of the universality of children's behavior. Indeed, as Schneider (1993) notes:

While one important contribution of cross-cultural research is to trace links between various characteristics of a society and the social behaviour of its members, cross-cultural research is also useful in demonstrating that certain aspects of social behaviour are replicated in virtually all cultures (pp. 119–120).

This chapter is guided by the belief that cultural patterns impact the social behaviors observed in the classroom. With acute awareness of the individuality of personalities within "groups," an attempt will be made to note elements that may distinguish group members from the mainstream culture. Some understanding of cultural distinctions is a prerequisite to planning and orchestrating a program that ensures the total integration of all children. The four largest minority cultural groups in the United States will be discussed: Hispanic Americans, African Americans, native Americans, and Asian Americans. Some cultural distinctions for each group will be outlined, followed by ways these distinctions may influence social behavior, with implications for social skills instruction.

Hispanic Americans

Hispanic Americans, defined as Americans of Spanish-speaking descent (Zeleny, 1991), are the second largest and most rapidly growing culturally diverse group in this country. The majority of this group (62.8 percent) are Mexican Americans. For the most part, they are descendants of Mexican people who lived in the Southwest when it became part of the United States. Mexicans are of mixed Spanish and American-Indian heritage *(mestizos)*. Puerto Ricans are the next largest Hispanic unit in the United States (12.2 percent), representing mixed Spanish, African, and American-Indian roots. Another 11.2 percent, Latinos, have migrated from Central and South America. A fourth group, Cuban Americans (5.3 percent), are mostly of Spanish descent with some of African ancestry.

Cultural Distinctions

Although Hispanics are not a singular group, there are some prevalent features of the culture worth noting that potentially impact social behaviors observed in the classroom.

1. Strong gender roles are defined. The concept of maleness, or *machismo,* is related to courage, superiority, and sexual prowess. The ideal man is one who never breaks down or cracks (Maldonado & Cross, 1979). As a husband, the man is an authoritarian, the head and master of the household.

2. Family unity is one of the most sacred values. The unit is an extended family, with relatives interacting daily as friends, consultants, and financial and moral supporters.

3. It is considered shameful to deal with the law. The concept of "the law" includes legal services and government agencies.

4. Children are desired but are taught to give unquestioning obedience and respect to their parents and authority figures (Wells, 1990).

5. Interpersonal, affective, or emotional relationships are cherished. The orientation is expressive.

6. Passivity and deference to others are encouraged as the ultimate in civilized behavior, as opposed to the aggressiveness reflected in the larger society. Children are discouraged from fighting, even in self-defense (Henderson, 1979).

7. While interpersonal relationships are cherished, the integrity of the individual is not to be violated with group pressure. Ghali (1979) speaks of the fear of relinquishing one's individuality in order to conform, and Henderson (1979) notes the difficulty of accepting the concept of teamwork.

8. Members are protective of their Hispanic culture and are reluctant to adopt "American" lifestyles.

9. The culture is bilingual. Spanish is spoken fluently in the home. The primary language is characterized as earthy, direct, and unadorned with metaphors. Accented English is the second language for many.

10. There is an orientation toward satisfying current needs and enjoying life in the present. A zest for life has been noted by various researchers (Litsinger, 1973; Henderson, 1979; Lewis, 1979).

11. There is a fatalistic acceptance of destiny or life as it exists.

12. Hispanic Americans do not identify themselves with any specific racial background because they are a composite of many races and civilizations. Their Spanish, black, and native American heritage is reflected in all ranges of skin colors, hair textures, and features. For many, color becomes an issue for the first time when they arrive in the United States, when they are judged to be either black or white. Problems of identity within families often start when some members are considered white while others are regarded as black.

13. Nearly one-third of all Hispanic Americans live below the poverty level, and the rate of unemployment is significantly higher than the national average (The Commission on Minority Participation in Education and American Life, 1988).

14. Hispanic Americans have the greatest proportion of high school dropouts (Wells, 1990).

Social Skill Needs

Although Hispanic children are often viewed as well mannered, they are frequently described as being passive, shy, and less socially competent than their peers from other cultural groups, particularly Anglos (Figueroa & Gallegos, 1978). Linguistically based social skills tend to be targeted as the area of greatest need. Teachers frequently report that Hispanic students are slow to initiate conversations with their peers or others, interactions with peers are minimal, and receptive and expressive English language skills are weak (Carlson & Stephens, 1986).

In a study of culturally based social skills, Carlson and Stephens (1986) found language-based skills to distinguish Mexican-American and Anglo students with behavior disorders, according to teachers' ratings of social skills using the Social Behavior Assessment (SBA) (Stephens, 1980). Although the Mexican-American children received more positive scores than Anglo children, the researchers observed two areas of verbal behavior "deviance" for the Mexican-American students: failure to initiate verbal behavior, and failure to respond appropriately on cue. The classes of social behavior pertained to 12 specific skills within the SBA that these students lacked (Carlson & Stephens, 1986):

Failure to initiate verbal behavior

- Makes positive statements about the qualities and accomplishments of others
- Compliments others
- Apologizes for hurting or infringing on others
- Describes one's feelings or moods verbally
- Initiates and assists in conducting a group activity

Failure to respond appropriately on cue

- Answers when asked about wrongdoing
- Makes relevant remarks in class discussions
- Participates in class discussions
- Shares relevant items in class discussions
- Discusses contrary opinions in class discussions
- Provides reasons for opinions expressed
- Initiates and assists in conducting a group activity
- Participates in role playing (p. 197)

Difficulties with language-based social skills suggest that friendship-making and general peer interaction skills may be areas Hispanic-American children need to develop. Teacher ratings in this study also indicate that, in comparison with their Anglo counterparts, Mexican-American children had fewer problems dealing with conflict, perhaps reflecting their cultural orientation toward passivity. Although this characteristic may aid in avoiding conflict, extreme passivity becomes problematic when it interferes with the assertiveness needed to make friends or to avoid victimization. Caution needs to be exercised not to overgeneralize from findings such as the previously mentioned study.

Schneider (1993) points out that there may be great variation of behaviors within cultures based on environmental and developmental factors. For example, Schneider reports an observational study conducted by Fry (1988) on the aggressive behaviors within two Zapotec communities in Mexico. One community, evidencing twice as much aggression as the other, also exhibited greater tolerance for play-fighting among its youth and more corporal punishment of children.

From a developmental perspective, Schneider (1993) cites cross-cultural studies showing young children interpret social events in very similar ways, but by adolescence noticeable differences are observed in their social perceptions, suggesting that the child has internalized the values and mores of the immediate culture.

At the secondary level, for Hispanic-American youth in this country, conditions of poverty, inadequate schooling, urban living conditions, psychological alienation, and other negative influences converge, causing a slight shift of focus to issues of aggression and violence (as typically displayed in gang behavior) for many of these young people. Hispanic youth make up approximately 33 percent of the 120,636 current gang members in the United States (Soriano, 1993). Accompanying this gang membership is the typical array of destructive behaviors—interpersonal conflict, aggression, violence, and criminal acts. Homicide rates for Hispanic youth are estimated to be three or four times greater than those of their nonminority age-mates (Hammond & Yung, 1993). Programs designed to strengthen positive, productive peer relationships and reduce the attraction of gangs are critical for many Hispanic adolescents.

Instructional Implications

Language problems are considered a major barrier to academic and social success; thus, in states densely populated with Hispanic Americans, teachers are being required to learn Spanish. Even without such mandates, teachers need to be sensitive to the fact that students may not understand nuances of the English vocabulary or comprehend explanations based on assumed out-of-school experiences. The language factor is articulated by Leonardo Olguin, now a Mexican-American educator:

> A Mexican American kid . . . goes to school . . . and discovers that the teacher can't talk! He can't understand a thing, and no one can understand him. He can't talk either! It's horrible! The school is make-believe and the real world is at home. I went through the first two years of school in a cloud—going to school, eating lunch, and going home. I didn't know until the second grade that there were two complete languages. I just thought I didn't know all the words! (Litsinger, 1973, p. 36).

Communication problems also create barriers with peers and severely limit home–school collaboration. Lessons in Spanish for non-Hispanic students make the learnings mutual exchanges. A one-sided effort to teach English and only mainstream customs reflects an attitude of superiority and disinterest in the other culture. Furthermore, fluency in more than one language stimulates intellectual development.

Hispanic-American children appear to be negatively impacted by the schooling experience, with large competitive classrooms and low teacher expectations. Nieto (1992) cites research indicating that Hispanic-American and other minority group students tend to receive less positive teacher attention, fewer direct questions, fewer cognitively demanding expectations, and less encouragement than their Anglo counterparts. The net effect for these Hispanic-American students, who are expected to be compliant and passive, is to render them invisible and undermine their academic and social competence.

Foremost in this discussion is the need for teachers to take a personal interest in the Hispanic-American student. To illustrate, personal interest may begin with knowing the names of all students; it is critical for teachers to learn the correct pronunciation and usage of children's names. They should be aware that the surname lists two units—the surname of the father first, and then that of the mother. For Hispanic individuals, the practice of calling an individual by only the first and last name eliminates the father's name (and position) in the process. "Antonio

Gonzales Lopez," for example, indicates the complete first and last name of this individual.

Personal home contacts may be effective if language and cultural issues are addressed. Hispanic Americans often prefer leisurely, warm, and informal beginnings to meetings. To initiate a meeting with an immediate discussion of serious and controversial affairs may seem confusing and even discourteous to most Mexican Americans (Maldonado & Cross, 1979). Also, to leave out the husband would put the wife in an "improper" role and would jeopardize the father's role as head of home affairs. It is highly desirable to communicate directly with parents. An interpreter should be used if the teacher cannot speak Spanish. It would be unwise to use the student in this role because this would contradict the normal child–parent relationship, and because weak skills on the part of the child might result in partial or inaccurate transfer of information.

To facilitate feelings of acceptance and mutual respect for the child and his or her family, Hispanic culture should be integrated into the total curriculum, including lessons on social skills. Inclusion of information about the history and symbols of the culture will not only help students gain a sense of pride and belonging, but will aid in cognitive skills by providing meaningful associations.

Having established a supportive and inclusive classroom context, teachers can more effectively use direct instruction to teach the social skills needed for positive interaction and school success. Employing the teaching procedures specified in Chapter 3, teachers can draw on Hispanic culture to identify possible social models. In their literature-based social skills curriculum for elementary students, Cartledge and Kleefeld (in press) used several Hispanic folktales or children's stories to provide a rationale for the targeted social skill. Many more such stories could be used in learning groups with significant numbers of Hispanic students. Or teachers could highlight the prosocial or socially skilled actions of current or past major Hispanic personalities, making sure to provide a broad spectrum and not to limit these profiles to stereotypical figures such as athletes or entertainers.

Culture-based instruction gains importance for the emerging adolescent who, becoming more aware of the dissonance between his or her own and the mainstream culture, is likely to develop feelings of alienation and resort to self-destructive and antisocial behaviors. Building on traditional cultural values—*personalismo* (people-centeredness), *allocentrism* (preference for group participation), and *simpatia* (avoidance of interpersonal conflict)—teachers might structure social learning experiences that foster positive peer interactions within a cooperative group context (Marin & Marin, 1991). This instruction should reflect collaborative efforts rather than authoritative dictates. That is, minority youth—particularly males, who are inclined to develop a heightened sense of identity with their subculture (Schneider, 1993) and peer group (Hare, 1979)—may be more receptive to lessons they help to devise and that they feel represent them and their culture. Thus, involving these youth in the selection of skills to be taught, the development of scenarios to be presented, the appropriate skill components and enactments, as well as the standards and means for evaluating and monitoring skill performance, is recommended.

Educators must be sensitive to the fact that some instruction delivered in school may contradict what children learn at home (teaching them to be assertive, to be critical thinkers, or to question authority). Students can become aware of new alternatives without the teacher minimizing or undermining the children's respect and affection for their parents' instructions.

African Americans

African Americans are largely descendants of West Africans who were brought to the United States as slave labor beginning in the 1600s. Since the abolition of slavery in 1863, African Americans have been native-born Americans and currently comprise the largest minority group in the United States. The wide range of features and skin tones among African Americans is partially accounted for by the mixture of native Americans and Anglo Americans in their heritage.

Cultural Distinctions

Representing every geographic region and every socioeconomic stratum in the United States, African Americans are a diverse group. An attempt to outline distinctions of the group as a whole "is treading a thin line between glossing over differences and promoting stereotypes" (Turnbull & Turnbull, 1986). Recognizing inadequacies of any such list, there are certain benchmarks that may be considered African-American cultural expressions and traditions.

1. The role of the church has been influential in the lives of the people. Largely Protestant, African Americans have been observed to attend church in greater proportions and with greater regularity than other groups.

2. Group members are noted to be xenophilous—comfortable with strangers—as opposed to xenophobic (fearful of outsiders) people.

3. Although comfortable when associating with different people, there is a reluctance to reveal personal information freely.

4. Music plays a functional role—as a means of communicating with God, for courtship, and for comfort. Black culture brings to mind spirituals, gospel, blues, jazz, soul music, and rap.

5. The black family traditionally has been an extended family "stretched horizontally in every direction as well as vertically . . . taking into account all members of the community" (Goode, 1979). The orientation is a sense of oneness with the community, and toward the survival of its members.

6. Emphasis is placed on respecting one's elders. Older generations orally relate the history of the family, serve as babysitters for working parents, and volunteer wisdom that comes with their years.

7. Children are encouraged to be "tough" to survive and overcome disparities in the real world. They may be conditioned not to unquestioningly trust all authority figures.

8. A sense of pride in self is encouraged. Educational and occupational milestones are greeted with special recognition and celebration.

9. Time is thought of in two dimensions—past and present. Potential time, or future time, is considered "no time." Henderson (1979) classifies the experience of blacks and time as an "African Survival": Time begins when an event is performed. This is in contrast to setting a specific time prior to the occurrence of an event.

10. The group is monolingual. Nevertheless, members understand a variety of usages for a single word or phrase, and some communicate in a special dialect that is different from the mainstream usage of English. Parallel to communicating with words, African Americans closely observe gestures, intonations, and facial expressions.

11. Life expectancy is less than that for other cultural groups, and the mortality rate among infants is higher and rising.

12. Academic achievements are below the levels of the majority-group peers, and students are disproportionately represented in special education classes (as are Hispanic Americans). Nationally, African-American children represent 17 percent of all students, but constitute 41 percent of the special education population. Of the African-American special education population, 85 percent are males (Kunjufu, 1989).

13. Cognitive styles vary, but many students are reported to achieve maximally when instruction is interactive and "hands-on," as opposed to passive, or in the hear–write channel exclusively.

14. Childrearing practices of most families would be labeled as "controlling" (or "authoritarian") as opposed to "democratic." In the controlling orientation, parents tend to stress obedience, respect, neatness, cleanliness, and staying out of trouble. They are more likely to use physical punishment and are sometimes arbitrary in their discipline. This practice may have resulted from three centuries of slavery where physical aggression was modeled as a principal means of control and compliance. According to Maccoby (1980), this style seems to be more damaging to boys than girls, based on research showing boys in these families display more dependent, angry, and defiant behaviors. A similar effect on boys appears to result from permissive parenting.

Social Skill Needs

Few studies systematically analyze the social skills of African-American students, particularly as they compare to their non-African-American peers. Indeed, some authorities contend that, despite obvious differences, ". . . social skill researchers have failed to attend to the variable of race" (Turner, Beidel, Hersen, & Bellack, 1984, p. 474). Among the few such studies, ethnicity emerged as a factor influencing the raters' perceptions of the subjects' behaviors (Lethermon, Williamson, Moody, Granberry, Lemanek, & Bodiford, 1984; Lethermon, Williamson, Moody, & Wozniak, 1986; Turner et al., 1984).

Keller (1988) compared the adjustment scores of white, black, and Hispanic seven-year-old students and found that black children consistently received lower teacher ratings than their non-black peers. Although the ethnicity of the teachers was not identified, bias was suspected because teacher and parent correlations "overlapped" only for white children, and significant correlations among all teacher ratings and measures of ability and achievement were found only for the white sample.

This finding supports evidence showing that not only low-achieving students but, surprisingly, high-achieving black students are singled out by teachers as having behavior problems. Shade (1979), for example, studied gifted African-American students and found that they were less praised and more criticized, even when compared to their nonachieving black counterparts. She described the situation as an unexplainable tendency of black achievers to induce negative reactions from their teachers. Girls received a somewhat better response than boys, but in general, both genders were objects of rejection.

A possible effect of racially based social perception is psychological alienation in minority students. In comparing alienation scores among black and white high school students, Moyer and Motta (1982) found an inverse relationship between alienation scores and academic performance for both groups, but high alienation scores were associated with behavior problems (school suspensions) only for the black students. This alienation may combine with the "castelike" social strata imposed on African Americans (Ogbu, 1981) and the declining economic and community conditions to push African-American youth into a "subculture of disengagement" (Taylor, 1988–89):

> This is evidenced by the rise of African-American teenage gangs and violent behavior, the spread of drugs and alcohol abuse, increases in teenage homicide and suicide rates, and the growing tendency among inner city youth to shun schooling and work for less productive, but more lucrative, criminal pursuits (p. 20).

The poorer overall school and community adjustment by African-American youth, particularly males from low socioeconomic groups, is profiled even more graphically by Prothrow-Stith (1991), who notes that for African-American males nearly "one in four between the ages of 20 and 29 is incarcerated, on probation, or on parole" (p. 163). They make up approximately 73 percent of all students in programs for behavior disabilities, and they are much more likely to be suspended or to drop out of school than other students.

The most dismal statistics of all, however, pertain to adolescent aggression and homicide rates. Prothrow-Stith (1991) points out that the homicide rate for young males in the United States is 4 to 73 times that of other industrialized nations and that of African-American males is four times greater than the U.S. average. Homicide is the number one cause of death for African-American males, resulting primarily from circles of friends and acquaintances.

This phenomenon of "primary relationship violence" indicates a need for programs to emphasize social relationships (Hammond & Yung, 1993, p. 150). The circumstances of low socioeconomic environments undoubtedly contribute to these events; however, Luthar (1991) and Luthar and Doernberger (1992) found that even under high stress conditions, socially skilled youth functioned better than their less skilled, less stressed counterparts. Although no single institution or program is adequate to address these concerns fully, in terms of school-based interventions and social skills instruction, there is no question that positive peer relations, stressing conflict management and behavioral alternatives to aggression, is one area of great need.

Instructional Implications

Several curriculum programs exist to teach prosocial behaviors and ways to manage aggression (e.g., Goldstein, 1988; Hazel, Schumaker, Sherman, & Sheldon-Wildgen, 1981). As noted in the preceding chapter, the Skillstreaming curriculum (Goldstein et al.) contains a list of skills and related activities designed to help adolescents constructively and nonaggressively handle potentially volatile situations. Although these programs provide the requisite skills and pedagogically sound strategies, a special issue for African-American youth centers on the most effective means of presentation so that the message not only will be heard, but received and employed. A study by MEE Productions (1992), entitled "Reaching the Hip-Hop Generation," underscores this point:

> This music-centered, male-dominated, rebellious, assertive voice of urban youth shapes (and is shaped by) the language, culture, fashion, hairstyles and worldview of a generation alienated not only from the Eurocentric dominant culture, but, to a surprising degree, from its own African-American heritage (p. 2).

The researchers note that even though there were indications of individual acceptance of some mainstream values, the ". . . strongest claim to allegiance of this audience is to its own subculture. Messages perceived as being from outside the culture have very little chance of getting in . . ." (p. 5). They observed that, to be effective, messages need to be peer-based, authentic, entertaining, delivered in the language of the street, and devoid of evidence of mainstream origins. This may be seen in the aftermath of the Los Angeles uprisings during the spring of 1992. Although community officials and leaders had long attempted to persuade gang leaders to stop the violence, it was not until the peer group (i.e., respected gang leaders) sanctioned this message (given credibility by the obviously senseless carnage) that the African-American gangs began to explore this option seriously. Ogbu (1981) suggests that this attitude among urban black males is rooted in their observation of generations of African Americans who subscribed to the rules and behaviors of mainstream society yet failed to reap commensurate gains.

Empirical documentation of the unique importance of the peer group is provided in research conducted by Hare (1979), as cited by Kuykendall (1992). In contrast to African-American females who related more strongly to academic achievement, African-American males were more inclined to base their self-image on their social ability and peer acceptance. Many activists have observed that the African-American male is prone to view "goodness" and academic achievement as feminine attributes, and therefore strive to establish his masculinity by proving that he is "bad" (Cross &

Foley, 1993). In an effort to counter these nonproductive perceptions, the Detroit Urban League devised a Male Responsibility Program (MRP) to develop culturally based personal/social skills in African-American males. The program focuses on the following characteristics:

- Have goals and aspirations identified early
- Show positive self-concept
- Show a strong sense of racial identity
- Exercise self-control and channel rage
- Benefit from someone's close supervision
- Have solid communication skills
- Become positive risk takers and reward themselves
- Have a spiritual foundation (Cross & Foley, 1993, p. 33).

Prothrow-Stith (1991) proposes school-based instructional programs to help urban youth deal constructively with anger and devise healthy alternatives to aggression and violence. In her book, *Deadly Consequences*, Prothrow-Stith describes a Peacemakers program in the Brooklyn, New York, schools where children and youth are first taught conflict resolution skills such as using assertive or "strong" language rather than aggressive statements when provoked. Children would learn to say, "'Don't bother me,' instead of 'Get your ugly face out of here'" (p. 174). The second component of the Peacemakers involves peer mediation—teachers help children reconcile disputes among their peers. Prothrow-Stith (1991) notes that many acts of violence and aggression are escalated by incendiary statements from peers, such as, "Don't let him talk to you like that," whereas peer mediation emphasizes that "Friends for life don't let friends fight" (p. 190). The peer mediation program is presented as follows:

> . . . each side is allowed to air its grievance, uninterrupted; mediators help each side clarify its grievance—often the issue at the heart of the dispute is not immediately apparent; the mediators keep both sides talking to one another until together they agree on the nature of the problem; the mediators help the two sides work out a balanced settlement that each side accepts as fair; the mediators write up the settlement and have it signed by both sides. Students who have had a fight settled by mediation may be asked to become mediators (p. 175).

Prothrow-Stith (1991) also outlines her 10-session curriculum on violence prevention. Students are first given information on violence and homicide to help them realize that all persons, including themselves, are vulnerable to commit such acts if they use poor self-management skills. This is followed by lessons on emotions (anger) and recognizing ways one typically handles anger. Students then conduct a "cost/benefit analysis" of fighting to determine if the actual returns were worth the fight. They are engaged in a discussion listing the good points (e.g., winning) versus the bad outcomes (e.g., killing someone or getting killed) of fighting. A resulting list, where the negatives of fighting far outweigh the beneficial effects, is used as the basis for helping students to question the wisdom of fighting and to begin to explore constructive alternatives to fighting. Through teacher prompting and guidance, students devise their own strategies for stopping or avoiding fights.

The strategies suggested for dealing with daily conflict situations are a salient and critical component of this curriculum. Many adolescents may at least covertly recognize the importance of avoiding aggression but are unaware of ways to defuse volatile situations effectively. With an overriding concern about losing face, how does a minority youth resist peer pressure to display manhood through aggression? Or how does one address obvious acts of "disrespect" in nonaggressive ways and maintain one's status in the peer group? These kinds of subtle issues, often hidden from the larger society, are the ones that tend to drive much of the maladaptive behavior in these communities. To be successful, instructional programs must address these issues explicitly and thoroughly.

Observing a paucity of research documenting successful social skills instruction with African-American subjects and the absence of culturally sensitive social skills curricula, Hammond and Yung (1993) assert the need for programs that incorporate culturally based instructional approaches. According to the authors, these include procedures such as using ethnicity-specific folktales with children, home-based therapy or education, indigenous outreach workers, and role models from the targeted cultural group.

Hammond (Hammond and Yung, 1991) built on the violence prevention program of Prothrow-Stith (1987) and the adolescent social skills training program of Hazel et al. (1981) to develop a social skills program—Positive Adolescents Choices Training (PACT)—for African-American youth. This is a cognitively based program, emphasizing communication, negotiation, and problem-solving skills. To address the interest and needs of its targeted audience, Hammond used African-American youth as models and devised role-playing scenarios that most likely reflected their daily experiences. Professionals involved with the students on a daily basis, as well as the student participants, provided suggestions for the conflict scenes. The modeling displays were presented on videotapes and students were given opportunities to role-play and practice desired behaviors.

This instructional program is commercially available in a set of three tapes and leader's guide entitled, *Dealing with Anger: A Social Skills Training Program for African-American Youth* (Hammond, 1991). The tapes address:

1. *Givin' It*—Constructive ways to express strong emotions.
2. *Takin' It*—Appropriately reacting to criticism and the anger of others.
3. *Workin' It Out*—Learning to negotiate and compromise in problem situations.

Hammond describes the tapes as follows:

> Each tape begins with a vignette of a conflict that escalates into a potentially violent confrontation. The narrator freezes the action and describes a skill that could have been used to defuse the violence. The same situation is played out again, but this time the

appropriate skill is used and the problem is solved without resorting to aggressive behavior.

A sample from Tape 3, *Workin' It Out*:

SUMMARY OF CONFLICT: Chad notices that the pump shoes Lamont is wearing are the ones that were stolen from his locker. Lamont says that he bought the shoes from a friend.

SKILL LESSON: How to negotiate a solution or work out a compromise to a conflict without resorting to aggressive or violent behavior. Explains that some situations are not negotiable (p. 371).

Hammond (1991) reports using these procedures with 14 African-American adolescent males. Training consisted of 37 to 38 sessions over a period of six months. "Success dollars" (paper money), which could be exchanged for backup rewards of cassette tapes, jewelry, t-shirts, and games, were used as reinforcers for participation and appropriate behavior. Observer ratings of videotaped role-plays, teacher ratings of daily behaviors, and school records of student suspensions/expulsions were more favorable for trained than untrained students.

Despite the foregoing discussion, it is important to point out that aggression and violence are not inherent in African-Americans; quite the contrary. Rather, the conditions of poverty and the messages of the popular culture cause a disproportionate percentage of these youngsters to be predisposed to acts of violence and aggression. Although African-American children are as capable as other children of behaving in socially appropriate ways—and the majority do already—"the decisions about drugs and other forms of behavior are made much earlier than the mainstream culture imagines on these hard streets where childhood can be very, very brief" (MEE, 1992, p. 2). This indicates a need for early intervention and continuous instruction throughout the grades. Teachers of preschool and primary-age children need to begin teaching alternatives to aggression, emphasizing the use of assertive language over verbal and physical aggression. This instruction needs to be schoolwide and include parents and other family members so the skills can be reinforced in the home and community.

Beyond direct instruction, teachers need to recognize the importance of establishing good relationships and a positive classroom climate to facilitate social skills development. To gain trust and rapport with African-American students, teachers must consistently demonstrate warmth and interest. Nonverbal clues are important. Soriano (1993) and other authorities point out differences in communication style between middle-class mainstream individuals and low socioeconomic minorities. Instead of verbal expressions of feelings and behavior, African Americans are more likely to rely on nonverbal communication. Children may perceive ambivalence when the teacher's tone and manner conflict with the spoken message. Also, because styles of body language may differ, children may receive the wrong message. To maximize chances for successful school experiences, teachers are encouraged to make an extra effort to convey concern. Blank or expressionless affect will likely be registered as indifference, remoteness, or superiority. Like all students, African-American youth thrive emotionally and cognitively when frequently reinforced. Programs with incentives for preestablished behavior and academic goals are effective. Verbal praise and physical demonstrations for approval (pats on the back, thumbs up signs, winks, hugs) are reassuring and motivating.

The beliefs of significant adults in the child's life are another often overlooked factor. Prothrow-Stith (1991) points out that these adults often possess attitudes similar to those of their students: the belief that the world is made up of victims and victimizers; in order not to be a victim one must be the aggressor. To be effective, teachers, parents, and other caretakers need to shed such fatalistic attitudes in favor of the belief that individuals have choices and can be proactive and respond constructively to threatening situations. By taking this position and becoming committed to preventing violence, teachers can communicate effectively to youth through both words and actions.

Finally, to be most effective, teachers must understand and build on the culture of African-American students. Literature, models, and role-play scenes should reflect their heritage and current experiences. Community mentors, particularly African-American males, should be recruited to help reinforce appropriate social and academic behaviors. Beginning early in their lives, children should be guided to problem-solve in conflict situations and to devise prosocial solutions. Every effort needs to be made to help students assume ownership for these solutions by creating constructive response repertoires that emerge from within the group rather than being superimposed by mainstream society. The use of the students' own language, styles, and music as a means of communication should be encouraged.

Native Americans

Native American refers to descendants of persons who were living in North America before the time of Columbus's landing. There are over 400 recognized native-American nations in the United States today. Language, religious beliefs, customs, and childrearing practices differ significantly among the nations. Recent literature searches reveal few studies that are tribe-specific. The terms *American Indian* and *native American* are often used generically without delineating memberships.

Cultural Distinctions

Trying to make generalizations about all native American nations would simply perpetuate stereotypes, while overlooking intra- and intertribe diversity. Another limitation of current research is the lack of long-term, in-depth qualitative studies that investigate multiple dimensions of a group of people. A presentation of various tendencies related to social skills will be qualified whenever possible by identifying specific tribes associated with the social behavior. Patterns of social behavior that have emerged are not only tribe-specific, but may be age- and gender-specific as well.

Nature of Interactions

Play Behaviors. Young native Americans of various nations are described as socially active. Little boys and girls, ages two through seven, play together freely with enthusiasm under the watchful care of an older sister. Clear lines are then drawn between the genders around age eight (Navajo, Hopi). Vogt, Jordan, and Tharp (1987) found that the formation of same-gender dyads and triads was a culturally appropriate classroom adaptation that enhanced the effectiveness of motivation management. This kind of separation of genders persists throughout life.

Games are spontaneous and creative. Children are prevented from hurting themselves but otherwise are not restricted from teasing, tagging, and so on. They are observed interacting like mainstream children. In fact, fifteen active native-American first-graders (no tribal distinction provided) served as a model group for increasing the social interaction of a Caucasian first-grade male in a successful study (Bergsgaard & Larsson, 1984).

When many native Americans reach age 10, however, they are expected to distinguish themselves physically and behaviorally from younger children. Young men do not play with little boys, and it is at this time that they would be expected not to engage in any one-on-one physical confrontations as younger children do. It is not manly to do so (Hopi). A spirit of cooperation and harmony with peers and others is strongly valued and reinforced not only for the Hopi, but for the Navajo, Creek, and Choctaws as well (Vogt et al., 1987; Scruggs & Mastropieri, 1985; Greenbaum, 1985). Greenbaum (1985), using videocameras to record data in four fifth- and sixth-grade classrooms in Mississippi, notes that Choctaws would not compete against peers for grades or criticize classmates.

Close Friends. It is worth noting that for many native-American children, the closest friends typically are not found and made in the classroom. Best friends very frequently are close relatives (Schneider, 1993). Alexander (1991) lived across the street from a child her age and attended public school classrooms in Tulsa. Yet her "best friend who was like a sister" was a first cousin who lived 20 miles away. The two families got together at least once a week, and she recalls those visits as "special times" with partings that were difficult. For the Creek and others (e.g., Hopi), a value stressed from the early years is to know who your larger family is and to respect its members (Alexander, 1991; Saslow & Harrover, 1968; Henderson, 1979).

Verbal Behavior. For the very young, many accounts report that singing, talking, and role-playing, in concert with traditional parenting practices, are uncensored. Various researchers report older children's "reticence" or unresponsiveness in the classroom (e.g., Mahan & Criger, 1977; Schneider, 1993; Youngman & Sadongie, 1974). Hopi children, and those of many other nations, are inclined to be silent in class. They may be labeled shy or uncommunicative: teachers report that questions directed to a native-American individual consistently may not be responded to, even though the student knows the answer.

In stark contrast, Choctaws speak out in the classroom setting. Compared to their Anglo counterparts, Choctaw students interrupt the teacher more often and must be taught the skill of alternating listening with speaking. Greenbaum (1985) refers to the need to teach them "switchboard participation." Although they speak out at will, it has been noted that Choctaw students use shorter utterances and gaze at their peers while the teacher is talking more than do students from the majority culture.

Various patterns of verbal behavior emerge not only by tribe but by gender within tribes. Alexander (1991) asserts that Creek women, for instance, are considered aggressive speakers, and that this characteristic "should not be viewed as an anomaly."

Prosocial Behavior. Demonstrations of anger or aggression are the exception rather than the rule for native Americans. Navajos are reported to value a sense of humor, laughing often and not taking themselves too seriously. In the culture, young men and women are trained to be good-natured in interactions with each other. This absence of aggression may be attributed partly to "the spirit of belonging" considered characteristic of native-American societies (Brendtro, Brokenleg, & Van Brockern, 1990, p. 37). Children are reared in communities where they are nurtured, taught, and supported by all members. Accordingly, they are helped to acquire a sense of belonging to all other individuals as well as to nature, which, in turn, encourages them to live in harmony with others and their physical surroundings.

Traditional native-American practices have undergone some marked changes in recent decades. Brendtro et al. (1990), note historical attributes of the culture, including (1) a sense of belongingness, (2) a spirit of mastery, (3) a spirit of independence, and (4) a spirit of generosity. From early childhood native-American children were encouraged to strive toward mastery in every human domain: physical, cognitive, spiritual, and social. Instructions came through stories that taught ways of behaving, games that encouraged competence and group participation, and work that fostered responsibility. In their quest for mastery, children were motivated to achieve personal goals, not to be superior to others. More skilled individuals were not viewed as competitors, but as models who were establishing a standard to be attained.

The development of independence and autonomy were extremely important features of the childrearing practices within native-American cultures. Although children were encouraged to make independent decisions, it was hoped that, through instructions and modeling, children would respect their elders and acquire a set of behaviors consistent with their community. Emphasis was placed on being self-disciplined rather than obedient, promoted largely through "kindly lecturing" rather than punishment.

Generosity or altruism completed this native-American circle of life. Acts of selfishness were frowned on. Although property was held privately, favor and prestige were extended to those who gave generously rather than to those who accumulated massive holdings. To some extent, the ability to serve and give to others was the reason for one's being. To illustrate this generous spirit, Brendtro et al. (1990) relate the following story:

> Another high-school boy will receive a new coat in the mail and wear it proudly to the next school dance. For the next three months the same coat will appear on cousins and friends at the weekly dances, and it may be several months before the original owner wears his new coat again. (p. 45)

Social Skill Needs

Researchers identify numerous problems in the native-American culture: high dropout rates, a disproportionate number of children classified for special education, higher rates of teen suicide, and substance abuse. These and other problems are undoubtedly caused or exacerbated by conditions such as these:

1. *Speaking English as a second language.* Different rates of verbal interactions are typical of individuals who are learning a different language that reflects a different culture.
2. *Being alienated from one's support system.* While the home and clan are highly valued for the inclusion and support of its members, legal sanctions force children to leave home and live in alien surroundings.
3. *Frequent moves.* Long-term relationships with peers or others are hampered when children are relocated as frequently as occurs in the native-American population.
4. *Forced assimilation into a culture.* Acculturation often includes practices in direct conflict with one's upbringing, including religious beliefs and rites of passage.

Educational Implications

Distinctions in patterns of behavior may be explained by the tenacious desire of many native Americans to be different. Although sentiments vary greatly, for many, an effort is being made to keep the good traits of their unique heritage. To maintain their identity is to separate themselves from the mainstream (Noland, 1991). The challenge for teachers and other professionals is to respect, understand, and build on the culture to bring about the successful inclusion of native Americans into their own and mainstream society. Toward this end, Brendtro et al. (1990) indicate the need to "mend the broken circle"—to interpret the child's problem behavior and prescribe actions according to the previously described four components of the circle of life:

1. Children acting out feelings of rejection might be helped through trusting, intimate relationships to produce a sense of *belonging.*

2. Those frustrated by a lack of *mastery* would benefit from well-designed success experiences.

3. Aberrant behaviors resulting from feelings of impotence and lack of self-control could be addressed through activities that promote self-determination and self-discipline to bring about *independence.*

4. The pitfalls of selfishness and self-serving behaviors can be overcome through *generosity*—opportunities to give and care for others.

Some specific structures and learning are indicated. Often forced to leave home for public schooling, native-American children are exposed to conditions that can easily lead to feelings of alienation and rejection. Creating accepting, belonging environments (which might be fostered through cooperative learning activities such as those discussed in Chapter 5) becomes most critical. Scruggs and Mastropieri (1985), for example, found that native-American children performed better in cooperative groups than with individual assignments.

Native culture and literature can be used to provide "kindly lectures" or direct instruction on desired social behaviors. As noted, native Americans traditionally used stories both for entertainment and lessons in human behavior. Two of these stories are provided by Cartledge and Kleefeld (in press) in their literature-based social skills curriculum for elementary-age students. A Cherokee tale, "The Animals' Ball Game" (Scheer, 1968), tells about how one set of animals helped less competent animals become skilled in playing a ball game. The story focuses on developing good play skills by including and helping rather than excluding others. Through a series of activities provided in curriculum, children identify and act out ways to help peers become more skilled in play activities.

Similar lessons can be explored in adolescent literature such as *The Education of Little Tree* (Carter, 1976). This book describes growing up as a Cherokee in the 1930s and provides in-depth and moving insight into the values and principles guiding the lives of these native Americans. For example, in the second chapter, one sees how self-discipline and independence are fostered when the grandfather, who knows his grandson wants to accompany him on the high trail, tells Little Tree that he could go but that the grandfather would not wake him in the morning: "A man rises of his own will in the morning." Although the grandfather made some extra loud noises the next morning, the young boy took pride in arising and presenting himself to his grandfather on time.

Chapters 3 and 4 of this book describe direct instruction and the self-management procedures that can be used to help students develop the requisite discipline to be socially competent in modern society. Finally, a "curriculum of caring" may be particularly appropriate for native-American students. Altruistic acts not only provide a needed service but returns may be even greater for the benefactor. Through such activities children often develop empathic responses, commonly considered precursors to prosocial behaviors. Group activities with a central goal also may contribute to a sense of community and belonging that aids in overall social development. As noted in Chapter 3, caring activities may take various forms, ranging from peer or cross-age tutoring to aiding the homeless.

Hall (1993) describes the National Indian Youth Leadership Project (NIYLP), which builds on the native-American heritage and promotes a concept of "servant leadership":

> The model of a servant leader has been passed down in the ancient languages of our people. It is available to a world too often broken by selfishness, exploitation, and domination. The lesson we must teach our young is simply stated in these old Navajo words, Yaa joobaa': "Having compassion for others above all" (p. 29).

At the seventh and eighth grade, youth attend a multicultural Leadership Camp to acquire skills and experiences they are to apply when they return to their respective communities. Training sessions vary, ranging from whitewater rafting to leadership seminars. An understanding grows that true leadership results from helping and empowering others. Sample community projects that have emerged from such training include adopting kindergarten students for reading and tutoring services and painting murals on the walls of a senior center. Reported effects on the native-American youth include increases in self-esteem and the development of higher-level thinking and problem-solving and conflict-resolution skills.

Asian Americans

As with the other groups discussed in this chapter, Asian Americans are a diverse population representing several different nations, languages, and subcultures. The most populous group in the United States from East and Southeast Asia include Japanese, Chinese, Koreans, and Vietnamese. A smaller related set of people from the Asia Pacific are immigrants from the Philippines, Guam, India, Indonesia, Laos, Burma, Cambodia, Malaysia, Pakistan, Samoa, Singapore, Sri Lanka, Thailand, and Tonga. With the exception of the Vietnamese and Cambodians, who came in the 1970s and 1980s as refugees of war, most Asian Americans were voluntary immigrants, beginning with the Chinese in the mid-1800s. Many, such as launderers and cooks, came to supply menial labor, but numerous others, particularly in recent years, have come to assume positions as businesspersons or professionals. Asian Americans tend to be concentrated in Hawaii and California, but representative groups are found in every region of the country at all socioeconomic levels.

Cultural Distinctions

The same reservations apply here as with the preceding culturally diverse groups. Asian Americans certainly are not a monolith, and there are sufficient inter- and intragroup differences to warrant extreme caution in discussing cultural common-alities. Nevertheless, there are some frequently occurring patterns that impact the child's social development and need to be addressed in the context of social skills instruction for Asian-American students. Based on the literature describing Asian and Western (U.S.) cultures, Table 10-1 compares the two. The Asian cultural traits

TABLE 10-1 Asian Cultures versus Western Culture

	Asian cultures	Western culture (U.S.)
Traditional worldview	* Revere and appease the ancestors or the spirits of the deceased.	* God is the creator and controller of the world.
Social control	* Restraint is internalized according to family values; feelings of guilt or shame can act as a powerful means of social control.	* More external restraint; achievement as well as failure are attributed to the individual.
Behavior rules	* Harmony is the basic rule guiding interaction with others. * Behavior should be based on role expectation. * Self-expression or feelings that may cause conflict are not encouraged but are restrained to maintain harmonious relations.	* Sincere people should behave on the basis of openness and the individual's feelings. * Self-expression and feelings are encouraged with an emphasis on the value of the individual.
Family role	* Family members have clearly defined roles, and the individual acts in accordance with role expectation.	* American families tend to relate to each other in an intimate fashion without emphasizing individual roles.
Parent–child relationship	* Parent–child relationships are bound tightly and continue through the whole life. * Individualism is thought of as selfish or not considerate of other family members.	* The individual is encouraged to break away from the family and go his or her own way. * Individual-centered society, individualism, independence, and self-sufficiency are stressed.
Parenting practices	* The child's behavior is the reflection of the family's dignity and "face." * Filial piety and deference to elders are stressed. Child's rights are not emphasized. * Children's obligations to the family also are emphasized by their parents or elders.	* Children are taught to take responsibility for their own behavior. * Children are encouraged to develop in their own way. * Rearing children is the parents' duty, but the child's obligation to the family is not stressed.

described to here pertain largely to the far eastern countries such as China, Japan, and Korea.

As shown, a major distinguishing feature of Asian societies is the central focus of the family and the greater emphasis placed on the family than on the individual. In Asian cultures, the family bond is systematically strengthened over one's lifetime, exercising considerable control over the individual's relationships and social behaviors. The reverse is more likely to be the case in the U.S. mainstream culture. Asian cultures tend to socialize their children to subjugate themselves to the will of the family, to be compliant, and to avoid any actions that would bring shame or disgrace to the family.

Social Skill Needs

The popular stereotypical image of the Asian American is that of the "model minority" (Sue & Morishima, 1982; Sue & Sue, 1972); however, research with Chinese- and Japanese-American students reveals that they are more likely to be isolated, lonely, nervous, anxious, less autonomous, and possess poorer self-concepts than their non-Asian peers (Asamen & Berry, 1987; Sue & Frank, 1973). Other researchers note that Asian Americans spend considerably more time doing homework than participating in social activities. They are not inclined to start dating until their late teens, with little interest in popular music, television, or athletics (Reglin & Adams, 1990).

Although their industry and academic achievement are laudatory, for some Asian Americans the disproportionate emphasis on academic performance may be costly in terms of lost opportunities to interact with peers and develop critical social behaviors. When placed in mainstream environments, many Asian-American students isolate themselves by ignoring social interactions and engage mainly in academic tasks. Social interactions are likely to be limited to their ethnic peers. Their usually compliant and on-task behavior in the classroom causes teachers to view them as well-adjusted. As a result, needs for personal adjustment or interpersonal skills may be overlooked by the school system or the larger U.S. society. Silence and extreme passivity, however, are not necessarily indicative of overall social adjustment.

An example of this can be seen in the following personal account given by an Asian-American college student. She did not like to go to school, she had no friends, she talked to no one, and no one talked to her. She recalled being teased and called names by her non-Asian classmates, and although she was deeply hurt, she made no response. Later she would cry when alone in her room. She described herself as being so shy it was difficult for her to make eye contact or speak to peers. She had equally limited interactions with teachers, who occasionally sent notes home on her report card stating, "She is very quiet at school." Perhaps her most positive recollections centered around the times she was assigned to help other students with academic assignments. The students expressed gratitude for her help, but that was all. According to this student, she felt best about herself when she was assisting one of the other students; otherwise, she did not like herself because she felt shy, lonely, and didn't have any friends. Things improved a bit in high school when she was assigned to edit the yearbook and got the opportunity to talk more to her teachers. At that point, she began to express herself more to other people.

Although not universal, the school experiences of this student may typify those of many Asian-American students inclined toward self-isolation. In the absence of academic and acting-out problems, such students are less likely to be identified for intervention. Yet the extreme social isolation, moderate peer rejection, and limited opportunities to try out and practice interpersonal skills are predictive of emotional and social difficulties.

Social communication with an emphasis on friendship-making and self-assertion skills is probably most critical for students corresponding to this profile. Several curriculum programs referred to previously in this text provide skill listings and instructional activities in these areas (e.g., Cartledge & Kleefeld, 1991; Stephens, 1992; Walker et al, 1983). Among others, instruction might include skills such as these:

Social Communication Skills

- Making eye contact
- Smiling
- Greeting others
- Starting a conversation
- Keeping a conversation going
- Asking questions
- Asking for help from peers
- Asking for help from the teacher
- Gaining attention from peers in appropriate ways
- Naming feelings in self and others
- Expressing feelings
- Speaking assertively

Friendship Making Skills

- Making positive statements to others
- Taking turns
- Sharing
- Joining the activity of others
- Inviting others to join
- Suggesting a group activity

Instructional Implications

Direct Instruction

Asian Americans have generally been found to be unreceptive to Western-style counseling, which often relies on unstructured talking or indirect methods. Instead, they prefer a more structured counseling environment and direct suggestions (Hartman & Askounis, 1989; Sue, 1981; Sue & Morishima, 1982). Therefore, a skills training model, such as that detailed in this book, may be the most effective way to help Asian-American children catch up and learn facilitating behaviors in the mainstream environment.

For Asian-American students who are characterized by passive, quiet, and shy behaviors, teachers may have to prompt extensively to help them initiate new social skills. Teachers need to encourage such students to respond more in class under formal and informal conditions, structure and provide more opportunities for formal and informal interaction with other students, and praise attempts to act out newly acquired behaviors. To facilitate the learning of the Asian-American students, non-Asian students can be prompted, encouraged, and reinforced to interact with their Asian-American classmates. Viewing parents and teachers as symbols of authority, the Asian society tends to respect teachers highly. Thus, teacher praise alone may be a sufficiently powerful reinforcer for shaping social behaviors, discounting the need for tangible rewards.

Cooperative Learning

Cooperative learning, where students work together to achieve some common goal or produce one academic product, is another means for promoting peer interactions. Through cooperative learning, structured peer interactions may provide for meaningful interdependent relationships, increasing the students' feelings of belonging, acceptance, support, and caring. With this self-approval experience, and the acquisition of social skills, cooperative learning also can help children become more autonomous, which means they are able to consider both their internal values and situation requirements and to respond in flexible, appropriate ways (Johnson & Johnson, 1987). Children with a history of isolation or rejection by peers usually emit less autonomous and more behavior directed by others (Asamen & Berry, 1987; Johnson & Johnson, 1987)—a condition common to Asian-American students, due to their cultural influence (high conformity and meek behavior).

To bring about a better outcome for Asian-American students at risk, some cultural factors should be taken into consideration when structuring cooperative learning environments. The first pertains to specific instructional objectives. For Asian-American students, the emphasis should be on collaboration—which does not mean working independently within the group or one member doing the work for the group. Teachers need to identify collaborative academic behaviors and analyze them into specific responses, which include at least the following major skills: (1) beginning and talking about the assignment (on-task behaviors); (2) teaching peers how to perform an assignment, which may involve asking for help and giving help to group members; and (3) being able to reinforce each other's academic and social behaviors (Cartledge & Cochran, 1993). Each of these abilities needs to be taught in the same manner as any other social skill.

A second consideration is the size of the group. Johnson and Johnson (1987) suggest that when initiating cooperative groups, pairs or threesomes are a good start. The learning group needs to be small enough so each member in the group can join in the discussion. This is especially important for the Asian-American student who tends to retreat from mixed-group situations.

Assigning students to heterogeneous groups is the third concern. Students appear to gain more from group heterogeneity (Johnson & Johnson, 1987). Asian-American students, who are inclined to band together and segregate themselves from the mainstream environment, would benefit from groupings with non-Asian, socially appropriate students.

Finally, because Asian-American students tend to stress academics disproportionately, initial cooperative groups might place greater emphasis on group participation than on the completion of some academic task. Cartledge and Cochran (1990) found that cooperative behaviors occur more easily if the demands of the academic tasks are reduced when first establishing groups. The students in their study exhibited many more cooperative behaviors when practicing previously learned math facts in a game format than when attempting to complete worksheets on newly taught math skills. Creating cooperative groups where the focus is on full, equal, friendly participation by all members would be most advantageous for Asian-American students. Teachers should resist the temptation to put these students in the role of "teacher"; this further reinforces the stereotype that peer interactions with Asian Americans should be restricted to academic matters.

Summary

The U.S. population has more commonalities than differences, yet the diversity among the cultures mandates analysis of subcultures for instructional implications. Educators are challenged to help equip children and youth from culturally diverse backgrounds with social behaviors that will promote and preserve their personal integrity while simultaneously contributing to the common good. The cultural distinctions discussed in this chapter for the four minority groups point to some consistent themes.

First, the fierce desire to establish or maintain one's unique heritage or culture may cause many minority youth to reject mainstream teachings, particularly as they pertain to social behaviors. To increase receptivity: (1) instruction might be presented from the learner's cultural roots (established cultural teachings), (2) the learner should be helped to understand how the behavior is in his or her best interest, and (3) the learner should collaborate with the instructor on effective strategies for performing the behavior.

Second, a sense of alienation is common among culturally different children and youth and often manifests itself in both internalizing and externalizing maladaptive behaviors. This indicates the need for teachers to become skilled in ways to validate their learners. Social skills trainers must take the time and effort to learn and understand the culture and language of their students. Beyond being able to speak in Spanish, for example, trainers need to understand the jargon and nuances of meaning in the language used by their students. Instruction needs to be presented in a nonjudgmental manner, reflecting an acceptance of the students, if not their behavior. Through creating the appropriate atmosphere, instructors can collaborate with students to devise strategies to promote interpersonal and school success and minimize peer rejection.

A sensitive instructor is aware of the different backgrounds of the students and makes a systematic effort to recognize prior learnings that may differ from the experiences of the majority group. Each student is allowed the dignity of being expected to learn and is empowered by being taught the skills essential for school and adult success. Effective teachers can communicate with the students and their parents. Being products of their own cultures, teachers may fall short in attaining total fluency and understanding of another culture, but sincere caring for a child rarely will be misinterpreted.

Finally, the cultural roots of each of the groups discussed here are grounded in "collectivistic" rather than "individualistic" societies characteristic of the United States and other major English-speaking countries (Schneider, 1993). Despite some differences and changes over time, members of these cultural groups typically are oriented to group/family goals rather than individual goals and competitive achievements. Minority students tend to learn well through group, peer-mediated activities. Cooperative learning groups should be mixed according to cultural backgrounds, academic performance, and social skills. The effective teacher acknowledges the distinctions of a cultural minority, but sees individuals as foremost. While affirming the contributions of diverse peoples, special experiences need to be orchestrated for the entire learning group so that each subgroup can feel commonly bound with a collective, greater whole.

References

Alexander, M. (1991). Unpublished interview. Columbus, OH: The Ohio State University.

Arnold, B., & Orozco, S. (1989). Acculturation and evaluation of Mexican Americans with disabilities. *Journal of Rehabilitation, 55*(1), 53–57.

Asamen, J. K., & Berry, G. L. (1987). Self-concept, alienation, and perceived prejudice: Implications for counseling Asian Americans. *Journal of Multicultural Counseling and Development, 15*(4), 146–159.

Bergsgaard, M. O., & Larsson, E. V. (1984). Increasing social interaction between an isolate first grader and cross-cultural peers. *Psychology in the Schools, 21*(2), 244–251.

Brendtro, L. K., Brokenleg, M., & Van Bockern, S. (1990). *Reclaiming youth at risk.* Bloomington, IN: National Educational Service.

Carlson, P. E., & Stephens, T. M. (1986). Cultural bias and identification of behaviorally disordered and learning disabled students. *Behavioral Disorders, 3*(11), 191–199.

Carter, F. (1976). *The education of Little Tree.* New York: Delacorte Press.

Cartledge, G., & Cochran, L. (1990, November). *Developing cooperative learning behaviors in students with behavior disorders.* Paper presented at Annual Conference for Ohio Federation for Council for Exceptional Children, Cleveland, OH.

———. (1993). Developing cooperative learning behaviors in students with behavior disorders. *Preventing School Failure, 37,* 5–10.

Cartledge, G., & Kleefeld, J. (1991). *Taking part: Introducing social skills to children.* Circle Pines, MN: American Guidance Service.

————. (in press). *Working together.* Circle Pines, MN: American Guidance Service.

Cartledge, G., & Milburn, J. (1986). *Teaching social skills to children: Innovative approaches,* 2d ed. New York: Pergamon Press.

The Commission on Minority Participation in Education and American Life (1988). *One-third of a nation.* Washington, DC: American Council on Education.

Cross, M., & Foley, R. (1993). Reclaiming an endangered species: The male responsibility program. *Journal of Emotional and Behavioral Problems, 1*(4), 33–36.

The Encyclopedia Americana: International Edition (1980). Danbury, CT: Americana Corporation; Vol. 14, 370–371.

Figueroa, R., & Gallegos, E. A. (1978). Ethnic differences in school behavior. *Sociology of Education, 51,* 289–298.

Fry, D. P. (1988). Intercommunity differences in aggression among Zapotec children. *Child Development, 59,* 1008–1019.

Fuentes, J. (1988). *The effects of social background, Spanish use, and English proficiency on codeswitching attitudes and behavior.* Paper presented at the Annual Meeting of the National Association for Bilingual Education, Miami, FL.

Ghali, S. B. (1979). Culture sensitivity and the Puerto Rican client. In G. Henderson (Ed.), *Understanding and counseling ethnic minorities* (pp. 232–250). Springfield, IL: Charles C. Thomas.

Goldstein, A. P. (1988). *The Prepare curriculum.* Champaign, IL: Research Press.

Goldstein, A. P., Sprafkin, R. P., Gershaw, N. J., & Klein, P. (1986). The adolescent: Social skills training through structured learning. In G. Cartledge & J. Milburn (Eds.), *Teaching social skills to children: Innovative approaches,* 2d ed. (pp. 303–336). New York: Pergamon Press.

Goode, K. G. (1979). From Africa to the United States. In G. Henderson (Ed.), *Understanding and counseling ethnic minorities* (pp. 32–42). Springfield, IL: Charles C. Thomas.

Greenbaum, P. E. (1985). Nonverbal differences in communication style between American Indian and Anglo elementary classroom. *American Educational Research Journal, 22*(1), 101–115.

Hall, M. (1993). In our own language: Youth as servant leaders. *Journal of Emotional and Behavioral Problems, 1,* 27–29.

Hammond, W. R. (1991). *Dealing with anger: Givin' it, takin' it, workin' it out.* Champaign, IL: Research Press.

Hammond, W. R., & Yung, B. R. (1991). Preventing violence in at-risk African-American youth. *Journal of Health Care for the Poor and Underserved, 2*(3), 359–373.

————. (1993). Psychology's role in the public health response to assaultive violence among young African-American men. *American Psychologist, 48*(2), 142–154.

Hare, B. (1979). *Black girls: A comparative analysis of self perceptions and achievement by race, sex and socioeconomic background.* Baltimore: The Johns Hopkins University Press.

Hartman, J. S., & Askounis, A. C. (1989). Asian-American students: Are they really a "model minority"? *The School Counselor, 37*(2), 109–112.

Hazel, S., Schumaker, J. B., Sherman, J. A., & Sheldon-Wildgen, J. (1981). The development and evaluation of group training program for teaching social and problem-solving skills to court-adjudicated youths. In D. Upper & S. M. Ross (Eds.), *Behavioral group therapy.* Champaign, IL: Research Press.

Henderson, G. (1979). *Understanding and counseling ethnic minorities.* Springfield, IL: Charles C. Thomas.

Johnson, D. W., & Johnson, R. T. (1987). *Learning together and alone: Cooperative, competitive, and individualistic learning.* Englewood Cliffs, NJ: Prentice-Hall.

Keller, H. R. (1988). Children's adaptive behaviors: Measure and source generalizability. *Journal of Psychoeducational Assessment, 6,* 371–389.

Kochman, T. (1981). *Black and white styles in conflict.* Chicago: The University of Chicago Press.

Kunjufu, J. (1989). *A Talk with Jawanza: Critical issues in educating African-American youth.* Chicago: African American Images.

Kuykendall, C. (1992). *From rage to hope: Strategies for reclaiming Black and Hispanic students.* Bloomington, IN: National Educational Service.

Lethermon, V. R., Williamson, D. A., Moody, S. C., Granberry, S. W., Lemanek, K. L., & Bodiford, C. (1984). Factors affecting the social validity of a role-play test of children's social skills. *Journal of Behavioral Assessment, 6*(3), 231–245.

Lethermon, V. R., Williamson, D. A., Moody, S. C., & Wozniak, P. (1986). Racial bias in behavioral assessment of children's social skills. *Journal of Psychopathology and Behavioral Assessment, 8*(4), 329–337.

Lewis, O. (1979). The Rios family. In G. Henderson (Ed.), *Understanding and counseling ethnic minorities* (pp. 207–215). Springfield, IL: Charles C. Thomas.

Litsinger, D. E. (1973). *The challenge of teaching Mexican-American students.* New York: American Book Company.

Luthar, S. S. (1991). Vulnerability and resilience: A study of high-risk adolescents. *Child Development, 62,* 600–616.

Luthar, S. S., & Doernberger, C. H. (1992, August). *Resilience among inner-city teenagers: Further empirical insights.* Paper presented at the meeting of the American Psychological Association, Washington, DC.

Maccoby, E. E. (1980). Child rearing practices and their effects. *Social Development.* New York: Harcourt Brace Jovanovich.

Mahan, J. M., & Criger, M. K. (1977). Culturally oriented instruction for Native American students. In G. Henderson (Ed.), *Understanding and counseling ethnic minorities* (pp. 318–328). Springfield, IL: Charles C. Thomas.

Maldonado, B. M., & Cross, W. C. (1979). Today's Chicano refutes the stereotype. *College Student Journal, 11,* 46–152.

Marin, G., & Marin, B. V. (1991). *Research with Hispanic populations.* Newbury Park, CA: Sage Publications.

MEE Productions, Inc. (May, 1992). *Reaching the hip-hop generation.* Executive Summary of a Study by MEE Productions, Inc. to the Robert Wood Johnson Foundation. West Philadelphia Enterprise Center, 4601 Market Street, Philadelphia, PA.

Moore, H., & Porter, N. (1988). Leadership and nonverbal behaviors of Hispanic females across school equity environments. *Psychology of Women Quarterly, 12*(2), 147–163.

Moyer, T. R., & Motta, R. W. (1982). Alienation and school adjustment among black and white adolescents. *The Journal of Psychology, 112,* 21–28

Nieto, S. (1992). *Affirming diversity.* New York: Longman.

Noland, K. (1991). Unpublished interview. Columbus, OH: The Ohio State University.

Ogbu, J. U. (1981). Origins of human competence: A cultural-ecological perspective. *Child Development, 52,* 413–429.

———. (1990). Literacy and schooling in subordinate cultures: The case of Black Americans. In K. Lomotey (Ed.), *Going to school: The African-American experience* (pp. 113–131). New York: State University of New York Press.

Prothrow-Stith, D. (1991). *Deadly consequences.* New York: HarperCollins.

Reglin, G. L., & Adams, D. R. (1990). Why Asian-American high school students have higher grade point averages and SAT scores than other high school students. *High School Journal*, 73(3), 143–149.

Saslow, H. L., & Harrover, M. J. (1968). Research on psychosocial adjustment of Indian youth. In G. Henderson (Ed.), *Understanding and counseling ethnic minorities* (pp. 291–306). Springfield, IL: Charles C. Thomas.

Scheer, G. F. (1968). *Cherokee animal tales*. New York: Holiday House, Inc.

Schneider, B. H. (1993). *Children's social competence in context: The contributions of family, school and culture*. Oxford: Pergamon Press.

Scruggs, T. E., & Mastropieri, M. A. (1985). Cooperative vs. competitive performances of behaviorally disordered American Indian adolescents. *Journal of Instructional Psychology*, 12, 31–33.

Shade, B. J. (1979). Social-psychological characteristics of achieving black children. In G. Henderson (Ed.), *Understanding and counseling ethnic minorities* (pp. 60–69). Springfield, IL: Charles C. Thomas.

Smith, C., & Brewbaker, J. (1989). Ms. Smiff and Rodriguez bridge the crain-cracks gap. *English Education*, 21(2), 88–91.

Soriano, F. (1993). Cultural sensitivity and gang intervention. In A. Goldstein & C. R. Huff (Eds.), *The gang intervention handbook* (pp. 141–161). Champaign, IL: Research Press.

Stephens, T. M. (1980). *The SBA technical manual*. Columbus, OH: Cedars Press.

———. (1992). *Social skills in the classroom*. Odessa, FL: Psychological Assessment Resources, Inc.

Sue, D. W. (1981). *Counseling the culturally different: Theory and practice*. New York: John Wiley & Sons.

Sue, D. W., & Frank, A. C. (1973). A typological approach to the psychological study of Chinese and Japanese-American college males. *Journal of Social Issues*, 29, 129–148.

Sue, D. W., & Sue, S. (1972). Ethnic minorities: Resistance to being researched. *Professional Psychology*, 20, 142–148.

Sue, S., & Morishima, J. K. (1982). *The mental health of Asian Americans: Contemporary issues in identifying and treating mental problems*. San Francisco: Jossey-Bass.

Sugai, G., & Maheady, L. (1988). Cultural diversity and individual assessment for behavior disorders. *Teaching Exceptional Children*, 21, 28–31.

Swisher, K., & Deyhle, D. (1989). The styles of learning are different, but the teaching is just the same: Suggestions for teachers of American Indian youth. *Journal of American Indian Education, Special Issue*, 1–14.

Taylor, R. (1988/89). African-American inner-city youth and the subculture of disengagement. *The Urban League Review*, 12, 15–24.

Turnbull, A. P., & Turnbull, H. R. (1986). *Families, professionals, and exceptionality: A special partnership*. Columbus, OH: Merrill.

Turner, S. M., Beidel, D. C., Hersen, M., & Bellack, A. S. (1984). Effects of race on ratings of social skill. *Journal of Consulting and Clinical Psychology*, 52(3), 474–475.

Vogt, L. A., Jordan, C., & Tharp, R. G. (1987). Explaining school failure, producing school success: Two cases. Special Issue: Explaining the school performance of minority students. *Anthropology and Education Quarterly*, 18(4), 276–286.

Walker, H. M., McConnell, S., Holmes, D., Todis, B., Walker, J., & Golden, N. (1983). *The Walker social skills curriculum: The accepts program*. Austin, TX: PRO-ED.

Wells, S. E. (1990). *At-risk youth: Identification, programs, and recommendations*. Englewood, CO: Teacher Ideas Press.

Youngman, G., & Sadongie, M. (1974). Counseling the American Indian Child. *Elementary School Guidance and Counseling*, 8, 273–277.

Zeleny, R. O. (1991). *The World Book Encyclopedia*, 9, 248–253, Chicago: World Book, Inc.

Appendix *A*

Resource Materials for Teaching Social Skills

This appendix presents materials that could be employed by the teacher or clinician as stimuli to set the stage for social skills instruction, as vehicles for teaching, or as ways to provide practice and generalization of skills. It is organized into categories corresponding to the principal medium through which the material is presented. These include: curriculum programs and kits, printed materials and books, audiovisual presentations, dramatic play materials, and games. The materials are organized into age levels as nearly as possible. This list is not exhaustive, and its intent is to make the reader aware of materials available rather than to endorse any specific items.

Curriculum Programs and Kits

My Friends and Me

Preschool. Kit includes teacher's guide, 2 activity manuals containing instructions for 190 activities; metal carrying case; 24" x 32" freestanding activity board; six 23" x 29" full-color activity pictures; 59 magnetic shapes in various forms and colors; two 10" x 12" storybooks with 40 stories and 232 color illustrations; two fuzzy 12" dolls; three inked print blocks of adults, children, and the above-mentioned doll figures; five cassettes or twelve 7" records containing 16 recorded activities, narration, dialogue, and 23 songs; miscellaneous equipment—ink pad, ink, sponge, four liquid-chalk pens, eraser; song cards (7" x 9 3/4"); and spirit masters of 38 illustrated family activities. Kit assists personal and social development. (American Guidance Service)

*Arizona Basic Assessment and Curriculum Utilization
System (ABACUS)*

Learners with disabilities—developmental ages 2 to 5-1/2. Comprehensive
program designed to screen, assess, program, and monitor the progress of disabled
children, relative to their body management, self-care, communication, preaca-
demic, and social skills. Socialization: (1) awareness of self and others, (2) awareness of feelings, (3) social information, (4) play behavior, and (5) interactive
behavior. (Love Publishing Co.)

*I Can Problem Solve: An Interpersonal Cognitive
Problem-solving Program: Preschool (Myrna B. Shure)*

Spiral-bound manual containing 59 lessons designed for three- and four-year-old
children to teach problem-solving skills through use of games, stories, puppets, and
role playing. Lessons grouped into (1) pre-problem-solving skills focusing on learning
a problem-solving vocabulary, identifying one's own and other's feelings, and
considering other people's point of view; (2) problem-solving skills, focusing on
thinking of more than one solution, considering consequences, and deciding which
solution to choose. (Research Press)

D U S O Kit D-1 (Revised)

Kindergarten and lower elementary. Activities designed to aid in learning words
for feelings; learning that feelings, goals, values, and behavior are dynamically
related; and learning to talk more freely about feelings, goals, values, and behavior.
Materials are manual, 2 storybooks, 33 posters with easel, 21 records or 5 cassettes,
6 handpuppets, 11 puppet props, 2 character puppets, 33 puppet-activity cards, 5
group-discussion cards, 33 role-playing activity cards. (American Guidance Service)

Taking Part

Introducing social skills to children, preschool to grade 3. Uses a skills training model to teach activities for identifying, developing, and practicing the skill.
Also includes procedures for skill maintenance and transfer. Program contains
instruction manual, puppets, reinforcement stickers, and skill posters. (American
Guidance Service)

*I Can Problem Solve: An Interpersonal Cognitive
Problem-solving Program: Kindergarten & Primary Grades
(Myrna B. Shure)*

Spiral-bound manual containing lessons adapting material in preschool manual to
early primary grades. Teaches skills through use of games, stories, puppets and role
playing. Lessons are grouped into two major categories: pre-problem-solving skills
and problem-solving skills. (Research Press)

D U S O Kit D-2 (Revised)

Upper primary to grade 4. Activities to develop understanding and valuing of oneself; understanding of interpersonal relationships and purposive nature of human behavior; and understanding of interrelationships among ideas, feelings, beliefs, behavior, and competence. Materials include: manual, 33 posters with easel, 27 records or 5 cassettes, 6 handpuppets, 2 character puppets, 33 puppet-activity cards, 5 group-discussion cards, 33 role-playing activity cards. (American Guidance Service)

I Can Problem Solve: An Interpersonal Cognitive Problem-solving Program: Intermediate Elementary Grades (Myrna B. Shure)

Spiral-bound manual containing lessons for teaching pre-problem-solving and problem-solving skills to intermediate elementary children. Includes material similar to preschool and kindergarten and primary grade curricula adapted to older children. (Research Press)

Getting Along with Others: Teaching Social Effectiveness to Children

Elementary. Instructional program consisting of guide, skill lessons and activities, and videotapes. A skills training model is employed to help elementary-age children develop specific skills pertaining to introductions, following directions, verbal and nonverbal communication, sharing, helping, problem solving, giving and responding to feedback, responding to teasing, and resisting peer pressure. (Research Press)

Learning the Skills of Peacemaking

Elementary. Includes 56 lessons designed to teach children that peace begins with the individual and is spread through an understanding of ourselves and others. (Childswork/Childsplay)

I Can Behave

Elementary. Self-management curriculum designed to teach self-control and independent work skills. Includes storybook, student workbooks, and assessment materials. (PRO-ED)

Think Aloud: Increasing Social and Cognitive Skills— A Problem-solving Program for Children

Elementary. Structured learning activities are provided, designed to help children think through social situations and cope with various problems. Children are trained in problem-solving techniques and ways to use self-speech to direct social behavior. Program divided into three levels: (a) grades 1–2, (b) grades 3–4, and (c) grades 5–6. (Research Press)

Social Skill Strategies (Books A and B)

Grades 5 through 12. Two books of strategies on social communication skills. Includes lessons on introductory skills, peer interaction skills, and emotional expression skills. (Thinking Publication)

ACCESS Program

Grades 6 through 12. Comprehensive curriculum to teach interpersonal and self-management skills to adolescents. Designed for regular and special education settings. (PRO-ED)

Personal Power

Grades 6 through 12. Comprehensive curriculum designed to teach school-related, self-related, and peer-related social skills. Lessons include games, stories, artwork, and group exercises. (PRO-ED)

Toward Affective Development (TAD)

Grades 3 through 6. A social skills program consisting of 191 sequenced lessons, posters, discussion pictures, audiocassettes, and pupil worksheets. Emphasis is on feelings and peer relationships. Activities include role-playing, modeling, simulations, problem solving, and games. Organized into five sections:

1. Reaching In and Reaching Out—sensory awareness and creative thinking.
2. Your Feelings and Mine—labeling and interpreting feelings.
3. Working Together—cooperative participation.
4. Me: Today and Tomorrow—relating personal traits to world of work.
5. Feeling, Thinking, Doing—conflict resolution. (American Guidance Service)

Transition

Elementary and junior high. Emphasizes social and emotional growth of middle school and junior high school student. Appreciation of human differences is stressed by presenting a wide range of racial, ethnic, and economic groups and physical handicaps. Activities for students to write out and act out scenarios about personal conflicts and decision making, simulated encounters, directed observation and analysis of human behavior, and large and small group discussions. Program consists of five units: (1) Communication and Problem-solving Skills; (2) Encouraging Openness and Trust; (3) Verbal and Nonverbal Communication of Feelings;

(4) Needs, Goals, and Expectations; and (5) Increasing Awareness of Values. (American Guidance Service)

Asset: A Social Skills Program for Adolescents

Adolescents. A social skills training program that addresses giving and receiving feedback, resisting peer pressure, problem solving, negotiating, following instructions, and conversing. The program consists of 8 films or videocassettes, leader's guide, and program materials. (Research Press)

The Walker Social Skills Curriculum: The Accepts Program

Children with disabilities. A social skills curriculum, employing the skills training model, to ease the integration of children with disabilities into less restrictive settings. Specific instructional scripts are provided for the following classes of behavior: (1) classroom skills, (2) basic interaction skills, (3) getting along skills, (4) making friends skills, and (5) coping skills. Program also includes videotape that provides an overview of curriculum program and videotape that demonstrates positive and negative modeling of target skills for trainees. (PRO-ED)

Social Skills for Daily Living

Adolescents with or without disabilities. Curriculum program designed to teach personal interaction, social communication, and problem-solving skills. Comic book space adventure series used to provide practical strategies to help learner develop critical social skills for home, school, and on the job. Instruction also includes workbook and role-play activities. (American Guidance Service)

Social Skills on the Job

Ages 15 and up. Learner with mild mental retardation and behavior disorders. Video vignettes are used to model and develop appropriate work related behaviors. Curriculum addresses 14 skills and provides for individual practice through interactive materials. Materials include videotape, manual, worksheets, and computer discs. (American Guidance Service)

Aggression Replacement Training

Adolescents. Three-part training program designed to teach students to understand and replace aggression and antisocial behavior with positive alternatives. Training focuses on the development of prosocial skills, anger control, and moral reasoning. (Research Press)

Scripting

Adolescents. Short plays for adolescents to read/perform to reinforce social skills instruction. (Thinking Publications)

The Waksman Social Skills Curriculum

Adolescents. Program for teaching adolescents appropriate assertiveness skills. Contains specific lessons, homework assignments, and student workbooks. (PRO-ED)

Printed Materials and Books

Printed Materials

I Have Feelings

Ages 4 to 9. Pictures and narrative of boy experiencing different emotions. (Human Sciences Press, Inc.)

Emotions Poster

Elementary. Poster containing pictures of children displaying 28 different emotions. (Childswork/Childsplay)

Activities for Exploring Conflict and Aggression

Secondary. Instructional activities focused on means for conflict resolution. Can be used as separate unit or integrated into regular curriculum. (J. Weston Walch, Publisher)

Books—Practitioner

The Bookfinder

Ages 2 through adolescence. Three volumes: Volume 1—through 1974, Volume 2—1975 through 1978, Volume 3—1979 through 1982. Provides references and descriptions for children's books according to more than 450 psychological, behavioral, developmental topics. The referenced books may be useful in helping the reader develop insight and possible alternatives for problem situations. (American Guidance Service)

Rational Emotive Education: A Manual for Elementary School Teachers, Knaus

Elementary. A curriculum guide that adapts the principles of Rational Emotive Therapy for application in the elementary classroom. The program includes the principles of RET, irrational belief systems, feelings of inferiority, learning, catastrophizing, responsibility, perspective taking, stereotyping, teasing, bullying, protesting, and friendships. (Institute for Rational Living, Inc.)

Talking, Listening, Communicating

Elementary. Curriculum guide designed to teach social communication skills through group activities. The chapters are: (1) Preparing Yourself, (2) Understanding Self, (3) Communication, (4) Building Groups, (5) Relating to Others, (6) Developing Creativity, (7) Making Decisions, (8) Solving Problems, (9) Ending a T.L.C. Group. Skills to be developed include group leadership, social interaction, creativity, problem solving, decision making, and how to end the group positively. (PRO-ED)

A Rational Counseling Primer

Elementary. Young, H. S. (Institute for Rational Living)

100 Ways to Enhance Self-concept in the Classroom

Elementary. Canfield & Wells. (Prentice-Hall, Inc.)

Teaching Interpersonal and Community Living Skills

Adolescents and adults with disabilities. This book provides a guide for devising objectives and instructional activities to develop community living skills among handicapped adolescents and adults. Emphasis is placed on skills relating to work, consumerism, citizenship, transportation, family living, learning, and recreation. (PRO-ED)

Leisure Programs for Persons with Disabilities

Moderately/severely disabled. Curriculum useful for developing instructional programs for the leisure-time activities of children with disabilities. Contents include: (1) normalization, (2) leisure skills assessment, (3) leisure instruction, (4) adapting leisure skills, (5) curriculum design and format, (6) hobbies, (7) sports, (8) games, (9) object manipulation, and (10) program implementation. (PRO-ED)

Creative Conflict Resolution

Grades kindergarten through 6. Contains over 20 conflict resolution techniques designed to help teachers deal creatively and constructively with conflict situations typically occurring in elementary classrooms. Also includes reproducible worksheets and numerous activities and cooperative games. (Scott, Foresman and Company)

Records and Cassettes

Ideas, Thoughts, and Feelings—The Learning Party

Primary. Musical album helps the young child understand growing, senses, family, and relating to others. Includes guide. (Constructive Playthings)

Relaxation—The Key to Life

Elementary. Goldsmith, Rachell C., and Barry Goldsmith. Recorded on Kimbo L.P. 9080. Manual. (Kimbo Educational Activities, 1973)

Peace, Harmony, Awareness

All ages. Audio program that teaches relaxation, self-confidence, and control, and helps improve relationships. Can be used with individuals, groups, and children with special needs. Consists of a manual, six audiocassettes, and seven 8" by 10" color photographs. (Teaching Resources Corporation)

Socialization Skills—Adaptive Behavior

Children with disabilities. Sixteen songs on record or cassette presenting concepts involving sharing, emotional awareness, social skills, manners, and listening. (Kimbo Educational)

Films/Videos

Learning Values with Fat Albert

Elementary. Set of 16 animated films with the live presence of Bill Cosby as host. Films address real-life problems typically experienced by young people and means for problem solving. Subject matter of these films includes: animal care/protection, misjudgment, individuality, drugs, doctors/hospitals, nutrition, honesty, alcoholism, smoking, new people/places, shoplifting, death/dying, deafness, and friendship. (McGraw-Hill)

Delicious Inventions from Willy Wonka and the Chocolate Factory

Elementary. Five children tour Wonka's wonderful factory and receive a sweet lesson in manners. 15-minute full-color film. (Films Incorporated)

Positive Interactions for Success with Children

Elementary. Series of five 17-minute color videotapes available in 3/4", VHS, or Beta. Designed to accompany written program *Getting Along with Others*. Includes step-by-step outline of major program components, including setting expectations for social behavior and using specific teaching strategies. (Social Effectiveness Training)

Catch 'em Being Good

Elementary. Presents ways to use behavioral approaches in the elementary classroom. Developed to help teachers and students solve problems such as aggression, disruptive behavior, and lack of attentiveness. 30 minutes. (Research Press)

Worry: I'm in Big Trouble Now

Intermediate to junior high. Billy, who is in charge of his little brother, loses him while exploring a barn with a friend. Provokes discussion on responsibility, guilt, fear, and worry. Color, 12 minutes, videocassette. (Guidance Associates)

The Transformation of Mabel Wells

Intermediate to junior high–secondary. A cranky old woman returns from the hospital to find get-well cards and gifts from many people. Provokes discussion of loneliness, helping, and friendship. Color, 12 minutes. Cine Golden Eagle Award. (Guidance Associates)

Loneliness: The Empty Tree House

Intermediate to junior high. Tony sees his best friend spending more and more time with a new boy. Provokes discussion on demands we make on friends and how we can prepare for changes in a relationship. 13 minutes. (Guidance Associates)

Learning to Manage Anger

Junior and senior high. Designed to teach students the seven-step RETHINK method for controlling anger and resolving conflict. Student actors dramatize real-life conflict situations which are used to demonstrate the RETHINK model. Video allow for viewer group discussions and role-playing. 33 minutes. (Research Press)

Who Did What to Whom?

Secondary. Film for improving human relations. Introduces principles of human interaction to almost any group. Principles covered are positive and negative reinforcement, punishment, and extinction. Film shows 40 short scenes that occur every day at home, in school, and around the office. Discussion time is provided after every scene. Film is $16\frac{1}{2}$ minutes in length. Sufficient for a full two-hour session. Also includes a leader's guide. (Research Press)

The Skillstreaming Video

Demonstrates how social skills trainers might use the Skillstreaming model to teach social skills to children and adolescents. Instructional procedures include modeling, role-playing, performance feedback, and transfer training. 26 minutes. (Research Press)

Dealing with Anger

A secondary violence prevention program for African-American youth. Uses vignettes, language, and dress specific to African-American culture to teach three conflict-resolution skills: (1) expressing anger nonaggressively, (2) accepting criticism appropriately, and (3) negotiating a problem situation. Program includes three videotapes, leader's guide, and skill cards. (Research Press)

Dramatic Play Materials

The Magic of Puppetry

Primary. Set of four puppets: a mother, a father, a boy, and a girl, with a 142-page manual providing instruction on staging puppet plays and making puppets. Designed to facilitate communication and social skills in young children. (American Guidance Service)

People Puppets

Elementary. Set of eight cotton puppets, includes father, mother, boy, girl, policeman, farmer, and fireman. (Constructive Playthings)

Games/Game Construction

Creative Games for Learning: Games for Parents and Teachers to Make

Ages 3 through 8. Fifty games to make that promote social, motoric, cognitive, and academic learning. Includes objective for each game, drawing of game, materials needed, steps for construction, and rules for playing. Spiral bound, 160 pages. (The Council for Exceptional Children)

Games

The Social Skills Game

Ages 6 through 14. Board game that uses cognitive principles to develop peer-related positive interaction skills. Activity cards target specific social skills such as asking for help, taking turns, and introducing oneself. (Childswork/Childsplay)

The Good Behavior Game

Ages 4 through 12. Includes board containing colorful cartoons depicting various good and bad behaviors, chance cards, and dice. Designed to help children distinguish good and bad behaviors. Children receive or lose tokens depending on whether they land on a good or bad behavior. Adaptation for older children permits the learner to discuss the value of being good. (Childswork/Childsplay)

The Good and Bad Feelings Card Game

Elementary. Deck of 48 cards depicts 24 different emotions. Manual describes three different games that can be played to help children learn about their feelings and take responsibility for them. (Childswork/Childsplay)

The Classroom Survival Game

Ages 6 through 14. Board game that deals with specific task-related behaviors such as attending to class instruction, participating in class discussions, independent work habits, staying on-task, and completing assignments. (Childswork/Childsplay)

The Ungame

Ages 5 through 105. Board game designed to facilitate communication while teaching cooperative and listening skills. Contains two decks of cards, one with lighthearted questions the other with more serious questions. (Childswork/Childsplay)

Communicate Junior

Elementary. Educational board game designed to reinforce social skills instruction. Game played in cooperative manner. (Thinking Publications)

Communicate and Communicate Expansion Cards

Grades 5 through 12. Board game and expansion cards designed to teach social communication skills. (Thinking Publications)

Wipe-Off Game Boards

Elementary. Set of four boards. Each is sturdy 14" × 22" plastic coated board and wipes clean. Use together with game pieces to create game for individualization and small-group learning. (Constructive Playthings)

Game Maker Set

Elementary. Includes items for making your own games: wipe-off spinner, 40 cards and game field, 15 game pieces, 4 dice, crayons, and idea book. Packed in storage carton. Helpful for individualizing for special needs. (Constructive Playthings)

Talking-Feeling-Doing Game

Elementary. A board game primarily for use in counseling or therapy with children; also has some potential for social skills training. (Creative Therapeutics)

Stacking the Deck

Adolescents/adults with mild to moderate mental retardation. A social skills game designed to teach skills related to general social skills, social/vocational skills and social/sexual skills. Game consists of a deck of 48 cards that contain social situations to which the players are to react. The format is a table game that involves successive turns and progressive movement around the game board. (Research Press)

Socialization Games for Adolescents and Adults with Mental Retardation

Adolescents and adults with disabilities. Contents include a description of use of socialization games, organizational and environmental requirements, uses with groups, and specific games. (Charles C. Thomas)

Appendix *B*

List of Publishers

American Guidance Service
Publishers Building
4201 Woodland Road
Circle Pines, MN 55014

Childswork/Childsplay
Center for Applied Psychology
P. O. Box 1586
King of Prussia, PA 19406

Constructive Playthings
1040 East 85th Street
Kansas City, MO 64131

The Council for Exceptional Children
1920 Association Drive
Reston, VA 22091

Creative Therapeutics
155 County Road
Cresskill, NJ 07626

Films Incorporated
733 Green Bay Road
Wilmette, IL 60091

Guidance Associates
Communications Park
Box 3000
Mount Kisco, NY 10549

Human Science Press
72 Fifth Avenue
New York, NY 10011

Institute for Rational Living
45 East 65th Street
New York, NY 10021

Kimbo Publications
P. O. Box 477
Long Branch, NJ 07740

Love Publishing Company
1777 South Bellaire St.
Denver, CO 80222

McGraw-Hill
Cedar Hollow & Matthews
  Hill Rd.
Paoli, PA 19301

PRO-ED
5341 Industrial Oaks Blvd.
Austin, TX 78735

Prentice-Hall
Englewood Cliffs, NJ 07632

Research Press
Box 31773
Champaign, IL 61821

Scott, Foresman and Company
1900 East Lake Avenue
Glenview, IL 60025

Social Effectiveness Training
P. O. Box 6664
Reno, NV 89513-6664

Teaching Resources Corp.
100 Boylston Street
Boston, MA 02116

Thinking Publications
1731 Westgate Road
Box 163
Eau Claire, WI 54702-0163

Charles C. Thomas
2600 S. First Street
Springfield, IL 62794-9265

J. Weston Walch, Publisher
Portland, ME 04104

Appendix *C*

Social Skills List

Environmental Behaviors (EB)

Care for the Environment (CE)

- To dispose of trash in the proper container.
- To drink properly from water fountain.
- To clean up after breaking or spilling something.
- To use classroom equipment and materials correctly.
- To use playground equipment safely.

Dealing with Emergency (DE)

- To follow rules for emergencies.
- To identify accident or emergency situations that should be reported to the teacher.
- To report accident or other emergency to the teacher.

Lunchroom Behavior (LR)

- To use eating utensils properly.
- To handle and eat only one's own food.
- To dispose of unwanted food properly.

Movement Around Environment (MO)

- To walk through the hall quietly at a reasonable pace.
- To enter classroom and take seat without disturbing objects and other people.
- To form and walk in a line.
- To follow safety rules in crossing streets.

Interpersonal Behaviors (IP)

Accepting Authority (AA)

- To comply with request of adult in position of authority.
- To comply with request of peer in position of authority.
- To know and follow classroom rules.
- To follow classroom rules in the absence of the teacher.
- To question rules that may be unjust.

Coping with Conflict (CC)

- To respond to teasing or name-calling by ignoring, changing the subject, or using some other constructive means.
- To respond to physical assault by leaving the situation, calling for help, or using some other constructive means.
- To walk away from peer when angry to avoid hitting.
- To refuse the request of another politely.
- To express anger with nonaggressive words rather than physical action or aggressive words.
- To handle constructively criticism or punishment perceived as undeserved.

Gaining Attention (GA)

- To gain teacher's attention in class by raising hand.
- To wait quietly for recognition before speaking out in class.
- To use please and thank you when making requests of others.
- To approach teacher and ask appropriately for help, explanation, instructions, etc.
- To gain attention from peers in appropriate ways.
- To ask a peer for help.

Greeting Others (GR)

- To look others in the eye when greeting them.
- To state one's name when asked.
- To smile when encountering a friend or acquaintance.
- To greet adults and peers by name.
- To respond to an introduction by shaking hands and saying how-do-you-do.
- To introduce oneself to another person.
- To introduce two people to each other.

Helping Others (HP)

- To help teacher when asked.
- To help peer when asked.
- To give simple directions to a peer.

- To offer help to teacher.
- To offer help to a classmate.
- To come to defense of peer in trouble.
- To express sympathy to peer about problems or difficulties.

Making Conversation (MC)

- To pay attention in a conversation to the person speaking.
- To talk to others in a tone of voice appropriate to the situation.
- To wait for pauses in a conversation before speaking.
- To make relevant remarks in a conversation with peers.
- To make relevant remarks in a conversation with adults.
- To ignore interruptions of others in a conversation.
- To initiate conversation with peers in an informal situation.

Organized Play (OP)

- To follow rules when playing a game.
- To wait for one's turn when playing a game.
- To display effort to the best of one's ability in a competitive game.
- To accept defeat and congratulate the winner in a competitive game.

Positive Attitude Toward Others (PA)

- To make positive statements about qualities and accomplishments of others.
- To compliment another person.
- To display tolerance for persons with characteristics different from one's own.

Playing Informally (PL)

- To ask another student to play on the playground.
- To ask to be included in a playground activity in progress.
- To share toys and equipment in a play situation.
- To give in to reasonable wishes of the group in a play situation.
- To suggest an activity for the group on the playground.

Property: Own and Others' (PR)

- To distinguish one's own property from the property of others.
- To lend possessions to others when asked.
- To use and return others' property without damaging it.
- To ask permission to use another's property.

Self-Related Behaviors (SR)

Accepting Consequences (AC)

- To report to the teacher when one has spilled or broken something.
- To make apology when actions have injured or infringed on another.
- To accept deserved consequences of wrongdoing.

Ethical Behavior (EB)

- To distinguish truth from untruth.
- To answer truthfully when asked about possible wrongdoing.
- To identify consequences of behavior involving wrongdoing.
- To avoid doing something wrong when encouraged by a peer.

Expressing Feelings (EF)

- To describe one's own feelings or moods verbally.
- To recognize and label moods of others.

Positive Attitude Toward Self (PA)

- To say thank you when complimented or praised.
- To be willing to have one's work displayed.
- To make positive statements when asked about oneself.
- To undertake a new task with a positive attitude.

Responsible Behavior (RB)

- To be regular in school attendance.
- To arrive at school on time.
- To hang up one's clothes in required place.
- To keep one's desk in order.
- To take care of one's own possessions.
- To carry messages for the teacher.
- To bring required materials to school.

Self-Care (SC)

- To use toilet facilities properly.
- To put on clothing without assistance.
- To keep face and hands clean.

Task-Related Behavior (TR)

Asking and Answering Questions (AQ)

- To answer or attempt to answer a question when called on by teacher.
- To acknowledge when one does not know the answer to a question.
- To volunteer an answer to teacher's question.
- To ask a question appropriate to the information needed.

Attending Behavior (AT)

- To look at the teacher when a lesson is being presented.
- To watch an audio-visual presentation quietly.

- To listen to someone speaking to the class.

Classroom Discussion (CD)

- To use tone of voice in classroom discussion appropriate to the situation.
- To make relevant remarks in a classroom discussion.
- To participate in a classroom discussion initiated by teacher.
- To bring things to class that are relevant to classroom discussion.
- To express opinion in classroom discussion even when contrary to opinions of others.
- To provide reasons for opinions expressed in group discussion.

Completing Tasks (CT)

- To complete assigned academic work.
- To complete assigned academic work within the required time.
- To continue working on a difficult task until it is completed.
- To complete and return homework assignments.

Following Directions (FD)

- To follow teacher's verbal directions.
- To follow written directions.
- To follow directions in taking a test.

Group Activities (GA)

- To share materials with others in a work situation.
- To work cooperatively on a task with a partner.
- To carry out plans or decisions formulated by the group.
- To accept ideas presented in a group task situation that are different from one's own.
- To initiate and help carry out a group activity.

Independent Work (IW)

- To attempt to solve a problem with school work before asking for help.
- To find productive use of time while waiting for teacher assistance.
- To find acceptable ways of using free time when work is completed.

On-Task Behavior (OT)

- To sit straight at desk when required by teacher.
- To do a seatwork assignment quietly.
- To work steadily for the required length of time.
- To ignore distractions from peers when doing a seatwork assignment.
- To discuss academic material with peers when appropriate.
- To change from one activity to another when required by the teacher.

Performing Before Others (PF)

- To participate in a role playing activity.
- To read aloud in a small group.
- To read aloud before a large group of the entire class.
- To make a report before a small group.
- To make a report before a large group or the entire class.

Quality of Work (QW)

- To turn in neat papers.
- To accept correction of school work.
- To make use of teacher's corrections to improve work.
- To go back over work to check for errors.

Source: From Stephens, T. M. (1992). *Social Skills in the Classroom.* Odessa, FL: Psychological Assessment Resources. Copyright 1978, 1992 by Psychological Assessment Resources, Inc. Reproduced by special permission.

Author Index

Subject Index